SO-ATF-582

THE
GREAT
BRAIN
SUCK

THE GREAT BRAIN SUCK

AND OTHER AMERICAN EPIPHANIES

EUGENE HALTON

THE UNIVERSITY OF CHICAGO PRESS

Chicago and London

EUGENE HALTON is professor of sociology and American studies at the University of Notre Dame and the author of *Meaning and Modernity: Social Theory in the Pragmatic Attitude* and *Bereft of Reason: On the Decline of Social Thought and Prospects for Its Renewal*, both published by the University of Chicago Press.

The University of Chicago Press, Chicago 60637
The University of Chicago Press, Ltd., London
© 2008 by Eugene Halton
All rights reserved. Published 2008
Printed in the United States of America

17 16 15 14 13 12 11 10 09 08   1 2 3 4 5

ISBN-13: 978-0-226-31465-5 (cloth)
ISBN-13: 978-0-226-31466-2 (paper)
ISBN-10: 0-226-31465-0 (cloth)
ISBN-10: 0-226-31466-9 (paper)

Library of Congress Cataloging-in-Publication Data

Halton, Eugene.
The great brain suck: and other American epiphanies /
Eugene Halton.
p. cm.
Includes bibliographical references and index.
ISBN-13: 978-0-226-31465-5 (cloth : alk. paper)
ISBN-10: 0-226-31465-0 (cloth : alk. paper)
ISBN-13: 978-0-226-31466-2 (pbk. : alk. paper)
ISBN-10: 0-226-31466-9 (pbk. : alk. paper) 1. United States—
Civilization. 2. National characteristics, American. 3. Popular
culture—United States. 4. United States—Intellectual life.
5. United States—Social conditions. 6. United States—Politics
and government. 7. Political culture—United States. I. Title.
E169.1.H225 2008
973—dc22
2007043181

♾ The paper used in this
publication meets the minimum requirements
of the American National Standard
for Information Sciences—Permanence
of Paper for Printed Library Materials,
ANSI Z 39.48-1992.

TO MY MOTHER, LORRAINE HALTON,
AND TO THE MEMORY OF
MY FATHER, EUGENE HALTON

CONTENTS

PREFACE

These diverse essays consider the ways a variety of ideas, works, and practices reveal uniquely American themes. They delve into American life in all the varied senses the term *epiphanies* might suggest: bodyings forth of ideas, showings, manifestations, even visionary appearances. I harvest ideas from familiar settings and more obscure and unexpected terrain—including my own epiphanies—to expose neglected masters, narratives, and artifacts, and to reveal central motifs of American life in a new light.

The "quintessential American" can be found in exemplary people or their works, to be sure—a number are portrayed here. But that person can also be found in the Joneses next door, or in your own back yard or living room—or mine, or in your local tavern, the nearest mall, nuclear bombs, or even in The Parthenon in Nashville, as I discovered to my amazement on a couple of occasions.

The essays range freely in style as well as content over a broad, varied territory and are not intended to develop a single story line. I am not attempting a linear tour of American culture, but rather what Kenneth Burke called "perspective by incongruity," of lateral and nonlinear developments both in the ordering of chapters and the organizing within them. Feel free to roam the book, nonsequentially. The term *epiphany* (Greek epiphaino, "to appear upon, manifest," from the prefix epi-, "upon," and the verb phaino, "appear") connotes "perspective by incongruity," wherein an unexpected illumination or manifestation brings a new way of seeing, kaleidoscopically.

Moving, for example, from considering nuclear America of the 1950s in chapters 2 and 3 to early twentieth-century St. Louis and Chicago in chapters 4 and 5, backtracks how the power structure that emerged in the fifties was already prefigured in the dynamos and cultural energies Henry Adams presciently described. It is a peeling away of historical materials rather than a chronological narrative of them, in order to provide, as Lewis Mumford once put it, a "useable history" through which to consider contemporary American culture.

Chapter 4, "The Hunter-Gatherers' World's Fair," juxtaposes Geronimo and Ota Benga at the St. Louis World's Fair with Max Weber and Henry Adams at the same fair: quite an unlikely quartet! Yet incongruity through juxtaposition provides a way to develop the story of Ota Benga and to contrast the hunter-gatherers with the civilized power structure that confronted them. One of the major points of the chapter is to view America and modern civilization through the very different eyes of the hunter-gatherers assembled at that world's fair.

Epiphanies are not only subjects for describing; they also constitute a varied form of expression. James Joyce's free-associative writing from the inner life of some of his characters in *Ulysses* and other works is but one example of the boundless possibilities of epiphany as form. Joyce's narrator in *Stephen Hero* offers Stephen's view: "By an epiphany he meant a sudden spiritual manifestation, whether in the vulgarity of speech or of gesture or in a memorable phase of the mind itself. He believed that it was for the man of letters to record these epiphanies with extreme care, seeing that they themselves are the most delicate and evanescent of moments." Joyce manifests one perspective here, but there are many others, some not so sudden, some not so spiritual—all radiant, perhaps, but some radioactive as well.

I use the form of epiphany as a means of being free, free in the sense in which Ralph Waldo Emerson described the American scholar: "The world,— this shadow of the soul, *or other me*, lies wide around. Its attractions are the keys which unlock my thoughts and make me acquainted with myself. I run eagerly into this resounding tumult. I grasp the hands of those next [to] me, and take my place in the ring to suffer and to work, taught by an instinct, that so shall the dumb abyss be vocal with speech." The American scholar of today, sadly, has become a quite different creature from the one envisioned by Emerson. Ingrown with expertise, hidebound by "peer-reviewed" juggernauts and university standards designed to insure bureaucratic conformity, intellectuals too easily shrink from the "resounding tumult" in which free thinking thrives. Reader be warned: I prefer to take the "life" part of "intellectual life" seriously, wherever it takes me.

In the rise of technological and acquisitive materialism in twentieth- and twenty-first-century America, one recurrent theme is the tension produced between the ideals of technicalism and consumerism versus that of a democratic public life. Early chapters focus on some key symbols of materialism in post–World War II America, including the automobile and its transformative effects on social life; radioactivity as master symbol for the materialization of the transcendent in the twentieth century; and on the increasing influence of mechanical and electronic domestic devices of all sorts in the home (particularly relating to the mass media and entertainment industries).

I view America since World War II as problematically guided by a power-oriented culture, which, in the names of national security and convenience, has tended to reshape America toward a hierarchical machine model of society—toward *megatechnic America*—and against the requirements of democratic community. The history of nuclear power alone, from the increasingly lethal and expensive development of weapons in the cold war and the ways in which they dictated American foreign policy, to the promises of virtually cost-free energy, suggest that radioactivity has functioned as the invisible specter of the old American dream of the New Jerusalem.

Radioactivity, which perhaps defines twentieth-century materialism as bronze, silver, and stone did for earlier ages (and which silicon may do for the twenty-first century), proved to be a seemingly immaterial but deadly power that we have yet to harness. Yet both public and domestic life in a democratic society demand that technical products and the technical way of thinking serve as means to the good life, and not usurp their place as means to become the intended or unintended goals of life. Hence a crucial question dealt with throughout the book, despite a wide range of content, is how American culture—and indeed world culture—can regain human autonomy in the face of a seemingly irresistible automatic culture.

Conservative Republican president Dwight D. Eisenhower, former general and allied military forces commander in World War II, used the term *the military-industrial complex* in his farewell speech as president on January 17, 1961, to describe the dangerous expansion of bureaucratic purposes taking on a profit-making life of their own. The Left later used the term to criticize the United States as an out-of-control imperial power during the Vietnam War. Despite the criticisms, the power complex has continued to expand its reach both globally and especially in America, outwardly and inwardly, so I have updated the term to *the postdemocratic military-industrial-academic-entertainment-sport-food complex*. I like the way it rolls off the tongue.

Currently, American culture—and global culture more generally—seems bent on extending machine ways of living without limit. The epiphany of the robot as deus ex machina—the god out of the machine—is a delusion that may prove our final undoing, as life becomes ever more dominated by electronic devices. Although techno-mania is a defining feature of American life, there is another America, rooted in the vision of the organic, that has inspired Americans since long before there were Americans or America, and that continues to animate the American vision today.

The same American culture that has promoted "automatic" ways of living also provides alternatives, ranging across the possibilities for meaning found in the artifacts and activities of domestic and public life, the problematic quest for spontaneity in a range of postwar arts and in relation to earlier American artists and thinkers, and unlikely connections between American themes and non-American artists and thinkers.

One sees this, for example, in the uniquely American visions of Lewis Mumford (1895–1990) and Wharton Esherick (1883–1970), both of whom could be regarded as exemplars and nodal points of American culture. Esherick, who has been called "the dean of modern American furniture design," was a twentieth-century Thoreau in wood and a friend of writers Sherwood Anderson and Theodore Dreiser and of architect Louis Kahn, among others. Although central to the emergence of the "art furniture" movement in America, and a major influence on his younger contemporaries such as Sam Maloof and Wendell Castle, Esherick has only recently begun to be recognized. Heavily illustrated "coffee table" books on furniture are now mentioning him as a central figure, but are only beginning to show photographs of his work. His life and place in American culture has languished in obscurity. Of particular interest to me is Esherick's vision of domestic life, realized in the structure and life-history of his own home.

Similarly, the actual home of Lewis Mumford in Amenia, New York, where I visited with him and his wife Sophia over a few years before his death, provides a take-off point for recollections of and reflections on his life and work as a public intellectual. Here I am primarily interested in Mumford as a manifestation of American culture as well as a thinker now strangely neglected. His work extended far beyond his better-known writings on cities and architecture, and included a general philosophy of life. Mumford has been criticized by some as a Luddite, by others as excessively pessimistic and moralistic. Yet a number of his dark observations resonate with those of Herman Melville and philosopher Charles Peirce, two other Americans who seemed to break with American optimism. Chapter 12 explores why such views can be seen as distinctively American, and what the limitations and possibilities of such visions are.

Early chapters deal with embodiments of public and domestic life in America and of the tensions in maintaining each in the face of a culture oriented toward mass consumption and automatic convenience. These chapters include discussions of a number of public symbols, such as the Vietnam Veterans Memorial and the International Airstream Travel Trailer convention, of how the artifacts and activities of the domestic environment symbolize "home-life," and of the dual public and private place of electronic media in what I am terming *pax electronica*, the "peace" induced by the matrix of electronic devices that increasingly permeate everyday life and consciousness in America and globally. *Pax electronica* as a *pox electronica*.

The theme of a *pax electronica* also appears in later chapters that consider manifestations of invisibility, immaterial materialism, and secrecy. Radioactivity again emerges as a master symbol in American culture since World War II, as the invisible specter of the New Jerusalem, along with the cult of celebrity and consumption culture. To give one example, a critical analysis of the novel *His Master's Voice*, by Polish writer Stanislaw Lem, which deals with a fictional secret research project modeled after the old Manhattan Project, provides a take-off point for my discussions of the place of secrecy in science and public life, and of the American victims of nuclear testing, whose numbers by most estimates are greater than the American dead of the Korean, Vietnam, and Iraq wars combined.

Epiphanies, as incandescent manifestations, also include the visionary, and I have included, to be true to this aspect of the form, some of my own American epiphanies. Our age tends to denigrate the inner life as "merely" subjective, as though "insight," in the literal sense, cannot also be insightful, opening felt portals to self and world. In my case, visions of a world's fair, of The Parthenon in Nashville, and of hurricanes, made manifest sensings of things of which I was not consciously aware, and ideas worth weaving. But are they objective knowledge, the modern rational reader might well ask. Why do you think the subjective is cleanly separated from the objective, I might reply, for all that is now known was first imagined, sensed, and felt, however darkly. Read them as openings, not closures, as invitations to run eagerly into the resounding tumult.

1

THE GREAT BRAIN SUCK

The 1990s ushered in a new phase of postmodern decay in America: virtuality as virtue. The year 1990 is a convenient decade marker for the change, when superstores begin to blitz already mall-crazed America, when cheap imitation ethnic restaurants give way to high quality virtual "local" ethnic restaurant franchises—and gluttony spawns an obesity epidemic—when high quality superbookstore and supercafe franchises colonize city and mall alike, when Americans finally and voluntarily surrender those chunks of time not already owned by television to their newly purchased smart typewriter contraptions. Could anyone imagine just twenty-five years ago the extent to which mass quantities of the leisure classes of the advanced industrial nations would spend significant leisure time "typing?" Or "mousing?"

The great fear of "y2k" was that computers would not function after the new millennium began. But that was a minor problem in comparison with the absorption of people by machine-system activities. The old vision of the human of the future was a spindly creature with an enormous brain. Now we know that vision was wrong, because we are making the human of the future right now, "it" is already well underway—that pathetic genderless creature—and we know in what remains of our Internetted souls that it will eventually be an

1

obese, pinheaded creature with huge, thick typing fingers. Evolution has selected carpal tunnel syndrome as the means of weeding out the mechanically weak stock, and the Internet as the means of brain sucking the populace, of increasing its dependency on externally derived information that bypasses the need for actual thinking, feeling, and experiencing. We've already witnessed the brain suck of checkout attendants, who formerly possessed the ability for common arithmetic, by calculating machines.

More and more information is pumped into the world every minute of every day and yet America dumbs down: more and more information about the world, and yet people know less and less about it; more and more sources of history available and less and less knowledge of history; more and more information about the cultures of the world and yet less and less awareness.

Do people accumulate this information by day, and have it removed, like night soil, by dark? There is a vast brain suck occurring. But from where? How can you flood brains with information, and by doing so, precisely in the act of doing so, suck them dry?

How is it that we can look at and listen to so much information bombarding our eyes and ears, yet apparently see not and hear not? It is not simply a physiological problem but a cultural and moral one, which involves all the fibers of our being, including the physical. It is the same problem, I suppose, that causes me misgivings when I see those people in health clubs reading on bicycle machines, iPods engaged, abstracted from the pure being of their bodies. You know when you look at them that they cycle away more miles on those indoor machines than the ones they passed while driving in their automachines to get to the health club. But these are physiologically measurable and paid-for miles.

My technical term for this neuro-metaphysical disorder is *brain suck*. It derives from a techno-culture bent on replacing self-originated experience with rationally derived commodity forms, and on colonizing the inner life with substitute emotions, embedded to function like Internet "cookies," linked to the system. The result is what might be called, only half-fancifully, "brainoid tissue," surrogate synapses all linked to and ultimately produced by the Great and Powerful Machine. This is not the same as "brain drain," which means the flight of intelligence to other countries. A drain is a leak, but brain suck is a kind of vacuuming effect, sucking awareness from one's life into the void of the undead zombie-zone. One might think that this process occurs by brainwashing, and in a sense it does. But the chief means by which brain suck operates is what I prefer to call *brain rinsing*, a seemingly kinder, gentler approach that is no less effective. Brainwashing is usually through forcible punishing torture, aiming at a total conversion. But brain rinsing achieves brain suck piecemeal, usually through repetitive, pleasurable miniactivities, none of which alone may be compromising, but all of which together add up to a compromised self running on automatic.

In contrast, by *self-originated experience*, I mean that the self, though conditionable and though developed through habits of conduct, involves a spontaneous, sensing reasonableness not reducible to its habits and conditioning, one whose purport is self-determination. This self requires bodily involvement in the moment and the availability of feelings, needs, desires, and goals to make sense of that moment. It requires the awareness needed to continue to be itself in the moment, that is, to determine itself in its environment as a socially autonomous being. I want to explore now some of the varieties of brain suck with reference to the colonization of the human self by consumption culture—mostly in its American version—with some gear shifts.

GEAR SHIFT

Let us imagine a day in the life of "techno-colonized person," who, in the spirit of H. L. Mencken's term "boob-oisie," I will call BIG Zombie. In the American version, BIG Zombie moves by machine, spending an average of sixty-seven minutes a day for males and forty-four minutes for females a day driving an automobile, according to a study by the U.S. Department of Transportation.[1] BIG Zombie enjoys this time in the auto, and perceives hurtling speedily down the road as his or her "time to think and enjoy being alone." This auto-meditative attitude is more pronounced among the young, declines with age, and also increases with wealth.[2]

Far from the view of modern culture as a purely rationalizing system, there is this other side to it, its need to make connection to the human soul. American consumer culture, for example, represents a fully techno-totemic system in place. Do you need to make up a personal name for your automobile when it's already a Mustang, a Stingray, a Cobra, a Jaguar? If you want to display your luxus, what better way than through a Lexus?

The American car system functions as a crucial part of this consumer techno-totemic system. It is a pure example of a technical system at work, and yet it needs to attach irrational symbols of desire, either predatory or sexual, to itself, to a machine. Driving becomes a technical form of hunting or eroticism or luxury or musical emotion or even meditation, and the auto experience is supposed to confer those qualities onto the owner or the driver.

The word *automobile* means self-moving, and that is an important part of the symbolism of cars. You can not only move in a solitary place, seemingly away from the rat race even while you are driving in it, but it is also supposed to give you the freedom to move within the social system.

American culture today highlights the more general battle between autonomy and the automaton. The great dream of the modern era has been to provide for and enlarge the autonomy of humankind through technical invention and control over the necessities of life. As that dream has been realized it has all too frequently revealed itself in diabolical reversal. The vast technical culture and wealth of America have not led the way toward the good life, but instead toward the goods life, toward a reified culture centered in commodities rather than citizens, toward an ultimate goal of automatic things and away from human autonomy. This is not the necessary outcome of the development of technology but the consequence of the withering of human purpose in the face of the "magic" of technique. The 1980s signified the new phase of the electronics revolution underway, but I would suggest something more sinister. It was as if the long-held human tension between fear of and fascination for the robotic finally dissolved, as if the fascination for the magic of the automaton overwhelmed the understandable fears for its power to alienate the human and left only the ideal of a fusion of humans with the powerful instruments of the automatic: humanoids, terminators, carbon-based units.

Perhaps the small child playing with "transformer" robots or video games, the larger child mall cruising or earlocked in an iPod or similar audio device, the adult in a health club exercising on an electronic bicycle while watching a video display of a route or a large screen television set, are all symbols of an emergent creature that willingly would prefer to live in "virtual reality" rather than the real thing. Yet who can deny the conveniences the machines launched in the 1980s and 1990s afford? Still, the question is whether they truly enhance autonomy or automatism, and clearly both outcomes are possible.

Probably you, dear reader, and surely I, would defend the word-processing computer as providing greater autonomy. But talk to an office worker whose keystrokes are being monitored or who has suffered repetitive-motion damage. Talk to the marketer or secret police person who may be monitoring which Web sites you have visited. What books are the video-game-expert child not reading? Consider Morgan Pozgar, the thirteen-year-old girl who won the LG National Texting Championship and its $25,000 cash reward in April, 2007, by typing the following lines from a *Mary Poppins* tune on her cell phone in a mere fifteen seconds: "Supercalifragilisticexpialidocious! Even though the sound of it is something quite atrocious. If you say it loud enough you'll always sound precocious." The technical information she had absorbed and technical facility she had developed to achieve this feat by sending an average of over eight thousand text messages a month resulted in a girl with a lot of money and a typical 'tween's dream of consuming. When asked what she wanted to do with the money, she said, "I'm going to go shopping and buy lots of clothes." She wants to go into fashion when she grows up.

Or consider what a woman college student said after breaking up with a boyfriend and fellow student who played video games four hours a day, and said he was trying to reduce to fifteen hours a week: "He said he was thinking of trying to cut back to fifteen hours a week. I said, 'Fifteen hours is what I spend on my internship, and I get paid $1,300 a month.' That's my litmus test now: I won't date anyone who plays video games. It means they're choosing to do something that wastes their time and sucks the life out of them."[3]

What drain does each additional device put on time spent together in the home? The fact that the family meal has been increasingly fragmented through individualized microwaved meals, through the intrusion of television, through increased dependence on fast-food restaurants ought to be taken as a sign of how increasingly difficult it is to do simple activities together, relatively unintruded upon by high tech. It is now a dietary commonplace that meals made at home from scratch are healthier than processed foods, and the shared family meal is good for the soul as well as for the body. Yet Americans have been shrinking away from homemade meals. This is not simply a class issue, as though the poor can only afford unhealthy foods, for the best diets in the world tend to be "peasant" diets. It is not cheap rice, beans, and greens that are causing massive obesity, but high-fat, high-fructose unhealthy diets leveraged by the heavily subsidized industrial-food complex, manifest in processed foods and especially in fast food, which still remains more expensive than home cooking.

The presumed purpose of the high-tech household is to transfer everyday necessities—heating, cooking, cleaning, and so forth—to machines, in order to increase "leisure time." Yet leisure is largely a machine activity in America. Consider that the average American spent three thousand hours consuming media in 1988, of which 1,550 hours were devoted to television, and 1,160 to radio. Yet the average American household has steadily increased television time over the decades, most recently going from an average of seven hours and seventeen minutes in 1995 to just under eight hours (seven hours and fifty-eight minutes) in 2003 according to Nielson surveys. And this occurred in the decade when the epiphany of the computer screen materialized throughout America, compounding "screen time." Exposure to advertising has also expanded drastically in the past twenty years, as has sexual content of programming.

These numbing numbers suggest that Americans devote an enormous amount of time to the daily habit of listening and watching. Americans seemed to enter the 1980s as "joggers" and to exit as quasi-stationary "couch potatoes," going on to computer jockey status in the 1990s. Perhaps the great tendency to sit—in autos and in front of televisions—was perhaps offset somewhat by a reported rise in the "standing breakfast," eaten next to a kitchen counter, or by stand-up eating in fast food restaurants. But these standing and sitting patterns only testify to overly mechanized life.

As part of the larger dynamics of the modern era, American culture has transformed technique from a means to the good life to a virtual goal unto itself, with the result that Americans have increasingly seemed to be willing to sacrifice the art and practice and struggles of concrete life to the conveniences of abstract technique: to give up the active cultivation of home life to the passive consumption of TV, TV dinners, take-out and fast road food; to give up multipurpose centers for civic life and local commerce to self-enclosed, privatized, behavior-monitoring shopping malls; to surrender the pursuit of autonomy to the accumulation of dollars and the identity-confirming rituals of consumption.

In real life, as the expression goes, shit happens. Virtual automatic consumption culture is designed, in stark contrast, to habituate us to an idealized techno-kitsch realm immunized from the necessary baggage of human life. To the extent that it does, it sucks from us the anchors of everyday life, those problematic face-to-face relations with family, friends, neighbors, and co-workers that are anything but ideal, and that, precisely in their limitations, force us to find our way in a common world. And for people living on the edges of sanity, those social anchors may be all that is keeping them from plunging, lemminglike, into the abyss.

GEAR SHIFT

The Triumph of Pottersville

In the 1946 Hollywood Christmas film, *It's a Wonderful Life*, George Bailey (played by Jimmy Stewart), depressed and suicidal, experiences a vision of what it would be like if he had never been born. His small town becomes a glittery sin city, Pottersville, named after the heartless town millionaire. Bailey sees that his job as town banker has been crucial in keeping the community spirit alive, and not only the economic welfare of his neighbors and fellow citizens. He returns from his hopelessness, renewed as the solid-guy-who-holds-the-town-together, and succeeds in the end in staving off Pottersville. Decency overcomes unbounded capitalistic greed and human baseness.

Moving from the image of late Depression and wartime America to 1950s postwar prosperity America, something far worse happens to the small town myth. In the sci-fi classic *Invasion of the Body Snatchers* (1956), Dr. Miles J. Binnell, the lead character played by Kevin McCarthy, cannot hold the center together and loses everything, his town, his patients, his neighbors and friends, and even the object of his love, Becky.

Worse, the town is not lost to the tyrant, but to the postpersonality system of emotionless, conforming drones. Just as Vaclav Havel depicted the ascendance of *the posttotalitarian system* in communist countries after Stalin's death, we have the coming to being of what could be termed *the postdemocratic system* in America. By posttotalitarian he meant that totalitarianism, far from being over, had entered a new phase, shifting from the cult of personality characterizing the first generation of totalitarianism—with its Stalin, Hitler, Mussolini, Franco, and Attaturk—to a system running on virtual automatic pilot. Similarly, by postdemocratic system I mean a society that has lost its grounded democratic processes—ranging from vital neighborhood institutions to national political culture—in favor of the "automatic pilot" of media, commercial, and celebrity system requirements.

Like its posttotalitarian counterpart, the postdemocratic system that was under assembly in the fifties, and that shifted into higher gear by the nineties, selects for an elite of cool-thinking functionaries, expanding their vegetative ways. Perhaps Microsoft Man would be a good term for this being, though the suggestion of a gender—male or female—however diminished, still seems beyond the capacities of this neutered creature. If the fifties had its "organization man," who pledged allegiance to his company, perhaps we have seen since the nineties the emergence of postorganization person, whose only allegiance is to the system in general, regardless of the particular company or country.

The upper middle class and up has been becoming increasingly independent of both locale and public services through its money. Consider that 1 percent of American households own one-third of the private wealth, and the top 20 percent a full 84 percent of it; that if one moves to general financial wealth, 10 percent own about 80 percent of general financial wealth; and that average CEO pay (adjusted for inflation) between 1990 and 2005 skyrocketed almost 300 percent. During the same period, production workers' salaries increased a mere 4 percent, and, with inflation factored in, the federal minimum wage actually declined by 9 percent.[4] Maximum wages soared, minimum wages suffered: the stairway to heaven got a lot longer.

The advantaged class can claim it got there by its own rugged individual effort, and that it is not racist, and in individual cases perhaps this can sometimes be the case. But the American elite are living increasingly in class-segregated enclaves, and their "public" school districts become means for class segregation, and class segregation largely overlaps with race segregation. Hence the ideology of rugged individualism can become blindness, not only to how class structure imposes advantages and disadvantages unequally, but also to how much more than individual merit goes into living in a democracy. The basis of democracy is an inclusive common life, the opposite of exclusive distinction.

As Christopher Lasch said in his book *The Revolt of the Elites*, "meritocracy is a parody of democracy. It offers opportunities for advancement, in theory at least, to anyone with the talent to seize them, but 'opportunities to rise,' as R. H. Tawney points out in *Equality*, 'are no substitute for a general diffusion of the means of civilization,' of the 'dignity and culture' that are needed by all 'whether they rise or not.'"[5]

Lasch was not criticizing individual effort, the means by which many in America found ways to prosperity. His point was that meritocracy has become both a way for Americans to deny realities of class and one of the names for a deformation of democracy that gives up the local rootedness of life for the greater cosmopolitan Ladder of Success. "The meritocrat" also used to be called yuppie (though perhaps now, no longer "young," the new acronym should be "uppie?"). I prefer BIG Zombie.

Surveys on materialism, such as the Roper Center's study of what people think constitute the good life, reveal material indicators, such as swimming pools, "a lot of money," and "a job that pays more than average," have increased while "quality of life" indicators, such as "happy marriage" or "interesting job," have declined. In the same time period between 1975 and 1991 when dreams of material bounty increased, the percentage of people who think they can actually attain the good life declined from 35 to 23 percent.[6] It seems that as people's expectations for indicators of material wealth ballooned, that process was crowding out their expectations for actually living the good life. "Living large" has been replacing living well, and living large is proving to be a way of living unwell.

Invasion of the Body Snatchers got it right, for alien vegetating forces were stalking Americans. Yet the aliens were neither McCarthy-era paranoia-induced communists nor vegetable pods from outer space, but literally vegetable stalks from the mind of megatechnic America, which were en route in the second half of the twentieth century to absorb the American body. Through the progressive industrialization of corn products, and especially high fructose corn syrup from 1980 on, Americans began to overconsume ever-greater amounts of corn-based products, from soda pop to corn-fed meats, so that, as Michael Pollan points out, the American body today incorporates more corn than the Mexican body (which has a more varied diet on average). As Berkeley biologist Todd Dawson told Pollan, "When you look at the isotope ratios, we North Americans look like corn chips with legs."[7]

Corn, considered a traditional staple of the American diet, of healthy corn flakes, of traditional Native Americans who originally developed maize in Central America, was a key ingredient in the transformation to megatechnic America, in the sugar-opiating of kids and adults through high fructose corn syrup and other corn-based sweeteners, and in the obesity and diabetes epidemics underway. Key to the expansion of corn culture was the decision to transform ammonium nitrate from the postwar munitions industry to fertilizer in 1947, setting the stage for radical increase in yield.[8] Industrial corn culture is in this sense a direct product of the military-industrial complex.

Corn has colonized the American body through corn-sugaring, corn-fed cowburgers, and through pervasive industrial corn-based food, producing an overweight population numbed by food. The invasion of the body snatchers, in short, has actually happened; only it was corn fused to the megatechnic complex that ripped open a new niche: the industrial eater, BIG Zombie, capable of eating more and more. Consider that one-quarter of Americans eat fast food on any given day, that one in eight Americans are estimated to have worked for McDonald's, or that, as Eric Schlosser reports in his book *Fast Food Nation*: "In 1970, Americans spent about $6 billion on fast food; in 2001, they spent more than $110 billion. Americans now spend more money on fast food than on higher education, personal computers, computer software, or new cars. They spend more on fast food than on movies, books, magazines, newspapers, videos, and recorded music—combined."[9]

BIG Zombie can live in the fantasies of the BIG McMansion in the gated surveillance community, the BIG SUV, the BIG amounts of mall-gotten gains, the BIG obese body from believing the "merit" system of overconsumption, and feel no responsibility to anything more than his or her BIG butt plunking down in all of this excess, increasingly insulated from the common life. Meanwhile BIG Zombie Jr. is learning how to conform to the system properly, so that, clothed in the exquisite brands of success, Jr. will know how to press the merit buttons of the cage, and feel that he or she deserves all of these merit badges, and that those less privileged do not.

One could take the various *Star Trek* TV series and movies as personifying this rootless elite, alienated from family, friends, and neighborhood, living in a purely artificial convenience enclosure, militaristic, progress oriented, and propelled by extreme, bewildering mobility. These are precisely the elites Lasch spoke of in *The Revolt of the Elites and The Betrayal of Democracy*: "Those who covet membership in the new aristocracy of brains tend to congregate on the coasts, turning their back on the heartland and cultivating ties with the international market in fast-moving money, glamour, fashion, and popular culture. It is a question of whether they think of themselves as Americans at all. . . . The new elites are at home only in transit, en route to a high-level conference, to the grand opening of a new franchise, to an international film festival, or to an undiscovered resort. Theirs is essentially a tourist's view of the world—not a perspective likely to encourage a passionate devotion to democracy."[10]

Although the elite pictured by *Star Trek* grew more gender-equal and multicultural over the years, not much changed regarding their alienation from their home planet or their colonizing—while appearing not to interfere— "prime directive." What is their real prime directive? To extend the federation of machines.

GEAR SHIFT

From Metropolis to Dark City: The Triumph of Post-Pottersville

Metropolis: "Rotwang, give your robot this girl's (Maria) likeness."

Fritz Lang's classic silent film *Metropolis* was a remarkably prescient insight into the brain suck that characterizes our time, as well as the megamachine of modern life. Released in 1927, the story traces the path young Freder—son of the master of Metropolis Joh Fredersen—takes after seeing poor worker children. They are brought to the leisure gardens of the elite by Maria, who Freder falls for. He sets off to find out more and enters the undercity of factories, literally set below the surface, where he ends up changing places with a hapless worker. The city is a haunting class structure literalized, with the workers' city deep below factories, and cryptlike ruins below it. There, Maria counsels the workers in their suffering: "Between the brain that plans and the hands that build there must be a mediator." Cut to Freder, hands beating on chest.

Lang's *Metropolis* can be viewed through numerous lenses. From a Marxist view Freder looks a lot like Freder-ick (Friedrich) Engels, who similarly came from the wealth of a Manchester factory his father co-owned to a passionate commitment to relieve the plight of workers. Engels moved from Germany in 1842 as a twenty-two-year-old radical to work at a cotton mill his father co-owned, and which his father hoped would steer him away from his radicalism. While there Engels met Mary Burns, who introduced him to Manchester and to the plight of the English working class. He lived with her until her death in 1862.

Yet despite a revolt of the workers, resolution occurs through mediation, not Marxist overthrow. The hands of the workers and the head that is literally the word "capital" meet in a final handshake between the foreman and

Freder's father at the entrance to the cathedral, and only after Maria says to Freder, who has saved the children, "It is the heart that must bring about an understanding between them." So it involves a kind of Christian resolution rather than Marxist revolution.

But then one can see the film through a Freudian lens of the oedipal family. At one point the father fires his assistant, Josef, who is the emotional mentor to Freder; in Freudian terms, the father imago regressively splits into aggressive and empathic elements. And it gets better. The father, Fredersen, has Rotwang, the mad scientist, make a robot Maria, which will be used to mislead the people. Rotwang has built a prototype to resemble his ex-lover, Hel, who he lost to Fredersen, and who died giving birth to Freder. Whew, does this get Freudian, or what?

Now, the term "robot" had only been coined a few years earlier, in Karel Čapek's play *R.U.R. (Rossum's Universal Robots)*, but Lang's robot Maria is no mere shiny piece of tin. She's a full-blown sex machine.

There is a scene where Freder enters his father's office to see him embracing the robot Maria. Freder, not knowing of the robot, hallucinates into psychosis. He has witnessed the Freudian "primal scene." We see here two oedipal families: the Unholy Family of heartless, aggressive father, soulless, robot mother, and psychotic son-savior-would-be lover; and the Holy Family of warm, empathic father (Josef the assistant), soulful Maria, and savior-son, who by successful heartfelt mediation of warring factions will also get to be savior-lover.

What is also fascinating in this modern epic is how deeply Fritz Lang understood the need for the rational-mechanical system of modern life to clothe itself in the appearance of flesh. Robot Maria is brain suck woman par excellence, her calculating cranium and shapely metal-bod encased in flesh copied from the original Maria in a dazzling special effects "body-suck." She can inflame feelings of hatred from the male workers, as an electro-rhetorician masterfully appealing to their resentment. And she can shake her seminaked booty in hot exotic dance "at the club" and suck feelings of love from the urbane male elite, who will even duel to death for her favor. She will mirror whatever you desire. She is, as Lang understood so well, the deal that the machine must make in order to be effective: the appearance of the human.

Rational metal, plastic, and silicon just don't cut it by themselves; they require the appearance of flesh, as contemporary consumption culture amply reveals. Look at how high a percentage of video rentals are sex-driven: the appearance of flesh. Or ask Americans what emotions they associate with McDonalds, as I have asked my students. "Happy meals," family, fun—these are a few of the responses. When asked to associate words to "rational," answers such as calculate, quantity, and cold turn up frequently. I point out to them that McDonald's is a rationally based corporation, yet one in which people have been conditioned through advertising to associate emotional feel-good words to a process and product that disguises the rational enterprise and conditions of production, one example of how people are conditioned to kitsch, armored in ready-made, idealized feelings and low-grade experience, of how they are brain sucked.

The science fiction film *Dark City* (1998), chillingly pictures a virtual bee-hive of drones, soullessly searching for the enigmatic human soul while "experimenting" tortures through nightly identity changes. Unlike medieval or modern torture chambers and their consciously induced pain, this urbanoid zone practices its experiments painlessly, taking its victims' identities instead of their physical lives through a form of circadian colonization. It is a kind of photo negative of Albert Camus' absurdist novel *The Stranger*, whose strange hero, Meurseult, inhabits a world in which, as he puts it, "nothing matters," not even his shooting a man to death at the beach. In *Dark City*, by contrast, nothing matters to anyone except to the one falsely accused of murder, John Murdoch.

Instead of a public concerned more with the keeping of convention than justice, here it is the strange chorus, insectlike, for whom nothing seems to matter. Known as "the strangers," they are dressed in trench coats ominously resonant with the dream sequence in which the trench-coat-clad character played by Leonardo DiCaprio in the movie *The Basketball Diaries* storms into his classroom and shotguns his teacher. It also resonates with the group of alienated students who called themselves the "trench coat mafia" of Columbine High School in Littleton, Colorado, two of whose members would explode in a murderous and suicidal rage a year after the release of *Dark City*. They apparently modeled themselves after the scene in *The Basketball Diaries*.

In seeing the film I suddenly imagine the strangers in the movie as a kind of cloned colony of Meurseult, the antihero of *The Stranger*. They gather every midnight in this night world to "tune," to chatter shrill little sounds, the result of which is a continually altering memoryscape projected into the city and into the shifting postmodern identities of its inhabitants. Buildings expand or shrink, new features appear, all is an unconscious mobility of place and identity, like a time-lapse film of contemporary life, a postmodern, constantly shifting Potemkin village.

The hero, Murdoch, somehow shares their "special" ability to tune. He is the individual, pitted against the mass of drones and power elite, somehow able to transcend the roles into which he is nightly projected. The only other human immune from the nightly transformations is the doctor Daniel Schreber, a name taken from an actual person, a judge from the nineteenth century. Schreber was the son of a physician whose widely read books advocated extremely harsh, constrictive methods of parenting, including devices to rigidly fix the posture of the child at the dining table. Many of Hitler's generation were raised on these methods of childrearing. Schreber the son published a book in 1903 titled *Memoirs of My Mental Illness*, which detailed his paranoid schizophrenia and described "fleetingly improvised men," forms sent in catastrophe to aid the one who would survive. "Fleetingly improvised men" rings as an apt name for postmodern identity, not to mention the character John Murdoch.

Freud used Schreber's memoir to describe schizophrenia. The doctor in the film is played by Kiefer Sutherland, the actor who a few years later went on to fame as secret policeman Jack Bauer, a commando capable of torturing or killing anyone at any time to get quick, violence-induced, adrenalized information. You know, like the kind that fans of the series get when watching it.

The landscape of *Dark City* is utterly claustrophobic: an old-time Hollywood grade B detective movie feel, set in a New York of the 1930s or so. There is no nature throughout the movie, not even urban nature: no trees, no fountains, not even a lawn. When Murdoch finally uses his tuning abilities in the finale, he creates a sun and an ocean beach. But it too is an illusory reality, set on a flat plane with swirling clouds, but no glorious globe of earth. Murdoch, who shares that alien power, remains unable to conceive a natural planet, or to return home again from virtual land. He gets the girl in a sentimentalized virtual reality through the same tuning powers that the aliens possessed: mind power, but no real soul power.

This theme also pervades *The Matrix* series, where the brain suck is amped-up to a level in which humans are reduced to virtual placental-like batteries for the machines, in a world devoid of natural wildness:

Neo: What is the Matrix?

Morpheus: The Matrix is everywhere. It's all around us, here even in this room. You can see it out your window, or on your television. You feel it when you go to work, or go to church or pay your taxes. It is the world that has been pulled over your eyes to blind you from the truth.

Neo: What truth?

Morpheus: That you are a slave, Neo. That you, like everyone else, was born into bondage . . . kept inside a prison that you cannot smell, taste, or touch. A prison for your mind.

The all-enveloping matrix is fought against by humans who by the end of the third film in the series seem themselves to be not much more than primitive kinds of machines, mass-rallying in a cavernous underground moshpit. Only the savior-figure, Neo, seems to be possessed of more. In the end, though, he is just another variant of Murdoch in *Dark City*: narcissistic grandiosity, able to leap walls in a single bound, locked inside his brain. He lacks the heart of Freder.

As in the 1982 film *Blade Runner*, there is the sci-fi fantasy of false memory, lost identity, everything the life of the "false self." And *Blade Runner*, which was based on Philip K. Dick's 1968 novel *Do Androids Dream of Electric Sheep?* and which continued a theme from Karel Čapek's 1921 play, *R.U.R.*, shows the machines to be more human than the humans who lost themselves through mechanistic master-slave delusions.

In *Blade Runner*, four advanced androids return to earth, the home they are forbidden to see because they are too indistinguishable from humans, in order to find their maker and learn how to prolong their lives beyond their allotted four years. They have all been programmed with false memories of childhoods and with special abilities by their genius "father," the head of the Tyrell Corporation. These creatures have no maternity and function as one might expect humans deprived of the early childhood narcissistic phase of mother attachment and separation that occurs between the ages of two and three. They search desperately for the empathic connection that never was, for the gaze of care and warmth, using "special gifts" they possess. They embody *The Drama of the Gifted Child*, as psychoanalyst Alice Miller put it in her book of that title, the narcissistic giftedness children develop to compensate for unempathic mothering.

Their extraordinary abilities of strength, sexuality, and cunning were "installed" as survival mechanisms, but function psychologically in the all-too-human androids as compensations for abandonment. For they have unexpectedly begun to experience real human emotions, real empathy for one another if not for humans, and their desperate need to extend their lives before dying becomes murderous narcissistic rage. This is most poignantly illustrated when Roy Batty, the android played by Rutger Hauer, penetrates the high-security high-rise corporate ziggurat of the Tyrell Corporation and confronts Tyrell about his origins and soon-to-be expired life span.

Tyrell: I'm surprised you didn't come here sooner.
Roy: It's not an easy thing to meet your maker.
Tyrell: And what can he do for you?
Roy: Can the maker repair what he makes?

Tyrell's response is basically no, that the life-span sequences cannot be altered. On hearing this, Roy cradles his surrogate "father's" head in both of his hands, looks him lovingly in the eyes, kisses him, and then proceeds to crush his skull in cold rage.

THE GREAT BRAIN SUCK

Čapek's play *R.U.R.* similarly involves a play on Nietzsche—showing the potential dark consequences of Übermenschen—as the following dialogue illustrates:

Harry Domin: I wanted to turn the whole of mankind into an aristocracy of the world. An aristocracy nourished by milliards of mechanical slaves. Unrestricted, free, and consummated in man. And maybe more than man.
Alquist: Superman?

In 1921 Čapek saw the false promise of the machine and "progress": the old Mephisto deal in shiny metallic clothing. Fritz Lang pictured it well, too, in *Metropolis*. The pure exercise of the will to power releases powers beyond the ability to limit them, such powers become "agents" unto themselves: robot nuclear weapons dictate world politics; robot automobiles dictate automotive habits of life; robot computers, televisions, bank tellers, and sex machines liberate us from direct experience in the name of convenience.

Machines are the latest episode of the old master-slave relationship, and the world today is like the Jewish stories of the golem that were prominent in Čapek's Prague. In one variant a rabbi made a golem, which grew throughout the day and served him. At the end of the day the rabbi would erase the name of God on the forehead of the golem (or under the tongue in other variants) and it would die. One day he forgot to eradicate the golem, which continued to grow through the night, monstrous, and when the rabbi awoke, he found his "will to power" willed to a superhuman level, which then annihilated him.

Dark City and *The Matrix* series strike me as important cultural indicators that picture the dire state of virtual lives people exhibit today in America and beyond, and that also find expression in the ideas of the leading lights of social thought and philosophy. The last surviving rogue android of *Blade Runner*, Roy, found his humanity at the conclusion of the film in saving his hunter named Rick Deckard, the blade runner played by Harrison Ford, by grasping his hand (even if the Harrison Ford character turns out to have been a 'droid as well, as the movie makes explicit in its 2007 director's cut release, *Blade Runner: The Final Cut*). But John Murdoch, protagonist of *Dark City*, merely assumes the power of the inhuman strangers, using it to project his own narcissistic, sentimentalized fantasy: a happy sunshine beach. *The Matrix's* Neo similarly soars to the heart of the matrix by excelling at its machine magic, which ultimately reveals itself as a jazzed-up version of the wizard in *The Wizard of Oz*, the deus ex machina.

The antithesis of creation, of the spontaneous life of the soul, is the automatic, which is equivalent to death. We live in the time of the automatic, for which these movies are symptoms of the "progressive" contraction of humanity. In *Metropolis* there was still the hope of the heart, represented by unmothered Freder. There, the narcissistic hero discovers empathy through his resolution of his Freudian-Christian-Marxist oedipal conflict, which also gets him the mother replacement, Maria. In *Blade Runner* a faint echo of the heart remained in the last human touch of the unmothered android. But by the time of *Dark City* and *The Matrix*, all that is human has all but melted away, leaving the empty narcissistic delusion of grandiose electronic mind magic, salvation by deus ex machina. And the God out of the machine has a final purpose in mind, being perfected in our time: to "save" humanity by replacing its organic qualities and capacities for self-originated experience with a machine-formatted substitute. That is "the myth of the machine," as Lewis Mumford put it, that we live in, the myth that denies myth and final purposes, even while enacting them.

The highly efficient, highly stratified economy of the hive was discovered 60 million years ago by bees and ants, and now humanity thinks its own technological version of it represents "progress," caring little for the simple fact that as we become antlike and beelike we forfeit all those qualities of empathy, spontaneity, and freedom that helped make us human.

GEAR SHIFT

What is normal in the consumption system we have today may not be normal for a rich home life, neighborhood life, and civic life, because these things require qualities such as love, friendship, trust, sharing, and forgiveness, and an ability to engage in self-originated experience. These things are not as easily bought and sold, yet are crucial for truly being normal in a vital way. They are the most valuable "things" one can possess. Even more basically, a home is a place where memories should be far richer than any computer could store, where the home-cooked meal should be a prized standard of cooking, where intimacy requires a self not completely encased in a commodity-driven identity, where things are means or testaments to the practice of life rather than emblems and trophies of some great baboon hierarchy.

GEAR SHIFT

Enscreening Consciousness

The telescreen received and transmitted simultaneously. Any sound that
Winston made, above the level of a very low whisper, would be picked up by

it; moreover, so long as he remained within the field of vision which the metal plaque commanded, he could be seen as well as heard. There was of course no way of knowing whether you were being watched at any given moment. How often, or on what system, the Thought Police plugged in on any individual wire was guesswork. It was even conceivable that they watched everybody all the time. But at any rate they could plug in your wire whenever they wanted to. You had to live—did live, from habit that became instinct—in the assumption that every sound you made was overheard, and except in darkness, every movement scrutinized.

—GEORGE ORWELL, *1984*

Any sufficiently advanced technology is indistinguishable from magic.

—ARTHUR C. CLARKE

In the 1960s, Lewis Mumford proposed the term *megamachine* to account for the transformation to the centralized, bureaucratized power structures associated with the advent of civilizations. The manifestation of specialized labor, standing military institutions and mass-killing warfare, and bureaucratic scribal institutions associated with settled city life, as well as a radical increase in social hierarchy, form a large-scale machinelike structure whose "parts" were mostly human.

In his view, the rise of the modern West is a reactivating of the ancient megamachine, with an added element: the progressive elimination of human parts by mechanical parts. Actually existing science today thus remains mythic in Mumford's perspective. Unlike traditional myths, it is an anti-mythic myth: the myth of the machine, the delusion of a machinelike universe, in which love, life, and purpose are mere contingencies. The "ghost in the machine" consciousness claimed to eradicate teleology from nature, but in fact retains a crypto-religious teleology of its own: to divest the human world of which it is a projection ("spectre" as William Blake put it) of human attributes, replacing them with machine virtual substitutes until all humanity is gone; further, to divest the world of nonmachine properties, such as spontaneity and biological variescence. Yet, as Charles Peirce put it, we live in a psycho-physical universe, one requiring a science that can understand that the signs that are its medium are themselves irreducibly real. Thus science may have achieved precision in particulars, but it has tended to unnecessarily exclude realities because of its contracted materialism.

The myth of the machine, as Mumford termed it, is similar to Marx's discussion of commodity fetishism: the treating of human purposes embodied in social institutions—including the machine elements—as though they were outside of human purpose, following independent mechanical rules. I take the establishment of both the ancient and modern megamachine as contractions of consciousness, first to anthropocentric mind, which encounters the world as the mirror of itself, and mechanico-centric mind, which encounters the world—and itself—as though it were a machine.[11]

Mumford described three stages in the myth of the machine, bridging the advent of civilization as the first "megamachine" to our own time:

If the first step in the rule of the Sun God was the unification of power and authority in the person of a Divine King, the second was the displacement of the actual king, who was still a living person, by a bureaucratic-military organization. But the third step, the fabrication of an all-embracing megamachine itself, could not be completed until an equivalent supreme ruler wholly of a "mechanical" nature, without human parts or attributes, could be invented.[12]

This description parallels Vaclav Havel's idea in his 1978 essay, "The Power of the Powerless," of a transition from totalitarian to posttotalitarian society. By "posttotalitarian" Havel meant that totalitarianism went on automatic, as a system no longer requiring an all-powerful dictator. But Mumford added a third stage, the completely dehumanized system, whose chief avatar would be the computer. In 1970, Mumford already foresaw not only the likely expansion of the computer to all facets of society but also the dire consequences for a world run ever more by and for automata.

Today the computer has become the virtual brain of the body electric, of the great robot. There are the other organs as well. As the head of Fritz Lang's futurist city *Metropolis* says to the mad scientist who serves him: "Rotwang, give your robot this girl's (Maria) likeness." Yes, the shiny metallic robot is not enough, it should have the appearance of the flesh, of seducing eyes, of that which will enable it to "pass" for human and enact its dehumanizing rituals, substituting virtual emotions for self-originated experience. It should have the happy glow of McDonald's, the magical beauty of commercials.

Although the increasing colonization of social life by computer is a key system requirement of the megamachine, I wish to focus here on a more specific question: How does such a megamachine inculcate its values? How does it mold selves through societal socialization? As Mumford described the emergent virtualization of the American child's world in 1970:

American children, who, on statistical evidence, spend from three to six hours a day absorbing the contents of television, whose nursery songs are advertisements, and whose sense of reality is blunted by a world dominated by daily intercourse with Superman, Batman, and their monstrous relatives, will be able only by heroic effort to disengage themselves from this system sufficiently to recover some measure of autonomy. The megamachine has them under its remote control, conditioned to stereotypes, far more effectively than the most authoritative parent.[13]

Mumford suggested in 1970 that the next phase of megamechanical dehumanization would be the creation of an elite deliberately deformed from birth by reduction or elimination of "inconvenient human attributes":

The next logical step, as with the Janissaries, would be to select for the "elite" in their cradles and deliberately deform them for the purpose in hand, so that no inconvenient human attributes will lessen their unconditional loyalty to the megamachine . . . nothing less than the selection of the elite from a bank of frozen spermatozoa and ova for gestation, under control, in an artificial womb . . .[14]

Mumford saw cloning as one possible means, and given the spread now of genetically altered animals and vegetables for commodification purposes, there is every reason to see human genetic modification for commodification purposes as the next phase in human "development": witness the $50,000 paid some years ago for "Ivy League" eggs. Even donated human organs have been commodified for profit by "harvesting" businesses—an interesting update on old-fashioned grave robbing.

Yet the genetic solution remains merely a literal one, and one need not necessarily change the hardware to alter the software. One can go directly to the software, to "man's glassy essence" itself, our neotenic nature, to train the megamachine's elite. This is a time-honored technique, the socialization into civilization and its discontents. But now the *degree* and *speed* with which the power complex indoctrinates its followers represents the most ominous sign of phase shift in dehumanizing system requirements.

As contemporary culture well knows, and is now perfecting, one can simply *brain rinse*, colonize, and deform children from infancy into becoming *consumers*. A consumer identity guarantees a being dependent on ceaseless acts of consumption through which that identity is maintained. A society that would permit such a systematic self-deforming socialization process, effected through relentless advertising and marketing, can be truly said to consume its own young. Need I remind you that Dante reserved the lowest rung of Hell for those who engaged in such behavior?

In the days of totalitarian communism, George Orwell could write, "Big Brother is watching you." But that system became obsolete; 1984 came and went, and by 1984 totalitarian had already given way to posttotalitarianism, as

Havel termed it, running on automatic. The Soviet Union lost the cold war to the superior machine of the West, not to democracy. America discovered that it is more efficient to pleasure the populace into submission than to beat them outright with truncheon. It is not so much that Big Brother is not watching you. You better bet that "he" is, in the "democratic" guise of Little Brother and Sister security, surveillance, and "national security" systems. That is simply not the main point.

Big Brother performs surveillance the other way around—one might say: "You is watching Big Brother," or better, Big Matrix, a synonym for mother. Big Matrix pounds, hammers, chisels the soul, killing it softly, not by brain-washing but by that seemingly gentler process *brain rinsing*, by conditioning deformity-conformity from birth on in virtual human software programmed to believe that every purchase is an act confirming one's identity.

Corporate consumption culture beams out its advertisements thousands of times per day into the minds, hearts, and souls of Americans, especially children, drilling them that they are fundamentally inadequate until they make an act of consumption, and that even then they can never hope to consume enough to be adequate beyond their consumption-colonized virtual identities. Puberty is another bio-cultural developmental process that can be altered to "brand" children by consumption dictates, as marketers have not only discovered but have also honed and expanded to intense marketing campaigns directed toward "'tweens."

Through its ever more pervasive advertising—which doubled over two decades to now expose Americans to between three and five thousand ads per day—the system indoctrinates people to identify commercial desires as their own materialistic fantasies, as the dreams of which their selves are made. It has created a culture of branded youth, for whom clothing labels function as ID cards, a time frame in which an obesity epidemic has imprisoned the bodily self. Contemporary corporate culture in America, as well as globally, may be the true other "superpower" enemy of America, more than equal to the task of undoing the United States than the Soviet Union and its inferior machines ever were, or even al Qaeda and related terrorists are, from within.

The old-fashioned brainwashing, propagandizing through negative reenforcement that seemed the principle approach of totalitarian states, did not seem as effective in producing a regulated, nonresistant order as the use of positive reenforcement through entertainment, sugar, kitsch, and endless conditioning by the commercial consumption machine. That is the "flesh" of the mechanico-centric mind, a virtual body depleter. And that is why I call this new, improved, seemingly softer but ultimately more effective technique *brain rinsing*. It clearly works better than traditional forms of education in imparting values, judging by how little resistance there is to progressive commercial colonization in public and private domains, in schools and homes in America. In this sense, America is virtually the avant-garde of the perfection of the megamachine, which is the complete inversion of Eden, of the aboriginal body-mind we evolved over hundreds of millennia and yet inhabit.

In a culture dominated by images of desire, buying, and instant material gratification, perhaps contemporary consumption can also be seen as directly concerned with socialization, education, and spirituality, albeit in sardonic inversion. Advertising is a vast effort to teach people the way of the commodity, not by rational persuasion so much as by endowing the commodity with a seductive, magic aura: the SUV that walks on water, the latest mythic movie figures connected with burgers, the talking toilet paper. These scripted images bespeak the contemporary philosophy of corporate sophists, seeking, like their ancient Greek counterparts, to persuade you to their view, not to the truth of things. But can this be called education? Spirituality? Perhaps indoctrination might be a better term, but then again much of what goes by the names "education" and "spirituality" in universities and churches today is but institutional indoctrination.

What if the whole thing, the whole fabric of contemporary civilized life, of universities and SUVs and religion and talking, glowing commodities is of one piece? What if we are truly locked in the illusory matrix of modern materialism, of the terminal perfection of the megamachine, of a contraction of consciousness, sleepwalking with eyes wide shut? What if the whole history of progress, of civilization and history, is a progressive lockstep march of one step forward, two steps backward, into The Lie?

The rule seems to be that as the culture becomes progressively infantilized into mechanico-centric consumption dependence, infants become progressively rationalized to the goals of the system. But can toddlers and young children be said to be agents of this process? Aren't the parents the agents?

GEAR SHIFT

Here's Looking at You, Kid: Turning an All-Seeing Blind Eye

We live in a camera civilization. Our entertainment is camera entertainment. Our holidays are camera holidays. We make them so by paying more attention to the camera we brought with us than to the waterfall we are pointing it at. Our science is almost entirely a camera science . . . and it is already becoming self-evident to camera man that only camera words have any meaning.
—OWEN BARFIELD, "The Harp and the Camera"

The dream of biological artificial "intelligence" has been a key theme of the computer age, but reaches back to robots and Mary Shelley's *Frankenstein* as well. From computer chip implants to genetically modified bodies and cloning, the theme of new, improved bodies has captivated modern consciousness. To some, these ideas may seem like the new paradise, to others, just plain scary, but from one perspective they may already be obsolete. They tend to focus on high-tech means of changing the hardware, but as Microsoft has amply demonstrated, the software may be more significant.

Software is the key, and what could be softer than a baby's head? That is where the bio-social Janissaries have already been in production for some time, though production methods are always improving.

Thanks to our biology as "degenerate monkeys" with prolonged neoteny, born with unfinished brains, one simply needs to substitute a bad mother early in the socialization process to alter the brain. The proven, efficient way to do this is to replace the gaze and frequent touch of the mother. How can one replace the gaze and frequent touch of the mother today? This is achieved by placing a big eye in every home, which is gazed at but does not touch, and which demands that children meet its needs. This artificial eye is what we call television, or more broadly, The Screen.

Although already highly efficient, the megamachine has become more effective in colonizing the developing brain in the past few years, reaching in from birth to two years old with specifically designed "Teletubbies," "Einstein videos," "BabyFirst TV," and the sugaring and toy grasping ads. A recent Kaiser Foundation study found that fully 61 percent of babies one year or younger view TV or videos every day for at least an hour on average. Eighty-three percent of children under the age of six watch about two hours of combined screen media per day, including TV, videos/DVDs, video games, and computers.[15] As Vicky Rideout, a coauthor of the study put it, "There has been this sense that it is kids clamoring for media and parents trying to hold back the tidal wave. But what came out is that parents themselves are very enthusiastic about using media in their children's lives. Many feel like they can't make it through the day without the assistance it gives."[16]

Parents enthusiastically support the colonizing effect of television, placing TVs in young children's rooms so that family members can view their own shows, as more than 50 percent reported. This is occurring during the crucial bonding with and separation from the mother, that developmental phase from between ages one and a half to three, wherein the bases for empathy and autonomy are established, undoing the biosocial requirements of the self. And even more ominously, it is reaching back to birth, intruding on the most basic development of the infant in establishing borders between itself and world.

When one considers the eye as an opening to the soul, as an organ that conveys the spontaneous self, the limitations of the camera/screen view become more apparent. And this is particularly true for the relations between mother and infant, where the empathic gaze and the "holding environment" provided by the mother and her touch, her literal and emotional structuring of the infant, are crucial not only for the initial development of the self but also for its later maturation.

It is a virtual system requirement that empathy, a key goal of primate mother-infant bonding process, be replaced with megatechnic loyalty. It makes for better "batteries" for the donamatrix of postdemocratic society. As the former president of the Kids-R-Us clothing store once famously put it, "If you own this child at an early age, you can own this child for years to come. Companies are saying, 'Hey, I want to own the kid younger and younger.'"

Think of it this way: the megamachine colonizes the self of the young child in its infancy, substituting for the empathic gaze and touch of the mother, the commercial empathy-substitute of the television's gaze, the gaze of the machine. The television, video game, and computer function as electronic idols, as elements of a great image apparatus, whose mirages promise all good things, all fables and desires of the child's imaginary world, if the child will only consume what the machine demands of it, including adrenalized button pushing.

Adrenalizing-attention culture is a form of electro-chemical stimulation that threatens to deplete indigenous attention, especially in at-risk children, much as bio-chemical stimulation depletes indigenous brain functions. As another recent Kaiser Foundation study shows, about 60 to 70 percent of all food ads kids see are for sugar! Thirty-four percent are for candy and snacks, 28 percent are for cereal, and 10 percent are for fast foods (ok, "fast foods" is fat, salt, other processed ingredients, and sugaring). And remarkably, out of 8,854 ads considered, "there were none for fruits or vegetables targeting children or teens."[17] The absence of vegetable or fruit ads is not even a new phenomenon, but has been noted for at least a generation. Even sweet fruits remain invisible in advertising to kids, eclipsed by sweet fruit juice. The matrix is not only what you see, but also what remains hidden.

American children born in 2000 have a one in three chance of developing diabetes (two in five if they are African American) as reported in the *Journal of the American Medical Association*, and are primed to have lower life expectancy than their parents. High fructose corn syrup first appeared in Coca Cola in 1980, a sweet psycho-toxic epiphany spreading throughout the food industry quickly, and as Michael Pollan describes it: "Since 1985, an American's annual consumption of HFCS [high fructose corn syrup] has gone from forty-five pounds to sixty-six pounds. . . . During the same period our consumption of refined sugar actually went up by five pounds. What this means is that we're eating and drinking all that high-fructose corn syrup *on top* of the sugars we were already consuming. In fact, since 1985 our consumption of all added sugars—cane, beet, HFCS, glucose, honey, maple syrup, whatever—has climbed from 128 pounds to 158 pounds per person."

Pollan goes on to say that much of the high fructose corn syrup is consumed in soft drinks, and that the increase in consumption was enabled by both what I'll call the supersizing and cheap calorie epiphanies, which made high caloric but not healthy, foods easier and cheaper to obtain: potato chips and cookies, but not carrots. He concludes, "That corn-made calorie can find its way into our bodies in the form of an animal fat, a sugar, or a starch, such is the protean nature of the carbon in that big kernel. But as productive and protean as the corn plant is, finally it is a set of human choices that have made these molecules as cheap as they have become: a quarter century of farm policies designed to encourage the overproduction of this crop and hardly any other. Very simply, we subsidize high-fructose corn syrup in this country, but not carrots."[18]

This strange invisible domination of American life by the alchemy of corn, brain sucking by high fructose sugaring—excess calories in, awareness out— is also mirrored in the socialization of children by advertising. Kids' TV ads communicate fantastic, magical minidramas of sugaring, peopled by cartoon figures and superhero demigods, all minions of the sugaring complex. The world of the hunter-gatherers through whom we evolved into humans is now completely reversed. They taught their children to believe in a fantastic world, revering and learning the varieties of the plants and animals that gave them life, ruminating over them in play and ritual—consider the place of maize in aboriginal America, for example, in Central America or in the Pueblo Corn Dance. We teach our children to believe in a world of fantastic appearances that mask an underlying rational-mechanical construct, and to revere the toxins that deprive us of nutrition and indigenous imagination, the toxins of death. We banish the plants, and impose a multitude of toxic brands, producing obesity, diabetes, and "A prison for your mind," as *The Matrix*'s Morpheus put it.

The gaze of the machine, through TV and computer screens and the whole plethora of consumption props, instills the sense of basic inadequacy, which can then be remedied through the latest thing to purchase. The gaze of the machine, in short, is a bad mother, a genuinely unempathic mother, to whom the child must respond, but who will not respond to the genuine needs of the child, of this particular child.

Television is a virtual bad mother who never gets charged with child abuse, despite the fact that her gaze is the gaze of violence and sexual desire and wanton greed without limit. If a babysitter were to say the things that TV says to young children, or to show them the endless images of violence and sexual desire, she or he would surely be charged with child abuse. Juliet Schor's book, *Born to Buy*, ominously reveals how marketing has channeled vast corporate resources toward children, using ploys of gaining trust that strike me as uncomfortably resembling those of child predators.[19] Marketers deliberately seek to disable mothers and parents generally, by associating antiadult values with sugared and enscreening commodities, interposed between children and their parents: the commodities bestow "cool," the parents are portrayed as "uncool."

Consumption culture illustrates the ghost in the machine mentality in the way its advertising apparatus fuels a magical fantasyland of consumption, socializing its participants into lives of daydreaming acts of consumption. Schor describes a study by Fournier and Guiry in her book *The Overspent American*, which revealed that 61 percent of adult respondents *always* have something in mind that they look forward to buying. And in her own recent study of children between the ages of ten and thirteen, fully 88 percent of the kids responded that they usually have something in mind they want to buy or get.[20]

These fantasies of "sacred" or magical consumption seem to offer a contrast with mundane or "profane" everyday life, even as they become the dream-stuff of everyday lives of quiet desperation. Unfulfilled desires function as the basis for making an unfulfillable, consumption-addicted self. The ancient Sacred Game of the hunter-gatherer, reverentially and imaginatively attuned over hundreds of millennia to the wild Other in the here and now, is now inverted to the self-depleting fantasies of Commodified Other, which is supposed to fulfill the self even as it empties it of self-originated experience.

When a consumption culture trains people from infancy to feel inadequate until an act of consumption is made, commodifying their identities, the grounds are laid for an unself-trustworthy populace. Such an insecure, dependent, conforming-to-consumption-dictates, indoctrinated populace represents a system requirement of the techno-consumption-machine: ever more dependent upon its pseudo-solace, its metallic-silicon mothering.

In his books *The Culture of Narcissism* and *The Minimal Self*, Christopher Lasch drew attention to the ways in which consumption culture represents a cultural manifestation of clinical narcissistic disturbance. It tends to select for an empty self, to promise that the self could only be fulfilled through acts of consumption, acts that leave the self emptier and more dependent on consumption: a culture predicated upon a minimalized self, contracted from its two-million-year evolutionary legacy.

Psychoanalysts such as D. W. Winnicott and Alice Miller have described narcissistic personality disorders as involving the development of a "false self," a defensive projection used to protect a person against the pathologies of bad mothering. The false self meets the needs of an inadequate mother, whereas a "good-enough mother," in Winnicott's usage, meets the changing needs of the emerging self of the infant and child.

I wish to argue for the reality, if I may use that term, of the false self as a requirement of contemporary megatechnic America. That false self created by the consumption machine is not arbitrary, but is a rationalized projection of the system, dependent upon it, a genuine agent and apparatchik of its system requirements. It grows into adulthood, a frozen false consumer self, tragically seeking its connection to the mega-mechanical-Mommy, indoctrinated into its/her "goodness," defended against its/her usurpation of the self's deepest spontaneous feelings and genuine needs. In short, the alien clones are already here, have been with us for some time, living their vicarious virtual existence through the programmed selves they inhabit. They "R" Us!

Is it any wonder that they are capable of shaping the body today so quickly to mechanico-centric system requirements through the obesity epidemic? Of displacing direct, face-to-face, eye-to-eye encounter, a tactile public space, which is far more than a mere linguistic practice, with an escapist, antipublic sphere, privatization culture? Of projecting into McMansionized surveillance suburbs, whose money often support elite "public" schools, into shopping malls, where free speech can be regarded as trespassing, into the utopian *ou topos*—nowhere—of computer space, where anonymous interaction often trumps person-to-person contact? Of a consumptive evaporation from democracy? True, computer and related electronic technologies are also openings for communications, as television can be for learning. But the tendency is to displace primary *face-to-face relations*, and secondary person-to-person *role relations*, to what I term *tertiary relations* of person-machine mediated interaction.

It would seem that the movement from a jogging to a couch-potato America in the 1980s signals part of the problem, garnished by 1990s computer jockeying. When anthropologists discuss *nomadic* versus *sedentary* peoples, do they have any idea of how "*sedentary*" is being perfected in our time? Mammon seems to be exacting pounds of flesh, all rendered unto consumption. What could be better than to colonize the human body into a benumbed sedentary state, substituting low-intensity virtual experiences, usually involving massive amounts of commercials, for real life? Sugar the brain, fatten the body, brain rinse the soul. Alienate people from their bodies in the act of encasing them in them—and with the speed, as the American Medical Association put it, of a communicable disease.

Whatever religion Americans preach, it is the religion of consumption they practice. The rise of American fundamentalism, especially the evangelical movement, may be understood as what rushed in to fill the brain sucked, belly-busting void created by the cult of consumption: pseudo-certainty as seesaw compensation for the carnival of commodities. And Mammon exacts a heavy toll, indeed, substituting fat for one's autonomous identity through "normalizing" a culture of overeating and undernourishment.

Then there is the sleeplessness epidemic, the extraction of the imaginative inner life of mammalian dreamtime and bodily renewal by techno-activities or sleeping pill consumption. Sleeping pill prescriptions have risen dramatically with about a 60 percent increase in prescriptions since 2000, following the 1998 Federal Drug Administration decision to allow drug advertising directly to consumers. This trend follows the coffee trend led by the spread of Starbucks since the nineties: caffeinate up, sedate down. Then there is walking deprivation (goodbye bipedalism!), and machine-dependent exercise programs, and numerous other system devices that insure that self-originated experience is minimized. This is truly a devolutionary drama of "status survival of the unfittest," whose techno-opiated bodily, mind, and soul sleepwalking conformity insures their fitness as cogs of the system.

What do you get when you devitalize humans in such ways? Drones on automatic. This is no accident but reflects the direct targeting of the human body by mechanico-centric mind seeking to perfect itself through its own bodily "software." The regressive removal of body-mind from living habitat into walled cities, sacred books, and now machines and screens, seems to be an infernal law of devolution: The great dream of liberation from the struggles of life has unwittingly brought us to the very real possibility of the extinction of humane and organically rooted life.

How can such system requirements be overcome? Can children today be taught the courage to not consume as a way of life, or to value local entrepreneurs and nonfranchised local life? Can adults find their way back to their bodies, their souls, their own minds, untrammeled by imposed brain suck?

I submit that the prospects are not too bright, but neither is it hopeless. It might be that for such an overcoming of the vast dehumanizing power complex at work today, the humane powers that are rapidly going into virtual extinction are the very ones that can best offset the *postdemocratic military-industrial-academic-entertainment-sport-food complex*. Consider the words of Havel, from "The End of the Modern Era":

It is my profound conviction that we have to release from the sphere of private whim such forces as a natural, unique and unrepeatable experience of the world, an elementary sense of justice, the ability to see things as others do, a sense of transcendental responsibility, archetypal wisdom, good taste, courage, compassion and faith in the importance of particular measures that do not aspire to be a universal key to salvation. Such forces must be rehabilitated.

Things must once more be given a chance to present themselves as they are, to be perceived in their individuality.[21]

Allowing people and things to present themselves as they are involves a reawakening of what it means to be human, a task as simple as telling the mechanico-emperor that it has no clothes, and as difficult as acknowledging oneself as a colonized element of that materialistic power structure. First and foremost in reawakening is to take seriously the developmental requirements of infants for frequent touch, empathic gaze, good-enough mothering, good-enough parenting. Taking our neotenous nature seriously means rethinking our institutions of education too, including, for example, the needs of puberty both physiologically and in rites of passage as something schools should be directed toward in learning, and not as something "extracurricular." But the problems go even deeper, in my opinion, requiring a questioning of the whole fabric of civilization, especially in a world where bio-global devastation threatens the health of the planet.

GEAR SHIFT

Man is a giant robot created by DNA to make more DNA.
—SCIENTIST HERMANN MULLER

Science cannot stop while ethics catches up.
—SCIENTIST ELVIN STACKMAN[22]

Scientists have discovered many amazing things in the past century, but might it be possible to be precise in the details and fundamentally wrong in the big picture? The ancient Hindus described a cyclical picture of the universe whose decline, the "Kaliyuga," is a time of childish rampant destruction. It is a good metaphor of our present scientific age, when overweening rationality, cut loose from passionate mind, proclaims itself the only proper guide to knowledge.

How is it that these "unscientific" ancient philosophers, using subjective sensing of the human creature and its follies, allow for regressive delusions, while "wise" scientists have been proclaiming unending progress throughout the past century? Think of that worldview of the religion of modern science, which flowered in mid-twentieth century with its hydrogen bombs and totalitarian scientifically planned societies, with its cult that society could be governed by scientific principles: by bomb makers, by replacing mother's milk with "formula," by building more and more roads and cars, more and more technology, by transforming all "undeveloped" forests and lands into modern, scientifically planned agricultural centers, by exterminating bugs with DDT, by transforming universities into research grant junkies, by building ever more complex machines that would free us from our drudgery through our increased dependence upon them. Here is an example of the power of science for you, from one of its deadliest temples, the Atomic Energy Commission, which in 1971 proclaimed, "Large nuclear explosives give us, for the first time, the capability to remedy nature's oversights."[23]

This is indeed a world vision of infinite possibilities, where, as Dostoyevsky's Grand Inquisitor predicted, "Everything is permitted." Only we have discovered that everything is not permitted, that one cannot format natural finitude according to scientistic megalomania.

This is what the big-picture of science and technology has showed itself time and time again in the past century to be: a crypto-religion of arrogant cult scientism, led by emotional infants (albeit intelligent and skillful infants). I don't think such views express the real essence of science, but that is how the culture of science, institutionally, has repeatedly revealed itself.

Where were the scientists during the first half of the century who should have seen the dark and dangerous possibilities of the powers science was releasing? Why did it take a "fool" like Henry Adams, using logically incorrect methods on the rise of power over the last few centuries, to predict in 1905 that it would not take another half century for there to be "bombs of cosmic violence," and conditions in which morality would become police, and disintegration overcome integration?

Why did humans evolve under conditions of reverence and awe, conditions that have sustained humans until modern "scientific" times? Do you think hominids could have evolved into humans under the kinds of scientific, technical, bureaucratic, economic, ideological, academic, and artistic thinking that predominated in the past century? The answer is no. This would have been a starvation diet to the fierce passionate creatures who created us.

GEAR SHIFT

I am Not a Number, I am a free man.
—THE PRISONER

Normal Man normally kills that which does not fit into Normality. Traditionally he kills the inspired wise man. The wise man's followers form a religion or school. Then that religion or school becomes normal, and kills its own original impulses to insure that no genuine inspirations will happen again.

Creativity seems to me to work like that. Normal people like to steal the creativity and kill the creative one, so that they can possess the creativity. Then their very possession and use of it renders it normal and no longer creative. But they often do appropriate the worldly success.

Take *The Death of al-Hallaj*, a depiction of a tenth-century Muslim from Baghdad who allowed his religious passion to flow. So of course he had to be put to death. Why was al-Hallaj, with his wonderful sense of play and irony, not a founder of a religion like Jesus and Mohammed, who both seem to me so earnest? Then again, the recently translated Gospel of Judas has Jesus laughing a couple of times. Perhaps Jesus was killed a second time—and for me this would be his real death—by his Normalizing followers and their idealized Christ, who deleted his sense of play and other unacceptable qualities, and "earnesthetized" him.

This battle goes on in us, individually, too. And that is why the poet and painter William Blake proposed a marriage between heaven and hell. Without those corrosives and fiery inspirations, we would go inert. Maybe that's why the bumper sticker says, "I like heaven for the climate, hell for the company."

Consider contemporary image consumption culture in this light. It takes as its task the absorption of human emotion through its projection of virtual transcendence, of appearances of corrosives and fiery inspirations whose sources run deep in sex, war, and religion, of magic celebrities whose images and actions are so many stimuli producing emotion-like responses in the spectatorial lonely crowd. Consider a populace socialized into this world from early childhood, carefully trained to experience the extremes of human emotion in virtual scenarios of TV violence and commercial abundance. These bright images of contemporary consumption culture are beacons shining dark lights upon the human soul, the old Faust deal done under slow habituation. It is the dance of the bees, the simulated scents of simulated flowers, compelling the populace to the rules of the hive, making them feel as if they're alive!

As Dr. Miles J. Binnell shouted out at the end of *Invasion of the Body Snatchers* over a half century ago, "THEY'RE HERE ALREADY! YOU'RE NEXT! YOU'RE NEXT! YOU'RE NEXT..."

GEAR SHIFT

Materialism and Normalcy: Why Be Normal?

I probably don't need to tell the reader that the word normal means norm or average. Norms that set healthy limits are necessary to any society. You can't live without some norms. Yet if one's ultimate goal is to become normal, one gives up on one's own possibilities of development. A healthy individual, on average, needs to be immersed to varying extents within family, household, work, and larger community. Everybody has different levels and degrees by which they identify themselves and find balance.

We the American people tend to like to believe that—although it is a fantasy, we are a rugged people as we drive our mechanical broncos and otherwise named totemic chariots. So we live these fantasies of rugged individualism, while in reality we reduce ourselves to a pathologically "normal" existence. We become the norm of a vast, mega-technic machine. We produce and are trained to consume mass quantities of *low-grade experience* as a key system requirement of postdemocratic society, weaning us from real life. The effect may very well be that . . .

You Are Getting Sleepy

you wish to become more aware
you watch the news
you are getting sleepy
very, very sleepy
sleepy pill seductions. . . .

you see the Lunesta butterfly cartoon
and you are getting sleepy
floating back to your cartoon childhood
you watch a little news
sandwiched between the drug ads
sandwich!

blood to stomach . . . cartoon to brain . . .
aware of the news
the politician is . . .
very, very sleepy

you dream Ambien dreams
drowsy dreams of
unaware
trademarked winds
the storm has . . .
no survivors were . . .

sleepy dopey couchy potatoey
grouchy

you are . . .
dreaming Tinkerbell butterflies
floating in the violence
drive-by butterflies
sleepy in your stomach
warding off the day
warding off the night
like news of nothing

you feel . . .
very sleepy
no rest for the living dead
wary of your weary

Dormatil, Restoril,
Melloril, whooperwill,
the night-fix
Peter Panned

eye prod
urge to yawn
sleep to dawn
dimming down
tv pill. . . .

you are getting . . .
electro-chemical brain rinsed
all wired tapped
sleepy anxiety
of wish-world fantasia

perchance to . . .
buy the drug
sleep on it
awakening
very, very sleepy
drugged with unaware

take me
O Lunecstatic Ambulance
alleviate Bolivia
obliviate Namibia
enumerate amphibia
when sleep is twinned to death.

GEAR SHIFT

*Mourning and Melodrama: Reflections from 1997 on
Media Narcissism and Substitute Emotions*

What is the proper place of heroes and celebrities in social life? Public figures are supposed to be people who do things that, for various reasons, place them in the public eye. But what happens when an excessive emphasis on commercially produced celebrity takes over the socialization process and defines who counts as public figures and heroes?

Take, for example, the way artificially manufactured celebrity replaces genuine achievement, as in the rise of so-called entertainment news, whose purpose is to promote celebrities and their nonnews, or the way normal news excessively panders to celebrity sensationalism. The normal process of having role models in the environment, with whom we can either identify or internalize in the dialogue of the self, gets replaced by the elevation of celebrities and the kind of virtual world that celebrities inhabit.

Instead of contributing to the cultivation of the self, the system infiltrates the self at the core of the identification process, that "glassy essence" of which Shakespeare wrote, mirror of the soul, binding its images to those processes the psychoanalysts call "object-relations" and the social psychologists call "role modeling." It taps the roots of human emotion with its image/sound/product scenarios of ecstatic sex, violence, death, and the longings for transcendence, installs them, and presto! It turns people into replicas of human beings, brain sucked of their spontaneous life.

CUT TO COMMERCIAL

Consider the following statement issued by CNN, concerning the funeral for fashion designer Gianni Versace:

33

MILAN, Italy (CNN)—Naomi Campbell, one of Gianni Versace's favorite models, wept openly Tuesday as she, Princess Diana, Elton John and scores of international celebrities came here to say goodbye to the murdered fashion designer at the first public memorial in his native land.

Some 2,000 people, including Versace's brother Santo, his sister Donatella and his companion Antonio D'Amico, packed Milan's Gothic Roman Catholic cathedral for the service, one week after the Italian designer was gunned down outside his Miami Beach home. Authorities continued their hunt for the shooter, believed to be spree killing suspect Andrew Cunanan.

Famous Faces in Mourning

Those from the fashion world in attendance included model Carla Bruni and designers Giorgio Armani, Karl Lagerfeld, Carla Fendi and Tai Missoni. Also present were singer Sting; Carolyn Bessette, the wife of John Kennedy Jr.; and Italian ski star Alberto Tomba. Sting and Elton John were to sing a setting of Psalm 23, "The Lord is my shepherd." Italian opera star Luciano Pavarotti also was expected.

Campbell, wearing a black dress and jacket and dark glasses, had to be supported prior to the service as she walked to the Versace empire headquarters in Milan. She was doubled over and crying.

Princess Diana, a lover of Versace's glamorous, sexy clothes, wore a black dress and white pearls. The designer had named a handbag after her—the Lady Di. The princess was seated next to John. The pop singer, a fan of Versace's flamboyant outfits, was dressed in a dark suit.

END COMMERCIAL

GEAR SHIFT, IN A DARK SUIT

Killing the Creator

Some time after the murder of Gianni Versace I received one of those phone calls from a journalist, the one where they solicit your expert opinion on a subject not even remotely connected to your expertise. My call came from Christopher Mason, who was writing a biography of Versace.[24] I told him I was no expert on celebrity, but if I had anything to say I would. In fact, the first part of our conversation was more me interviewing him. He told me how the supermodels who attended Versace's funeral had been feuding with the company for the previous year. Nevertheless, their agencies flew them to Milan, and when they arrived at their lavish hotel suites each found a black Versace dress in her size waiting for her—a kind of gift from the grave. He also told me of the friendship between Versace, Princess Di, and Elton John, and how they too had been feuding before Versace's death. As we spoke I improvised a theory of Versace's murder: that Andrew Cunanan, his murderer, had a rage toward his father, who never recognized him, and transferred it to Versace, who Mason said apparently met Cunanan at the San Francisco Opera a few years earlier and recognized him from seeing him at some earlier time with an old friend.

I would like to take Cunanan as an example of the colonization of the self by consumer celebrity culture. He was someone who liked money and its luxuries, the "visibility" it makes possible, and who acquired them by being a "kept man," his expenses paid for by wealthy gay lovers, who typically were older men. He seems to be a textbook case of a narcissistic false-self disturbance, someone whose identity was largely based not only on the commodity forms it desired and acquired but also by him becoming a commodity for his lovers: "someone's amusing trinket" as the *Miami Herald* put it in an editorial.

As forensic psychologist Reid Meloy stated in an interview, Cunanan's rage and wanton killing spree exhibited, "The horrible flowering and self-destruction of a high-velocity young psychopath. . . . No one would know the name Sirhan Sirhan unless he killed Robert Kennedy. No one would know Mark David Chapman unless he killed John Lennon. Destroying a figure of that stature links you to that figure in perpetuity."[25]

If Cunanan illustrates a self extrinsically shaped by exhibitionistic markers of prestige, masking an underlying narcissistic rage and psychopathic manipulativeness, then the breakdown of that false self—and consequent release of the rage—might be expected to find its target in the self-images it could destroy: ex-lovers, older wealthy men, finally by a celebrity who once paid him attention by recognizing him. One can see how a narcissistically disordered self whose real feelings had been replaced by those of the consumption and status and celebrity world could be led by his self-images and released rage to destroy a celebrity, his Creator, the creator of his false self. In destroying the celebrity self-image, he could simultaneously merge with it, as another well-known raging American, Captain Ahab, did with his grandiose self-image, the whale, Moby-Dick.

Cunanan's creator, personified by Versace, was, like himself, a poor kid from a Catholic country who made it big in America, made it big in the world, and was in a close friendship triangle with the megacelebrities Princess Di and Elton John.

And a month after Versace's celebrity murder, his friend Princess Di topped his death with an even more perfect celebrity death, resulting from the infamous chasing of her auto by the Parisian paparazzi. Her death provided an international outpouring of emotions, a perfect synthesis of mourning and celebrity, tapping the traditional idealization of royalty and fusing it with a woman whose image bridged Mother Teresa's Eastern world of poverty and suffering with *la dolce vita* of the West—not to mention a genuine "playboy of the Western world," of middle-eastern extraction, Dodi Fayed. No soap opera could come close to this script: talk about "global village"! But let us return to the American melodrama, the killing of the Italian celebrity in Miami by the Philippine boy-toy.

When Mason told me that Versace's everyday friends sat in the back of the funeral services in Milan because of the celebrities filling the front rows, I asked, "He wouldn't have wanted that, would he?" Mason replied enthusiastically that, quite to the contrary, a celebrity funeral would be precisely what Versace would have wanted, that he basked in the celebrity spotlight, thoroughly enjoying surrounding himself with other celebrities.

Think about it. You can buy your identity by buying a fine set of clothes, by watching the celebrity images of fashion. This is the profane level of everyday consumption culture.

Or you can go to the sacred level by appropriating the Creator himself, instead of buying through the medium of money, killing through the medium of a gun. You attain immortality in this act of identification with the Creator. If "clothes make the man," merging in death with the Clothes Creator makes the man immortal.

Cunanan had an intermediary step: he killed a Chicago businessman "father," and stole some of his suits with the car—a Lexus—and money. He acquired clothing through the bullet method of down payment, which also helped point the way toward the Creator.

The Christ killed sex and aggression: no sex with the Holy Mary Oedipal Mother, no sex with the prostitute Mary "lover." No aggression toward the Heavenly Father who condemned him to death, no aggression toward the carpentry inflicted upon him on the cross, which cut close to his earthly and absent father's own profession.

Cunanan the "altar boy," as his father described him in denying his son's homosexuality, could not act against his earthly father, who had come to America, failed financially, and returned home. But when all mediating defenses were undone, he could go straight to the heavenly father, the former altar boy Versace, who had risen from poverty and made it big in America. Like the androids in *Blade Runner*, Cunanan could seek out Versace and merge with him and his immortal celebrity in a final act of murderous, suicidal aggression. He could merge as the antiprodigal son with the Creator, the Father, the Godfather of the extrinsic identity!

Ironically, in doing so, he provided his earthly father with a potential for windfall profit. The elder Cunanan responded to the media by making virtually immediate plans to have a film made about his son.

America is not only the land of democratic virtual royalty, it is also the home of celebrity virtual Olympus, of a virtual heaven that is nevertheless becoming increasingly globalized. Perhaps in this strange global media melodrama Princess Di, whose death anniversary again made the media headlines in 2007, is the new celebrity female Jesus; Versace is the good thief; Elton John—though not yet dead—is the bad thief; Mother Teresa is Holy Mother; Georg Solti—who also died in 1997—conducts in the background; while Madonna dances in her autoerotic "truth or dare" virtual video world on the actual grave of her mother. Meanwhile, real human dramas and tragedies go unnoticed, thousands die in auto accidents—like the friend of an acquaintance who died in an auto accident in Spain two weeks before Princess Di, and whose body required weeks of waiting before it could be returned to England for the funeral—and millions and millions of lives of unquiet desperation remain attuned to the Great Broadcast of the techno-maniacal media cult.

Ten years after Cunanan's celebrity murder, the Virginia Tech killer, Seung-Hui Cho, added his Columbine copycat variation, mass-murdering fellow students and professors. The young man who hardly ever spoke, and who signed his name in class as a question mark, burst out in a terminal volley of bullets and words. Between his first two murders and the thirty more that followed two hours later, he put together a package of videos, photos, and writings—some family members even said it was the first time they remembered him speaking whole sentences—and sent them to NBC. He would finally be seen and heard. It made for great news.

GEAR SHIFT

Consider the irony in this large claim I am making: the mechanical system of nature that replaced the Aristotelian worldview by the seventeenth century, did so by ejecting goal-directed conduct—teleology—from nature. Yet, I am claiming, it secretly retains that teleology in its mythic goal of dehumanization. But how is it possible for a nonteleological mechanical system to do this?

It is possible, in my opinion, because that entire system, the basis for modern science and civilization, is a grand social construction, a mythic projection of that automatic side of the human psyche onto the world, a mythic projection that must fundamentally deny that not only are the machines of humans themselves projections of the human mind, but also that the machine image of the universe is a projection of a portion of the human mind, of its automatic aspects, which must necessarily exclude the autonomous aspects.

So much of human life is engaged in the tension between the automatic and the autonomous, the rote habitual and the spontaneous engagement of the moment. And the course of modern civilization has also been the simultaneous development of the automatic and the autonomous, of the mechanical features of existence one sees in the developments of natural science and the subjective dimensions of existence one sees in the rise of the novel, of perspective in painting, of tonality in music.

In the twentieth century, it was as if the cultural "corpus callosum" joining these two sides of the modern mind broke, leaving parallel but relatively incommunicable courses for each. Modern art embodied this split in its tendencies, especially by midcentury, toward purely "objective" or purely "subjective" works.

What Arnold Schoenberg intended in his serial, or twelve-tone, music was one thing, what it resulted in—institutionally—was a rationalization of music, an objectivism comparable to the rationalization of architecture in the "international style," to the rationalization of philosophy in logical positivism and Anglo-American "language analysis," to psychological behaviorism, to scientism, to hyperrationalized, bureaucratized corporate and communist culture, all particularly dominant in the fifties. Simultaneously, the other split-brain opposite in the twentieth century was formlessness; for example, John Cage's aleatoric, or chance, music. From the burst of energy at the beginning of the century came an unviable legacy: lifeless forms and formless life; subjectless objects and objectless subjects; the "originality" of nothingness. Disconnected objectivism and subjectivism mapped the terminus of the modern era: the ghost in the machine.

Although a number of artists—some yet to emerge to visibility—did not capitulate to the "advanced" image of pure subjectivism or objectivism, the majority of "avant-garde" artists did, only to find themselves on a dead-end street, damaged goods. Even postmodernism, as a movement, again, with exceptions, could not provide an alternative. If modernism culminated ultimately in a dead-end, postmodernism was the "no exit" sign at the end of the dead-end street.

One insect uses all the known aerodynamic methods that anybody has con-
jectured. Rather than progressing from one sort of wing stroke to another
as flying speed changes—the way horses go from walk to trot to canter—the
butterflies behave more like Olympic gymnasts doing floor exercises. If the
average human being moved like the average red admiral [butterfly], city sidewalks would be filled with people progressing by hop, skip, jump, cartwheel
and back flip, in no particular order.

—DR. ADRIAN L. R. THOMAS[26]

Give me those city sidewalks, alive with "average people" progressing hop-
ping skipping jumping cartwheeling back-flipping in no particular order
other than the groove of life presenting itself to them as the airflows do to the
butterflies.

> Give me a life as free as the flap of a butterfly wing!
> For I would perpetually
> float like a butterfly
> and sting like a bee,
> And that's why I will always revere
> Muhammad Ali!

Muhammad Ali boxed the way a butterfly flies, *live to the moment!* You see . . .

We humans, in our current perverse separation from life, can take the
absolute free beauty of these butterfly flappings, spontaneously beating the
rhythms and aerodynamics of life, and turn them into this evil opportunistic
thought written into the discussion of butterflies cited above by James Gorman: "There is also a challenge and an opportunity for the creators of micro-air
vehicles, small autonomous flying machines that could be used for spying."

Why does Gorman's mind need to go there? It's not that what he says is
false, it is, indeed, "the future" that the old military-industrial complex has
finally come around to seeing as viable: no mere drive-bys, but butterfly-by
killings. The military machine was locked for so long into "biggest is beautiful," into wasting billions and billions of dollars into Dr. Edward Teller/Dr.
Strangelove large-scale hydro-incendiary hell-bombs, that it ignored the
military effectiveness of small-scale warring. And it killed and will have killed
into the millions, innocents, radioactively speaking, by the end of this century (see the book *Atomic Audit*).

But life doesn't wait for military-industrial science types to do their Faustian magic, it gets there way before them, way before "science" or even "philos-

ophy," in quotes, do. Consider Stanislaw Lem's fictional account of weapons of the twenty-first century, in "The Upside-Down Evolution," first published in 1984:

... the twenty-first-century synsect weapon is not a swarm of insects just like the ones in an entomologist's atlas, only made of metal.

Some of the pseudo-insects could pierce the human body like bullets; others could form optical systems to throw sunlight over wide areas, altering the temperature of large air masses so as to produce heavy rainfall or fair weather, according to the needs of the campaign. There existed "meteorological insects" corresponding to nothing we know today. The endothermic synsects, for example, absorbed large quantities of energy for the sole purpose of causing a sudden drop in temperature over a given area, resulting in a thick fog or the phenomenon known as an inversion. . . . New weapons dictated new conditions of combat and, therefore, new strategy and tactics, both totally unhuman. . . .

The cruel pressure to unhumanize the armies did away with the picturesque traditions of war games, the pageantry of parades (a marching locust, unlike a procession of tanks or rockets, is not a grand sight). . . . In various countries, at that time, a resistance movement developed among career officers. In the desperation of unemployment, they even joined the terrorist underground. It was a malicious trick of history—no one deliberately planned it—that these insurrections were crushed by means of microspies and minipolice built on the model of a particular cockroach.[27]

Perhaps one could say that one day Gregor Samsa, Kafka's character from "The Metamorphosis," awoke in his bed of uneasy dreams to find his cockroach self transformed into a computerized synsect. Lem already envisioned our microchip world-in-the-making, microchipping away at the spontaneity of life.

Long before the Manhattan Project and Hiroshima, the first atomic war took place in 1913, in the Balkans, using what H. G. Wells in his novel *The World Set Free* called "atomic bombs." It is a story, and it is a prophecy of the two great wars—the first that started in the Balkans in the next year, the second that ended with "atomic bombs"—and of the ungodly release of power in the twentieth century.

Why could H. G. Wells imagine in 1913 the implications he derived from the physicist Rutherford and see the possibilities for a weapon of mass destruction—which it took decades more for physicists to see? More, why could Wells see the consequences that the physicists who made the atomic bomb could not, until they stood back from the horror of its incandescent power: beginning with the Bomb of the initial Los Alamos test at the Trinity Site that caused physicist Robert Oppenheimer to quote from the *Bhagavad Gita*, "I am become Death, destroyer of worlds." And then that was only the physicists with conscience, such as Oppenheimer and Einstein, and they gave way in the fifties to the madmen, to Dr. Edward Teller and his hydrogen hell of Bigger Bombs.

Yes, we are the earth come alive to self-reflection, and also now in our civilized, infantilized hubris, we are slouching toward self-destruction, unless we can regain the touch of the earth and return to the purpose of life, not simply some "scientifically correct," mechanical homeostasis, but continuing self-creation, as beautiful as the flap of the butterfly wing, harmonized with life.

Being free involves choice. Perhaps that is why the system needs so much to appropriate it away from us by substituting virtual choice. The belief that you have a choice, that you can choose between Brand X or Brand Y, is the apparent choice advanced consumption capitalism "gives" us as it seduces freedom away from you and me. A mass is a de-individualized collective, one that, in America, has "individual choice" as its de-individualized mass collective belief. Call it "supermarket choice," the belief that somebody's commodity will confer on you an identity through its consumption, a life.

Free markets assume free individuals, but the reality of contemporary all-consuming capitalism is the requirement of unfree "individuals," brain rinsed functionaries of calculation, disabled from that free exercise of generosity, of empathy, of discretion, of neighborliness, of freedom to be participant in ongoing creation as reason for being. Why do American children never see vegetable or fruit ads as they are bombarded with sugaring ads? Why are indicators of materialism soaring in America as indicators of simple happiness are declining?

What is endless profit in comparison to the free creation of life: More excessive things that alienate us from life's realities, from real relations? What is it in comparison to the question, How do we live best together? "We" being that continuum from our own individual self and close relations to the entire community of life.

Count your electro-mechanical devices on one hand, and hold it out in front of you. Now count your blessings on your other hand, and hold it out too. Which hand holds more? Which hand holds more of your real life?

Real choice involves meeting the situation, sensing and being alive to the possibilities it holds out, and grasping the right one. It means being alive to the simple realities that surround one, in family and friends, and the local anchors of everyday life. There is also real community spirit, in which one's consciousness is in communion with community. In music we call it "groove," not mechanical rhythm but the feel of the rhythm, which is more than the beat per se. Being in the groove is speaking a common voice in the music.

In the beginning is the groove. Ceaseless groove. Ceaseless creation. In every flap of a butterfly's wings is the groove of creation and the possibility of "the butterfly effect," capable of producing great unforeseen consequences, not at all reducible to the cause. To be alive as a human being should mean to be as aware as the beating wings of a butterfly, freely sensing the drafts. Be alive in the creation! Or be brain sucked, as the living-dead. It is your choice. And mine too.

The celebrity-advertising-consumption machine functions as a great fantasia, providing all the virtual requirements of life, while it quietly absorbs the self as its "soul food." There is nothing new in this, perhaps. The ancient Romans knew that bread and circuses kept the population subservient. But what is different in the new *pax electronica* is that the entire mechanical universe of modern civilization has as its hidden teleology the absorption and ultimate replacement of human life with its own humanoid image: brain suck.

UPGRADE: DOWNLOAD: DOWN SHIFT: ARE YOU READY TO QUIT?

2

OUT OF THE FIFTIES

A few years ago I found myself playing a blues gig with a group of musicians in their twenties, and the former Muddy Waters band drummer Willie "Big Eyes" Smith, who was in his sixties. I sat out a couple of songs at one point, and when I looked at the stage, I suddenly realized that the shirts and hair of the young musicians—Nick Moss, Little Frank Krakowski, Brian Cook, Brian Combs—were right out of the fifties, that all of the guitars and amplifiers on stage were out of the fifties, that the music was all that fifties early Muddy Waters band sound that created Chicago blues, and that the only giveaway that this was not the 1950s—other than that the young musicians were white—was Willie Smith, who was dressed in a more contemporary shirt. Now, Willie was, in fact, the only person there who really was from that Muddy Waters era.

For a decade that was supposed to be about conformism, blandness, and nothing much happening, this picture didn't quite fit. Sure, there was a retro-fashion movement these young musicians had tuned into—and, I must confess, me too—but if you ask them what it all means to them, as I have on different occasions, they tell you it is about the music of that time, about the kinds of feelings that were released in Chicago blues in the fifties that still speak to them, feelings that are hard to find now, even in the blues.

And when you begin to think about the flowering of Chicago blues in the fifties, and of jazz—of bebop and cool and hard bop jazz, of Charlie Parker,

Dizzy Gillespie, Miles Davis, and John Coltrane—and of the birth of rock and roll and the apparent death of high modern music and art, of the "spontaneous bop prosody" of the beat generation, of the explosion of sexuality in Marlon Brando, Marilyn Monroe, and the invention of "the pill," of murdered Emmett Till and wronged Rosa Parks and the rise of Reverend Martin Luther King Jr., of Ralph Nader putting the brakes on the auto industry and Rachel Carson's breakthrough environmental book *Silent Spring*, of the harvest of sociological books critical of the times—of David Riesmann's *The Lonely Crowd*, William H. Whyte's *Organization Man*, C. Wright Mills's *White Collar* and *The Power Elite*, of Sloan Wilson's novel *The Man in the Gray Flannel Suit*—and of republican Dwight Eisenhower's invention of the term *military-industrial complex*, when you think of these things and of other phenomena mistakenly linked to the sixties, you begin to realize a lot more was going on in the fifties than the nostalgic images carried by TV reruns. Many of the leading ideas of the sixties, such as the civil rights movement and more open sexuality, were given birth in the fifties, just as many of the phenomena that flourished in the fifties, such as atomic bombs, bebop and baby boomers, sprang out of the forties. In speaking of "the fifties," like most decades, I mean the spirit of the time, not the literal decade, and so for some purposes a few years before and after.

Megatechnic America: Beginnings of a Beautiful Friendship

The 1950s were a time of fundamental transformations in American society, a time when the United States went fully megatechnic. Since the Second World War America has been problematically guided by a power-oriented culture, which, in the names of national security and convenience, has tended to reshape America toward an increasingly hierarchical model of society based on the system requirements of a machine. Although this same era gave birth to a generalized economic prosperity in the United States, to the civil rights movement, to feminism, and to other openings of public equality, the magnification of bureaucratic-corporate structures in that postwar, cold war prosperity has ultimately tended to restructure America against the basic requirements of democratic community. The power complex has expanded since that time, seemingly unabated, its electro-tentacles reaching ever deeper into body-mind-soul, which is why I have updated the term, to highlight newer ingredients of the *postdemocratic military-industrial-academic-entertainment-sport-food complex*.

The predicament of America after the Second World War was an enviable one: a victor, unlike Great Britain or the Soviet Union, physically untouched by the ravages of war, in sole command of devastating nuclear weaponry, launching into an age of unmatched prosperity. All the powers of American technical know-how had pulled together to win the war and now were poised to move on to the promised land that scientific-technical progress would make possible.

Megatechnic America has been highly successful in capturing much of the world, not simply by its overt and covert cold war military policies but also by its economic and cultural pizzazz. The rest of the world often seems to exhibit a love-hate relationship with America, resenting its vast power coupled with shallow commercialism, while mesmerized by the cornucopia of products of that culture. There are any number of criticisms of American "colonizations" of other countries during the second half of the twentieth century, of "Americanization," but it is important to see how the building of the megatechnic apparatus already underway successfully made America its first colony.[1]

Some might want to take that colonization back to the civil war, when industry and its North defeated agriculture and the South. We tend to think of this as a triumph of democracy over slavery, which in part it was, but the triumph of the machine, of industrial society over agrarian society, is crucial. It set the trajectory that culminated in our time with the victory of the machine over democracy.

In 1990 the superior machines of the West triumphed over the worn-out machine of communism, but to call it a victory of democracy may be too much. Totalitarianism had long since been replaced by what Vaclav Havel has called *posttotalitarianism*, a deadening system running on automatic, no longer needing the domineering presence of the dictator, and democracy in America, sadly, had long since been replaced by what I term *postdemocratic society*. The hugely increased power of military, corporate-industrial, and "BIG science" institutions developed during the 1950s signaled the transformation to megatechnic America, just as certain devices, such as hydrogen bombs, automobiles, and televisions, were key symbols of that transformation.

The automobile industry, for example, and its efficient mass-production techniques ushered in by Henry Ford decades earlier, had been instrumental to the Allied victory. But the postwar era saw the firm establishment of the cult of the automobile, led by an auto industry creating ever bigger, more powerful, inefficient, and unsafe autos—"the dinosaur in the driveway" as then American Motors president George Romney called them—whose chief reason for being that way was to create grossly inflated profits for the corporate oligarchy. "Sloanism," named for General Motors' president Alfred P.

Sloan, reproduced the American class structure in its design, pricing, and yearly model changes, making the auto a totemic object and ideal of consumption and identity.

In a peculiar way the public works projects of the New Deal in the 1930s gave way with the Second World War to the "secret works project": in the Depression workers built public bridges and post offices and writers wrote, but in that isolate Manhattan Project of the desert, there was an atomic epiphany, not simply the bomb of the initial Los Alamos Trinity test in New Mexico that caused physicist Robert Oppenheimer to quote from the *Bhagavad Gita* "I am become Death, destroyer of worlds," but the construction of scientific socialism in America. The bomb that would protect the United States from communism would be the center of a centralized, secret bureaucracy, which, like communism, tolerated no criticism of its ideology, its economics, its disinformation. This birth of the scientific-military-industrial welfare state, would over the course of the cold war suck massive resources into its ever-growing belly, and help define the addiction to government funding of "research universities." Enormous resources were channeled into basic scientific and computer research by the military, justified by fears of Soviet totalitarianism, but also pursued for domestic power, money, and because there was a buoyant culture of scientism that most Americans ardently believed in. Science was achieving remarkable breakthroughs, and it seemed to many that there were no limits to progress.

Fundable social science also bloomed in this era, riding the prosperity and the scientistic ideal that survey research could replace mere social critique. Today the commodification of scholarship in the academy is so debased that departments actually list the ability to procure money as a consideration in hiring someone. Universities hold amounts of monies and grants as ideals for researchers to pursue, even humanities scholars, and corporate bureaucratic structures have become models that universities increasingly emulate. What a far cry from "The American Scholar," who is, as Ralph Waldo Emerson put it: "In the right state he is *Man Thinking*. In the degenerate state, when the victim of society, he tends to become a mere thinker, or still worse, the parrot of other men's thinking." Surely the elevation of procuring money to a virtue of scholarship represents the "degenerate state" signaled by Emerson, not only for militarized scientific research but also the corporatized models of "intellectual life" in general.[2]

The history of nuclear power alone, from the increasingly lethal and expensive development of weapons in the cold war and the ways in which they dictated American foreign policy, to the promises of virtually cost-free energy, suggest that radioactivity has functioned as the invisible specter of the old American dream of the New Jerusalem. Radioactivity, which perhaps defines twentieth-century materialism as bronze, silver, and stone did for earlier ages, proved to be an apparently immaterial but deadly power we have yet to harness. Its power is invisible, and yet, like money, one of the most potent symbols of materialism.

When one considers the growing dependence of universities from the fifties onward on government funding for "BIG science" research, often, as in the case of computers, with military interests; the absorption of public intellectuals into the academy in the postwar period; the transformations in family life and political life effected by television, in diet by the industrial-ization of corn and meat, and by the rise of fast food and franchising; and the mushrooming growth of professional sports and a virtual requirement that major cities must have multiple major sporting complexes, the outline of megatechnic America becomes clearer. The military-industrial machine was a component of a vaster bureaucratic complex, a megamachine, whose requirements included bread-and-circus spectacle.

The BOMB as God Symbol and the Voice of Reason

If the radiance of a thousand suns were to burst into the sky, that would be like the splendor of the Mighty One. . . . I am become Death, destroyer of worlds.
—ROBERT OPPENHEIMER, QUOTING THE *BHAGAVAD GITA* WHILE OBSERVING THE FIRST DETONATION OF AN ATOMIC BOMB, THE LOS ALAMOS LAB'S TEST AT TRINITY SITE IN NEW MEXICO

Did you ever hear about the secret nuclear war conducted by the United States and the Soviet Union? Probably not. Nobody calls it that, despite the massive numbers of deaths it has caused. It has been an odd kind of war, a hot war conducted by each side in secret against its own populations in the name of national security. And it is a war far from being over, even though the Soviet Union dissolved some time ago.

At some nuclear tests, U.S. servicemen crouched in trenches one or two miles from ground zero, practicing combat under the mushroom. Those bombs bursting in air gave proof in the night of infernal light: the soldiers, eyes closed, literally seeing the bones in their hands and arms covering their faces. In the words of Marine second lieutenant Thomas Saffer, two miles from ground zero:

I was shocked when, with my eyes tightly closed, I could see the bones in my forearm as though I were examining a red x-ray. . . . Within seconds, a thunderous rumble like the sounds of thousands of stampeding cattle passed directly overhead, pounding the trench line . . .

Overcome by fear, I opened my eyes. I saw that I was being showered with dust, dirt, rocks, and debris so thick that I could not see four feet in front of me. . . . A light many times brighter than the sun penetrated the thick dust, and I imagined that some evil force was attempting to swallow my body and soul. . . . I was immediately conscious of an offensively strong smell and taste. The odor reminded me of that of an overheated electrical unit and the metallic taste in my mouth was foul and would not go away.

If that weren't bad enough, Lieutenant Saffer and his men then moved through swirling clouds of radioactive particles, under the great mushroom, to within three hundred yards of ground zero, which was radiating a deadly 500 roentgens per hour instead of the expected 50 per hour. He found himself again two miles from ground zero in a later test named Hood, which unfortunately was a 74-kiloton hydrogen bomb. Although fusion weapons were not supposed to be tested on U.S. soil, physicist Edward Teller and two other scientists had assured President Eisenhower two weeks before the test that they could eliminate 95 percent of fallout. A congressional investigation decades later revealed that it was the "dirtiest [nuclear] explosion in the United States."[3]

I spent an evening a few years ago with one atomic veteran, Reason Warehime, hearing him tell of his 1950s "close encounter" with the nuclear inferno. Warehime is an American Rasputin, an amazing patriot whose military experiences should have made him dead many times over. He spoke of how a Japanese bullet went through his arm and into his chest during World War II, how he was saved only by a steel-plated bible he had been given earlier and kept in his shirt pocket. Some damage to his wrist was permanent. But he survived the bodily damage.

Reason served as a soldier in Nagasaki after the atomic bomb, keeping people out of the irradiated zone for their safety while living in it for nine months. But he survived bodily damage.

Later, during the Korean War, he was riding as a passenger in a jeep when a nonuniformed North Korean threw a hand grenade into the jeep. Warehime alertly dove out of the jeep into a trench. Unfortunately, the driver grabbed the grenade off the floor and tossed it into that trench. But Reason survived the bodily damage.

That was not all that happened in Korea, though. Out in the field in combat, he described hearing a mortar launch, and had a feeling that no matter what he did it would be coming for him. He ran for cover, but the mortar did indeed get him, fracturing a vertebra in his spine. A medic soon arrived, but asked him if he could walk, because Chinese troops were closing in fast. He told the medic, "Hell, I can run!" And he somehow did, collapsing when they reached a line of safety. He survived the bodily damage.

But all these reasons to die were but trifling preludes. Reason Warehime, who had given so much for America in World War II and in the Korean War, made an even greater sacrifice after Korea. Previously he had merely given chunks of his body, but the American war machine demanded more from Reason. In its arrogant, boundless scientism, it wanted the body-soul, it wanted to flex power beyond human limits, it wanted not mere cannon fodder, but nuclear bomb fodder.

And so Reason Warehime—was ever a soldier so well-named, dear reader? —found himself dug into a Nevada desert trench for "Shot Simon," some 2,500 yards from what was measured by the officers in a trench even closer to ground zero to be a 56-kiloton blast. It was officially listed for decades as a blast in the low 20-kiloton range (raised to the 40s more recently), to make it seem "safer," and to prevent suspicions that hydrogen bomb testing, forbidden on U.S. soil, might have occurred. After all, Edward "Dr. Strangelove" Teller, self-proclaimed "father" of the hydrogen bomb, had promised President Eisenhower that 95 percent of the fallout could be contained! Perfectly safe, no?

"The dumb thing goes off and it just compresses your whole body," Reason said. "It's so noisy you can't hear anything. Once the heat wave hits you, and the light, you can see the bones in your hand. It's like they were being X-rayed."

Within weeks after that test, Reason Warehime's hair had fallen out, his teeth had blackened, and he had become permanently sterile. Within a year all of his teeth had fallen out, and the eight officers who had been in the trench ahead of him were all dead. But he survived the bodily damage.

But this was more than bodily damage. This was soul damage; this was American auto-genocide.

Reason went on to work for nuclear veterans, patiently working over decades attempting to get just recompense for medical injuries soldiers received as nuclear guinea pigs, as military science's nuclear cannon fodder. The U.S. government denied the extent of the damage it inflicted for decades, unwilling to do justice to those it called for no good reason to fry themselves with cellular damage. But the story goes further than that, with weird twists.

Reason's nuclear veterans' group published a full-page advertisement with an image of a nuclear blast in a major East Coast U.S. newspaper calling attention to the medical plight of nuclear veterans. Soon Reason's phone began to make strange noises, as though it was being tapped. Then he began to feel as though he was being followed when he drove. Was he paranoid? No, he was under surveillance. While being followed one day, he decided to pull over and confront the secret police. He went back to the FBI agents' car and asked them what the hell was going on. They didn't tell him, but helped arrange an interview.

After some questioning, it finally came out that the reason the FBI had Reason under surveillance was not due to the nature of the protest or the cause of nuclear veterans. It turned out that the image of the atomic bomb that was used in the advertisement, an image arbitrarily picked because it looked like a classic nuclear mushroom cloud, an image that was in the public domain, free, and so used, well, it turned out that this particular image happened to be a beautifully formed mushroom cloud from an *underground nuclear test*! You know, the kind of "test" that produces no fallout. Whoops.

This was one big atmospheric boo-boo that megatechnic America needed to cover up. It needed to cover it up by harassing one of its heroic patriots, Reason Warehime. For no citizen, however virtuous, shall stand in the way of scientistic "progress" and national security in megatechnic America. Not even a citizen who had given so much of his body and soul to national security and to his comrades in war in that day of nuclear inferno and in the afterlife of it, as Reason Warehime did, is immune from its tentacles of deception.

A flood of materials was released in the 1990s that showed how thousands of American families living near bomb-making factories and reactors, such as those in Fernald, Ohio, and Hanford, Washington, were exposed to appallingly high levels of radiation while the government of the United States officially employed deception by claiming that there was no health hazard—even though it very well knew the dangers. And there were public health officials who knowingly allowed uranium miners to breathe polluted air while they studied them, rationalizing that the increased lung-cancer deaths from lack of breathing masks were the cost of not risking alerting the Russians to the mining.

Dr. Victor E. Archer, the principal investigator for the study from 1956 until he retired from the Public Health Service in 1979, was quoted in the *New York Times* in 1989: "Looking at it with the standards of today, you could take the attitude that the miners were being used as guinea pigs, and we were essentially watching them die." When other medical researchers, such as Dr. Wilhelm C. Hueper, a scientist at the National Cancer Institute, were prevented from traveling west after drawing attention to the radiation problems, Archer stated, "That was enough to scare me. I wanted to stay out here and make studies. I had to officially take the position that we suspected that uranium miners may have health problems, and we were doing the study to find out what they were and how severe they would be. But we knew what they would be."[4]

If Archer were less of a coward, he might have taken the idea of Public Health Service seriously, and risked his secure research position to save lives. And he could have worked publicly over the decades before he retired in 1979 and after on behalf of all the Americans poisoned by the Great American Bomb Machine: the miners, the servicemen, all the people downwind from the tests. Reason Warehime did dedicate himself to the issue and also familiarized himself with the scientific data on the tests and on the effects of radioactivity. I saw Reason make a physicist from the University of Notre Dame, who in 2001 remained a committed ideologue to the idea that the military tests did no damage, and who insulted Reason by saying that bad hygiene might have been the cause of his hair falling out and teeth turning black after the nuclear test, seem like an ignorant schoolboy.

But Dr. Archer was himself also a guinea pig in the great deception perpetrated by the Atomic Energy Commission (AEC) and military. He quietly made his worthless, because already proven, death studies while men died and their descendants became potentially poisoned. I see no difference between those Atomic Energy Commission scientists and Dr. Josef Mengele, except that perhaps the chief difference between the American Archers and Nazi Mengele is that Archer and other researchers passively watched people die, while Mengele actively helped them to do so.

Archer stated in a letter to me in 1990, "Although I recognize that what I did was the only real way to achieve control of the hazard, I am not especially proud of it, since many lives were sacrificed. But that has frequently been the way of human progress—some must be sacrificed for the greater good of all. This has been true in war and peace. Modern ethics and morality may soften this path to progress, but only at the cost of slowing the process." Let no ethics or morality slow down the machine of scientific progress: the typical voice of modern scientism, perfuming itself.

The war he refers to was the undeclared cold war, advent of the age of undeclared wars, the war wherein $5.5 trillion, a cost of $21,646 to every American citizen, was spent on nuclear weapons alone, while the country was also building a secret government, whose covert CIA, FBI, and other agencies could suppress Americans' freedoms and rights under a mantel of "national security," free from public scrutiny.[5]

The wannabe genius, Edward Teller, is a classic study of scientific arrogance in the 1950s. Resentful of the director of the Manhattan Project, Robert Oppenheimer, who resigned a few months after the atomic bombs designed by the project successfully ended the war, Teller attempted to discredit him in public testimony and in secret interviews with the FBI.

While Oppenheimer was being discredited, former Nazi SS officer and V-2 terror rocket scientist Wernher von Braun and other Nazi scientists, such as Arthur Rudolph and Hubertus Strughold, were rising in the American rocket program, thanks to the secret Office of Strategic Services' (OSS) Operation Paperclip, which cleansed the files of ardent Nazis brought to the United States at the conclusion of the war. Von Braun, whose V-2 rockets rained terror on London during the war and who was immortalized in Tom Lehrer's song named for him—"Once rockets go up, who cares vhere zey come down, zat's not my department, says Wernher von Braun"—went on to become assistant director of NASA in the 1960s.

Strughold, "the father of U.S. space medicine," who designed astronaut John Glenn's spacesuit, was involved in aviation research during the Second World War in which numerous victims in Dachau concentration camp were pressurized until their lungs burst. As documents from the Nuremberg trials indicated, other victims were subjected to extreme conditions of freezing temperatures, water immersion, being forced to drink seawater, and other scientific tortures.

When the first astronaut landed on the moon, Rudolph was asked whether he saw this as a German or American achievement, and he responded that he saw it as a German achievement, by which he did not mean a "Federal Republic of Germany" achievement. Rudolph was chief operations director of the underground Mittelwerk complex where slave prisoners of the Mittelbau-Dora concentration camp were used for production of V-2 rockets. Memos with Rudolph's name show requests for 1,800 more slave laborers at one point. By war's end an estimated twenty thousand workers died.

A French survivor, interviewed in the documentary *The Nazi Connection*, described some of the brutalities, including how men were hanged by a slowly raising crane in groups of twelve, slowly twisting to death, in front of the offices of the scientists, and of how the "civilians," the scientists, were utterly indifferent. An initial report on Rudolph at the end of the war, later censored by Operation Paperclip, stated: "100 percent Nazi, dangerous type, security threat!! Suggest internment." When the Office of Special Investigations finally raised questions about his involvement in mass-murder war crimes, he was allowed to flee to Germany in 1984, agreeing to surrender his U.S. citizenship while retaining full pension and social security benefits, in exchange for no further proceedings against him.

Edward Teller could play the role of objective scientist well, but he was a man obsessed with his own self-interest, and he was intensely vindictive toward anyone who did not agree with him or who he perceived as standing in his way. He took Oppenheimer's reservations about the development of the hydrogen bomb as a personal attack. In the midst of the McCarthy era, on March 1, 1954, the "super," the hydrogen bomb developed under Teller's supervision, was detonated on Bikini atoll in the South Pacific, and about a month later, Teller publicly denounced Oppenheimer as a security threat in a political show trial put on by the Atomic Energy Commission and its director Lewis Strauss. That trial resulted in Oppenheimer losing his security clearance, effectively barring his participation in nuclear weapons issues and research. The only real threat that Oppenheimer posed to nuclear power mongers was that he was a patriotic scientist with a conscience, which led him to question the building of the hydrogen bomb. Could a fiction writer get away with such a story of a tattletale and paranoid snitch named "Teller"?

With the complete displacement of Oppenheimer by Teller, we see the corruption of morally concerned science by the mentality of the self-aggrandizing ego, a crucial ingredient in the building of megatechnic America in the fifties. Little power lords with huge egos were attempting to establish themselves across the board: Senator McCarthy and his paranoid witch hunts, J. Edgar Hoover's abuse of the FBI as a secret police, Robert Moses and his pavings of New York City, Ray Kroc and his politics of franchised hamburger totalitarianism, a view expressed best in his own words, "The organization cannot trust the individual; the individual must trust the organization."

Kroc's statement defines the new creature coming into being in the fifties, what William H. Whyte termed *organization man*. Mechanized standardization bestowed by benevolent bureaucracies would be the means by which mobilized citizens could drive themselves in their new autos on their new highways with their new motels and their new franchised fast food joints, and eventually their new privatized public shopping zones—that great epiphany of the fifties that is the mall—to the New Jerusalem of postdemocratic, conformist, megatechnic America. But if you make a world more and more machinelike, you run the risk of making yourself more and more machinelike. What was so perplexing for organization man, as Whyte noted, was that, "it is not the evils of organization life that puzzle him, but its very beneficence. . . . We are describing its defects as virtues and denying that there is—or should be—a conflict between individual and organization. . . . What it does, in soothing him, is to rob him of the intellectual armor he so badly needs."[6] Megatechnic Russia brutally terrorized its people into submission, but megatechnic America would pleasure its people into submission, through an unprecedented material abundance.

If you don't believe me, I dare you to deviate from conformity at your "local" mall, from the extremely narrow range of accepted behaviors that now run public places. Dress up as though you are homeless and beg for money, or try reading the constitution of the United States of America and see how long it takes the surveillance police to stop you. Or if you are too docile, sit yourself down at a mall and imagine you are doing these things, and look your fellow citizens square in the eyes as they pass by, and then imagine their response to you. I bet you that you will see what the evacuation from freedom in America looks like.

Consider one example from the "plowshare" project to use nuclear bombs for peace and prosperity. Teller propagandized heavily for a demented project cooked up at his Livermore laboratory in the late 1950s to set off a series of detonations in Alaska near Point Hope and create a new international harbor. Hoping to gather Alaskan support (and to continue his unrelenting obsession for weapons testing), Teller said in his commencement address of 1959 at the University of Alaska: "Please God, that by making harbors here in Alaska, perhaps near coal deposits, by exporting this coal cheaper to Japan, the Japanese might become the first beneficiaries of atomic explosions as they have been the first victims."[7]

God may not have appreciated the unintended irony in Teller's plea—given that only five years earlier, Teller's baby, the hydrogen bomb, was first tested on the island of Bikini. Along with Bikini natives, that bomb had murderously poisoned the Japanese fishermen of *The Lucky Dragon*, publicly reopening all the radioactive war wounds of Japan. No, God may not have appreciated the irony, but the devil would have gotten a good laugh, as he surely must when he remembers that fireball every time a beautiful bikini walks by!

Documents uncovered decades later by Daniel T. O'Neill reveal that the Atomic Energy Commission poured in more than $100,000 in grants for biological studies to the University of Alaska—big bucks in 1959. But as those studies pointed to the devastating effects the explosions would have, university officials, smelling MONEY, pressured, censored, and fired researchers and rewrote their reports. There were numerous other inconvenient facts, such as that since the region around Point Hope is icebound for months the railways needed to get to the coal would have been far too costly. In this one case alone one sees a glimpse of the transformation of American universities into the search-for-money bureaucratic grant-getting machines they have now become. Screw truth.

The many impracticalities of Teller's Project Chariot, not to mention the human costs the Atomic Energy Commission and Livermore officials sought to suppress, forced officials to adopt "scientific" rationalizations for the project, but these also failed to attract the funds needed. Yet the test also secretly intended to study the effects of fallout on the ecosystem—which would mean including the Native American "elements" of that ecosystem, the people of Point Hope, thirty miles north. Although the project officially fizzled, "dedicated" scientists working for the AEC went ahead anyway and secretly released forty-three and a half pounds of highly radioactive waste, brought up from a recent Nevada test, along the creek that ran into the proposed harbor, "to determine the extent to which irradiated soil would dissolve the fallout radionuclides and transport them to aquifers, streams, and ponds."[8]

Test done, the efficient scientists buried the now fifteen thousand pounds of contaminated soil and left without a word of warning to the inhabitants. Presumably out of the way Native American guinea pigs would not become as visible as the inhabitants of, say, Saint George, Utah, where heavy fallout fell even when weather conditions were "good" at the Nevada test site. John Wayne, Susan Haywood, Agnes Moorehead, Dick Powell, and a remarkably high percentage of other cast and crew members of the film *The Conquerors*, filmed in the desert outside St. George, died of cancers—in Wayne's case, from stomach cancer. Wayne's sons Michael, who acted in the film, and Patrick, who was present for the filming, each developed cancers later. Statistically, if not individually, as a member of that film cast and crew who breathed the desert sands on location, John Wayne was a casualty of the American nuclear war on itself.[9]

Imagine a map of the United States where, with prevailing westerly winds, most of the country east of Nevada is darkened to indicate areas covered by two or more fallout clouds, plus a good part of the California coast. The technical ingenuity that could build the Bomb and test it in an "isolated" desert never figured that its poisons would simply continue to drift predominantly eastward until it rained.[10] Current estimates of deaths due to nuclear bomb testing in the United States exceed more than 300,000 Americans, including large numbers of children, who were more susceptible to the invisible radioactive blasting of the cells of holy life. The numbers from the Soviet Union's military nuclear program are probably even worse.

Current estimates of deaths due to nuclear bomb testing in the United States easily exceed the number of Americans killed in the Korean, Vietnam, and Iraq wars combined, including significant numbers of children. *Atomic Audit*, a historical and financial account of the cold war, gives a conservative range of 70,000 to 800,000 deaths worldwide due to American fallout alone, a figure that doubles when you use zero threshold of radioactive effects, to which must be added deaths in high-risk populations and their offspring, such as the 500,000 to 600,000 workers in the nuclear weapons complex, the 220,000 military personnel who participated in atmospheric tests, those citizens who lived downwind from nuclear weapons plants, and the more than 23,000 men, women, and children who were subjects of radiation studies, often unwittingly.[11]

Deliberate deception was employed by the U.S. government against the American public and against any scientists courageous enough to release information showing the deadly probabilities. In 1970, for example, former Manhattan Project member and medical physicist John W. Gofman was threatened by Congressman Chet Holifield, chair of the Joint Committee on Atomic Energy, for his work showing that there are no "minimum" levels below which radioactivity has no effect. Holifield warned Gofman: "Listen, there have been others who have tried to cross the AEC before you. We got them and we'll get you." The AEC worked hard to prevent the accumulating scientific realities of radiation from becoming public, repressing reports and blackballing scientists responsible enough to research the human effects. Over the next couple of years Gofman's funding at Livermore laboratory was cut through pressure from the AEC and he was forced to leave.

The actions of the Atomic Energy Commission and by certain military, political, and scientific officials—such as Edward Teller—in deliberately misleading servicemen and the public about the dangers of radioactive fallout amount to mass murder, worthy, as Gofman has put it, of a "Nuremberg trial," and they should be dealt with accordingly, as "cold war" criminals. But don't hold your breath waiting for that.

What one sees in the nuclear culture of the fifties, in its arrogant scientism, in its effects on political, popular, and commercial life, is the scientific materialization of ultimate power, of God. Early in the century, in his autobiography Henry Adams had shown the connection in the title of his chapter "The Dynamo and the Virgin," where he argued that the electric dynamo had taken the pivotal place in society that the virgin held for medieval Europe.

When one reads of the delusions of a Teller, or of nuclear pimp Herman Kahn, author of *Thinking about the Unthinkable*—on how to "win" all-out annihilating nuclear war—and a proposal, similar to Teller's project, to detonate nuclear bombs underground in Pennsylvania coal deposits in order to create "natural" gas (albeit highly radioactive gas for tens of thousands of years)—when one reads of such things today, they are of a piece with the science fiction films of the times. Indeed both Teller and Kahn figured into the character of Dr. Strangelove, in the film of that title by Stanley Kubrick. But those movies were saner than Teller or Kahn, because they typically, however poorly done, recognized that the apparent ULTIMATE POWERS unleashed by man were destructively out of control.

Godzilla or Guernica?

When I first began encountering modern art as a young adult, I realized that some of my friends had been raised on the stuff that I was just discovering, that they had done the museums, heard the concerts, knew the names. I was just a new kid on the block, so to speak. Then I suddenly realized one day that, like my sophisticated companions, I too had ingested "the modern experience" as a child, at an even earlier age than they had. But the way it first got to me was in the drive-in movies my parents used to take me to in the fifties, where, as sunset gave way to darkness over New Jersey, all the children ran terrorized from the playground located just under the giant screen, knowing that momentarily Godzilla (1954, U.S. release 1956) or Rodan (1957) or some other menacing prehistoric nuclear terror beast would be looming above them.

I've carried this little pet theory for years that though we bombed the Japanese with the unholy terrors of atomic bombs in 1945, they retaliated in the fifties by bombing our psyches with those monstrous beasts, which were usually released by nuclear testing. Those beasts were the primal, reptilian darkness that civilization was supposed to repress, now suddenly released into consciousness, Yeats's beast "of laughing, ecstatic destruction" slouching toward Bethlehem. The Japanese released the gigantic repressed prehistoric beasts—Tyrannosaurus and Pterodactyl—perhaps influenced by the 1933 American film King Kong, while postwar America tended to release horrendously enlarged insects—ants in the film Them! (1954), or Tarantula (1955), or grasshoppers attacking Chicago (The Beginning of the End, 1957)—and radioactively enlarged or shrunken humans. The Incredible Shrinking Man (1957), for example, began his shrink to infinitesimal-tude after a nuclear cloud passes by his boat—an event strikingly similar to the thermonuclear dousing of the Japanese fishing boat The Lucky Dragon. The Amazing Colossal Man (1957) was titled after an American soldier who began to grow uncontrollably after being overdosed at a nuclear test site while trying to rescue civilians, ultimately enlarging into a demented monstrosity. This film expressed in crude grade-B form the hidden truth that the American government could never admit: soldiers really were disastrously overdosed, unlimited power really was like an uncontrolled cancerous growth.

These films were pop culture versions of what much of modern art was about: the release of those extremes of emotion in the outburst of modernism in the early twentieth century. In those years, avant-garde music ruptured its connections to tonality and painting broke out of the traditions of perspective and representation. Although this art may still seem abstruse to traditionalists, these artists were revealing the explosive energies of the new century, in the pagan forces of Stravinsky's *The Rite of Spring* (1913), Picasso's cubism—and later, of his epic painting of the first use of saturation bombing by the Nazis, *Guernica* (1937). Picasso's *Les Demoiselles d'Avignon* (1907) drew from African tribal masks to break with perspective, as later, racial stereotypes of African tribal life were used in *King Kong* to project the "primitive" into modern epic.

But both in these artistic breakthroughs of modernism and in the pop low-budget effusions of the fifties films there was a picturing of energies released that transcended pure power per se: Stravinsky and Picasso harnessed the energies in their showing of them, the sci-fi films were morality plays about the dangers of unharnessed power.

Return from Pleasantville

The only thing necessary for the triumph of evil is for good men to do nothing.
—ATTRIBUTED TO EDMUND BURKE

Why do the 1950s represent a golden age to many Americans? There was a genuine flush of optimism from the postwar age of prosperity America had embarked on. But does that explain it? Or is it rerun-itis, an overdose of 1950s sitcoms endlessly projecting those images of "swell times?"

In projecting its kitsch worldview of idealized families, TV was the means of "intimate depersonalization," of colonizing the home and enhancing the ways in which people came to feel personal connections to images performed by actors, celebrities, and politicians. Families gathered around their new televisions or those of their neighbors to watch projected images of families where all serious conflicts were removed, and where what problems that remained could be solved in a cheery resolution at the end of the half hour. As forties radio celebrity and one of the first casualties of TV, Fred Allen, put it, television was, "a device that permits people who haven't anything to do watch people who can't do anything." Perhaps he was a bit on the caustic side, but the sitcoms of the fifties pictured perfect kitsch families, Moms happy in their kitchens, Dads always employed in occupations hardly ever mentioned, boomer kids in little escapades. Swell times.

The 1998 film *Pleasantville* explores this nostalgic view of the fifties and of how its idealized self-image of perfection, portrayed in reruns of TV sitcoms, is not what it was cracked up to be. Dave, a self-conscious teenager, finds refuge from the arguments of his divorced parents and from the traumas of high school in the nineties through his fascination with reruns of a fifties sitcom. With his Mom going away for the weekend and his Dad refusing to visit, Dave wants to watch the all-weekend rerun festival of the show, with its call-in trivia quizzes. But a fight with his popular sister, who wants to watch MTV with her soon-to-arrive date, ends up with both of them projected into the black-and-white world of the series, thanks to a mysterious channel changer. Now they are "Bud" and "Mary Sue," an unbearable situation for his sister but clearly relished by "Bud," despite his anxiety.

In this kitsch-world, the families are all intact, all white, the high school basketball team never loses or even misses a shot, there is no sex, and there is no real feeling. It is a kind of reverse version of *Invasion of the Body Snatchers*, in which, as described previously, alien pod-spawned replicas are exact in every way except emotionally neutered. In Pleasantville, thanks to the intrusion of Bud and Mary Sue's 1990s view of things, people begin to change from a condition in which they are shielded from experience to one in which they are emotionally present. They literally become "colored," changing from black-and-white mannequin-like conformists, to being able to see and feel the world for all its color—a process that causes "racial" resentments to explode by the black and whites. Interestingly, however, Bud and Mary Sue are among the last to change, showing that even the sexual liberty that Mary Sue exhibits and the worldly savvy that Bud possesses are forms of conformism and masks that are every bit as alienated from true feelings as those of the Pleasantville people.

This is a movie that highlights the meaning of the spectatorial world TV has made. When one remembers how crucial for the formation of the self the gaze of a mother on an infant is, you realize that this film beautifully unmasks in comedic form the tragic substitution of that motherly gaze by the mechanical eye of television. In place of that motherly gaze is the television daze, the development of a relationship rooted in the deepest needs of the child, but based on the apparent attention the TV projects onto the viewer. There are some key scenes in which Bud, the TV junkie, directly encounters the gaze of his TV Mom, as, for example, when he applies make-up to her face so that his father and the mayor will not realize that she has become colored. Bud discovers that having feelings, even painful ones, is better than TV fantasy anesthesia, and he brings this insight back to his real world life. In place of the gaze and its empathy, the world of television has produced a Pleasantville of the soul in America, a culture in which one's identity is supposed to be completed by acts of consumption.

59

The Other Side of Optimism

It is easy to understand how the cult of perpetual, unlimited progress could flourish in postwar fifties America, given the outpourings of scientific discoveries, unprecedented economic prosperity, and the political superpower status the country had reached. But how does one explain the widespread hope that "things will get better" that is shared by disenfranchised African Americans in the South yearning for the "promised land" of the North?

In the forties and fifties, millions of African Americans moved north to escape the Jim Crow slave conditions of the South. It may not have been called slavery, but though legal slavery had been outlawed almost a century earlier the Deep South functioned as a slave police state for African Americans. Chicago, the North more generally, was the "promised land." In the Deep South a black man was either called boy, or, if older, uncle, but never a man, and could neither expect political or economic justice nor do anything to seek it without fear of severe retribution.

A drummer from South Bend, Bill Nicks, who in the mid-fifties founded the band that would later record on Motown as Junior Walker and the All-Stars, told me how his family moved to South Bend from Greenwood, Mississippi. One day the owner of the plantation threatened to beat his father, and his father stood up to him as a man, forcing the owner to back off. His father also knew that if they did not move that very night, he would likely be killed.

Some of these struggles were also recorded in the blues that found expression in Chicago in the 1950s. If Jimmy Reed's song "Big Boss Man" called attention to racism ("Big boss man, can't you hear me when I call?") and ironic ways of answering it (Well you ain't so big, you just tall, that's all), then Muddy Waters's "Hoochie Coochie Man" (1954) and Bo Diddley's "I'm a Man" (1955) celebrated the relatively freer conditions. At least in the North a man could call himself a man while being subjected to racial prejudice.

Take the tune "Chicago Bound" (1954) recorded by the blues guitar player Jimmie Rogers with fellow members of the Muddy Waters band, where you feel the energy and joy of northward migration in the lyrics and soloing by Rogers, harmonica master Little Walter, and piano player Henry Gray. After verses of "leavin' out of" Georgia, Memphis, and St. Louis, Rogers is "Chicago Bound":

> I'm gonna tell you somethin' that you all should know
> Chicago is the best place I ever know'd
> I'm gonna stay in this town

I'm gonna live in this town
I'm gonna live in Chicago
It's the greatest place around!

The Muddy Waters band was composed of Waters and Rogers on guitars, bassist Willie Dixon, and piano player Otis Spann. All had taken the road to Chicago from the Deep South. All were born in Mississippi except for harmonica ace Little Walter Jacobs, who was born in Louisiana. Drummer Willie "Big Eyes" Smith, who joined the band at the very end of the 1950s, was born near West Helena, Arkansas.

The success of the Muddy Waters band was unexpected—no one imagined that the raw country sounds of the delta would catch on in the sophisticated Chicago scene, not even Polish immigrants Phil and Leonard Chess, who first recorded the band. But with many new immigrants from the delta after the war, and with the new sound of electric guitars and Little Walter's cupping of the microphone while playing harmonica to create a kind of saxophone effect, the earthy intensity of delta life was transformed into the music of the promised land.

Little Walter's solos alone were remarkable for their rhythmic and melodic inventiveness, pure spontaneous improvisations that poured out from him like fresh water from a spring. He would listen to swing saxophonists, such as Gene Ammons, for ideas, and would play swing with his group, although, as his fellow band member Dave Myers once told me, the Chess brothers never let him record that material.

In the fifties there was a magnificent flowering of blues and jazz and rhythm and blues that was unprecedented and unmatched since. Perhaps it was simply the energies released by the war and by the massive migrations, but whatever the cause, the effect was sheer vital efflorescence, and it occurred, interestingly enough, when avant-garde "classical" music (which highbrows unfortunately call "serious music") was going belly up.

Avant-garde jazz was dominated by an aesthetic of spontaneity, heightened, perhaps, as a reaction to limitations big band structures had imposed on musicians. By contrast, avant-garde music from the classical tradition was dominated by a culture of abstraction in the form of serial chromaticism. First developed by Arnold Schoenberg early in the century, "twelve-tone serialism" institutionalized itself in the academy, "uptown" with Elliott Carter at Columbia University, at Princeton with Milton Babbitt, and elsewhere. Even Stravinsky began writing it. Its opposite, aleatory, or chance, music, was best represented by John Cage. But get this: both the rationally composed tone-row music and the virtually uncomposed chance music sounded alike,

61

having disallowed the repetitive elements so crucial to auditory memory and meaning. Both sides lost themselves in techniques and left the ear behind, revealing that cultural modernism was on the verge of decomposing.

One of the symptoms of deadness in institutionalized serial chromatic music and modernist architecture in the 1950s was their reliance on total symmetry. By contrast, blues and jazz musicians knew intuitively that exact duplication of a rhythmical or melodic line was simply a missed opportunity for a spontaneous variation on it. Look at any traditional African sculpture and you will see asymmetry in the body.

Avant-garde jazz pulsed with a wide range of vital emotions before it too went "outside" for a while to cacophonic meanderings in the 1960s. And that is not even to talk about the vital energies released in the fifties by the baby of the blues, rock and roll. How is it that jazz and blues and rock and roll were so alive in the fifties, while the modernist movement in music and architecture became so devitalized?

Begun by Charlie Parker, Dizzy Gillespie, and others in the forties, developed further by Miles Davis, John Coltrane, and many others in the fifties, bebop jazz found whole new means and moods of expression. Through unselfconscious collective improvisation—the lifeblood of African American tradition—it managed to speak a new language that was a genuine emergent of American culture. Perhaps of all the avant-garde art movements after the Second World War, bebop jazz best exemplifies the aesthetic of spontaneity, particularly "spontaneous bop prosody," the ways music speaks itself bodily —or, for writers, the ways words speak musically.

Segue to Spontaneity

Jazz was a powerful influence on well-known beat writer Jack Kerouac, and he and other beats drank heavily from the Dionysian fountain of bebop phrasing, breathing, and being, a fact perhaps undervalued today in the world of word writers who overvalue other word writers—especially beat writers— over musicians.

The spontaneity that jazz embodied also found its form in avant-garde painters, writers and poets in the fifties, such as poet Charles Olson (and other Black Mountain College artists), and in beats Kerouac and Allen Ginsberg.[12] Kerouac and Ginsberg, plus beat from the street Neal Cassady, formed one of a few unlikely trios of the fifties, such as the Tennessee Williams/Marlon Brando/Elia Kazan collaboration on *A Streetcar Named Desire*, or of planned parenthood Margaret Sanger/researcher Gregory Goodwin (Goody) Pincus/ and devout Catholic physician John Rock in making the birth control pill.

Neal Cassady, the street kid from Denver, appeared to the beats as a natural born con man and felon, mesmerized, I believe, by the literary versions of himself he found first in Kerouac, and then later in the 1960s in Ken Kesey. Cassady was like the dark mirror Kerouac could hold up to see himself in anti-idealized and even a kind of gregarious, antisocial form. In real life and in the character of Dean Moriarty in *On the Road*, Cassady functioned as Kerouac's imagined id, as Kerouac was Cassady's imagined superego.

If Kerouac showed Cassady the higher life of writing, then Cassady showed Kerouac the high life he never knew could exist in such intense, supercharged form. Cassady was the fast-talking streetwise hipster who found his doppelgänger in Kerouac's football playing athletic-literary fusion.

I suspect that Cassady found this same connection later with Kesey's wrestler-writer fusion: here were guys as nimble on their feet as he was, who also could sweat those vitalities into their writings, producing visceral, palpitating depictions of America, released from the dead Puritan grip. These were New World V-8 explorers, racing and conniving and screwing their way past all known speed limits, drugged with desire to live in the New Jerusalem of the uninhibited Holy Now: a no-holds-barred freestyle wrestling match with the demons of the fates.

Take that wistful rhapsody that ends *On the Road*:

So in America when the sun goes down and I sit on the old broken-down river pier watching the long, long skies over New Jersey and sense all that raw land that rolls in one unbelievable huge bulge over to the West Coast, and all that road going, all the people dreaming in the immensity of it, and in Iowa I know by now the children must be crying in the land where they let the children cry, and tonight the stars'll be out, and don't you know that God is Pooh Bear? the evening star must be drooping and shedding her sparkler dims on the prairie, which is just before the coming of complete night that blesses the earth, darkens all rivers, cups the peaks and folds the final shore in, and nobody, nobody knows what's going to happen to anybody besides the forlorn rags of growing old, I think of Dean Moriarty, I even think of Old Dean Moriarty the father we never found, I think of Dean Moriarty.[13]

Kerouac and Cassady—"Sal" and "Dean"—were a buddy movie unto themselves in *On the Road* (1957)—written initially in a three-week burst in 1951 on a single teletype roll of paper—but Kerouac was a man of other moods and contradictions as well. One can hear his great sense of phrasing, reading from *On the Road* on the Steve Allen show on TV, while accompanied by Allen's bluesy piano. One sees his more conservative tendencies—and alcoholism—in his appearance on William F. Buckley's TV show *Firing Line*.

When his spontaneous prose is on the mark, you feel the mood of his wild holy quest, whether it be a jumping jazz joint he is describing or the roadway epiphanies. He wrote from mania, often amphetamine or coffee driven, but Kerouac seemed in the end to be trapped by his depressive demons, his alcohol, his lost youth.

Did the beats find the New Jerusalem, or were their impulses to jettison the inner editor of consciousness, to go go *go* fast *fast* **fast**, to live in a limitless present, simply the subjective side of what rational, corporate liberal structure was undertaking with its fast cars, fast food, fast information, fast housing, fast suburbs, and oh so fast missiles?

In the drip paintings of Jackson Pollock, *painting*, literally, as an activity rather than an image, took precedence. In a strange way Pollock "pictured" the culture of **go!** of **go man go!** of America on the move. The art critic Harold Rosenberg called it action painting. But if an act involves its past, its future, and its situated context, perhaps *motion painting* might be more accurate than Rosenberg's term *action painting*. This was a reduction of action to pure motion painting: canvas virtual roadmaps, as though one could paint one's movement, thereby simultaneously mapping it. Is this what Jack Kerouac was doing in literary form in his *On the Road*, making a virtual roadmap?

Pollock's life ended sadly in 1956—as it did for James Dean in 1955 and Albert Camus in 1960—literally on the road, after he drunkenly raced his auto out of control. How did the expression go? Live hard, die young, and leave a beautiful corpse behind. Both Cassady and Kerouac also died early from the hard lives they led and celebrated, as did Marilyn Monroe, Charlie Parker, John Coltrane, Little Walter, and Elvis Presley, to name just a few.

I must confess that to my eyes, the vigor of abstract expressionism's "energy field" paintings developed in the forties—influenced by surrealism, by Native American palimpsest paintings and glyphs, by the Picasso of *Guernica* and other bold sources of ideas—had dissipated by the 1950s at the very time the artists were being anointed with success. There was a kind of reduction of painting to the act of gesture in abstract expressionism, which unnecessarily excluded other elements of what it means to paint. It proscribed the past and the image as possibilities, and tended to leave its adherents in the straightjacket of being "one-idea artists," as Rosenberg called them. In this sense abstract expressionism may have represented the culmination of modernism, or perhaps the cul-de-sac that modernism led to, as what I will term *the last gesture of painting*. It could turn into a mere exercise of technique—of the *technique* of spontaneity—every bit as much as the culture of abstraction it was supposedly a reaction against did.

Perhaps the elevation of the very concept of "advance-guard" as a guiding ideal of modernism, rather than a fact that happens to occur in history, an ideal that took the progressive jettisoning of the past in the name of originality as historical necessity, had to culminate in something like abstract expressionism, the last gesture of painting. It found its originality in the gesture of painting, and soon found itself painted into a corner by that very same gesture. True spontaneity, as the jazz musicians of the fifties well knew, deeply involved past and future in the moment. Spontaneity is not impulsivity of the moment, which is compulsive; rather, spontaneity is free. But like the apocryphal story of the hipster, who when asked "How do you get to Carnegie Hall?" responded, "Practice, man, practice!" spontaneity involves repetitive, day-in-and-day-out crafting. Like the musical scales John Coltrane would play endlessly in rehearsal, even between sets at a gig, the spontaneous gesture is a culmination of a practice rather than a starting point.

That Thing Called Freedom

When I remember that gig with Willie "Big Eyes" Smith and the twenties-something retro musicians, I think of that thing in America called freedom, of the great hopes and feelings in the fifties that everything was possible, and the various ways the limits of those ideas showed themselves, and will yet show themselves. Those young musicians that night, living their love of that music, despite the financial and personal toll it takes to try to live from playing blues music today, were so unlike the typical university students I encounter, who remind one of proto-corporate versions of pod-spawned, unemotional, prefabricated creatures from *Invasion of the Body Snatchers*. They look alive at first glance, but far too often they are brain sucked. But they know how to score well on tests and cheer well at mass spectator events.

Yes, those crazed and conformist, contradictory times of the fifties have found their ways very much into the present, even if that message of freedom has been formatted all too fatally into an evaporating mirage.

In thinking of the fifties, it may be good to remember that freedom was something very much in the air from a variety of perspectives—cold warriors, civil rights seekers, nascent feminists, teens cruising, artists seeking it or celebrating it through their work. Today, by contrast, the very idea of freedom seems to have been reduced to that of the "freedom" to consume, to a consumption culture that truly found its form in the very same automaniacal, franchising fifties.

Take the brain rinsing of children and their parents by television and its advertisements, by thousands of daily acts of anxiety relieved by the purchase of a commodity—the basic physiological stimulus-response formula of com-mercials—and by thousands of acts of unfelt violence, by endless images of overflowing magical luxury, by a world of disposable celebrities who provide the children who identify with them substitute emotions the same way that drugs promise substitute feelings. Buy me, eat me, drink me, drive me, and you can be spontaneous, says the new Moloch of megatechnic America. This is the reality of early education in America—mind-altering electro-chemical indoctrination—and why students can tell you everything from *I Love Lucy*, *Friends*, *The Simpsons*, and *Seinfeld* reruns to *American Idol* and reality TV while remaining clueless about the whys and whens of history, outside of the box of the celebrity-image machine.

Or take the ways preemptive behavior monitoring tests and surveillance in schools and the workplace are on the rise, or of surveillance in malls. I suppose the point is that if you indoctrinate schoolchildren into submis-sion to the surveillance state early on, they will grow up to be more docile to such losses of freedom at work and in the franchised consumption zones, and sheeplike in the loss of their neighborhoods when powerful and distant corporations so decree. Even more important to the surveillance sector and its agents and "educators" is to make students docile to the dictates of the bureaucratic consumption state and its technical devices of sedation. A con-forming, consuming, disenfranchised populace is much safer than a free and independent citizenry.

The fifties set into motion—with its autos and televisions and franchises and "military-industrial complex"—an increasingly megatechnic America, a machine that rules today increasingly on automatic. But there are those vast vitalities that poured out of the fifties, producing in a Rosa Parks or a John Coltrane or a Robert Oppenheimer or a Jack Kerouac enduring road maps of what America could be, "all the people dreaming in the immensity of it."

3

INTERLUDE: GO MAN GO

Go man go!
Don't you get it?
Just go!
Gettin' ain't goin'
and you got to go

Go from the get go
Go man
Gauguin
Go van Gogh
like Peter, the Rock
cut off an ear
but the voices won't stop
squeelin' like a stuck pig
like, crazy
like, kero-wacky

Go, go West, man!

Go to ground zero
to the diabolic void
like soldier in nuke test
Go from your safe trench
run like hell
go gung ho toward the celestial fire
desert the desert
go to Gomorrah
evaporate to shadows
be a goner, a go getter goner

Go, go like Buddha
beat a path
through the holy gone desert
to the beatific void
Gogo till you're gone!
gone man
gone to this visible world of **torment**
go and get nothing:
that's all there is to get
have you gotten any lately?

Dig your navel
conduct navel operations in the desert
cut through the visible
see the unseen

command the rocks to speak:
Lend me your ears!
hear the bad jazz they blow
molecular go-go dance
cellular chaos
pig-eat-pig world
nuclear winter of our discontent

go, go till you get there!
dig the groove of perpetual motion
going, going
Gone!
restless unto the night
violent nonaction
devoid

Figure 1. Loomis Dean, "Mannequins Used to Gauge the Effects of an Atomic Bomb on the Human Body," Yucca Flat, Nevada, 1955, Time and Life Pictures. Getty Images.

4

THE HUNTER-GATHERERS' WORLD'S FAIR

No Enclosures

I was born on the prairies where the wind blew free and there was nothing to break the light of the sun. I was born where there were no enclosures.
—GOYATHLAY, OR "ONE WHO YAWNS," A.K.A. GERONIMO

And Geronimo, fierce Apache warrior Geronimo, broken Geronimo, was led by the Creator, under armed military guard of the U.S. army, into the very shit of Civilization, where, in one of its strange rituals, he found himself living with the people of the dawn of man, though utterly surrounded by the people of the endtime of humanity. And he heard the songs of dawn, sung to Mother Forest for more than forty thousand years, and he scouted and played with the little people who made the songs, and he knew, that though on that fateful day that Civilization had once massacred his own mother, wife, and three children, along with the others of his people, had brought forth a few days later the vision that told him he need not fear bullet death and that his arrows would find their mark, he knew, in the midst of that Civilization's display of power, in the 1904 Saint Louis World's Fair, that true powers were to be found in this first gathering of the people of the earth, that the native peoples' brought in from around the world as human exhibits, in reality constituted *The Hunter-Gatherers' World's Fair.*

There were so many strange peoples. Yet there were so many more strange white eyes staring, paying him ten to twenty-five cents for photographs. But he felt at home in the high jinks of the Pygmies, and joked with them, and he heard the song of the dawn of man when Ota Benga and others played the sacred horn, the molima, the sacred horn that Pygmies have sounded for over forty thousand years. He felt at home with the Pygmy culture, which, with Australian aboriginal culture, reaches back to a time when Neanderthals still walked the earth, not yet eliminated by us anatomically modern humans, and which reaches back to the cultures who made their culture, to the origins of culture, reaches back to sacred ways of calling Mother Forest who called us into being. And it became clear to Geronimo that he was granted a time to live in this heaven and hell by the Creator, to experience the dawn of man and the dusk, the beginnings of our human heritage and the sad, human-all-too-human, civilized end, when all that had been given became no more than all that could be taken.

And you look into his face at the Saint Louis World's Fair, this Bedonkohe Apache shaman somewhere around seventy-five years old, holding one of the bows and arrows he made and sold there, and you see a man resigned yet resolute. Despite being wounded many times, he was not finally killed by bullet, though perhaps despair had a hand in his death. And you look into the face of Ota Benga at the Saint Louis World's Fair, holding his spear, smiling to reveal his fierce filed teeth, and you know that Pygmies have been conning the big people for millennia, yet you see a man in the game of it trying to figure out what the hell it is all about, this place swarming like an ant colony with people who Geronimo had called "White Eyes," all staring in the strange way that they do.

In that time of the St. Louis exposition there was made manifest in the symbolic heart of the civilized world a gathering of some of the last uncivi-lized humans, the last of the more fully aware ones. Most remain nameless, though visible in frozen photographs, prehistoric shards tossed into visible history. Some, like Ota Benga, emerge dancing in the debris: of the white eyes, of the zookeepers who would cage human as well as animal to display as goods of The Great Spectacle of Civilization, of the *muzungu*, Big People black and white alike, who would look down condescendingly on the ani-mate mind of hunter-gatherers as primitive, and on the Pygmy people of the most ancient of human ways of awareness as subhuman. What did those as-sembled peoples share? Did they rise to sing the dawn each day, seeing the

Figure 2. Geronimo, a.k.a. Goyathlay ("one who yawns"), Louisiana Purchase Exposition, 1904. Missouri Historical Society.

others celebrating diurnal life while the White Eyes slept under the tyranny of the clock? Did they speak of how White Eyes literally see through tiny focus vision, literally spectators, while they view the world in wide-angle vision, which feels as though one is in the picture? Did they trade stories of hunting, of animal mimicry, of stealth?

Sixteenth- and seventeenth-century Portuguese explorers gave extravagant reports of Pygmies, including powers to become invisible and, despite their diminutive stature, to kill elephants. They also claimed that Pygmies had tails. All three claims were true: Pygmies were experts at camouflage and hunting, and, as Colin Turnbull noted: "The pygmies today still kill elephants single-handed, armed with only a short-handled spear. And they blend so well with the forest foliage that you can pass right by without seeing

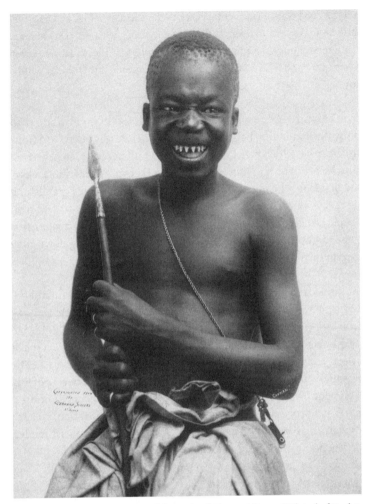

Figure 3. Ota Benga, 1904. Photograph by Gerhard Sisters. Missouri Historical Society.

them. As for their having tails ... the loincloth they wear is made of the bark of a tree, softened and hammered out until it is a long, slender cloth."[1] In living with the BaMbuti Pygmies of central Africa for a few years in the 1950s, Turnbull came to a deep respect for their wisdom and way of life:

They know the secret language that is denied all outsiders and without which life in the forest is an impossibility. The BaMbuti roam the forest at will, in small isolated bands or in hunting groups. They have no fear, because for them there is no danger. For them there is little hardship, so they have no need for belief in evil spirits. For them it is a good world. The fact that they average less than four and a half feet in height is of no concern to them; their taller neighbors, who jeer at them for being so puny, are as clumsy as elephants—another reason why they must always remain outsiders in a world where your life may depend on your ability to run swiftly and silently.[2]

Like Geronimo, Ota Benga had suffered massacre of his clan and enslavement, by the marauding Belgian Force Publique. He was purchased from the Baschilele tribe, which held him, by Samuel Phillips Verner, an American explorer who brought him and some pygmies from another tribe back to the United States for the 1904 Saint Louis World's Fair. Verner's grandson Phillips Verner Bradford and Harvey Blume have told the story in their remarkable book, *Ota Benga: The Pygmy in the Zoo*,[3] which I stayed up reading until 3 a.m. one night, awakening at dawn envisioning and writing down the first few paragraphs you have already read.

The Pygmies and a number of other indigenous peoples from around the world formed a major exhibit of the fair's Department of Anthropology. As the *New York Times* headline of November 16, 1903, stated: "To Exhibit Man at The St. Louis Fair, Dr. McGee Gathering Types and Freaks from Every Land." And the *St. Louis Republic* reported on March 6, 1904: "The three, the Ainus, the Pygmies, and the Patagonians will represent the lowest degree of human development. But many other strange races are included as typical stages of aboriginal progress by study of the white man's civilization."[4] Here was white man's civilization, not just in its normal American racist mode, but also in a genuine multicultural racist mode.

Along with a large number of Native Americans of various tribes, Geronimo was present, a prisoner of war. Later, a filtered biography of his life was published, which said little about the other peoples present at the fair. Also later, members of the secretive Skull and Bones Society of Yale University, including Prescott Bush, father and grandfather of the two Bush presidents, were said to have dug up Geronimo's remains from Fort Sill during World War I and brought them back to the stone tomb that serves as the society's headquarters at Yale. A letter from a member of the society, Winter Mead, dated from 1918, was discovered in 2006 that states: "The skull of the worthy Geronimo the Terrible, exhumed from its tomb at Fort Sill by your club . . . is now safe inside the [Tomb] together with his well worn femurs, bit & saddle horn." Mead was not at Fort Sill in 1918 however, so the story may still be apocryphal. But the disrespect shown to Geronimo and his people in his lifetime and after by white America, including the three generations of

Bush's, has continued in the legend the Yale elite still live, as does his vision that he would not return home.

Yet one day, or so the story goes, Geronimo approached the Pygmy enclave with his armed guard, and while chanting, gave to Ota an arrowhead he had made. He admired the Pygmies for their playfulness in the encampment, and no doubt for their awareness too. Like Geronimo, Ota Benga was a master of the sophisticated hunter-gatherer skills of tracking, camouflage, and awareness that Geronimo had practiced before surrendering. To those who consider such practices "primitive," consider Tom Brown Jr., who learned from the age of seven the arts of tracking and scouting from his teacher, a Lipan Apache named Stalking Wolf. Brown is widely known as a tracker, and has found numerous lost people and criminals over the years. Not as well known is the fact that Brown also taught U.S. commandos in the Special Forces, including Navy Seals. Some of his techniques can be seen in the Hollywood film *The Hunted*, which was loosely based on one of Brown's tracking cases.

In his book *Case Files of the Tracker*, Brown describes his introduction to a group of thirty-four elite American and non-American commandos around the 1970s.[5] Sensing their disrespect for his "primitive" skills, he invites them all to hunt him, capture him, and return him to base after giving him a five-minute head start. He also tells them to return silently to the base if they get a tap on their backs. The commandos laugh among themselves—they note that he doesn't even carry camouflage! Brown, of course, is a master of camouflage, who understands the superiority of using the local earth. As the men returned one by one to base, it began to dawn on them that if this were combat, they would be dead. None of them ever even saw Tom Brown, who not only dispatched all thirty-four in half an hour but also saved the "alpha male" for last, just for the fun of it. Brown's wilderness school today teaches the varieties of "primitive" skills, revealing them to be not only tools for survival but also entrees into sophisticated levels of awareness long since abandoned by most civilized peoples.

Alone and invisible, Ota Benga had hunted an elephant in the deep jungle in the days before his capture. The traditional way for a Pygmy to hunt elephant was to stalk invisibly and spear it from the side—get yourself out in the woods sometime with an enormous animal that can rip you apart in seconds and try this sometime—and then to allow the poison to do its work while tracking it. Traditional Pygmies looked down upon the ingenious traps used by the larger Bantu people of the villages, which lacked the up-close-and-personal involvement in the sacred game of hunting and respect for the game it entailed.

The successful hunt of an elephant is cause for great rejoicing and celebration among the Pygmies. And so a triumphant Ota Benga returned to his camp to bring news of joy, only to find his family and kin slaughtered by Belgians seeking booty. In his grief, he allowed himself to be captured. Now Pygmies, as Turnbull and others have documented, traditionally would live for times with villagers, playing dumb while reaping the benefits of village life. But the charade would only continue for a time, before they returned to the real world of the forest and its living freedom.

As is well documented, traditional hunter-gatherers worked much less and ate a much healthier diet than agricultural peoples. Until agriculture de-spoiled so much of the world, theirs was a life lived in the garden of paradise. Ota Benga had lost that freedom, but as Bradford and Blume note: "the key to this pygmy's confidence in his ability to survive a village is that he can leave. He can pass himself off as anything, play any role, assume any disguise, pro-vided his people, his hunting band, his family still exist and he can return to them. A pygmy can hunt even so large a creature as the St. Louis Fair, as the entire land of the *muzungu*, if his home still exists and if he knows he can still get there."[6]

Pilgrims of Power

> Modern man, the world eater, respects no space and no thing green or furred as sacred. The march of the machines has entered his blood.
> —LOREN EISELEY

This was indeed a spectacle, the Saint Louis World's Fair of 1904, officially known as the Louisiana Purchase Exposition. It brought, among others, two great interpreters of modern life. Historian Henry Adams would write of its energies in his book, *The Education of Henry Adams*. St. Louis also attracted so-ciologist Max Weber, who returned to worldly affairs after six and a half years of relative seclusion following a nervous breakdown. His lecture in St. Louis dealt with the historical increase of rationalized relations between German landowners and their workers. The ascent of rational culture in modern life more generally preoccupied him.

Weber had recently finished the work that would later be known as *The Protestant Ethic and the Spirit of Capitalism*, an analysis of modern capitalism and culture as products of the reformation. Weber showed there how the emergent religious ethos reversed the vice of organized profit making into a virtue, in effect cloaking the baby of rational capitalism until it could grow to throw off its religious cloak. Worldly asceticism, no longer sequestered, was a religious outlook that enabled rational calculation to be imposed upon ev-eryday life as religious virtue. The rationalized, ascetic life of the otherworldly monk was in effect loosed from the monastery by the reformation and imposed on all. Worldly success could be taken as a sign of grace rather than a motive for pleasure, a sign measured in profit, motivated by salvation. Sensuous bodily engagement and enjoyment could be taken as a source of sin. The bodily sources of human intelligence through which our hunter-gatherer ancestors evolved into humankind would be treated as suspect or sinful by the new modes of Puritanism.

Yet once this new worldview became institutionalized, it turned the tables and cloaked Christianity in its iron cage of rational-mechanical reason. The Christian Creator was reduced to a great clockmaker in the mechanical universe science was developing. The transformation of a philosophy of love into what Charles Peirce called the Darwinian "Philosophy of Greed," was one of the great sleight-of-hand magic tricks of history. Christian capitalists could love their neighbors for the profit they derived from them, could exploit the wide world for its riches, dominating its peoples, even exhibiting them in St. Louis, all framed in the ideals of the Western Christian tradition. Who needs a Mephistopheles when Faust could assume the spirit of capitalism as religious virtue?

Despite his deep interest in world religions and later meetings with Native and African Americans in his trip, Weber seemed not to take notice of the native peoples gathered at St. Louis. What we do know, at least from his wife Marianne's account, is that the Webers apparently found the light of German culture exhibited in St. Louis to be the most dazzling. As she recounted in the third person:

What delighted the Webers particularly in the brilliant vast panorama of the Exposition was the "German House," distinguishable from a distance by the mighty eagle with its pinions spread wide on the front. Here the achievements of interior decoration and furnishing, and of artistic expression generally, combined in a way that the companions had never before seen, and in the midst of products from all continents these achievements were unequaled. "All products of German arts and crafts are beautiful, and they have been so wonderfully combined into a total picture that it far surpasses every other nation; this is readily acknowledged by everyone." It struck them as strange that the Germans, whose way of life was often so plebian right up to the leading classes, should attain such perfection in their *plastic* achievement and become in this field the leaders of the West. Viewing these works Weber could be proud of his nation for whose shortcomings he had the painful clear-sightedness of love.[7]

The Webers found their mirror of civilization in St. Louis, and despite his tragic view of rationalizing modern culture—and the real possibility that it could result in rational barbarism, Max Weber was himself too locked within its logic to consider the possibility that aboriginal intelligence might provide clues to a way out of the dilemma. But that is another story.

The Saint Louis World's Fair was also an occasion for historian Henry Adams to observe the dynamos of power, as he had a decade earlier at the World's Columbian Exposition in Chicago. The power dynamos dynamited Adams's imagination with ideas of energy, leading him to his well-known reflections in his book *Mont-Saint-Michel and Chartres* on the transformation from the religious-social energies of medieval culture, symbolized by the Virgin, to the electro-energetics of the modern machine. In his sprawling memoir and book of essays, *The Education of Henry Adams*, this "pilgrim of power" returned to the theme in describing his visit to St. Louis.

The new American showed his parentage proudly; he was the child of steam and the brother of the dynamo, and already, within less than thirty years, this mass of mixed humanities, brought together by steam, was squeezed and welded into approach to shape; a product of so much mechanical power, and bearing no distinctive marks but that of its pressure. The new American, like the new European, was the servant of the powerhouse, as the European of the twelfth century was the servant of the church, and the features would follow the parentage.

The St. Louis Exposition was its first creation in the twentieth-century, and, for that reason, acutely interesting. . . . No prophet could be believed, but a pilgrim of power, without constituency to flatter, might allow himself to hope. The prospect from the Exposition was pleasant; one seemed to see almost an adequate motive for power; almost a scheme for progress. In another half-century, the people of the central valleys should have hundreds of millions to throw away more easily than in 1900 they could throw away tens; and by that time they might know what they wanted. Possibly they might even have learned how to reach it. This was an optimist's hope . . .[8]

Optimist's hope indeed! Adams was no Pollyanna; he understood that peoples may rise and peoples may perish, and that the challenge in his time was for Americans and humankind more generally to come to grips with the enormous energies being released by technical civilization. These energies act on people, and require the reaction of social institutions. This insight marks his distance from the simple belief in progress, though he was still implicated in it.

Adams sought to apply a scientific outlook to history, modeled after the natural sciences. He observed the acceleration of quantitative power in Western civilization since the Middle Ages and attempted to graph it as a universal development, as law. Ironically, his method was flawed from a quantitative perspective, based on a loose assemblage of dates to predict future accelerations of power. Yet his predictions were uncannily accurate. Adams sought a scientific basis for his predictions, but neglected the fact that his own sense of social energies, his intuitive feeling for events, was the chief instrument for his most profound insights. If he could have read what his contemporary, Charles Peirce, had written on the logic of *abduction*, or hypothesis creation, he might have realized that his subjective promptings were not only vital for the practice of life but also ingredients in a scientific outlook.

Further, the acceleration of quantitative energies he had observed and diagrammed were aspects of a progressively automatic rational-mechanical culture that was, as he sensed, unraveling vital social practices and institutions. But this was not due to necessary laws, as Adams assumed. It was rather a civilization locked into a rut of its own choosing, a rut it viewed as inevitable development. It was what Weber described as "rationalization." It was progress, defined as the unlimited expansion of mechanical invention, scientific inquiry, and bureaucratic control, and in which the human passions were treated as suspect, as merely "subjective." In this outlook the universe was increasingly defined as a machine to which human imagination, emotion, and purpose were reducible.

Although Adams assumed a necessary acceleration of physical energies, he did not assume human institutions develop so automatically. Many religious limits, social customs, and traditions that the Enlightenment sought to eradicate were accretions of human connection in some ways resistant to unlimited expansion. Adams saw that their erasure without corresponding development of new humane institutions would mean dehumanization, not progress. The new America lacked character but possessed prodigious force, as he wrote in a letter on December 20, 1904, and was "running very fast into the impossible." Consider his St. Louis view of the new American, coming into being:

For this new creation, born since 1900, a historian asked no longer to be teacher or even friend; he asked only to be a pupil . . . for he could see that the new American—the child of incalculable coal-power, chemical power, electric power, and radiating energy, as well as of new forces yet undetermined—must be a sort of God compared with any former creation of nature. At the rate of progress since 1800, every American who lived to the year 2000 would know how to control unlimited power. He would think in complexities unimaginable to an earlier mind. He would deal with problems altogether beyond the range of earlier society.[9]

Far from progress as utopia, as the end to all problems, those unimaginable complexities and unprecedented problems Adams foresaw would indeed characterize the twentieth century. Adams saw, as no progressivist did, that the new century was a Pandora's box of powers on the verge of opening and urgently required a new social mind:

No scheme could be suggested to the new American, and no fault needed to be found, or complaint made; but the next great influx of new forces seemed near at hand, and its style of education promised to be violently coercive. The movement from unity to multiplicity, between 1200 and 1900, was unbroken in sequence, and rapid in acceleration. Prolonged one generation longer, it would require a new social mind. As though thought were common salt in indefinite solution it must enter a new phase subject to new laws. Thus far, for five or ten thousand years, the mind had successfully reacted, and nothing yet proved that it would fail to react—but it would need to jump.[10]

When Adams wrote in 1904 that "the next great influx of new forces seemed near at hand, and its style of education promised to be violently coercive," he was describing a world that would be launching a year or so later in Albert Einstein's papers on relativity, in Picasso's African-influenced modern bathers, noses askew, perspective disregarded. This world was launching itself in Adams's, Einstein's, and Picasso's imaginations, but its promise to be "violently coercive" would be explodingly fulfilled during the course of the twentieth century.

About eight months after visiting St. Louis, on January 17, 1905, Adams wrote his remarkable letter to the historian Henry Osborn Taylor, in which he said,

The assumption of unity which was the mark of human thoughts in the middle-ages has yielded very slowly to the proofs of complexity. The stupor of science before radium is a proof of it. Yet it is quite sure, according to my score of ratios and curves, that, at the accelerated rate of progression shown since 1600, it will not need another century or half century to tip thought upside down. Law, in that case, would disappear as theory or a priori principle, and give place to force. Morality would become police. Explosives would reach cosmic violence. Disintegration would overcome integration.[11]

Adams not only accurately predicted the manifestation of "cosmic violence" in explosives, exemplified in the atomic bomb, but he also saw how the growing power matrix would tip social institutions upside down, amplifying force over law, reducing morality to police. Totalitarianism was the initial face of the power matrix, exemplified in the images of the great dictators, Stalin, Hitler, and the others. No nurturing Virgin Mother there. But the atomic bomb emerged as one "face" of the machinery that reshaped world society in the course of the cold war, making politics a servant of the logic of total nuclear devastation.

The ultimate "Big Brother" was the Power Complex itself, which would render the strong-armed dictator obsolete. However much their images were idealized, the great dictators still retained too much human personality, which proved an impediment to the system. So the system, the military-industrial complex, moved on. But the complex still required The Image, which would globally enscreen human consciousness in the second half of the twentieth century through the developments of television and computers, perfecting the mechanization of life. All that is human could be melted into machine: human awareness as input, human relation as interface.

So in the great gathering of native peoples of the world in St. Louis, where was Henry Adams, who so sensitively registered the degradation of social institutions by an accelerating power culture? Who documented the mechanization by dynamos of social energies formerly manifest in the Virgin? Who pleaded so eloquently for the powers of the feminine in his poem, "Prayer to the Virgin of Chartres," found in his wallet at his death in 1918:

> Help me to feel! Not with my insect sense,—
> With yours that felt all life alive in you;
> Infinite heart beating at your expense;
> Infinite passion breathing the breath you drew![12]

Why was he blind to the intense energies of the hunter-gatherers, who need neither dynamo, Savior, or Virgin, but only the naked relationship to the circumambient universe of life, establishing and attuning themselves to plants and berries, to the game, to one another, to the rocks and streams and sun and moon and all things through which the fantasia of life manifests. In ongoing attunement through all-encompassing awareness of the relation of me to the life I am immersed in, especially to the direct sources of life on which I depend, is to be found the original energy source and social life that powered us, through hunting and gathering, into humanity. It is the full awareness for which the human brain evolved, before we piecemealed our consciousness with the institutions and divisions of labor, and walled ourselves from direct participation in nature, which civilization, literally city-fication, brought about. And it was all right there for Adams to see: the original social dynamos of human awareness manifest in rich diversity on daily exhibition in St. Louis. It was there for anyone who had eyes to see and ears to hear. But he was too much immersed in "the noise," as the Pygmies put it, to feel those energies, the original dynamo of animate mind.

The veils of civilization have, from its very beginnings, been designed to mask the indigenous other, the wild self, without and within. Adams sensed the social power of the civilized medieval Virgin, embodied in the great cathedral of Chartres. But that she herself might be a repressed symbol, divorced from her sexual being as a mother, an abstract manifestation of the feminine in a patriarchal civilization, but also a cipher for what the Pygmies term "Mother Forest," were possibilities beyond Adams's reach.

Perhaps the power of the medieval Virgin was a sign of the rebirth of pagan vitalities in Christian symbol, vitalities that not only reanimated Christian Europe, but also Western patriarchal civilization. Perhaps those Paleolithic earth mothers—such as the Venus of Willendorf—bodied forth anew in a return of the repressed feminine, a return, though not without repression, when Venus became Virgin.

Similarly, the beloved animals of the hunter's imagination and art found form on medieval churches. As eco-philosopher Paul Shepard said, "Foraging peoples typically spend thousands of hours every year pondering and studying the animals around them and discussing the events of the day. The animals are numinous and oracular signifiers. In their most subtle moves, they are watched and studied with dedicated determination."[13] Our interaction with those animal Others informed the making of the human brain, the human brain we use today, despite ten thousand years of civilizing. Again, Shepard:

We are space-needing, wild-country, Pleistocene beings, trapped in overdense numbers in devastated, simplified ecosystems. . . . Whereas the sanctity of non-human life was a normal part of small-scale societies for thousands of years, the "world religions," with their messianic, human-centered, and otherworldly emphasis, trampled those traditions and now are beginning to recognize what they lost: sensitivity to human membership in natural communities and affirmation of and compliance with the biological framework of life.[14]

We domesticated animals and plants, we domesticated the world, and we domesticated our consciousness with the distancing shelter of civilization. But our bodies remain wild in constitution and wild in need. Adams longed for the human touch, but could not connect with the animate dynamos of indigenous peoples in St. Louis, still passionately alive. He could only gropingly implore his idealized medieval virginal dynamo:

> Help me to feel! Not with my insect sense,—
> With yours that felt all life alive in you . . .

Awakening at Dawn

Man is a queer beast. He spends dozens of centuries puffing himself up and drawing himself in, and at last he has to be content to be just his own size, neither infinitely big nor infinitely little.

—D. H. LAWRENCE

Ota Benga lived in New York City after the Saint Louis World's Fair, where he worked for a time at the Brooklyn Zoo as a zookeeper, before the director came up with the bright idea of exhibiting him as just one more caged animal. Although it soon caused a major scandal, it was a role Ota well knew how to play from his St. Louis experience, albeit more literalized. And besides, Pygmies had cultivated for generations how to play dumb for *muzungu*. So Ota ended up moving to Lynchburg, Virginia, where he had spent some time in the seminary school.

When he settled in Lynchburg, Ota found some means to live as a hunter-gatherer again, albeit with restrictions of civilization imposed upon him. He lived with the Others, which, for most dark skinned people in America, meant white people. But in Ota's case, it meant *muzungu*, big people, black or white. He had to follow the ways of the black *muzungu* to some extent, even as they had to live in the boundaries of racism imposed by the white *muzungu*. But even though he had to work various jobs, he could also practice the hunting and gathering skills of his Pygmy people.

In fact, Ota Benga formed a new tribe of "little people," not Pygmies, but of the town's children: "In Lynchburg, ten thousand miles away from home, Ota went some way toward recreating the traditional sociability and communalism of the hunt. The difference is this, that Ota's last hunting band, was not made up of peers. He was the only member of his age group, the only adult to be represented—all the rest were children. The band of hunters Ota led through Lynchburg's woods were boys from about five to eleven years old."[15]

He not only taught these boys his "primitive" skills of hunting, fishing, and honey gathering, but also the intense social bonding of hunter-gatherers. Some eighty years later an old man who had been one of those boys described Ota stringing a bow as long as he was tall as sounding like Beethoven. Others recounted his amazing abilities at mimicry, demonstrating quail and turkey calls, and how, "he said it was better to draw game to you than to have to go out after it. He stood still on rocks above a stream, the spear in his hand poised for passing fish. Once a bear cub stumbled into one of his traps. Ota released it; it would surely find its mother, he explained."[16]

Ota would bring herbs to Anne Spencer, a poet associated with the Harlem Renaissance, and who hosted Booker T. Washington, W. E. B. Du Bois, and many other notable black intellectuals at her home. He seemed to be getting along well in Lynchburg. But after a few years, he gradually realized that he would never be able to return to Africa.

Ota undertook one final ritual, celebrated in the way of a Pygmy, in song and in dance around a fire he built on March 20, 1916. There, as Bradford and Blume describe:

At the vernal equinox, outside the carriage house where he slept when it was warm, he built a fire and broke off the caps placed on his teeth. He stripped to a loincloth. A crowd gathered to see Otto dancing, singing around the fire. The boys tried to join him as always. This one time he chased them all away. . . . He had hidden a revolver he had stolen earlier that day. In March's afternoon shadows he retrieved it from under the hay in the carriage house and, still singing, turned the gun upon his heart and fired.[17]

As Moke, a BaMbuti Pygmy, once told Colin Turnbull, the forest, "is where we belong, and we shall return soon. We cannot refuse the forest."[18]

There was Geronimo, fierce free Geronimo, "born on the prairies where the wind blew free," enslaved by constant armed military guard, yet able to make and give an arrowhead to a man as inwardly free as he. Geronimo, whose sorrowful epiphany was that he would never be killed by a bullet, and who would never return to his homeland, was touched by the spirit of Ota Benga in this strange gathering of hunter-gatherers from the remote remnants of the free wild earth. Ota Benga's final epiphany was also tragic, his despair at his break from his homeland touched him at last with the bullet he put to his heart.

Despite staying up to 3 a.m. reading *Ota Benga*, I leaped awake just at dawn, infused with dream-world images of Geronimo, Ota Benga, and others, all grouped with their own peoples, welcoming the dawn in St. Louis as the "White Eyes" world slept, sharing their wide-eyed wonder in the face of the ant colony and perennial freak show that is civilization. I awoke compelled by this vision, realizing that this indeed was the first world gathering of hunter-gatherers, an event that felt to me worth far more than the insights of Henry Adams and Max Weber and the other great modern minds who attended, despite not being recorded into history. My vision urged me further, to see what was going on in my little city dawn, and so I watched a cardinal couple cover each other in my own back yard, alighting their way to my next door neighbor's bird feeder. I then went downstairs, now compelled to write notes, to body forth the first paragraphs and outline of this essay, and then I went back to sleep. It all seemed a bit obsessive-compulsive, though I am not an obsessive-compulsive personality.

About an hour to two afterward, as I discovered only later in the day, a neighbor just up the block from me shot himself to death. I must have been asleep when the shot rang out. The next time my inner wake-up call was to vision forth was the night before and morning of 9/11, when images of owls and a burned-out body jolted me wide-eyed awake at dawn. But that too is another story.

The inner voice we all hear speaks from time to time, if we but listen. If I could have listened more deeply to that which urged me awake, perhaps I could have been roused out of my house and up the block, and knocked at that neighbor's door to tell him this tale, and spare him his final nightmare.

5

LIFE, LITERATURE, AND SOCIOLOGY IN TURN-OF-THE-CENTURY CHICAGO

In describing the technological exhibits at the World's Columbian Exhibition in Chicago, of 1893, Henry Adams said, "Chicago asked in 1893 for the first time the question whether the American people knew where they were driving." Adams thought the American people did not know, "but that they might still be driving or drifting unconsciously to some point in thought, as their solar system was said to be drifting towards some point in space; and that, possibly, if relations enough could be observed, this point might be fixed. Chicago was the first expression of American thought as a unity; one must start there." As Adams goes on to describe the political events in Washington surrounding the battles over the gold and silver standards, it becomes clearer that "the fixed point" toward which America was drifting was the mechanistic life of the machine and its economic extension in capitalism.[1]

Adams was wrong about Chicago as the first expression of unified American thought, if anything the "Golden Day" of transcendentalist New England in the early 1850s should count as the first flowering of "American thought as a unity." But he saw more clearly than his optimistic contemporaries that Chicago was a fast-beating pulse with which one could measure the new American dynamism: it was the city that in 1893 took as its motto, "I Will."[2]

Chicago was the quintessential American city of blind will, of the frenetic push to butcher, to stack, to railroad itself to some point in space, blindly drifting within the expansive dream of the machine. "I Will" the city said in its determination to rebuild after the Great Chicago Fire of 1871 and to hold the greatest exposition ever in 1893, but Chicago could easily have borrowed from Nietzsche for its motto and said: "I Will to Power," for power was its end and money its chief means.

Turn-of-the-century Chicago can be viewed as a dream of money, a dream shared by rich and poor alike, a dream that set out, for better or worse, to re-shape the world. What we now consider as Chicago literature and sociology both share a fascination with the profound social upheaval and energies cre-ated by the explosion of industrial capital. Both sought to document the life of the city, which was no small task in the chaos that was Chicago. The litera-ture of Upton Sinclair and Theodore Dreiser described the degradation that could be brought about by the new materialism. Similarly, Hull-House was a social settlement house for immigrants that opened in 1889 as one of the first in America, drawing attention to the stark conditions of life in Chicago while providing a humane alternative, and laying the groundwork for a new sociol-ogy in the process. "Chicago sociology," although now viewed as coming into its golden age in the 1920s, should be seen as rooted in these earlier efforts, and also in the broad social philosophies proposed by John Dewey, George Herbert Mead, and others who were not in the Sociology Department of the University of Chicago. The University of Chicago was built on the grounds of the Chicago World's Columbian Exposition of 1893. Yet academic sociology, although now equated with Chicago sociology, emerged out of these other milieus as well, and although it achieved a new emphasis on urban ethnogra-phy for sociology, it may be criticized for unwarranted "scientism" in its ef-forts to establish itself in the academy. And all of these efforts can be viewed as taking their cues from life itself, particularly from the peculiar new forms of life emerging in the chaotic expansion that marked Chicago. In this way I am interpreting Chicago literature and sociology as products of the city, and indicators of its culture of materialism.

Chicago reveals American materialism in the making, in which the city produced a critique of the rampant consumption of the Gilded Age that is, strangely enough, the legacy of that materialism. One question is whether Chicago literature and sociology remain forms of critique or whether they go further to create new insights or perspectives not reducible to their im-mediate milieu, although, perhaps, growing out of it. In other words, did Chicago literature and sociology provide a genuine and durable alternative to the consumptive materialism of Chicago?

Literature and sociology have been intimately related in Chicago since the end of the nineteenth century. Consider the irony that Upton Sinclair's

Figure 4. Chicago exerted an unmistakable influence on the books of its writers, who shared common concerns with the antisocial effects of the rapidly expanding industrial city and ways of reacting against those fragmenting conditions through social reform, literature, journalism, and social philosophy.

fiction produced immediate social reform, whereas Thorstein Veblen's social theory of the leisure class was regarded by some as literary satire. The novelist James T. Farrell began his Studs Lonigan trilogy in the late twenties while still a student at the University of Chicago, where he took courses in sociology during the central years of the department's urban ethnographical research. The list of his short stories for a composition class reads like the list of books published by members and students of the Sociology Department in the 1920s.[3] More recently, the most celebrated Chicago author of all, Saul Bellow, had his office not in the English Department, but in the Social Science Research Building at 1126 East 59th Street, where he was a member of the University of Chicago's Committee on Social Thought.

The relationship between literature and sociology is further illustrated by the careers of W. I. Thomas and Robert Park. Thomas began his sociological career at the University of Chicago as a graduate student in that key year for Henry Adams, 1893. Thomas had earlier taught English literature at Oberlin College, and he later introduced the use of "literary" materials—personal documents such as letters and life histories—in his research with Florian Znaniecki, published between 1918 and 1920 as *The Polish Peasant in Europe and America*. Park's complicated career included eleven years as a newspaperman, with his last assignment coming as a reporter and drama critic for the *Chicago Journal* from 1897 to 1898. During this time Park also wrote an unpublished novel and several plays. He was originally motivated by his study with John Dewey, who Park said inspired him, "to see and know what we call 'Life.'" Dewey also gave Park his "first great assignment": "to investigate the nature and social function of the newspaper." Park then went on to study philosophy with William James, Josiah Royce, George Santayana, and Hugo Muensterberg at Harvard, to take his only sociology course with Georg Simmel in Berlin, and to work for seven years as the personal secretary of black reformer Booker T. Washington in the South, a most unusual occupation for a white man with a doctorate in philosophy from the University of Heidelberg.[4]

The binding thread connecting Chicago literature and sociology is the newspaper. Noted Chicago writers such as Dreiser, Sherwood Anderson, Ben Hecht, Carl Sandburg, Nelson Algren, and Bellow all worked for newspapers at some point in their careers. One can say that literary "Chicago realism," although not perhaps reducible to journalism, shows strong influences of journalism. Likewise, the series of ethnographic studies in the 1920s by graduate students of Park and Burgess and the earlier researches of Thomas and Znaniecki not only point to the significance of communications media for sociological study but also can be seen as using methods common to the newspaper reporter for sociological purposes.

In Park's 1939 article, "Notes on the Origin of the Society for Social Research," he describes the centrality of Thomas to the development of academic Chicago sociology. The essence of Thomas's perspective was for Park its "literary" quality: "Thomas' interest was always, it seems, that of a poet (although he never, so far as I know, wrote poetry) and of a literary man in the reportorial sense, and not that of a politician or of a practical man. He wanted to see, to know, and to report, disinterestedly and without respect to anyone's policies or program, the world of men and things as he experienced it." Although it may not seem to follow that a "literary man in the reportorial sense" is necessarily a literary man, one must remember that much of what we think of as Chicago literature is precisely literature "in a reportorial sense." Also keep in mind how essential a reportorial sense is to Park's whole conception of sociology, as he described himself:

It happened that, having been for something like ten years a newspaper reporter, I knew a good deal about the city. In fact it was, as I have frequently said, while I was a reporter and a city editor that I began my sociological studies. It was under the guidance of an extraordinary personality, Franklin Ford, himself a newspaperman, that I got my first understanding of the significance and the possibilities of the social survey as an instrument for social investigation. That must have been as early as 1893 or 1894. In the article I wrote about the city I leaned rather heavily on the information I had acquired as a reporter regarding the city. Later on, as it fell to my lot to direct the research work of an increasing number of graduate students, I found that my experience as a city editor in directing a reportorial staff had stood me in good stead. Sociology, after all, is concerned with problems in regard to which newspaper men inevitably get a good deal of first hand knowledge. Besides that, sociology deals with just those aspects of social life which ordinarily find their most obvious expression in the news and in historical and human documents generally. One might fairly say that a sociologist is merely a more accurate, responsible, and scientific reporter.[5]

One sees in this statement how strongly the impress of the newspaper made itself felt on Park and why he believed sociology needed to turn from theoretical discourse to empirical observation. One might call this type of sociology and literature "reportorial realism." Park was a key actor in the drama of twentieth-century sociology, and his self-assigned role was to transform the sociologist from philosopher-historian to scientific reporter. He believed that sociology could become scientific through concrete reporting of empirical reality. Yet one of the potential problems in reportorial realism is that the empirical may have historical distortions embedded in it that remain relatively invisible to the reporter and that call for a different level of analysis. Chicago may not have been the generalizable model of the modern metropolis that academic Chicago sociologists believed it to be.

Park's scientific materialism was part of the same forces of materialism that were at work in Chicago, and more generally, in modern culture. Park's reportorial realism would in turn be supplanted by a statistical sociology that viewed only itself as truly scientific: the reporter gave way to the "accountant" as the dominant role model for scientific sociology, and the qualitative colors of city life that remained a part of the reporter's facts were excised from the quantitative conception of human science.

The Great Stockyard Machine

To understand Chicago, or "Porkopolis" as some of its citizens at the turn of the century were fond of calling it, one must appreciate to what extent it is a city of quantities. It was the fastest growing city in the world for over sixty years between the 1860s and the 1930s, frequently doubling its population in a decade. Although only incorporated in 1837, Chicago had acquired 29,963 residents by 1850, 112,172 in 1860, 503,185 in 1880, and 2,701,705 in 1920. In 1892, the year before Chicago asked, as Adams put it, whether the American people knew where they were driving, Chicago drove approximately two and a half million cattle and almost five million hogs to slaughter. The railroad made possible an unprecedented aggregation of capital and labor in the stockyards, one that the rationalizing tendencies of the megamachine quickly maximized, not only over the mode of production—as in the early use of assembly-line techniques—but also over every aspect of life possible, reducing everything to quanta of profit.

Chicago gave birth to the modern skyscraper, enabling a more rationalized use of limited land in the business district, and an increase of light and window space. The new ideas growing out of Chicago had a profound influence on European modernist architects, which culminated in the glass and steel skeletal structures of the "second school" of Chicago architecture led by émigré Mies van der Rohe. Skeletal buildings are perhaps apt symbols for a city that built its reputation on flaying and the skinning of hides. As Max Weber remarked after visiting Chicago on his way to the 1904 Saint Louis World's Fair, "With the exception of some exclusive residential districts, the whole gigantic city, more extensive than London, is like a man whose skin has been peeled off and whose entrails one sees at work."[6]

Of a somewhat more modern, but equally first class Chicago pork packing and canning establishment, Rudyard Kipling remarked around the same time as Weber, "Then that first stuck swine dropped, still kicking, into a great vat of boiling water, and spoke no more words, but wallowed in obedience to some unseen machinery, and presently came forth at the lower end of the vat and was heaved on the blades of a blunt paddle-wheel-thing."[7]

Chicago fires of the soul burned in this "singing flame of a city," as Dreiser called it. As Upton Sinclair's *The Jungle* so searingly showed, the one quality left unquantified and uncapitalized was the death-squeal of the doomed pig. The good citizens of Porkopolis liked to boast, "They use everything about the hog except the squeal!"

Sinclair's novel is set primarily in and around the Union Stock Yards of the South Side. The Union Stock Yards were by no means named because they were organized labor unions. Presumably named for the United States, they were founded in 1865 to consolidate meat packing in Chicago, which had risen in importance during the Civil War because Chicago was in the war zone. In many ways the Union Stock Yards can be seen as part of the victory of the machine in the Civil War, which defeated not only the human slave labor of the South, but also the American vision of democratic vistas, of a free life as Walt Whitman said, "copious, vehement, spiritual, bold," that could transcend the merely material. It was the machine of industry that indeed appropriated the copious, vehement, spiritual, and bold to itself, leaving to life the meager,

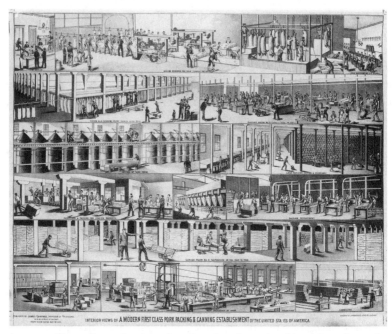

Figure 5. Lithograph, *Interior Views of a Modern First-Class Pork Packing and Canning Establishment of the United States of America*, printed by Shober and Carqueville, Chicago, 1880, ICHi-04064. Chicago History Museum.

insensate, spiritless, and submissive. The Union Stock Yards, described in relentless detail in *The Jungle*, were quite united and cold-bloodedly efficient in attempting to destroy any opposition from the workers' unions.

In the industrialization of the American vision after the Civil War the tensions between the romantic and the technical that characterized the exploration of the New World swung decidedly toward the technical, and a great inversion occurred. Henceforth it would be the mechanism—money and the machine—that would be endowed with the romantic, leaving the hollowed-out human form to assume the qualities of the machine. When Jurgis Rudkis, the Lithuanian protagonist of *The Jungle*, toured the Durham meat packing plant with his family shortly after their arrival in Chicago, it seemed, "impossible of belief that anything so stupendous could have been devised by mortal man." That was why to Jurgis it seemed almost profane to speak about the place skeptically as others did: "It was a thing as tremendous as the universe—the laws and ways of its working no more than the universe to be questioned or understood. All that a mere man could do, it seemed to Jurgis, was to take a thing like this as he found it, and do as he was told."[8]

This "thing as tremendous as the universe" was the great machine of modern capitalist industry, transcendent and omnipotent, that Sinclair later pits against a fiery socialism also transcendent and capable of defeating the bigness of the capitalist machine with the bigness of organized labor. There was a kind of transcendence in the massiveness of emergent industry, in its raising of human activity to the level of the gigantic, in the smooth-flowing and metallic way it seemed ritually to transform life itself into bloodless carcass and packaged product. Perhaps only the Aztec ritual sacrifice, in which the human victim's still-beating heart was plucked out on the high steps of the pyramid and displayed to the populace, could match the ritual tours of the slaughter factories. Or perhaps the Spanish bullfight, in which living beef is agonistically skewered to the delight of the spectators, or its inverse, the annual running of the bulls in Pamplona, in which the spectators are occasionally skewered by the stampeding bulls, are somewhat analogous. How many modern cities have made of their local blood baths a major tourist attraction?

There is something more honest in that Chicago slaughter spectacle than in American consumption culture today, where slaughter factories, and production more generally, are hidden from view, like the underground slaughter/production factories of the Morlocks in H. G. Wells's *The Time Machine*. The stockyards were, after all, a key ingredient in the culture of display in Chicago, and they impressed on the many thousands of tourists who visited them the bloody hog-squeal symbol of a city seemingly dedicated to the mechanics and commerce of death, to the modern mechanical Meat-Moloch.

But Meat-Moloch moved on, upsizing to today's postindustrial Meat-Moloch, concentrating from the big six or so of Sinclair's time to the big four mega-corporations today, led by ConAgra. The unions gained by workers after Upton Sinclair's novel were undone by Reaganism, and workers' pay and benefits began a long downward spiral, abetted by the heavy use of illegal migrant labor. Meat-Moloch uses meat Morlocks, laborers hidden, so to speak, from public view or organized labor, to serve up the burgers to the unsuspecting Eloi of consumption culture, who, like their counterparts in Wells's novel, think that food somehow arrives on its own, as packaged happy meal.

Today's slaughter factories are tied to massive urbanoid feedlots far from the city, where cattle are fed on corn rather than grass, which works against their digestive systems and requires massive amounts of antibiotics to keep them from getting too sick. Tens of thousands of cattle are tightly packed in their own manure and pumped with steroids to speed up their growth, corn to fatten them quickly, and antibiotics to keep them alive just long enough for slaughtering. The new feedlot-slaughter factory system is an advanced breeding ground of antibiotic-resistant bacteria, imperiling not only the workers but also Americans generally, while fattening the pockets of the meat profiteers. These rationalized-for-money-efficiency breeding grounds are a chief source of the appearance of the deadly E. coli O157:H7 epiphany and of a variety of pathogens. As Michael Pollan notes: "The Centers for Disease Control and Prevention estimate that our food supply now sickens 76 million Americans every year, putting more than 300,000 of them in the hospital, and killing 5,000. The lethal strain of E. coli known as 0157:H7, responsible for this latest outbreak of food poisoning, was unknown before 1982; it is believed to have evolved in the gut of feedlot cattle. These are animals that stand around in their manure all day long, eating a diet of grain that happens to turn a cow's rumen into an ideal habitat for E. coli 0157:H7. (The bug can't survive long in cattle living on grass.)"[9]

If McDonald's and other fast food brands embody Milan Kundera's definition of kitsch as the denial that shit happens, the feedlot-slaughter factory is the reality being denied. As Eric Schlosser tells it in *Fast Food Nation*: "In the USDA study, 78.6 percent of the ground beef contained microbes that are spread primarily by fecal material. The medical literature on the causes of food poisoning is full of euphemisms and dry scientific terms: coliform levels, aerobic plate counts, sorbitol, MacConkey agar, and so on. Behind them lies a simple explanation for why eating a hamburger can now make you seriously ill: There is shit in the meat."[10]

The Home as a Sign of Chicago Materialism

Two representative works of Chicago literature, Sinclair's *Jungle* and Dreiser's *Titan*, illustrate the consumptive culture of the city through opposing trajectories. *The Jungle* moves from the joys of a wedding ceremony for a newly arrived immigrant couple to the depths of jail, death, destruction, and dissolution, while *The Titan* rises from divorce and jail to the upward reaches of unlimited power and wealth. Spiritually, however, both tell of the domination by power and bigness over purpose and life. *The Jungle* does so through the perspective of the underclass, and *The Titan* from that of the capitalist overlord.

Key to both works, and to an understanding of the consumptive culture of accumulation and conspicuous display, is the significance of the home. *The Jungle* begins with the promise and hope of Jurgis and Ona Rudkis's wedding, the finding of jobs for the extended family, and the purchase of the family's new home near the stockyards. Yet the stench of the power complex can be smelled even in these happy beginnings. The family soon realizes that they have only signed to *rent* their home for the next eight years with a down payment of all their savings, and that they must pay more monthly than they had thought, or else forfeit everything. The legal butchery of the real estate officials and lawyers is every bit as much a rationalized slaughter as that of the stockyard factories. The house is poorly constructed, as the family discovers when the cold Chicago winds begin to blow through it. The great stockyard machine devours the life-energies of its workers, and does so with admirable efficiency, creating a progressive deterioration leading inevitably to the loss of the home and of all human attributes, and eventually of human life. Jurgis is at one point released from jail, where he had been sent for a month for attacking the boss who had forced Ona into prostitution. He returns to find that while he was in jail, his house had been sold and his family evicted. The new tenants had been told, like Jurgis and his family, that the house was brand new. Reflecting on the house, Jurgis realizes:

Why, they had put their very souls into their payments on that house, they had paid for it with their sweat and tears—yes, more, with their very life—blood. Dede Antanas [the grandfather] had died of the struggle to earn that money—he would be alive and strong today if he had not had to work in Durham's dark cellars to earn his share. And Ona, too, had given her health and strength to pay for it—she was wrecked and ruined because of it; and so was he, who had been a big, strong man three years ago.

That first lying circular, that smoothed-tongued slippery agent! That trap of the extra payments, the interest, and all the other charges that they had not the means to pay, and would never had attempted to pay! And then all the tricks of the packers, their masters, the tyrants who ruled them—the shut-downs and the scarcity of work, the irregular hours and the cruel speeding-up, the lowering of wages, the raising of prices! The mercilessness of nature about them, of heat and cold, rain and snow; the mercilessness of the city, of the country in which they lived, of its laws and customs that they did not understand! All of these things had worked together for the company that had marked them for its prey and was waiting for its chance. And now with this last hideous injustice, its time had come, and it had turned them out bag and baggage, and taken their house and sold it again![11]

But this was not the last hideous injustice, for shortly later Jurgis's precious Ona dies in childbirth because of lack of money to secure adequate medical treatment. Still later, when his only son drowns in the mud of the street where the family lives, the last intimate tie is cut and Jurgis abandons his remaining relatives to wander as a tramp. The process of depersonalization is complete, and Jurgis joins the homeless, with yet further depths of hell to pass through before he is redeemed by the vision of socialism.

The Titan (1914) forms the second book of Dreiser's Trilogy of Desire, along with The Financier (1912) and The Stoic (1947, posthumous). The entire trilogy is closely modeled on the life of Charles T. Yerkes, the financier and street railway magnate who dominated the transit industry in late nineteenth-century Chicago. Yerkes practiced a capitalism of corruption, documented not only in Dreiser's trilogy but also in Lincoln Steffens's earlier muckraking classic, Shame of the Cities (1904), and William T. Stead's even earlier If Christ Came to Chicago (1894), both of which might have influenced Dreiser. Stead described Yerkes in part 3, titled "Satan's Invisible World Displayed," and how an inventory of his riches showed Chicago politics at work: "Mr. C. T. Yerkes, erstwhile of a Pennsylvania penitentiary, now the street railway despot of Chicago, a millionaire and a resident in a handsomely furnished mansion at 3201 Michigan Avenue. Mr. Yerkes, according to the oath of the South Side Assessor, has got $1,000 worth of personal property in his residence, excluding the piano.... The carpets on the floor, the pictures on the walls, the plate on the table to ordinary eyes would seem to be dirt cheap at $1,000." Stead commented further on Yerkes's role in society:

Of the predatory rich in Chicago there are plenty and to spare, but there is one man who stands out conspicuous among all the rest.... I refer to Mr. Charles T. Yerkes. Mr. Yerkes is a notable product of the present system. Of course, though Mr. Yerkes at an early stage in his career, before he was launched upon Chicago as a financier and street railway magnate, had served in a Pennsylvania penitentiary, I would not for a moment suggest that in his operations in Chicago he has brought himself within the clutches of the law.... It is probable, however, that Mr. Yerkes, grown insolent by the impunity with which he has ridden roughshod over the people of Chicago, has over-reached himself....

Mr. Yerkes is a significant sample of the class to which I refer. He lives in style, and apparently does not find it difficult to obtain the assistance of the gentlemen of Chicago in the managing of his companies.[12]

Stead saw Yerkes as a "significant sample" of the predatory, as opposed to the idle rich. This distinction was also used, somewhat differently, by Veblen in his Theory of the Leisure Class (1899), published shortly after Stead's book and written in, and frequently about, Chicago. The concept of a predatory elite may have been influenced by Lewis Henry Morgan's idea of evolutionary stages of savagery, barbarism, and civilization, but the metaphor of "civilized" pecuniary predation is an apt one.

The Titan begins with Frank Algernon Cowperwood, the Yerkes-based hero, leaving jail and relative homelessness in Philadelphia to begin his second career as a robber baron of Chicago. The novel is about power in its various manifestations in finance, sex, and acquisition, and depicts a transient world in which personal force means everything. From the beginning Cowperwood buys his way into Chicago, audaciously in business, and ostentatiously but not so successfully in high society. He builds a magnificent home and fills it with magnificent art. These material possessions are signs of his rise on the power and status ladder, and of the magical alchemy of money, which is capable apparently of transmuting base and corrupt materials like Cowperwood and his wife, Aileen, into the gold of "the gold coast," then located on South Michigan and Prairie Avenues.

The home in *The Titan* is, like that of *The Jungle*, a sign of achievement. But where the Rudkises' home is a center of family life and death, Cowperwood's home is the center of the "higher" aspirations, or at least of the aspiration to move higher into "society." In order to do this one must have the proper emblems and accoutrements, as described by Veblen. Perhaps the home and its belongings, including "the wife," together form the best trophy to display social standing and legitimize predatory wealth. This is particularly evident in the grand opening of Cowperwood's newly built house on South Michigan Avenue, a ritual feast of display featuring "music by a famous stringed orchestra of Chicago," "artists of considerable importance," "the important pictures" that Cowperwood had purchased in Europe, and of course the already-initiated members of high society, which the Cowperwoods were seeking to join. Most prominent of the paintings were a portrait of Aileen by a Dutch artist, Jan van Beers, and "a picture of nude odalisques of the harem, idling beside the highly colored stone marquetry of an Oriental bath." The nude was, "more or less 'loose' art for Chicago, shocking to the uninitiated, though harmless enough to the illuminati," who apparently have learned the correct pecuniary canons of taste.[13]

The illuminati in attendance at Cowperwood's affair would have known that a bunch of fleshy, naked women is what beauty is all about and that it probably cost a bundle. And the portrait of Aileen revealed much to the onlooker: the wife on the European trip painted amid the Dutch countryside that symbolized a famous style of art, dressed in the latest Paris fashion, seated before a brick palace that signifies her moneyed pretensions to aristocracy. "In the warm glow of the guttered gas jets she looked particularly brilliant here, pampered, idle, jaunty—the well-kept, stall-fed pet of the world." Both paintings perform their function of displaying conspicuous leisure, submission, and possession. They signify their owner's predatory manliness: He

Figure 6. Charles T. Yerkes, source for Dreiser's *The Titan*, standing in front of his fireplace at his home on 3201 Michigan Avenue, ca. 1890s, ICHi-13104. Chicago History Museum.

possesses "the wife" on whom he could waste conspicuously in life and in art, and he possesses "the harem" of the respectable man's desire, sublimated in the art, but also actually lived out in Cowperwood's endless romantic affairs. These paintings signify the ideal of woman and beauty in consumptive culture: "The well-kept, stall-fed pet of the world." And the paintings—all of them—indeed a harem, which Cowperwood increasingly turns to in the name of art, as his idealized narcissism increases.[14]

Although Chicago literature is usually thought of as related to the muckraking tradition, there are also peculiar positive relations to business and capitalism. "The business of art" and the "art of business" are intertwined in Dreiser's *Trilogy of Desire* just as they are in Sherwood Anderson's *Windy McPherson's Son* (1916), also set in and around Chicago. Perhaps one should view this attitude that business activity and art are intrinsically related and good for each other as part of the culture of gilded materialism in early twentieth-century America. This was, after all, the culture that produced such a successful businessman and great artist as Charles Ives, who combined in his person the statistical certainties of insurance with the atonal, transcendentalist longing of his 1908 musical composition *The Unanswered Question*. But "the might of money and the entanglement of art with it—the dollar as soul's husband," as Saul Bellow's Humboldt expressed it decades later in *Humboldt's Gift*, is better viewed as part of the wholesale capitulation of higher ideals in American life to the forces of the moment, the forces of uncontrolled industrial and capitalist expansion.[15]

The word *art* appears throughout Dreiser's trilogy frequently in inappropriate places, and usually as something lofty and redeeming. But it always translates into personal force: "Truth to say, [Cowperwood] must always have youth, the illusion of beauty, vanity in womanhood, the novelty of a new, untested temperament, quite as he must have pictures, old porcelain, music, a mansion, illuminated missals, power, the applause of the great, unthinking world." The accumulation and display of art was also Cowperwood's substitute for inner spiritual experience. Through his purchase of "important" paintings and affairs with "artistic" women he could appropriate beauty and apply it, like a salve, to the inner wasteland left by his calculating and externalist approach to life. "I satisfy myself" is literally Cowperwood's motto. All of life's qualities and life itself become mere "satisfactions," things to be momentarily possessed and discarded. Cowperwood's desire for art and beauty and Dreiser's nebulous understanding of them reveal why materialism, with its underlying faith in physical sensation as the foundation of reality, must move increasingly toward power and transience.[16]

Chicago Sociologists

Although the term *sociology* originated with Auguste Comte in Europe and many of its greatest early practitioners were European, sociology is usually acknowledged to have become a fully autonomous institution at the University of Chicago. When one speaks now of Chicago sociology, one thinks particularly of the urban ethnographies and studies of "human ecology" that flourished at the University of Chicago in the early decades of the twentieth century and culminated in the works of W. I. Thomas and the many publications of the 1920s by Robert Park, Ernest Burgess, and their students. Thomas is known today primarily for his development of "situational analysis" and for his multivolume series *The Polish Peasant in Europe and America*. This work used case studies and personal documents as evidence, methods later criticized as insufficiently empirical by number-crunching sociologists, who preferred statistical norms to situational facts. Yet *The Polish Peasant*, despite earlier controversy surrounding it, is still regarded as a pivotal work in the establishment of empirical sociology for its use of personal documents, including some 862 personal letters.

Thomas is also widely known today as one of the fathers of "symbolic interactionism" in sociology, especially for his emphasis on "the situation" as locus for sociological analysis. His most frequently quoted statement on the situation (from a piece coauthored with his wife, Dorothy Swain Thomas, who later confirmed that the words were his) is: "If men define situations as real, they are real in their consequences." Thomas saw that subjective factors need to be included in analysis, and symbolic interactionists interpreted this to signify that meaning is primarily subjectively based, despite the fact that Thomas went on to say in the next sentence that both subjective and objective factors are significant. "The total situation will always contain more and less subjective factors, and the behavior reaction can only be studied in connection with the whole context, i.e., the situation as it exists in verifiable, objective terms, and as it has seemed to exist in terms of the interested persons."[17]

Thomas provided a seeming alternative to sociological positivism, yet he shared with it a prejudice for the present that devalues history. Thomas is regarded today as a representative of a humanist sociology, and by the high-tech standards of robotic quantitative contemporary sociology, this view is perhaps correct. But it is important to see that Thomas not only sought to develop a scientifically grounded sociology, but also that his view of society was deeply imbued with the image of science wrought by the modern power complex.

According to Thomas, the nature of the individual, "demanding a maximum of new experience, is in fundamental conflict with the nature of society, demanding a maximum of stability." Here the ideas of maximization and conflict are foundational, just as, perhaps not by coincidence, they are in capitalism. The individual does not possess inner capacities for stability, and society does not possess outer resources for change in this modified form of Hobbesianism. And the human sciences should emulate the natural sciences, in Thomas's view, in order to learn the "fundamental human attitudes" and thereby create the possibility of social engineering. Only science, applied to a contemporary situation like Chicago, and not history (or, presumably, literature), can give us the answer:

The very disharmony of the social world is largely due to the disproportionate rate of advance in the mechanical world. We live in an entirely new world, unique, without parallel in history. History has not helped us. It cannot help us because we do not understand it: we do not even understand an election. We must first understand the past from the present. We must view the present as behavior. We must establish by scientific procedure the laws of behavior, and then the past will have its meaning and make its contribution. If we learn the laws of human behavior as we have learned the laws of mathematics, physics, and chemistry, if we establish what are the fundamental human attitudes, how they can be converted into other and more socially desirable attitudes, how the world of values is created and modified by the operation of these attitudes, then we can establish any attitudes and values whatever.[18]

Thomas believed that the "very disharmony of the social world" could be resolved by aligning ourselves with the disproportionately advancing mechanical world that created the disharmony, a very strange melody indeed. He thought that people must adjust situationally to the mechanical world of the present because history is inadequate. Only by scientifically discovering laws of behavior will "the past have its meaning and make its contribution." Then social engineering, could establish "any attitudes and values whatever," as though mechanism, and not purpose, was the motive and end of human conduct. This is the voice and victory of the machine.

Park's urban sociology combined the concrete observations of social life characteristic of his earlier work as a reporter, with "naturalistic" laws of ecology that underlie city life, stressing how the city is a product of human nature. The natural was the nonreflective, so that certain "moral regions" of the city—vice districts, saloons, brothels, race tracks, and the like—were unplanned "natural areas." Park viewed "moral regions" as "part of the natural, if not normal, life of the city," and the term was intended, "to apply to regions in which a divergent moral code prevails, because it is a region in which the people who inhabit it are dominated, as people are ordinarily not dominated, by a taste or by a passion or by some interest which has its roots directly in the original nature of the individual. It may be an art, like music, or a sport, like horse-racing. Such a region would differ from other social groups by the fact that its interests are more immediate and more fundamental."[19]

Park saw the modern city as lacking the controls to keep natural inclinations in place, so that natural needs become expressed in the chaotic manifestations of vice, crime, and family life. He attempted to include a concept of life in his urban equation, yet his view of nature, like Thomas's, was derived from Thomas Hobbes, who saw nature as an underlying chaos on which is superimposed social convention to keep order. In what ways, though, could Park's Chicago, with its constantly exploding population, be said to be "natural"? The city is a historical phenomenon, just as history is a city phenomenon, having originated in literate cities. Whatever the nature of a city might be, it cannot be divorced from its history.

The problem with Park's view of nature, as with Hobbes's, is that it assumed a one-sided, nominalistic view derivative of modern scientism, in which nature is nonrelational and nonpurposive, and culture in its highest forms is denatured. The implication of this view for Park was that he could not see that there may be intentions of the system operating in the so-called moral regions. In a more explicit way than Park's scientism, Sinclair's fiction caught the alleged natural basis of this system when he showed how the jungle of Chicago was anything but a natural ecology.

In the Packingtown neighborhood where Rudkis lived, there was a totalistic system of exploitation with an intentionality of its own. This systemic intentionality, the logic of unlimited rational capitalism, could be seen clearly in the planned stockyards, but it was also operating in the establishment of the check cashing bars that lined the streets near the stockyards, the real estate people who would "eat you alive," the men who would attend a traditional wedding feast, eating and drinking according to tradition, but not giving money to the bride as was also traditional. I have always found it peculiar how the attempt to be "naturalistic" because it is "scientific" caused Park and the academic sociologists of the Chicago school to ignore or devalue the glaring historical, economic, systemic purposes that were creating geographical and social areas in their own image.

Chicago, the city without a history, was used as a "laboratory" for a universal scientistic-urbanism without history. It is strange that despite Park's discussion of the tension between history and natural science, which formed the basis of the opening chapter of the widely influential introductory textbook he published with Ernest Burgess in 1921, he developed a view of the city that ignored the shaping and formative forces of history. Just as Freud generalized from turn-of-the-century Vienna psyches to claim a universal psychology, Park and the academic Chicago sociologists such as Thomas, Burgess, and, later, Park's student, Louis Wirth, generalized from the unique and rapidly industrializing turn-of-the-century Chicago to claim a universal scientific sociology of urban life. Their fear of history and fervor for positive science were symptoms of scientism, of an ideology of science that was the product of modern materialism.

In seeking to legitimize sociology as a science, academic sociologists at the University of Chicago had to distinguish sharply their efforts not only from social workers and settlements but also from the research of settlement workers. Urban ethnography, demography, and ecology are now associated with academic Chicago sociology, though efforts in these areas were begun earlier in Chicago in nonacademic works such as *Hull-House Maps and Papers*

(1895), works themselves influenced by Stead and earlier English social surveys. One finds sparse reference to this earlier research by the academic sociologists, and when references are made, they are frequently to distinguish
the scientific nature of the academic sociology. Thus Burgess (who had actually lived at Hull-House at one point) cites *Hull-House Maps and Papers*, with
some other works, as "illustrations of the careful study and keen observation
of these early efforts to determine and to take account of the many and different conditions affecting neighborhood work. This interest in the discovery
of factors in the social situation may therefore be called the second stage in
the trend of neighborhood work toward a scientific basis. Science, however,
is concerned not with factors, but with forces."[20]

Burgess's conception of what constituted science falsely "naturalized"
such forces as competition, which was supposedly an example of an ecological force rather than a by-product of industrial capitalism. Academic Chicago
sociologists legitimately sought to broaden the base of sociology beyond practicing social work, but they did so with crude ideas of scientism ultimately
derived from the same power complex that created the peculiar forces of
life in Chicago and that sought to repress the force of purposive community
life. Even though academic Chicago sociology of the 1920s seems humane by
today's standards of number-crunching machine sociology, it is the nascent
technocrat of the power complex we hear when Burgess recommends:

The work of neighborhood centers, like that of all other social agencies, must increasingly be placed upon the basis of the scientific study of the social forces which with
they have to deal. Especially are studies desired of the actual effect and role of intimate
contacts in personal development and social control. . . . Neighborhood work, by the
logic of the situation, if it is to evolve a successful technique, will be compelled more
and more to depend upon research into the social forces of modern life.[21]

It was precisely the scientizing and bureaucratizing of social work that
devitalized the settlement concept. The model of the home was transformed
into the model of the bureau as a center for social work. And the sense of a
public life, embodied both in neighborhood centers such as Hull House and
in a public intellectual such as Jane Addams, is rooted in a sense of democracy not reducible to bureaucratic technique. We see in Burgess's words the
blueprint for the destruction of the organic life of Hull-House by the machinelike social forces of sociological scientism.

As Mary Jo Deegan has pointed out, that sense of public life and its responsibilities in Jane Addams grated against the bureaucracy of the University of

Chicago in its early days, causing the administration to deny her an honorary degree.[22] The world would later award Addams a Nobel Peace Prize, and the university finally came around over twenty years later to offer an honorary degree. But the university preferred technocrats, who, under a banner of "science" could appear legitimate and politically neutered.

The academic sociologists wanted to be newspaper reporters with white laboratory coats, detached documenters. They were, in their way, every bit as reformist as the Hull-House, but they saw humanism as unscientific. The people associated with Hull-House depended on the method of life, not positive science. They used the activities of life—play, art and craft, drama, work and its conditions in Chicago—as the basis of their ideas. For this reason they were in many ways more empirical than the academics precisely because they allowed life in its potential fullness to determine their observations rather than a reductionistic model of science.

Jane Addams and Ellen Gates Starr opened the doors of Hull-House in 1889 with lofty ideals: they would uplift their poor neighbors in the South Halsted Street area with "object lessons" drawn from the art objects they had acquired in their European travels and through discussion of serious literature. Their initial ideas of settlement work seemed to be based on the model of bourgeois respectability, as if Dreiser's Cowperwood were to invite Sinclair's Rudkis to view his art collection! But Addams and Starr quickly readjusted their ideas, not so much by lowering their ideals as by broadening them. Hull-House, influenced by the English model of Toynbee Hall, may have been among the first settlement houses in an emerging movement in America, but no other settlement house so caught the fires of the imagination.

Art and social reform were interwoven in the life of drama cultivated at Hull-House. The Hull-House Players developed into the leading avant-garde theater in Chicago within about a decade after the group's founding, performing plays by George Bernard Shaw and Henrik Ibsen by 1905 and later social realist plays of John Galsworthy and Gerhart Hauptmann.[23] Art was not merely a tool of counseling or a "practical activities" slot on the daily calendar; rather, it achieved a genuine life of its own that cultivated the participating community.

New forms of thought that were in the process of being created in Chicago found their forum at Hull-House. Frank Lloyd Wright gave his famous lecture of 1903 there, "The Art and Craft of the Machine," wherein he challenged industrial society to take control of and put to right uses its machines, and John Dewey's close involvement with the activities of Hull-House concretized his developing social philosophy and philosophy of education (which was also influenced by his connection to the laboratory school of the University of Chicago). Both Wright's architectural outlook and Dewey's philosophy were rooted in the centrality of organic life to genuine human culture. Both believed in democratizing society and in the cultivated individual as a necessary ingredient to a living democracy.[24]

Wright specifically denied that he was giving a "sociological prescription" in his Hull-House address, yet he uttered a far better sociological description of the relations of life, individual, and society than the Hobbesian academic sociologists at the University of Chicago. Wright described how civilization could be characterized as a "dramatizing of an object," or "conventionalization," and cited the artistic use of flowers as expressions of a civilization: the acanthus and honeysuckle of ancient Greece, the chrysanthemum of Japan, or the lotus of Egypt. Far from contemporary theories of convention as inert or arbitrary code, Wright saw that conventionalizing consisted of finding in a substance "the pattern of its life-principle" and embodying it. Using the metaphor of the artist-craftsman who seeks to dramatize a "beloved flower" in stone and applying it to society, Wright remarked, "But the true Democrat will take the human plant as it grows and—in the spirit of using the means at hand to put life into his conventionalization—preserve the individuality of the plant to protect the flower, which is its very life, getting from both a living expression of the man-character fitted perfectly to a place in Society with no loss of vital significance. Fine art is this flower of the Man." According to Wright, art does not simply imitate life but also creates its own life out of it. Life is not formless and anarchistic, as a Hobbesian might say, but is the creative source of form and function. And democratized society is not the faceless aggregate of the "mobocracy" or "machine-made moron," but it is a dramatic conventionalization that preserves and nourishes the life of the individual.

It is an understatement to say that life flourished at Hull-House: life infused everything Hull-House touched. For any serious investigation of the mind of Chicago, all roads lead eventually to Hull-House, the institution through which almost all the vital energies of Chicago seemed to pass. In the end, however, Hull-House did not remake Chicago. Yet the image of Hull-House, like the Greek acanthus or the Japanese chrysanthemum, remains as a "guide to the imagination." Walter Lippmann wrote in 1913, "If Hull-House is unable to civilize Chicago, it at least shows Chicago and America what a civilization might be like. Friendly, where our cities are friendless, beautiful, where they are ugly; sociable and open, where our daily life is furtive; work a craft, art a participation—it is in miniature the goal of statesmanship."[25]

The Triumph of Antilife

The journalistic realism found in turn-of-the-century Chicago fiction and academic sociology provides a picture of society in which the events of the moment loom large, but history and the sense of inner vision are given short shrift. In the end then, Chicago literature and academic sociology of the early twentieth century can be seen as products of the city and as the traces left by the culture of materialism; they document the unchecked tendencies to bigness and power of modern materialism and sometimes even celebrate it, but they do not provide an imaginative or critical alternative. They take their cues from life in the city, from the massive social upheaval, but they are stamped with the same problems. They cannot account for the metropolis as producer of enduring human values or for the human capacity to regain and create purposive organic life and form in the modern city.

Sinclair's socialism was humane but did not provide checks against bureaucratization or the centralizing tendencies of the machine that could offset the utilitarian power complex. Dreiser took the power complex to be that which animates the art of life. Art does not so much imitate life as it imitates the will to power: the movers and the takers are the makers and the shakers. Much the same view permeates Chicago's academic sociology. Human nature is Hobbesian in the ecological views, always seeking more and now, and the concept of life is but the philosophy of greed. The city is largely a play of transience and self-interest, a mirror of uncontrolled capitalism, and in Louis Wirth's essay, "Urbanism as a Way of Life," it becomes associated with the tendency toward bigness itself.[26]

American thought had indeed reached a "unity" in turn-of-the-twentieth-century Chicago—the unity of the mechanistic Archimedean vanishing point: the "ghost in the machine." The glowing, confident White City of beaux arts buildings at the Columbian Exposition that had provoked such dark thoughts in Henry Adams had the same effect on another psychic seismograph of the time, master architect Louis Sullivan:

These crowds were astonished. They beheld what was for them an amazing revelation of the architectural art. . . . To them it was a veritable Apocalypse, a message inspired from on high. Upon it their imagination shaped new ideals. They went away, spreading again over the land, returning to their homes, each one of them carrying in the soul the shadow of the white cloud, each of them permeated by the most subtle and slow acting of poisons; an imperceptible miasma within the white shadow of a higher culture. A vast multitude, exposed, unprepared, they had not had time nor occasion to become immune to forms of sophistication not their own, to a higher and more dexterously insidious plausibility. Thus they departed joyously, carriers of contagion, unaware that what they had beheld and believed to be truth was to prove, in historic fact, an appalling calamity. For what they saw was not at all what they believed they saw, but an imposition of the spurious upon their eyesight, a naked exhibitionism of charlatanry in the higher feudal and domineering culture, conjoined with expert salesmanship of the materials of decay.[27]

Sullivan—who, like Adams, knew that the built environment was a visible sign of a civilization—saw the death of the democratic vision in the nostalgic revivalism of the exposition's architecture. Sullivan was, in the main, correct about the downward slope of democracy, even though he could not see that those emerging nostalgic images of empire would later be replaced by a stark, ultramodern image of empire—the so-called international style—that also denied the democratic vision, but in the name of the almighty grid. Nor could he see that the two images of empire would then fuse in the postmodern style of the late twentieth century, signifying the domination by desiccated technique and desensualized nostalgia to which the American dream had sunk. The plague foreseen by Sullivan grew to full virulence in this "post-" time when America traded its sense of history for virtual substitutes and forfeited its dreams to the fetishism of technical commodities. Still, there remain the organic, modernist visions of democracy left by Sullivan and Wright, the pragmatic philosophies of Dewey and Mead, and the memories of Hull-House.

As the logic of modernity, by no means necessary but surely sufficient, raced toward closure, even Chicago's academic sociology had to give way to more machinelike ways of thinking, to "abstracted empiricism," and to "grand theory," exemplified by sociologist Talcott Parsons. The turn toward abstracted empiricism was characteristic of American sociology in general but was signaled in particular within the Sociology Department of the University of Chicago by the arrival of William F. Ogburn. Ogburn not only championed quantitative technique, which in itself broadened the means available to sociology and which was the reason the rest of the department hired him in 1927, but he also went further to disparage that which did not fit his technical conception of science. He scorned social theory, social reform, "qualitative" methods, and seemingly everything that suggested that sociology has human interests.[28]

Oddly enough, it was Ogburn who played a significant role for the Committee on Symbolism for the Social Science Research Building, which in 1929 helped decide the symbolism of the new building that would house social science at the University of Chicago.

Figure 7. Social Sciences Building, 1126 E. 59th Street, University of Chicago.

Although the more prominent Chicago sociologists, such as Park and Burgess, had developed a sociology concerned with the physical environment and its symbolism, and although Ogburn had been at the university only less than two years, it was he who was instrumental in getting the positivistic symbolism layered on to the neo-Gothic "feudal" structure, especially expressed in a maxim derived from Lord Kelvin and incised under the large bay window of the common room: "When you cannot measure, your knowledge is meager and unsatisfactory." This inscription accurately set the tone of the rising quantifying sociology that would replace the older style of academic sociology.

The new Social Science Research Building not only symbolized the turn to social science research, but in picturing titans of laissez-faire capitalism (Adam Smith), utilitarianism (Jeremy Bentham), and positivism (Auguste Comte) over its doors, and in inscribing the utilitarian view of research as a measuring cup, also symbolized the coming capitulation of social science to the ideology of scientism. Only those aspects of social life that could be counted would be considered valid for the emerging style of "American" sociology. Or put differently, only those aspects of social life capable of being run through the machine of quantification—beginning with survey forms and simple counting machines and later achieving academic centrality in the form of the computer—only those quanta of the social grid would be viewed as valid objects of sociological research. Life in all its fullness would become too passionate for this dispassionate and bloodless conception of sociology. The dominant number-numbing sociology that assumed power by midcentury in America was, like the centralized stockyards that emerged in the nineteenth century, equally an avatar of the great life-denying dynamo of modernity.

It is interesting to speculate what might have happened if bureaucratic scientism and pedantry had not triumphed at the University of Chicago and the American university more generally. Charles Peirce, whose last years were lived in dire poverty, was a contender to be the first chair of philosophy but was denied it because he was divorced. Think of what Chicago pragmatism might have been with Peirce added to the mix of Dewey and Mead. What if Jane Addams had accepted a position in the Sociology Department? Could she have given her scientistic colleagues a better appreciation of the unnaturalness of power in Chicago? Perhaps not, since they did not show much response to her widely read books anyway.

The Chicago schools of sociology, philosophy, psychology, and Veblen's economics became widely influential, but oddly, seemingly evaporated at the University of Chicago. The clean-fitting grid of the academy replaced these modes of thought with ones stamped with the proper look of mid-twentieth-century science. The embarrassing optimism of Chicago thought was replaced by an arrogant scientism more blindly confident of its mission, one confirmed in the religion and sects of positivism.

The open-ended pragmatisms of Dewey and Mead, centering on the human being within a live social environment—a human capable of criticism, spontaneous conduct, and continued growth in the community of interpretation—was replaced by the closed positivist dream of the end of philosophy personified by Charles Morris and Rudolf Carnap and by the new technicalism of analytic philosophy that in turn replaced positivism. The critical symbolic economics of Veblen were replaced by a second Chicago school of economics, one that believed that "there is no such thing as a free lunch," to paraphrase its chief exponent, Milton Friedman. This second school, now assumed to be *the school*, blindly ignored the possibility that there may be no such thing as a free market in its deification of uncontrolled profit stripped of social context or human purport. Only more recently has the Sociology Department tried to revive some of its earlier traditions, but it still is dominated by bureaucratic, machine sociology.

It is no wonder that the economic and racist practices that nourished the corrosive sprawl of the ghetto have a stranglehold today on the city: totalitarian rationalism breeds its opposite. The blight of the megamachine and its

Figure 8. Hull-House sits today as a quaint relic of a forgotten past, a mere "display." But note that the real display is the dominance of the steel and glass box of the University of Illinois at Chicago student union looming over Hull-House, symbolizing the triumph of the rational machine bureaucracy over organic thought in Chicago.

institutionalized chaos that is Chicago's birthmark now control even those areas where organic thought once flourished as the city's own vital contribution to modernity. Perhaps the best symbolic expression of this state of affairs is the remnant of Hull-House, now a museum, dwarfed by the monolithic skeletal form of the black steel and glass student union of the University of Illinois at Chicago, which rises up behind Hull-House and reduces its physical presence to that of a quaint relic from the forgotten past.

Many of the Hull-House buildings were razed to make room for the university's campus in the early 1960s, and in the mid-1980s the settlement's library was absorbed by the university library, symbolizing the final etherealization of the organic intelligence that flowered at Hull-House. Books, this act seemed to say, must not be confused with life, and a venerable institution such as Hull-House must not be confused with living function if it is to be properly embalmed as a museum.

It is true that space was cramped in the two remaining buildings, one of which is the original structure on which the many additions to Hull-House were later added, and therefore the removal of books was perhaps "functional."

But if one literally "deconstructs" a structure to arrive at a building too small to be functional as anything other than a museum, then the problem is one not simply of physical space and function but of purpose. Apparently the purposes and history embodied in the physical structure of Hull-House were at cross-purposes with the modernist premises of novelty and nonintegration with neighborhood and past embodied in the design of the "circle campus," as the university is usually called.

"The city that works" had worked to destroy the tradition-saturated Hull-House physical structure, with its many meeting, recreation, theater, dining, art, and other rooms designed expressly for communal activities. In its place, the city erected a sterile structure housing a student union with precisely the same sorts of rooms. And in the 1990s Mayor Daley the second closed the nearby Maxwell Street Market, which for over one hundred years was the center of a free street culture of vendors of everything under the sun. Typical Chicago arrogance destroyed these great symbols of Chicago's vitality, opening the way to moneyed development in the Maxwell Street area. But perhaps it is fitting that the triumph of the academy over social work, of the bureau and bureaucracy over home and neighborhood democracy, of the machine over organic thought, of the rationalization of existence over the life of the street, be honestly symbolized.

When Aristotle said that man is by nature a political animal, he had in mind a view of social relations as fundamental to the human creature and the city, or polis, as the public organ capable of expressing those fundamental human capacities for speech and self-controlled purposeful conduct. Modernity developed quite antithetical views. In its manifestation as virulent, consumptive capitalism and the power complex, modernity held competition and rational calculation to be the original beliefs of the human soul and made the city to be the gladiatorial arena: every man for himself, winner takes all. In its manifestation as political communism and the power complex, modernity displaced speech and conduct with secrecy and expediency. We see the prophetic anticipation of this process in the inability of Raskolnikov of *Crime and Punishment* to break out of the secrecy of his crime, rationalized murder, and to confess his guilt in the public market.

In its manifestation as Chicago, modernity rediscovered Aristotle's maxim, but diabolically inverted the meanings of *political* and *animal*. The activity of life itself was turned into a thing to be possessed. The life of the public, as *The Jungle*, *The Titan*, and the human ecology of Chicago's academic sociologists showed, was one dominated by machine politics, machine economics, machine bureaucracy. And despite all the settlement work and muckraking, the muck has enjoyed a settled existence right down to the present.

6

COMMUNICATING DEMOCRACY: OR SHINE, PERISHING REPUBLIC

Kitsch-R-US: Remembering Reagan Forgetting

You making haste haste on decay: not blameworthy; life is good, be it stub-
bornly long or suddenly a mortal splendor: meteors are not needed less than
mountains: shine, perishing republic.
        —ROBINSON JEFFERS, FROM "SHINE PERISHING REPUBLIC," 1925

We should declare war on North Vietnam. We could pave the whole place over
by noon and be home by dinner.
        —RONALD REAGAN, 1976[1]

When one looks at recent presidential elections, political symbolism appears
to be so powerful in the United States as to have utterly annihilated politics.
Not only has political discourse been gutted by hype and media sensationalism, but also the very nature of the public sphere—including the communicative practices that constitute a public life as well as the physical places
in which these take place—has been corroded by the dual materializing and
etherealizing processes of megatechnic America. By examining two different
kinds of public spaces as self-representations of democracy, I hope to bring

to light some of the dark tendencies that have transformed the American vision of autonomy into the dream of automatic culture and kitsch.

The commanding images of American media culture have taken on a life of their own, so that celebrity and slogan have long since replaced substance. As was clear in the election of Ronald Reagan and his continued popularity throughout the 1980s despite widespread cynicism concerning his policies, the American people love having a star—especially a "Teflon president" on whom nothing bad ever sticks—and would seem to prefer entertainment to popular democracy. Yet when one contrasts a President Reagan to a President Vaclav Havel of Czechoslovakia, it is clear that playwrights who can write their own scripts are to be preferred to actors.

In the presidential election of 1988, George H. W. Bush overtook and defeated Michael Dukakis on the basis of superior "sound bites"—fifteen-second slogans that could be easily fit into the evening news programs and advertisements. One of the most widely known was the expression "read my lips, no new taxes," where Bush pledged not to raise income taxes if elected, a pledge he subsequently broke. This sound bite appeared in a campaign that also used the face of a black rapist, with racist overtones, to suggest that Dukakis was too soft on criminals. Bush also tried to give the appearance of slight distance from Reagan's policies by calling for a "kinder, gentler America," a sound bite widely lampooned in newspapers along with the "read my lips" sound bite.

Sixteen years further down the road, having given up his "compassionate conservatism" sound bite, an updating of his father's "kinder, gentler, America," George W. Bush successfully ran for a second term as a "war president." During the campaign he enabled false stories denigrating the military record of John Kerry, his opponent—a tactic Bush had also carried out against republican John McCain four years earlier during the primaries, while dodging facts concerning his absences from the National Guard. Although it had not worked so well for Bill Clinton's sexual foibles, Teflon was now so institutionalized that Bush could brush off the policy of deliberate torture of prisoners of war and violation of the Geneva Convention his administration had endorsed, the falsified information concerning weapons of mass destruction as a pretext for invading Iraq, and the enormous economic slide of the U.S. economy into debt. His campaign pitched fear of terrorism as its primary hook, led by a "strong leader" who in reality on 9/11 had continued to read a children's book, *The Pet Goat*, with elementary school students for five minutes after being informed of the two attacks on the World Trade Center, unable to spring into action on his own, as any real leader would.

Bush completely bypassed a public campaign trail for "private," invitation-only gatherings, at which isolated citizens with t-shirts espousing criticisms of Bush were evicted by police while other citizens cheered. Public space had become redefined as private property, wherein police and celebrity image could replace politics and free speech.

American politics, and perhaps American culture more generally, seems to have become dislocated to the concept of the *empty symbol*, which mirrors back to the individual only what the individual will want to see. The empty symbol, as politicians use it, is perhaps similar to a technique in psychotherapy associated with Carl Rogers in which the therapist repeats the patient's statements as if saying something new, thereby prompting the patient to continue without having to take the lead. Similarly, if less empathically, the empty symbolist is one who attempts to signify anything while saying nothing. This is a smiling politics, the feel-good politics of Ronald Reagan, the sound bite and flag politics of the George Bushes, the politics that prevented Michael Dukakis from admitting he was a liberal in the 1988 presidential election and got Clinton to bypass it completely. It is a politics of entertainment, cynicism, and kitsch.

Kitsch is often thought of as bad taste, "cheesy" art, or "camp." But there are deeper meanings to the term as well. Kitsch, as Milan Kundera reminds us in *The Unbearable Lightness of Being*, is the enemy of art, being, and democracy. Consider some of Kundera's definitions of kitsch (he rejects the simple *bad art* understanding of the term): "Kitsch causes two tears to flow in quick succession. The first tear says: How nice to see children running on the grass! The second tear says: How nice to be moved, together with all mankind, by children running on the grass! It is the second tear that makes kitsch kitsch." Kitsch: "the need to gaze into the mirror of the beautifying lie and to be moved to tears of gratification at one's own reflection." With kitsch "all answers are given in advance and preclude any questions." Kitsch is, as he pointedly reminds us, the denial that "shit happens." In his words: "Kitsch is the absolute denial of shit, in both the literal and figurative senses of the word; kitsch excludes everything from its purview which is essentially unacceptable in human existence." American kitsch, usually dismissed as bad taste or cultural ignorance by Europeans, is also serious business. It is a crucial ingredient in the dehumanizing process of the megamachine, a means of both disguising the rationalization of life and of giving up real feeling for false substitute emotions.

Reaganism found the strength of its legacy in 2004, the year he died and George W. Bush was reelected. There were kitsch commemorations after Ronald Reagan's death on June 5, 2004, perhaps perfect realizations of his Hollywood kitsch presidency. Many Americans seemed to think Reagan single-handedly ended communism, forgetting Gorbachev's pivotal role in arms reduction and the desperately failing Soviet economy—killed by decades of its own stupidity, not by Reaganomics.

The reality of Reagan's legacy was something quite else, though brushed aside in Kitschland. Many Americans forgot or remained unaware that Reagan enabled Osama bin Laden, and that he funded mujahedeen fundamentalism in Afghanistan and Saddam Hussein in Iraq. Hussein was propped-up by America in the 1980s to play off against Iranians, who were also being armed by the United States, through Israel, of all places.

Reagan's presidency trained Latin American terrorist death squads, like the one trained in Fort Benning, Georgia, that raped and murdered four nuns in El Salvador, not to mention one hundred thousand others killed. It sold arms to Iranian fundamentalists who had just held Americans prisoners, and cocaine to Americans, all to fund the illegal contra squads in Nicaragua. Those terrorists killed sixty thousand people, and the United States was fined $60 million by the World Court for engineering and funding them (and refused to pay it).

Reaganism gave the United States more social inequality, thinning the middle class down and bloating the wealthiest, getting government off corporate America's backs. The top 1 percent went from an average of $280,000 in 1979 to $525,000 in 1989 in constant dollars. With the mining of Nicaraguan harbors and turning away from world court jurisdiction, Reagan paved the road that led directly to George W. Bush's state-sponsored torture of prisoners at Guantánamo, Cuba, and at other secret CIA prisons, dishonoring human rights and military professionalism, and illegal mass surveillance of American telephone communications and credit card transactions.

Reagan gave the United States the empty symbol of celebrity, perfected: government by image and handlers and Teflon; government of kitsch by kitsch for kitsch. Nixon was forced to resign under the threat of impeachment in the previous decade for attempting to subvert the Constitution, but Reagan glowed in a Teflon aura-shield. The Iran-contra scandal posed as deep a threat to American democracy as Watergate, but caused far less indignation. America seemed too kitschified to remember any of this in 2004: cultural Alzheimer's is now institutionalized. Remember Kundera's kitsch: the denial that shit happens, and a key lubricant for a postdemocratic order.

The scariest part of the 2004 memorials for Reagan was the realization of how Reagan-perfect it all was: pure kitsch form devoid of content, final resting place of the Teflon presidency. Kitsch-R-US. It was an ominous indicator that the numerous lies, scandals, and policy failures of the George W. Bush presidency would not stand in the way of his reelection later in the year.

Postmodern America had so emptied itself of reality that nothing except image mattered anymore.

The Bush torture scandal, secret prisons scandal, domestic spying scandal, and lies concerning weapons of mass destruction as a pretext for war with Iraq scandal could have resulted in his impeachment or resignation and criminal action against Dick Cheney, Donald Rumsfeld, and other administration officials *if* there were "Equal Justice Under Law" (as chiseled above the Supreme Court Building). These were far more grave breaches than Clinton's sexual indiscretions, for which republicans called for impeachment. But instead of equal justice under law, there was the Reagan legacy, still burrowing toward bedlam.

The Russian model of grim Stalin "Big Brother" was defeated by a superior American version, one that perpetually smiled and promised Goodfeel: the smiley-faced empty cipher as presidential essence, of which "Reagan" was perhaps the perfected full-Hollywood avatar, and George W. Bush a sometimes scowling, cheap imitation. Why have Big Brother watching you, when you can voluntarily bathe in the kitsch-fest of watching Big Brother, voluntarily enscreening one's consciousness and awareness within a perpetual soft indoctrination device of advertising and entertainment?

Even the brief awakening brought about after 9/11 turned quickly into a much greater expansion of and reliance upon automatic culture of various forms in the United States. America not only blundered into the Iraq quagmire unprepared but also lost the war on terrorism to the automaton within, which would prefer a false ideal of "invulnerability," technical, political, and personal, at any cost, even freedom. One cannot be truly alive without being vulnerable. Yet as the smiley face says: HAVE A NICE DAY! Or to update it to advice given by Vice President Dick Cheney after 9/11: GO SHOPPING! People today forget Reagan realities because cultural kitsch has become rigidly institutionalized throughout the culture, deadening memory. Here is another definition: Kitsch is the soul food of the living dead.

Given an atmosphere of utter kitsch and cynicism, one dominated by a television entertainment culture, it is no wonder that empty political symbols have assumed a central significance in electoral politics. I take these symbols of empty politics to be accurate indicators of a more widespread unraveling of the moral fiber of American culture, which in turn is part of the larger unraveling of modern life. Let us examine two self-representations of democracy from these times, in order to highlight the difficulties that democracy and its communication face in the United States today. These cases also illustrate how rational bureaucratic processes and kitsch sentimentalism eat away from opposite directions at the possibility of the public realm.

Despite what I see as a dangerous withering away of the democratic fabric of American life, I would like to point out an unlikely candidate for a symbolic self-representation of democracy in the best sense. Given the combination of cynicism and kitsch, the Vietnam Veterans Memorial stands as a remarkable public symbol of democracy in the face of overwhelming odds against it. After examining the Vietnam Veterans Memorial as a self-representation of democracy, I will turn to a contemporary cult of high-tech vehicular democracy that could almost have come out of the film *Dr. Strangelove*.

The Vietnam Veterans Memorial

When we remember that the Greek root *symballein* means literally "to throw together," we see how the Vietnam Veterans Memorial is perhaps the outstanding political *symbol* in America today. It not only manages to be a convincing public monument at a time when such things are difficult to realize, and for a war that produced bitter divisions in America, divisions that continued throughout the planning and realization of the Memorial and reerupted in the presidential elections of 2004, but it also achieves supremely what the chief task of a "symbol" is, to bind something together through a representation.

The memorial was commissioned with four criteria in mind: it had to be imposing, reflective, include all the names of the 58,175 Americans killed in the war, and make no political statement. Given these criteria, it is all the more remarkable that the memorial stands today as a powerful and moving political symbol that honors the dead while yet containing all of the ambiguities of the war.[2]

The memorial stands in a public park area of Washington known as "the Mall," whose vistas include the principal symbols of American democracy, including the Capital Building and the White House, and a number of monuments and memorials and museums. Despite the precipitous decline of many middle-sized American cities and the public space that they afford, due to the effects of suburban shopping malls and other factors, the Washington Mall area remains a visible national public space. The Mall area was part of the plan of the city of Washington submitted in 1791 by the French engineer Maj. Pierre Charles L'Enfant, a plan of grand baroque proportions oddly at issue with the ideals of the newborn American democracy.

Despite L'Enfant's intentions, the great static vista provided by the Mall evoked the absolute despotism of centralized power and control symbolized by Versailles instead of the bounded powers of a federal republic. L'Enfant's total plan also required a larger population than Washington possessed, and a public control over land that was not achieved. Hence his plan was only partially realized, aided by an attempt to renew the plan in 1901.

The Mall contains the ideal baroque broad vista, an ideal unfortunately better suited to the tourist's eye than the inhabitant's daily use. Nevertheless, the Mall provides the national public space for public demonstration and protest, and is capable of holding huge numbers of people, from those who marched on Washington during the civil rights and anti-Vietnam War movements of the 1960s to the pro- and antiabortion groups today.

At the center of the Mall stands the Washington Monument, a traditional obelisk raised to giant, phallic proportions, which dominates the downtown skyline. The cornerstone of the monument was laid on July 4, 1848, but due to a lack of funds—revealing a lack of foresight similar to that of the realization of L'Enfant's Washington city plan—the monument was not completed until 1888.

At the western end of the Mall is the Lincoln Memorial, which houses a large statue of Abraham Lincoln and words from speeches in which he proclaimed the end of slavery in America. On the steps of the Lincoln Memorial, Dr. Martin Luther King Jr. delivered his most impassioned and memorable speech of the civil rights movement on August 28, 1963, before more than half a million Americans. There are no visible physical memorials at this site, yet powerful images of it remain through filmed recordings, illustrating perhaps how evanescent public speech can sometimes be more enduring than weighty public monuments.

A couple of hundred meters from the Lincoln Memorial and its visible and invisible memories stands the Vietnam Veterans Memorial, which was unveiled in 1982. The design of the Memorial was based on a national competition, which was won by a twenty-one-year-old student at Yale, Maya Lin. In what could only be described as fate, the student was an Asian woman, whose design of a large open wedge was to fix for the permanent record a memorial of the American men who died in the Vietnam War. If the selection of L'Enfant for the Washington city plan symbolized both the American dependence on European civilization and perhaps admiration for the French Enlightenment and thankfulness to the French for help during the Revolutionary War, perhaps we can look at Lin herself as a representative symbol of the new generation of Asian Americans and women reshaping the face of America. In an interview after her design was selected, Lin said that she did not want to make a phallic symbol. And when one visits the memorial it is clear that she did not, for it is, if anything, the opposite, a vaginal symbol. I am not, in most circumstances, a Freudian, yet it was clear to me upon visit-

Figure 9. Vietnam Veterans Memorial by Maya Lin, dedicated in 1982.

ing the memorial that it is a *gash*, in the colloquial senses both of *wound* and *vagina*.

There is a fantastic tension between the great erection of the Washington Monument, which one can vertically ascend by foot or elevator, and the Vietnam Veterans Memorial, which one descends into by foot. The two walls of the Vietnam Veterans Memorial are intentionally aligned on a 120-degree axis with the Washington Monument and the Lincoln Memorial. When asked in 1983 whether her memorial "had a female sensibility," Lin responded, "In a world of phallic memorials that rise upwards, it certainly does. I didn't set out to conquer the earth, or overpower it, the way Western man usually does. I don't think I've made a passive piece, but neither is it a memorial to the idea of war."[3]

The memorial was marked with controversies from the beginning, with many veterans' groups resenting the abstractness of the design—for example, only the names and dates were listed—and the original design was later changed to add words stating that the names listed were veterans killed in the Vietnam War, to erect a flag over the juncture of the memorial, and to place a realistic statue by sculptor Frederick Hart of three soldiers, a black, a white, and a Hispanic, at a distance opposite the memorial. One veteran appeared before the commission on fine arts to complain that the design was "a black gash of shame." Because of lingering controversies regarding the Vietnam War, and controversies surrounding the memorial, President Reagan did not

attend the unveiling of the memorial in 1982, but did participate in the unveiling of the realistic statue in 1984.⁴ Reagan could only associate himself
with the kitsch realism, not with the real monument. One sees how Reagan's
"handlers" sought to associate him in the media with good news, and to distance him from the possibility of bad news. He stood his ground for kitsch,
shunning the reality that the real Vietnam Veterans Memorial expresses.

The memorial can be described as abstract, minimalist even. Yet it somehow contains both a quiet dignity and a nonabstract tangibility through the
names carved into the reflecting marble. In the controversy surrounding the
Vietnam Veterans Memorial, which many Americans simply call "the Wall,"
one sees a fascinating twist on the culture of the "empty symbol."

Again, by "empty symbol" I wish to draw attention to a curious tendency
in the right-wing politics and left-wing art of the 1980s to signify no quality or content—recalling the title of Robert Musil's novel, *The Man without
Qualities*—as most fully realized politically in Ronald Reagan and artistically
in minimalism. Artistic minimalism, despite its postmodernist pretensions
to novelty, can be seen to continue the earlier minimalizing tendencies of abstract expressionism as a "process art" in which the content does not matter,
and of pop/op as only signifying content, in which the form does not matter.
Perhaps the ultimate minimalist celebrity is Andy Warhol, hero of "art-lite"
and empty symbol, and like Reagan, avatar of the great spiral down the vortex of hyperunreality.

Lin was surrounded by the culture of artistic minimalism but had to confront the fact of death in her funerary architecture class at Yale University. She
created the empty object that reflects back the viewer's own image, which is
exactly the politics of Ronald Reagan, but with the opposite effect. What normally goes by the name of minimalism, what one sees in museums and hears
in music, is glorified banality. Somehow, by contrast, this memorial is real and
earnest; it carries death with dignity. Although deriving from minimalism, it
is clear that Maya Lin did not let the cynical and shrewd and blasé attitude—so
prominent in the 1980s—override her attempt to make a real memorial. When
one looks back at the controversy that surrounded the memorial, with the
Texas millionaire Ross Perot flying veterans to Washington and conducting a
skewed survey of prisoners of war (rather than veterans in general or families of
veterans), it is also clear that Lin's memorial is a triumph over schmaltzy sentimentalism as well as starved minimalism—it succeeds because it straightfor-
wardly fuses the human and epic proportions of tragic war.

Yet another of the contradictions of the Vietnam Veterans Memorial is its
frank acknowledgment of death. The tragic entry to the under-womb earth
symbolism works. Death seemed to contradict the 1980s "feel good" mental-

Figure 10. A man traces a name from the wall.

ity that Ronald Reagan celebrated and sold to Americans, so it is all the more remarkable that the Vietnam Veterans Memorial was able to speak so directly of the meaning and memory of death to a nation that only wanted to forget. To give one example, it seems fair to say that the significance of Memorial Day, a national holiday at the end of May intended to commemorate those killed in war, has declined in recent years. Originally begun as a tribute to the soldiers of the American Civil War, Memorial Day has been celebrated in most American communities by parades and public speeches. Perhaps the best discussion of the place of Memorial Day in American life can be found in W. L. Warner's book *The Living and the Dead*, the last of the five-volume Yankee City series, in which he describes the Memorial Day parade as a ritual pilgrimage to the town cemetery, to "the city of the dead" as he calls it.

Memorial Day seems to have declined in significance, just as cemeteries have declined in significance in America. Although Americans remain a highly religious people, American culture has turned away from the commemoration of death. Whether the decline in Memorial Day is due to the denial of death syndrome, or to the fallout of the Vietnam era and its moral ambiguities, or to its less readily "marketability" in contrast to other holidays, or simply that it expresses outdated sentiments, is unclear.

It is a common practice for people at the Wall to make rubbings of names, and tour guides will provide paper to make rubbings. Hence at any given walk through the memorial there will be people actively making a rubbing, thereby imparting a participatory atmosphere to the quiet stone to the dead. The only comparison I can think of is perhaps the graffiti on the old Berlin Wall, which signified the ridicule of communist absolutism and anything else imaginable. That symbol of the great divide, with exploding mines on one side and irreverent images and graffiti on the other, was, and I suspect will remain, the most powerful political symbol of twentieth-century Germany, with its "no man's land" around the remains of Hitler's bunker, where he burrowed his way back to hell, with its barbed wire and police guards and police dogs that stood as self-representations of the so-called German Democratic Republic, and with its images in the fall of 1989 of the concrete demise of communist concrete. This oval enclosure in Berlin was perhaps also a manifestation of the feminine in the twentieth century, but in its malefic aspect as vagina dentata, as a phobic Gaia. It said quite clearly: "Here is where the vice-grip closed on Nazi Germany." It also symbolized, to my eyes at least, how clearly Hitler's legacy had shaped the postwar world, where East and West, starkly divided, both made copious use of Nazi scientists and technicians in an ever-escalating arms race. "The Wall" signifies the twentieth-century battle between democracy and totalitarianism that continues to be fought in our century, even if every last piece of it is sold as a sacred tourist relic.

In the fall of 1989, a month before it fell, I suggested at a conference in Bonn, West Germany, that some of the Berlin Wall, including specifically the area of Hitler's bunker and other prominent sections from cold war history, be designated as a symbol of twentieth-century Germany. My reasoning was that although the Berlin Wall was a product of the cold war that testifies to the failures of communism, it holds a broader significance as well. The fact that Hitler's final bunker, a mound buried within the wall, out of which his body emerged to be cremated, struck me as a fantastic reality from some sardonic Disneyland—almost like the ancient Assyrian practice of burying enemies within the city's wall. This site also addressed twentieth-century hubris: "Here is German defeat, resulting from unbridled arrogance," just as other portions of the wall signify the divided postwar Germany and the continuing battle of totalitarianism versus democracy. The cold war virtually ended on top of the wall, at least in memorable images, in the celebrations.

For these reasons the Wall, even more than the Kaiser Wilhelm Gedankskirche (a church deliberately left in partial ruins), seemed to me to encompass the broadest span of twentieth-century Germany. Fifteen years later, in October 2004, I returned to Berlin to discover that the city has left at least one full city block of the wall intact (and individual sections elsewhere), and excavated a level down next to it. An outdoor photographic exhibit in the excavated section was titled *The Topography of Terror*. I walked the history of the Nazi times in Berlin, while occasionally looking up to the wall layer above, the literal topography of terror.

Berlin did something far better than I could have imagined. As I walked from the *Topography of Terror* exhibit and the Berlin Wall above it, ominous black clouds and wind suddenly materialized, a hard rain began, and I felt the strange topography of *nicht* and nowhere, of dead zone zombie history where that war ended and the cold war clinched its vice-grip on the Fatherland. A couple of blocks away I found the site of Hitler's bunker, now just a flat empty lot, unmarked, construction going on all around it. But something more was in the process of manifesting. I realized that soon the last under-earth of the Führer would become somebody else's office building, obliterate, as it should be, and as you read this, it now is. Then a couple of blocks farther, as I walked in the pouring rain, I came upon a huge field of stone monoliths in construction, thousands in lines, forming a sculptural cemetery, marking the Holocaust. So much for Nazi "blut und boden," "blood and earth." This was a kind of inversion of the final solution, a strange reverse of Hitler's demented vision of a thousand-year Reich centered in Berlin. *Steinenfeld (Field of Stones)*, was now bodying forth as a city of the dead, of Jews finally given that Berlin earth as memory ground, while a few blocks away Hitler's nameless, placeless bunker was en route to oblivion.

The Vietnam Veterans Memorial, which deliberately avoids the term "Vietnam War," also symbolizes defeat, and in the late twentieth century, defeat proved an important legacy of the modern era, an antidote to its boundless confidence and total wars. Both the Vietnam Veterans Memorial—the Wall—and what Germans called the Mauer (wall) can serve as stark reminders of misguided national purposes.

Somehow the Vietnam Veterans Memorial manages to bind together the feelings of those who died in or believed in the war with those who did not. It captures the ambiguity of the war and of the sixties in its seeming refusal to acknowledge the tradition of war memorials, yet also clearly honors the dead. Despite initial opposition to it by veterans groups, its subsequent popularity has prompted a life-sized replica to be displayed in major cities around the United States, so that more people can see it. It has also generated permanent "mini-walls" in smaller cities and towns, which seek to symbolize a connection to the great wall in Washington, but which also exemplify the franchising tendencies of megatechnic America and the ease with which heartfelt emotion can be turned to idealized kitsch.

One of the reasons this memorial seems to work so well, it seems to me, is because it is endowed with the binding power of the feminine. How odd that a monument dedicated primarily to dead male soldiers is so powerfully feminine! And yet it is precisely its feminine ability to encompass and nurture that helps set it apart. Henry Adams, and later Lewis Mumford, noted that the power of the feminine had been lost as a moving cultural symbol. Yet perhaps in this powerful contemporary symbol of American democracy and its failings we see the possibility of a renewal through the feminine.

My next case will take us from a self-representation of democracy that transcends kitsch to one that bathes in kitsch.

Airstream Amerika

Nothing, in my view, more deserves attention than the intellectual and moral associations in America. American political and industrial associations easily catch our eyes, but the others tend not to be noticed. And even if we do notice them we tend to misunderstand them, hardly ever having seen anything similar before. However we should recognize that the latter are as necessary as the former to the American people; perhaps more so.

In democratic countries knowledge of how to combine is the mother of all other forms of knowledge; on its progress depends that of all the others.

—ALEXIS DE TOCQUEVILLE[5]

In Italo Calvino's novel *Invisible Cities*, Marco Polo describes to an aging Kublai Khan the many strange and mysterious cities of Khan's empire he has seen. Fantastic in shape and frequently surreal in lifestyle, they together weave a picture of an empire in dissolution and decay. I shall describe for you an American association every bit as weird as some of those cities that Calvino's Polo depicts, and in some ways even more queer: an association that forms a city that, like Polo himself, is self-moving and filled with wanderlust.

It is a city that defines itself through techno-leisure and that embodies those now classic American values of rugged mass "individualism" and the auto. Indeed, one might say that it is literally an elaborate system of auto eroticism. It is a city that can be characterized as a landscape of signs, a transitory city whose entire existence is predicated upon mobility: upward and onward mobility. In its artificiality it is perhaps only rivaled by that great American desert mecca, Las Vegas. But where Las Vegas is a city dedicated to Mammon, in his manifestation as chance and uncertainty in gambling, the city I will describe is dedicated to hierarchical, rationalized, totemic order, in which the figure of Mammon is not always as immediately apparent.

If, as Émile Durkheim believed, "social life, in all its aspects and in every period of its history, is made possible only by a vast symbolism,"[6] then the contemporary cult of the Airstream especially serves as an indicator of American leisure culture. By exploring the strange traveling rituals of a club formed around the inventor of the Airstream travel trailer, Wally Byam, we see in actuality a group approximating an ideal of the values of leisure and retirement that are so central to the American so-called way of life, and a semiotic landscape that embodies these values and the larger mind they serve: megatechnic America.

In the Airstream city we see an anonymous aggregate of Airstreams, their possessors possessed by a vast power, property, prestige complex, a soulless never-never land where *things* and their ownership, not *citizens*, form the heart of the city. The Airstream cult provides one small opening to a discussion of the virtual dictatorship of the automobile in contemporary Western civilization, of commodity fetishism, of the myth of classless "rugged individualism" in the context of mass society, and of the stubborn ability of objects to retain animistic qualities in seemingly rational, technocratic society. But what of the earlier visions of America as the New World?

In many ways the traditional American vision can be characterized as the immersion of the individual in the community of nature. One sees this vision in the literary transcendentalists of the 1850s, such as Thoreau, Melville, Whitman, and Emerson, through the organic architecture of Louis Sullivan and Frank Lloyd Wright, through the founding of nature movements near the end of the nineteenth century—Audubon, the Sierra Club, and others—and even somewhat later in the spread of the Boy Scout movement. Just as Frederick Jackson Turner declared the frontier closed, and just as Americans were completing the program of genocide practiced on Native Americans, white, largely protestant Americans could adopt the totemic outlook of the Native Americans through the Boy Scouts.[7] Later the auto and professionalized sports would provide media for totemic mass cults.

One sees this vision as well in the poetry of Robinson Jeffers, the naturalistic philosophy of self and community elaborated by the philosophical pragmatists, the photography of Ansel Adams, the furniture, home, and sculpture of Wharton Esherick, and the organic vision of Lewis Mumford. A common feature of this New World vision is the attempt to strip the pretensions of Western civilization and its lusts for power and prestige by growing a new kind of individual and community, rooted in the organic environment. But that New World vision was already marred by genocide and slavery and fatally cracked by the Civil War. Industry triumphed over agricultural ideals, powering itself up ever since.

The grand vision of organic utopia has been paved over by another America, by the one most of us are familiar with. This other America is the one

Jean Baudrillard has referred to in his book *America* as the place where the lights are never turned off.[8] Who can deny the omnipresence of this omnivorous Disneyland empire and its Disney World view? Even if, I must say, Baudrillard's tourist-eye view of American culture runs about as deep as the view that French culture can be expressed in the law that all adult Frenchmen are required to carry baguettes under their arms at all times in public. Still, it is clear that "actually existing America" is far removed from the organic vision that animated its original peoples as well as its greatest artists and thinkers.

The Caravan

In June and July 1984, and again in 1990, four thousand silver Airstreams and almost ten thousand Airstreamers, all members of the Wally Byam Caravan Club, converged on the campus of the University of Notre Dame for their annual international caravan. Shining silver Airstreams occupied every available open space surrounding the campus, creating a city of wheels in which a rich system of totemic and hierarchical symbolism predominated. The Wally Byam Caravan Club is named after the inventor of the Airstream travel trailer, which the Airstream club describes as "the prestige units of travel trailers." Members are also quick to distinguish their "prestige" travel trailers from the more prosaic RVs (recreational vehicles). The term "caravan" evokes the nomadic life of travel and trade in the Middle East, but the Airstream club draws on the image of "wagon trains" of the American frontier, when settlers would travel with all of their worldly possessions in covered wagons.[9]

Most Wally Byam Caravan Club members, then and now, are retired, and a number of males are former career military men. The club is then predominantly a gerontocracy, and one in which one's rank and social standing is quite significant. Perhaps this indicates a need to recreate social roles lost through retirement, a fantasy microworld where roles are clearly delineated and where one can even dream again of "career" advancement. I was told, for example, of an electrician who found his much-needed services for the caravans brought him very quickly to a position of prominence. Alexis de Tocqueville was one of the first to note that, "Americans of all ages, all stations in life, and all types of disposition are forever forming associations."[10] Who knows but that the club might presage the kinds of organizations one might see developing in a demographically aging American population? At the times I observed the Airstreams, before campus construction prevented their return to the University of Notre Dame, I little realized that the four-wheel vehicles needed to tow the Airstreams presaged the reeruption of the big, gas-guzzling American car: the SUVs and vans that would dominate U.S. autos in the 1990s and on.

In the Wally Byam Club we see the hallmarks of the cult of ritualized leisure and prefabricated spontaneity, all in the name of a mythic mass individualism. Although international in name (there are a tiny number of foreign members, but the club has made foreign caravans), the community of the elect is linked by the means to purchase an Airstream (at an average 1990 price of $27,000 to $49,000), which serves to exclude lower-income classes and racial and ethnic groups more associated with lower income, namely African American or Mexican American. The Byamites are overwhelmingly white. Despite having many former career military males, the Airstream caravan city lacks the racial and ethnic diversity of the Vietnam Veterans Memorial primarily because it is based on the purchase of a large and expensive machine, the Airstream.

The Wally Byam Caravan Club involves an elaborate system of totemic hierarchy. Members arrive at the international caravan, for example, wearing ribbons they have received for attending regional caravans, and those with the greater number of ribbons enjoy greater prestige as being more active in the club. The membership number printed in red letters on Airstreams also signifies how long one has been a member of the Caravan Club. Those with lower numbers assume higher prestige than owners of Airstreams who do not join the club, and the lower one's number, the closer one is to the origin of the club and its mythic founder: to "the good old days" or, as Mircea Eliade put it, "in illo tempore," the time of "creation."

Perhaps there is some greater need in American culture to adopt totemlike classifications as a sort of echo of the native peoples crushed by the "American Dream." One only has to turn to that greatest symbol of the American way of life, the automobile, to see the elaborate totemic naming system of largely predatory animals, such as the Stingray or Cobra, or of prowess, such as the Mustang or Bronco, or of prestige, such as the Monarchs and Regals, to see how technology carries an animistic aura seemingly quite at odds with the modern ethos. Power, sexuality, prestige, mobility—the lethal ability to kill as many people in the United States each year as one would expect from a war—these are some of the primary values that cars carry both in America and more generally in the modern world. But how strange it is that high tech should have such primal urges and emblems attached to it. Dr. Freud, inventor of scientific psychoanalysis, might well understand how totemic symbolism and its taboo status in modern life might easily coexist. Photos of his office at Bergasse 19 in Vienna reveal a cultic semicircle of ancient statuettes surrounding the enlightened scientist. The Airstream is one of the highest of

Figure 11. Wally Byam Caravan Club Airstream panorama at the University of Notre Dame.

high-tech vehicles, and, as is clear from the Wally Byam Caravan Club, also a veritable social hieroglyphic.

In the flag symbolism, which reflects the Byamites' penchant for totemic emblems as well as traditional patriotism, and in the hierarchical alignment of the high-status vehicles near the "sacred" space of the University of Notre Dame, the football stadium, one sees the re-creation of the ancient concept of axis mundi. Although the University of Notre Dame is a private, Catholic university, whose religious center is "the golden dome"—the administration building on which stands "Notre Dame du Lac"—the university is universally known in America for its football teams, and is regarded by many as the symbolic center of American football. A famous film about Knute Rockne, the coach of the team during its golden years in the 1920s and 1930s, featured one of the star players, George Gipp ("the Gipper"), who was acted by Ronald Reagan. And Reagan, as is well known, later went on to a starring role in American political symbolism when he portrayed the president of the United States for an eight-year run. He drew quite consciously on the popularity of this film by retaining the nickname "the Gipper" throughout his political career.

So in understanding the political symbolism of the University of Notre Dame, it is important to keep in mind how it is more of a "religio-athletic" institution than a religious university. It is an academic institution that can and does use its sacred religio-athletic aura to great profit, not only through its professional "collegiate" football team, multimillion-dollar TV deals, and multimillion-dollar annual football coach's salary, but also through the intense merchandizing of its brand name and campus. And it is precisely that "sacred" athletic aura with which the Airstream cult chose to surround itself. Hence the highest-ranking vehicles, belonging to the officers of the club, were to be found next to the football stadium that Rockne built, between it and the huge indoor basketball complex. This configuration is no longer possible after the stadium was enlarged a decade later and especially after the security concerns after 9/11.

Most of these elite Airstreams were also distinguished by the large number of flags they flew—about five per vehicle—and by their low club membership

Figure 12. Highest-ranking officers' Airstreams parked next to Notre Dame football stadium.

numbers. The president's Airstream on the right of figure 12, for example, showed membership number 124. The next level, that of past presidents and officers, formed the rows slightly more removed from the stadium. Another pocket of prestige was an area reserved for the grandparents of regional "Miss Teen Stream" beauty contestants. On one perimeter of the Airstream city was a functional "neighborhood" reserved for dog owners, which was established because of prior experiences of barking dogs disturbing the peace. Both individual Airstreams and the collective city they form are paradigms of modern functionalism. When the architect and city designer Le Corbusier declared that the house is a machine, he expressed the modern dream of transforming human life into that of the machine. That dream clearly lives in the soul of Airstream Amerika, and in the ever-increasing dependence on machines.

The Auto, Autonomy, and the Automatic

The auto is made for the aged. The sense of going—going—going—in the open air, dulls thought, and induces a sort of hypnotism or mental lethargy, with swift visions of landscape and escape.

—HENRY ADAMS[11]

Around 1930, just when the "new capitalism" suddenly slumped down to earth, the motor car industry picked itself up by exchanging economy for style. . . . Within the next two decades, the motor car became a status symbol, a religious icon, an erotic fetish: in short, "something out of this world," increasingly swollen and tumescent, as if on the verge of an orgasm. What words other than Madison Avenue's can adequately describe these exciting confections, glittering with chrome, pillowed in comfort, sleepy-soft to ride in, equipped with mirrors, cigarette lighters, radios, telephones, floor carpeting; (liquor bars and tape-recorders are still optional).

—LEWIS MUMFORD[12]

Although not usually associated with political symbolism, I would like to suggest that the auto can be seen as a key antipolitical symbol in contemporary American life, and more broadly, as a symbol of the mechanization of life and consequent loss of organic human purpose and sense of limitation. The 1980s began with the prospect that the home office, through the personal computer, would achieve a far greater role in the "workplace," and ended with the automobile—that master symbol of American culture—as the model office of the future. Through cell phones, computers, and related devices the auto has supposedly been in the process of becoming the ideal high-tech traveling office in the age of gridlock as ever-increasing amounts of congested roadways reduce mobility to and from work. Taken together, all of these developments signaled an ever-greater reliance on automatic, technical culture.

The term *auto* means self—hence *automobile* or self-moving—but the meanings of Ralph Waldo Emerson's essay "Self-Reliance" and contemporary *auto reliance* could not be more disparate. Consider the irony of business people sitting in stalled traffic, diligently working with all the conveniences of home and office: the auto-immobile.

Perhaps it would have been better if another term, originally applied to one of the earliest self-moving vehicles, had been adopted, the *locomobile*. Given the increasing amounts of time Americans are spending in these "moving places," and given the effects cars have had in dominating and devitalizing cities through residential sprawl, workday congestion, and the sheer roadways themselves, and given the continuing subordination of organic human purpose and habitat to the requirements of the delocalizing, centralized machine mentality, the term "locomobile" also captures the "moving craziness" of contemporary American culture.

The Parade of Democracy

We're just one big happy mass of silver.
—AIRSTREAMER, CITED IN THE *NEW YORK TIMES*,
SEPTEMBER 25, 1990

Throughout the two weeks of the caravan, club members engage in numerous internal political and cultural activities, a number of which are significant for one's place in the hierarchy, as well as attending entertainment events, all centered in the huge University of Notre Dame indoor sport amphitheater. But the climax and central ritual of the entire caravan is the Fourth of July parade. Not only is the caravan timed to conclude on Independence Day, but all of the state groups also devote time during the two weeks to making symbolic floats and costumes. The theme of the 1990 international caravan, for example, was "The Good Old Days," around which a variety of images—from elderly people dressed as infants to antique autos—were constructed to reveal a nostalgic "history" that mirrors the self-image of the Airstreamers as friendly, fun-loving, patriotic explorers of America.

Indeed, the Airstream cult could be termed a *community of nostalgia*, in contrast with what Robert Bellah and the coauthors of *Habits of the Heart* have designated as *communities of memory*. A real community, according to Bellah and his coauthors, retells its past in order not to forget it. The stories and rituals through which a community's memories are made public must be more than mere positive idealizations:

A genuine community of memory will also tell painful stories of shared suffering that sometimes creates deeper identities than success. . . . And if the community is completely honest, it will remember stories not only of suffering received but of suffering inflicted—dangerous memories, for they call the community to alter ancient evils. At some times, neighborhoods, localities, and regions have been communities in America, but that has been hard to sustain in our restless and mobile society. . . . Where history and hope are forgotten and community means only the gathering of the similar, community degenerates into lifestyle enclave. The temptation toward that transformation is endemic in America, though the transformation is seldom complete.[13]

By contrast with a community of memory, the Airstream cult represents an ideal type of the opposite: all bad events are banished from its collective memory banks, and the ultramodern vehicle that the Airstream was and purports to remain is fused with sentimentalist nostalgia: "the good old days." One Airstreamer told the story of a small caravan through Mexico, and how every night the twenty or so Airstreams would form a circle as was done in the days of the pioneer wagon trains. He recalled the campfire and songs, but had virtually nothing to say about Mexico: his memories were made within his circle of the familiar, not from the unfamiliar world without. This was a tourism that traveled fully insulated by a bubble of American culture.

One saw in the Airstream caravan of 1984 (and 1990), an ironic inversion of Orwell's 1984. Here was no totalitarian dictatorship imposing a denial of real history while stifling dissent. Instead there was a society freely choosing to deny the real history one develops by being rooted to a community, to deny that anything might be wrong with itself. The Airstream cult might be regarded as a collective immune system to history. It was a collective embodiment of the "feel good" and forgetful ideals of Reagan America. Although the Airstreamers like to think of themselves as friendly and open, theirs is the friendliness of mass anonymity, the "gathering of the similar." As an owner of another brand of recreational vehicles told me about Airstreamers: "They're snobs. They look down on other kinds of vehicles."

The Fourth of July is, of course, the date of American independence from England, and so holds a patriotic significance in American "civil religion," as well as being perhaps the chief civic holiday of local communities. But there is an additional weird layer of symbolism beyond the obviously political: the heroic founder of the Airstream cult, Wally Byam, was born on July 4, 1898. Hence the parade also acts as a commemoration of the founding father, fusing national symbolism with the "creation myth" of the Airstream.

What could be a more appropriate form of ritual to signify the cult of mobility than the parade? When we examine some of the floats in the parade, the symbolic values of the Airstream cult become even clearer. A Brazilian former colleague, ethnographer Roberto DaMatta, studied Carnival in Rio, and showed how highly structured and authoritarian Brazilian society temporarily transforms itself into relatively nonhierarchical community in the Carnival parades. Such a temporary reversal of structure illustrates the "ludic" or "liminal" phase of rituals described by ethnographer Victor Turner, where normal roles are temporarily reversed.[14] But DaMatta has also noted how Mardi Gras in New Orleans, where all the groups are led by a king or queen, reveals the American desire for hierarchy beneath the egalitarian, democratic facade.

Similarly, we see in the organization of the parade the ritual exhibition of hierarchy through the initial arrival of elected Airstream dignitaries to the reviewing platform in the large, four-wheel-drive autos (as I then called them)—known as Broncos, Blazers, and Suburbans, but later popularized in the SUV craze that swept American highways—used to pull the Airstreams. As the parade proceeds, the teenage girls who are state winners of Airstream beauty contests and who are competing to become "Miss Teen Stream" arrive in Corvette Stingray automobiles rented for the occasion. Here one sees "auto eroticism" at its purest, as the sports cars symbolize the budding sexuality of youth. In this sense the ruling Airstream gerontocracy can vicariously express the blush of youthful sexuality through the girls and the potent Corvette Stingrays on which they ride.

Indeed, both the parade and the "city of wheels" represent the elevation of vehicles to cultic status, both in the Airstream microcosm and American culture in general, and the significance of one's "ride" as totemic symbol of one's standing. Throughout the parade many of the floats fused Airstream symbolism with the symbolism of the University of Notre Dame, whose football team is widely known as "the Fighting Irish."

One sees this in the group of older women dressed as Leprechauns resting before the beginning of the parade (figure 13). The contrast between age (the sitting Leprechaun women) and beauty (the standing Miss Teen Stream contestants in the sports cars behind them) is also striking.

Similarly, in the float named "Green Magic Carpet" one sees the combination of the mobile "magic carpet" of the Middle East, the land of caravans, and Irish green (figure 14). On the front of the float is a motto used by University of Notre Dame football fans: "Irish fever, We've got it." The twin domes

Figure 13. Airstreamers dressed as leprechauns for a parade, Miss Teen Stream contestants in background.

on the front of the float may appear to be a model of a nuclear reactor but are in fact a representation of the university's indoor sport complex.

When it comes to the power of symbols, neither learning nor religion conveys the main message of the University of Notre Dame. Rather, it is the mythic power of the American sport complex, perfumed by the faint aura of religion and higher learning, that provides energies for ritual expression. Here

Figure 14. "Magic Carpet" float with motto: "Irish Fever, We've Got It!"

too, one can see American society in microcosm. Georg Simmel observed that as the concept of God lost its mediating power as *coincidentia oppositorum* in modern culture, money arose to take its place in the hierarchy of modern values. If money best represents the materialistic symbol of transcendence in the modern age, then spectator sport perhaps best represents the materialization of religious ritual.

When we remember that most of the modern sports, including the major American sports of football (1869), basketball, and baseball, were invented in the last decades of the nineteenth century,[15] it is possible to see the great significance of modern sport globally, with its elevation of the human body and of large-scale spectacle, as deriving from the myth of materialism. The old gods may have been dying, as Durkheim lamented in *The Elementary Forms of the Religious Life*, but new ones were indeed being born all around him. Like sport, the auto and the airplane were powerful emergent symbols of modern materialism and culture.

All three symbols—sport, autos, and airplanes—crystallized as central institutions of American culture after the Second World War. Professional football and basketball rose to the prominence of baseball in America, and Americans became enthusiastic viewers of year-round televised sporting events. Somewhat later, airports became status symbols for cities in America and throughout the world. In the age of institutionalized modernism a city without its own airport was as deficient as a city without a skyscraper, symbolism that was transparent to Osama bin Laden. Transportation in America underwent fundamental changes in the 1950s due to policy decisions heavily influenced by oil companies and automakers to build a national highway system. Such decisions greatly empowered the auto and truck transport, while undermining mass transit systems nationwide. During this period of euphoria over the new Interstate Highway System the Wally Byam Club was formed and began to flourish, so that by 1959/60 it could caravan through Europe and Africa, meeting Haile Selassie and Ugandan witch doctors. And it is precisely this 1950s spirit of "on the road" that remains the core value of the club today. In this sense the club represents the ideal realization of the mobile society, where both home and city are in continual motion.

The Airstream city of wheels is nothing less than a utopia, a contemporary mobile analogue to the earlier utopian communities of the New World, just as the development of the city may have been the original utopia, as Lewis Mumford suggested, concretely realized at the dawn of civilization:

[A]s Fustel de Coulanges and Bachofen pointed out a century ago, the city was primarily a religious phenomenon: it was the home of a god, and even the city wall points to

135

this super-human origin; for Mircea Eliade is probably correct in inferring that its primary function was to hold chaos at bay and ward off inimical spirits.

This cosmic orientation, these mythic-religious claims, this royal preempting of the powers and functions of the community are what transformed the mere village or town into a city: something "out of this world," the home of a god. Much of the contents of the city—houses, shrines, storage bins, ditches, irrigation works—was already in existence in smaller communities: but though these utilities were necessary antecedents of the city, the city itself was transmogrified into an ideal form—a glimpse of eternal order, a visible heaven on earth, a seat of life abundant—in other words, utopia.[16]

The ancient city wall held "chaos at bay" and warded off "inimical spirits," just as the walled medieval city, whose success may have been the initial impetus to modern capitalism, warded off potential enemies. Americans seem to have activated these ancient functions of the wall in shopping malls, which ward off that which is "undesirable." But where the ancient wall served the life of the city, the modern mall serves itself, and privatizes the life of the city into itself. Americans have increasingly chosen to spend their time and money in walled malls instead of in cities, so that by 2003 there were 47,104 malls and shopping centers, a 29 percent increase just since 1990. Sales increased from $706.4 billion in 1990 to $1.277 trillion in 2002.[17] According to a looser measure of sales by the International Council of Shopping Centers, "shopping center-inclined sales" in 2003 amounted to $1,980 trillion, or 76 percent of nonautomotive retail sales in the United States.[18] About 14 percent of the nonagricultural workforce works in shopping malls.

The ancient gods of the city and of the home have not been dispelled by modern materialism, but have been reinstated in the ever-tightening cult of American consumerism. In this new way of worshipping, the organic seasons of nature have metamorphosed into extended indoor shopping seasons, and the ancestor cult transformed from an act of propitiation into a declaration of consumptive "independence." Americans practice consumption with the seriousness of a religion.

Malls represent a vision of utopia in contemporary American society, promising to free Americans from crime, urban blight, and uncertainty. But they do this by alienating people from spontaneous conduct, from voluntary association other than that of a consumer, and ultimately from a public life. As privatized public spaces they rigidly enforce the new American code of controlled and monitored behavior, the "culture of control."[19] They are not only *controlled* but also *controlling* environments. Malls promise that the good life is to be found in the life of goods, but their reality is that they are literal embodiments of the dark side of Thomas More's ambiguous term *utopia*, which suggests both *eutopia*—the good place—and *ou topos*, literally *no place*. They give ample testimony to the benumbed confusion in America that capitalism and democracy are synonymous, and to the continued atrophy of vital democracy.

Similarly, the Airstream city is a highly controlled environment: structurally it keeps poor people out; functionally it is monitored by its own security force, the "blue berets," who police the grounds on motorbikes; culturally it values the "like-minded" organization man, symbolized as much by the high numbers of retired career military personnel in the membership as by the official club songbook and "Wally Byam Creed." One sees virtually no poor, nonwhite, or sick Airstreamers, despite the myth of classless community that permeates the group. The loss of public spaces to private malls, where free speech can be treated as trespassing, raises the question: Just what is a city and how might the city symbolize democracy?

Conclusion: Perishable Democracy

As anyone familiar with American electoral politics and television knows, or as I hope the Airstream cult might illustrate, American culture frequently utilizes powerful symbols of democracy. Yet though these are self-representations of democracy, they rarely *represent* democracy. Rather, they are signs of the reduction of American political life to entertainment. They signify an antidemocratic mass society in which rituals of consumption, mass media, and leisure have largely replaced the cultivation of local, regional, and national public life.

The Vietnam Veterans Memorial stands as a curious exception in contemporary American life in how it has been able to channel powerful sentiments into the serious consideration of democratic values. It does not glorify the war, but it does call forth emotions of loss and of mourning. It raises, for many, the question of the purpose of Vietnam as well as the tangible specter of defeat, qualities that reerupted again as America's war in Iraq quagmired.

It is a symbol wedged between American kitsch sentimentalism and cynical "sound bite" politics, yet it somehow works. It grows out of an aesthetic of minimalism and postmodern "earth art," two vacuous styles that say more about the depletion of the human person in the late twentieth century as the living mediator of culture than about the making of art. Yet it transcends minimalism as a powerful testimony to the significance of the human person, collective memory, and all-too-human death. As earth art it can be seen to resonate with, whether intended or not, the Taoist idea of the "empty container," or that which paradoxically reveals itself in fullness out of its emptiness. As a public monument it provides an uncanny and unique solution to the great difficulty we face at the end of the modern era between rational architectural forms that severely limit the expression of human feeling and the lure of nostalgia to reduce human feelings to kitsch. One also sees in it the potential binding power of the feminine as a welcome and needed dimension of political and cultural self-representation today.

Old-time nationalistic self-representation will no longer do: the catastrophic events of the twentieth century repeatedly showed the dangers of political symbols that lack the capacity for self-examination and self-criticism, just as the disastrous twenty-first-century American war in Iraq has. The new world culture emerging in the American population, bringing the vision of America as microcosm of the world community to a new phase, has to go past the symbols of unquestioning national glory and private self-interest to those of self-critical and mutual responsibility. Yet the capacities for empathic connection, autonomy, and self-criticism, requisite for a healthy self and democratic culture, seem ever increasingly compromised in the electro-kitsch complex busily bodying into being in twenty-first-century America.

If democracy is to be anything other than a brief "mortal splendor" in the longer drama of American culture, it will need to undo the antidemocratic culture the word "Americanism" now communicates and which thoroughly dominates American life. It needs to undo the corporate-dominated, *post-democratic military-industrial-academic-entertainment-sport-food complex*. The great challenge that democracy has always posed in America—to create self-critical autonomous selves embedded within broader community purposes—is one whose survival in an ever more automatic America is questionable.

7

LEM'S MASTER'S VOICE

Decoding Science

Mankind has got rid of all its big predators and we think we're the top of the food cycle, but in fact the viruses are still at the top, and there's very little we can do about them.

—RON ECCLES, DIRECTOR OF THE COMMON COLD CENTER,
CARDIFF, WALES[1]

Nature has neither core nor skin: she's both at once outside and in.

—GOETHE

In his novel *His Master's Voice*, Polish writer Stanislaw Lem poses perplexing questions about the nature of science, life, communication, and cosmology, and most especially about the strange and perverse creatures we humans are. Written in 1967, the book is set in America in the form of a memoir of a mathematician, Peter E. Hogarth, and concerns his work on the "His Master's Voice" project. By setting the novel in America during the cold war, Lem could avoid possible Communist Party censorship, even though the book's message applies as well to the Soviet police state. I want to take the novel as another means of observing the epiphany of big science in American culture.

Through some contingent and crazy beginnings, it becomes known to scientists that a particular band of neutrino radiation from distant space is a nonrandom, repeating code. A group of scientists are secretly gathered together at an abandoned nuclear bomb test site in Nevada to decode the message. Because this event represents the first known communication with extraterrestrial life it is of momentous significance to science and the human race; and since there might be great powers to be tapped, it is of equal importance to the powers that be: hence the secrecy.

As I understand it, the original Polish title, *Głos pana*, means "master's voice," and can be interpreted as ambiguously referring to the voice of God or to the voice of one's personal master or lord. And Lem clearly wants to keep this ambiguity in the title to play on the tension between the message of a civilization so mature that it has entered into the process of universal creation—it is discovered that the code has ever-so-slight life-enhancing physical properties that over the eons would help enhance the planetary conditions for life to emerge—and a civilization so full of itself and its obsession with power that its potentially greatest discovery is placed under the authority of military secrecy. Science is shown to be the servant of two masters, with the expected tragic results. I am not sure whether Lem or his translator introduced "His Master's Voice"—the old RCA logo—into the English translation, but the image of the dog listening to a device beyond its comprehension, yet seemingly understanding, is apt for a wide range of contemporary research and debate—artificial intelligence, genome decoders, Darwinians and "intelligent design" evolutionists, and the philosophy of science.

Lem is saying that we, like the RCA dog, are listeners of something far beyond our comprehension. We hypothesize elaborate and complex theories with the same chances of success as the RCA dog. Hogarth, the mathematician, conveys through his autobiography a portrait of the self-projecting nature of science, showing us how our most advanced understandings and speculative hypotheses are simply a kind of complex Rorschach test response. He shows scientists who collectively embody the delusions of human hubris, seldom doubting the "objectivity" of their projections. In Hogarth's words, "The myth of our cognitive universality, of our readiness to receive and comprehend information absolutely new—absolutely, since extraterrestrial—continues unimpaired, even though, receiving the message from the stars, we did it with no more than a savage who, warming himself by a fire of burning books, the writings of the wisest men, believes that he has drawn tremendous benefit from his find!"[2]

The Kantian dilemma informs a central question raised by this book. Is humanity limited, as Immanuel Kant claimed, to knowing only its own faculties of mind that give form to sensory experience? Or can it go beyond these faculties to the thing-in-itself: the cosmic code? Or, as Lem suggests, do we possess in our faculties "similarities" to objective phenomena that give us the hope of truly knowing those phenomena? In Hogarth's words:

To such questions philosophy and religion are traditionally supposed to supply answers, not the natural scientist, who severs himself from the temptation of trying to divine the motives behind Creation. But here it was just the opposite: the approach of the guesser of motives, so discredited in the historical development of the empirical sciences, became the last hope offered for victory. Granted, the attributing of anthropomorphic motives to the Causer of the properties of the atoms remained methodologically prohibited; but some similarity—even the most remote—between Those Who Sent the code and the code's recipients was more than a fantasy to comfort the mind; it was a hypothesis on whose cutting edge hung the entire Project. And I was certain of this from the first, from the moment I set foot on the HMV compound—certain that a lack of any similarity would render futile all efforts to understand the stellar message. (98)

Hogarth put no stock in the myriads of conjectures about the signal proposed by his colleagues, saying, "all this was borrowed from the poverty stricken repertoire of ideas which civilization, in its current technological form, had at its disposal. These ideas were a reflection—much like the themes of science fiction novels—of society, and of society primarily in its American version . . ." Yet he was convinced that only through a "similarity" to the Senders would it be possible to project something objective out of our anthropomorphism. This is Lem's "Peircean turn," a view of science similar to that proposed by Charles Sanders Peirce, which appears as an alternative to Kant's inward faculty theory of knowledge, or at least confronts the Kantian view. It is by no means an "outward" as opposed to an "inward" view, but rather literally a theory of *insight*.

If we are fashioned from the same stuff as the cosmos then we may be endowed with the capacity for true insight into the nature of the cosmos. Narcissus looked outward to the water and could only see a mirage of the other, his own reflection, tragically. That is also the tragedy of the Kantian view. But insight means that we may be able to use our inward, tempered capacities and experiences to genuinely perceive nature and hypothesize its laws. Anthropomorphism in this sense is not only inescapable, but may also be our surest touchstone to reality, seeing the world through human filters, themselves bodied forth from the world—but only if we understand anthropomorphism as a branch of "mammalism," and of the earlier strata of life actively encoded in our brains.

In Lem's view, hypothesis making is essential to science and is neither simply a linguistic phenomenon nor even a primarily rational process. Following a brief but devastating criticism of positivism, Hogarth launches into an attack on language analysis, and on the underlying rationalism that framed so many philosophical accounts of science in the twentieth century:

I had to laugh, for instance, at the assurance of those who determined that all thought was linguistic. Those philosophers did not know that they were creating a subset of the species, i.e., the group of those not gifted mathematically. How many times in my life, after the revelation of a new discovery, having formulated it so solidly that it was quite indelible, unforgettable, was I obliged to wrestle for hours to find for it some verbal suit of clothes, because the thing had been born, in me, beyond the pale of all language, natural or formal?

I call this phenomenon surfacing. It defies description, because what emerges from the unconscious with difficulty, slowly, finds nests of words for itself; it exists as an entity before it settles inside those nests; yet I can give no indication, no hint, to explain in precisely what form that non- and pre-verbalness appears; it is heralded only by a keen presentiment that the expectation of it will not be in vain. (30–31)

One is again struck with the similarity of Lem's account of "surfacing" and Peirce's theory of "abduction," or hypothesis formation. Peirce articulated a logical theory of abduction as an irreducible mode of inference in addition to deduction and induction. Both Lem and Peirce describe a process that is logical—because it leads to valid results—yet extrarational.[3] Peirce's later description of the process in 1907 sounds very much like Hogarth's:

The whole series of mental performances between the notice of the wonderful phenomenon and the acceptance of the hypothesis, during which the usually docile understanding seems to hold the bit between its teeth and to have us at its mercy, the search for pertinent circumstances and the laying hold to them, sometimes without our cognizance, the scrutiny of them, the dark laboring, the bursting out of the startling conjecture, the remarking of its smooth fitting to the anomaly, as it is turned back and forth like a key in the lock, and the final estimation of its Plausibility, I reckon as composing the First Stage of Inquiry.[4]

Lem/Hogarth and Peirce quite plainly reject the rationalist view of science as limited to conceptual knowledge, and show why *preconceptions*, in the literal sense, are essential to inquiry, however much "the dark laboring" might be denigrated by the clear light of conceptual, verbal rationality.

The entire HMV project, and, to a great extent, the structure of this novel, come about through "surfacing." Two young astrophysicists recorded approximately two years worth of neutrino emissions at Mount Palomar in what turned out to be a worthless experiment. The tapes were then sold to a "physicist manqué," by the name of Swanson, who is a sort of scientific confidence man, and who markets the tapes as random number tables. A lunatic by the name of Dr. Sam Laserowitz—the "Dr." standing for the name Drummond but serving to give him the air of scientific respectability—purchases one copy of these tables. One also thinks Stanislaw Lem for Sam Laserowitz: a man of laser wit!

Laserowitz quickly makes the headlines with the false claim that the spaces between signals represents "Morse code," while independently a statistician charges Swanson with falsifying the tables, because a significant portion of volume two is found to be a perfect duplication of volume one. These stories happen to be published near each other in a newspaper, which happens to be read by a scientist at the Institute for Advanced Study, Dr. Saul Rappaport, and as he puts down the newspaper, "a thought came to him, a thought so queer that it was comical: Laserowitz, taking the sections of silence on the tapes for signals, was without question raving. And yet it was conceivable that at the same time the man could be right, seeing in the tapes a "communication"—if that communication was the very noise! . . . An insane idea, but Rappaport could not rid himself of it."

Rappaport's "insane idea" proves, through his further testing, to be a well-founded hypothesis, and the "Master's Voice" project comes into being. Hence the project is an act of "surfacing": from the perception of the senses, that is, the astronomical observations recorded on tapes, through the intervention of the "dark ones," the con man and the crazy, who, together with Rappaport, make the surfacing possible, to the institution of the project itself. As Hogarth says, "We really have no idea what a multitude of con men and crackpots inhabit the domain that lies halfway between contemporary science and the insane asylum."

Now it is said that art imitates life, but often it seems the other way around, and not only does life seem to imitate art on occasion, but also here is an instance where science imitates art. Consider this excerpt from an article in the *New York Times*, April 8, 2001, that reads as though it was taken right out of *His Master's Voice*:

Dr. Dembski said his rather vague doubts about Darwinism did not take scientific shape until he attended an academic conference in 1988, just after finishing his doctoral thesis. The conference explored the difficulty of preparing perfectly random strings of numbers, which are important in cryptography, in computer science and in statistics. One problem is that seemingly random strings often contain patterns discernible only with mathematical tests. Dr. Dembski wondered whether he could devise a way to find evidence of related patterns in the randomness of nature. Dr. Dembski eventually developed what he called a mathematical "explanatory filter" that he asserted can distinguish randomness from complexity designed by an intelligent agent. He explained this idea in *The Design Inference* (Cambridge University Press, 1998). Dr. Dembski has applied his explanatory filter to the biochemical structures in cells and concluded that blind natural selection could not have created them.

Dembski turned the random numbers game toward "intelligent design," the view embraced by Christians as an alternative to standard scientific theories.

Lem's lunacy model not only finds its echoes decades later in ongoing evolutionary debates concerning whether evolution involves "intelligent design," but is also an accurate insight into pure science. Lem's lunatic beginnings of the project amount to nothing less than abduction, as it really often functions, dark, ominous, "crazy," unwanted, unbidden even, subversively shattering conventional expectations. Conventional science, like conventional religion, will always prefer to put to death the mercurial voice of abduction, if it could. But the real scientific impulse, like the real religious impulse, will always be desirous of learning, of even undergoing a "conversion experience" to a new way of thinking or being. It will echo what physicist Niels Bohr once said to Wolfgang Pauli: "We all agree that your theory is crazy, but is it crazy enough?"

Darwin's theory of natural selection seemed crazy to many when he published *On the Origin of Species* in 1859, but opened up a whole new way of understanding life, which further research has confirmed in great detail. But was it crazy enough? It eventually became normalized in the sciences, to the point that skeptics today—not just religious fundamentalists, who are too crazy—are often regarded as crazy simply for questioning it.

Darwinian theory is by my lights not "crazy enough," so I find the attempts to consider natural design and purposiveness as elements of evolution to be a potential opening in the unquestioning acceptance of Darwinian evolution today. Who knows but that it might lead not only to an overthrow of the currently reigning biological God of Chance but also of religious fundamentalism? That is not what intelligent design adherents want, but if they don't want the peaches, they should stop shaking the tree: they cannot exempt their religious beliefs from criticism.

Perhaps it could even lead to what Peirce described favorably in an 1893 book review as the "Biologos religion":

Doubtless, everybody has, at some time, envied the condition of our domestic animal pets. A mother's love is passionate, physiological, forced upon her. But a man's love for his dog is at once disinterested and voluntary. Though the dog does not reflect much, he does so enough fully to understand his relation to his master. Great comfort he takes in his master's love; but his greatest delight is in the reflection that, despite the man's incomparable and incomprehensible intelligence (of which the dog is quite aware), he is yet neither omniscient nor omnipotent, so that he, dog, is, or may be, positively helpful to the man. Now, the Biologos religion makes of a man God's dog.[5]

Peirce, a practicing mathematician, physicist, and philosopher, and a political conservative, shared with Karl Marx, the political radical, a deep admiration for Darwin's observational abilities as a naturalist, and a sharply critical assessment of his theoretical abilities as leading him to project English political economy falsely onto nature. Marx and Peirce both preechoed, in the nineteenth century, Pyotr Kropotkin's claim that Darwin's theory ignored "mutual aid" as a real and irreducible factor in evolution. Kropotkin is more known as a political anarchist, but also spent five years as a geographer in Siberia, observing nature. He claimed that there is "Mutual Aid" in nature, genuine sociality, *as well as* Darwinian competition. This possibility of noncompetitive sociality was later dismissed by neo-Darwinians, when R. L. Trivers found a means to reduce it to a by-product of rationalized maximization, which he termed "reciprocal altruism." All that derives from the philosophy of Greed is Real, all that is not is reducible to the Greed Matrix.

Peirce claimed that when it came to Darwinism and Aristotelianism, the lion would eventually eat and incorporate the lamb into itself—only in the long run it would be the reacknowledgment of generality as real in the physical sciences after the age of nominalism exhausted itself that would make of a modified Aristotelianism the lion and of Darwinism the lamb to be devoured. Hence he viewed Darwin's as a partial view that ignored other real modalities of evolution. He proposed in his 1891 essay "The Architecture of Theories," that there are three modalities of evolution, that Darwin's corresponded to the modality of *Chance*, but that there was also *Catastrophe* and *Habit*.

Clarence King's nineteenth-century cataclysmic or catastrophe theory of sudden population shift was only one of many interesting challenges to Darwinism that faded as Darwinism became institutionalized and normalized. Stephen Jay Gould and Richard Lewontin's more recent theory of "punctuated equilibria," which challenged Darwin's idea of gradualism—slow changes in populations—can be viewed as a restatement of King's catastrophe theory rather than an original idea. Gould also claimed that one can view biological evolution as Darwinian and cultural evolution as Lamarckian. Some Darwinians were enraged with this claim, yet it seems to me that it merely rattles the cage of Darwinism while completely content to live within it. Gould was a public symptom of the orthodox nature of evolutionary thought in contemporary life, in my view, despite his popular style of writing.

Why should Lamarckian evolution be limited to culture and not our biology as well, especially when one considers how critical nurture is to complete our nature in childhood development? Gould seemed to think that humans physically emerged in cultural darkness, and suddenly used our giant uncultured brains to turn on the Lamarckian light of culture. Doesn't it make more sense to say that our physical evolution into humanity and its defining cultural "placenta" was also increasingly shaped by that very emerging purposiveness itself? The Lamarckian element, as cultural habit, was part of the process, not some empty afterthought, existing solely within ethereal "mind-culture." A century earlier Peirce had argued for a Lamarckian element in evolution, using habit as the modality that corresponds to what he describes as "evolutionary love":

Now it is energetic projaculation (lucky there is such a word, or this untried hand might have been put to inventing one) by which in typical instances of Lamarckian evolution the new elements of form are first created. Habit, however, forces them to take practical shapes, compatible with the structures they affect, and in the form of heredity and otherwise, gradually replaces the spontaneous energy that sustains them. Thus, habit plays a double part; it serves to establish the new features, and also to bring them into harmony with the general morphology and function of the animals and plants to which they belong.

Here is Peirce again, from his 1893 essay "Evolutionary Love":

The *Origin of Species* of Darwin merely extends politico-economical views of progress to the entire realm of animal and vegetable life. The vast majority of our contemporary naturalists hold the opinion that the true cause of those exquisite and marvelous adaptations of nature for which, when I was a boy, men used to extol the divine wisdom, is that creatures are so crowded together that those of them that happen to have the slightest advantage force those less pushing into situations unfavorable to multiplication or even kill them before they reach the age of reproduction. Among animals, the mere mechanical individualism is vastly re-enforced as a power making for good by the animal's ruthless greed. As Darwin puts it on his title page, it is the struggle for existence; and he should have added for his motto: Every individual for himself, and the Devil take the hindmost! Jesus, in his sermon on the Mount, expressed a different opinion.

Here, then, is the issue. The gospel of Christ says that progress comes from every individual merging his individuality in sympathy with his neighbors. On the other side, the conviction of the nineteenth century is that progress takes place by virtue of every individual's striving for himself with all his might and trampling his neighbor under foot whenever he gets a chance to do so. This may accurately be called the Gospel of Greed.

Much is to be said on both sides. I have not concealed, I could not conceal, my own passionate predilection. Such a confession will probably shock my scientific brethren. Yet the strong feeling is in itself, I think, an argument of some weight in favor of the agapastic theory of evolution—so far as it may be presumed to bespeak the normal judgment of the Sensible Heart. Certainly, if it were possible to believe in agapasm without believing it warmly, that fact would be an argument against the truth of the doctrine. At any rate, since the warmth of feeling exists, it should on every account be candidly confessed; especially since it creates a liability to one-sidedness on my part against which it behooves my readers and me to be severally on our guard.[6]

Peirce used the religious language of Christianity here, but he would be the last person to accept anything less than a fully scientific approach. His primary rule for science was: do not block the road of inquiry. His larger claim is that there is real social relation in nature, not reducible to competitive maximizing struggle. As a physicist, mathematician, and founder of semiotics and mathematical logic, he argued that there is real general relation in nature—namely sign-mediation or what he termed "Thirdness"—not reducible to underlying mechanical principles. Reality itself is inherently social, and of the nature of a general sign. Peirce claimed that ultimately, "every evolutionism must in its evolution eventually restore that rejected idea of law as a reasonableness energizing in the world."[7] Darwin's "Gospel of Greed" must give way to a fuller account inclusive of general social relation. Consider in this context the Gaia hypothesis, associated with James Lovelock and Lynn Margulis, the idea that the earth is a living organism, that all life is an interdependent whole. Lovelock accepted Darwin's theory of evolution, saying that Darwin would like Gaia, and that Gaia extends natural selection.

In my opinion the concept of Gaia does extend natural selection, but more than Darwin—or maybe even Lovelock—would allow. Darwin allows that competition is real, but not cooperation. Neo-Darwinists reduce cooperation to sublimated competition, to "reciprocal altruism." But cooperation, Kropotkin's "mutual aid," is a real fact of nature as well. Darwinism seems to hold that nature is antisocial. But why can't nature involve competition, and also genuine intraspecies and interspecies sociality? As evolutionary biologist Margulis said, "Life did not take over the globe by combat, but by networking."[8] Margulis has argued that many bacteria function cooperatively as "chimera"—diverse types of bacteria working together to create a larger entity that functions as though a unified creature—and that such symbiogenesis is the major cause of new speciation, not, as commonly assumed, mutation. This is an example of what she means by networking.

There is a fascinating Gaia novel from before Lovelock and Margulis's work, by Lem, called *Solaris* (1961). I first heard of Lem through Solaris, not the novel, but the space rock band I joined way back in a universe very far away, as a graduate student in Chicago. Then later I read the novel, then later I read about Gaia theory and realized that Lem the fiction writer had beaten scientists Lovelock and Margulis to the idea of the living planet. Like all alien life forms in sci-fi, Solaris is the alienated view of earth: We live on a planet that is a living organism; we are the earth come alive to self-reflection.

Solaris concerns a planet that is an intelligent organism, which incarnates beings from the memories and fantasies of the astronauts who are exploring it. The dream of journeying to a distant living planet is revealed as another symbol of our alienation from our own planet and inner life: fetalized astronauts, unable to breathe in outer space without their mechanico-umbilicus, aliens on Solaris, the planet of life. The water of its seas comes to meet your hand when you reach out to it.

Lem projects the living earth in alien form as the planet Solaris. C. P. Snow once wrote of "The Two Cultures," meaning the split between science and the humanities. David Lavery has updated the distinction, claiming that the "two cultures" prominent in the contemporary imagination are those of space versus earth, of those who would flee our swirling globe of life in a dream of unlimited progress and those who accept earth-limits as a condition of life. The former condition, space-age consciousness, manifests not only in literal technicalism but also in a wide variety of "spaciness."[9]

Why would people think that removing oneself from the planet that gave us life, that is literally incarnated in the very structure of our being, would likely mean progress, improvement, freedom? We live on a planet that is a living organism: we are the earth come alive to self-reflection, more, to continued self-creation. Touch anything living and you are being touched by Gaia, the living earth.

Scientists Lovelock and Margulis and novelist Lem described in their different ways what that Apache shaman I mentioned earlier, Stalking Wolf, wandering an amazing journey through the Amazon last century experienced through an epiphany at a unique waterfall called "life": the interconnectedness of all life and the living universe.[10]

The Devilish Pursuits of Dr. Einstein

I like Heaven for the climate, Hell for the company.
—BUMPER STICKER

Lem's inclusion of the fantastic within scientific inquiry and of the dark forces at work not only in the human psyche but also in the workings of science, is reminiscent of Dino Buzzati's short story "Appointment with Einstein." There, Albert Einstein, walking through the woods of the Institute for Advanced Study, imagines himself in the midst of curved space, and begins to wax proud with the power of man to comprehend the nature of the universe. The scene suddenly shifts and Einstein encounters a gas station attendant, who asks him for a match. The gas station attendant turns out to be the Angel of Death, the devil Iblís, come to take his life.

Einstein pleads for a delay, telling Iblís that he has almost finished a very important project. He is given more time, two delays in fact. Finally, Einstein appears at the appointed time for his death, and tells the Angel of Death that he is ready to go with him, that his work is completed, that "in a sense the universe is now in order." The Iblís gas station attendant suddenly breaks into a knee-slapping laugh and tells Einstein to go home, that his real purpose was to help Einstein finish his project. When Einstein quizzically asks why his work mattered to Iblís, the devil responds, "To me, it meant nothing. But downstairs the big devils run the show. They say your discoveries have already been extremely useful. You're not to blame for it, but it's true. Whether you're pleased or not, dear professor, Hell has profited greatly from your ideas."

Buzzati is suggesting that the good Albert Einstein in his pure research was yet part of the zeitgeist of the twentieth century, helping to open the doors through which greater, darker powers could pour through. Historian of science Gerald Holton has said concerning Einstein, "there exists a mutual adaptation and resonance of the innovative mind with portions of the total set of metaphors current at a given time."[11] Despite this statement on the connections of minds to their times, Holton tries to show how feeble the attempts to link relativity theory to movements in twentieth-century art and culture have been. He convincingly shows why cubism, for example, is not related to relativity theory, originally termed *Invariantentheorie* by Einstein, but simply to a nontechnical understanding of the term *relativity* that is at odds with *invariant theory*. Yet when we consider the revolutionary forces exploding all across the cultural spectrum in the first two decades of the twentieth century—the displacement of perspective and figure in Picasso; the displacement of rational ego in Freud, or of rational economy in Thorstein Veblen; the displacement of tonality in composer Arnold Schoenberg; the displacement of even the facade of humane values in World War I—we see that *Invariantentheorie*, or what came, through Max Planck, to be known as relativity theory, not only displaced the Newtonian world but also was in resonance with the revolution of displacement.

It is not mere chance, in my opinion, that Harlequin the trickster was to appear in Picasso's paintings at this time, or that Picasso would be so absorbed with the image of the Minotaur, the wildly sensual and unpredictable monster who lived within the rational cage of the labyrinth, destroying and devouring.

Picasso himself was both: Minotaur who devoured whole styles of painting, whose great released and restless energies produced an incomparable body of work; Harlequin who was many things at once, the trickster who dared the viewer to fit him into a frame of understanding, even while juggling the frames. Perhaps Einstein was right and God does not play dice with the universe, but that doesn't stop the devils from a good game now and then. And we should not forget the God who gambled with Satan over Job, betting that no matter what chaos they brought to poor Job, he would not curse God. Einstein must have forgotten this older Gambling God, who was not yet completely distinct from Satan, evil, chaos, and contingency. As Job put it, "Shall we receive good at the hand of God, and shall we not receive evil?"

In 1905, as Einstein was publishing his theory of relativity, as Picasso was beginning to displace noses on the face and discover cubism, Henry Adams wrote that remarkable letter to Henry Osborn Taylor: ". . . it will not need another century or half century to turn thought upside down. Law . . . would . . . give place to force. Morality would become police. Explosives would reach cosmic violence. Disintegration would overcome integration."[12]

A half century later, after Hitler and Stalin, after Guernica and Auschwitz and Dresden and Hiroshima, after Nazi scientists and technicians were effortlessly absorbed into the ranks of their American and Russian colleagues to continue their researches, thought indeed had been turned upside down. These were not moral questions for the American military establishment after World War II, because only expedient force mattered. Morality had become police, as it already long since had in the Soviet Stalinist Union, and big science only too gladly pimped itself to military purpose and money. By January 1955, a half-century after Adams's prediction, the United States and the USSR were actively polluting the biosphere with gigantic hydrogen bomb "tests," spewing deadly global radioactivity in bombs too powerful to be useful. Yet despite the replacement of the human ends of life with the mechanisms of "cosmic violence," with mechanism itself transforming human ends to its means, there remain many happy souls who believe in the sanctity of scientific/technological advance. Eighty years after Henry Adams's letter and after all that happened in between, Gerald Holton could still write in all seriousness: "The marriage of science and technology is undoubtedly permanent and beneficial to each. . . . It is not merely a question of the commonplace observation that our physical burdens have lightened, farm life has been transformed, and medicine improved, but of the direct and indirect influence that the results and attitudes of scientific/technological advance have had in extending the very conception of *human rights*. Since Thomas Hobbes, to whom the essence of such rights was merely the freedom to eat and be eaten, moral and legal rights have increased greatly."[13]

Holton sees very clearly the role of scientific/technical advance in extending "the very conception of human rights," but he is totally blinded to the dark side of scientific/technical advance as radically extending the possibilities for "human wrongs." Even so commonplace an observation as "our physical burdens have lightened" does not free us from *The Unbearable Lightness of Being*, to use Milan Kundera's title, of a world that can function as a frictionless, and feelingless, and meaningless plane through the powers of technology. Farm life has indeed been transformed by scientific rationality, but not toward the enhancement of the biosphere. Quite the opposite: rationalization and centralization of livestock and poultry have increased risks for a global bird flu pandemic, for antibiotic-resistant bacteria, for new toxic *E. coli* contaminations, mad cow disease, and a host of other inhabitants of Pandora's box yet to emerge. Medicine has improved, but so has the marketing of a medicated, increasingly obese society.

The possibility that scientific rationality, cut free from its moral obligations to human life and life in general, might be acting as a self-aggrandizing and destructive force, as an alienated voice of the power system, of the machine of modernity, seems to be beyond Holton's ken. It takes a fantasist such as Lem to offer a more realistic appraisal of the situation, twenty years before Holton's remarks:

We have wholly abandoned ourselves to the mercy of technological progress. The roles are now reversed: humanity becomes, for technology, a means, an instrument for achieving a goal unknown and unknowable. . . . The imagination of humanity has become, in a sense, frozen in place transfixed by the vision of atomic annihilation—which, however, has been sufficiently evident to both sides for them to abort its materialization. The fascination with scenarios of the thermonuclear apocalypse, written by strategists and scientific advisory councils, has paralyzed minds to such an extent that no attention is paid to other—and who knows if not ultimately more dangerous—possibilities hidden in progress. (124)

Lem's Hogarth then goes on in 1967 to predict the use of space-based missiles—what became known as "star wars" or "strategic defense initiative" in Reagan's 1980s. SDI was to be part of a strategy of "indirect economic attrition," of deflecting the Soviet economy, which was already well on its way to collapse, regardless of how America chose to continue to waste its money.

What lies in our minds and is projected out through the HMV project? Two groups of the scientists, biochemists and biophysicists, independently discover that a carbon- and silicon-based life form, a gelatinous blob, can be created from the signal. The life form, which one group terms "frog eggs" and the other calls satanically "Lord of the Flies," lives on internally generated micronuclear reactions, and it is discovered that in sufficient quantity it can produce "tele-detonations," or detonations at a distance from the object. This would seem to be an extension of quantum mechanics and its peculiar finding that minute particles can be described as being in two places at once. But here, it occurs in a living being. Once this fact becomes known to the research group as a whole, the governmental informers embedded in the project call Washington, and the military swoops in and takes total control of the project.

If this sounds too far-fetched a scenario, remember again the whitewashing of the records of Nazi scientists and technicians by the OSS and later the CIA in Operation Paperclip, and Edward Teller helping to discredit Robert Oppenheimer. Consider those scientists who worked for the Atomic Energy Commission (AEC) in the fifties and sixties who were threatened with dismissal or who were discredited when they attempted to make known their results on the lethal effects of nuclear bomb testing on thousands of American children. Scientist John Gofman, who researched effects of radiation at the government's Livermore Laboratory and whose research showed that there was no minimum threshold for exposure, was told by Congressman Chet Holifeld, an apparatchik of the Atomic Energy Commission, "Listen, there have been others who have tried to cross the AEC before you. We got them and we'll get you."[14]

Mirroring the Modern Soul

The foam is not cruel, neither does it crawl. The state of mind which attributes to it these characters of a living creature is one in which the reason is

unhinged by grief. All violent feelings have the same effect. They produce in us a falseness in all our impressions of external things, which I would generally characterize as the "Pathetic Fallacy."
—JOHN RUSKIN[15]

Get your facts first, then you may distort them as you please.
—MARK TWAIN

Lem reveals for us the mind of technical civilization, behind which lies the invisible dictator of POWER, ready to assume direct infantile control at will. As the Pentagon officials discover that the tele-detonations become randomly located and unpredictable at larger, bomblike sizes by occasionally blowing themselves up, Hogarth understands that even the "secret" HMV project was a mere facade of a far more secret enterprise.

Big science frequently serves as the veneer of the power complex, just as the opportunistic actor character in Heinrich Mann's novel *Mephisto* appears to be a true manifestation of German *Kultur*, but in actuality is a pawn, a fly to be crushed at the whim of the power-mad Nazis when his usefulness is over. Lem describes the "rational husbandry of scientists," based on the metaphor of how pigs were trained in the nineteenth century to hunt for truffles and were tossed acorns for their efforts, like so many research grants: "Availing himself appropriately of outlets here and there, the scientist-pig—explained Rappaport—can then, without further distraction, devote himself to the hunting of truffles, for the benefit of the rulers but to the undoing of humanity, as indeed the new stage in history will demand of him" (61). Ah yes, the undoing of humanity, that ultimate goal secreted beneath the veneer of the purposeless universe installed by the modern myth of the machine universe.

No artist works on the HMV project, possibly because no artist's findings could enhance the power complex. But what if a composer were to decipher the musical equivalent of Bach from the incredibly advanced Senders? What if the great code of life is more like a song, a fantasia, a pouring forth of beauty more than a computer code? What if the Senders were to decipher our message installed on the Voyager space probe? What would the Senders think of a civilization that sends Chuck Berry and Bach, as we did? The Senders would find our science incredibly primitive, perhaps no more advanced than single-cell organisms are to human bodies. But would the same be true of Bach? Or could they, from Bach or Berry, become truly aware of the human body in a way that the mere diagrams etched on the information disk could never begin to reveal? Does science render piecemeal what art bodies forth whole?

As Lem puts it: "The synthesis of Frog Eggs was preceded by the tearing, from the code, of its elements, which were then assigned atomic and stereochemical 'meanings.' There was a sort of vandalism in this, as if on the basis of *Moby-Dick* one were to begin slaughtering whales and rendering their blubber" (129). Written well in advance of the human genome project, *His Master's Voice* nevertheless draws attention to how a similar vandalism may be at work in that decipherment project. Although scientists have now mapped out the basic "notes" of the genome, what if they are missing the melodies, the harmonies, and rhythms that might be involved in it? What if there are meaningful patterns, involving "nonmeaningful" individual genes in ways similar to how blubber analysis cannot comprehend *Moby-Dick*? The human genome as blubber analysis?

One reading of the formless silicon blob of life with radioactive characteristics is that the two groups of scientists only understood so much of the cosmic message as to be able to create a mirror image of the modern soul. The modern soul, with its silicon-based computer mind and nuclear bomb body, is a composite of chance and calculation. It is an antisoul, being the antithesis of that pouring forth spontaneity that marks real soul. The great reality of the modern mechanical universe is its fiction of soullessness. Modern culture was the attempt to replace life with rational mechanism, an apocalyptic delusion of that crafty degenerate ape that is humanity, braining itself out of existence.[16]

From the observation of the skies, so central historically to the establishment of science and of that increasingly abstracting consciousness, there arose the idea of a clockwork universe ticking away, devoid of soul, accidentally producing life and consciousness. The living cosmos, which ethnographic and archaeological evidence suggests informs the lives of all aboriginal peoples—and in my opinion the very evolution into humanity—becomes anathema. Life becomes an accident, and reasonableness unreal.

The shapeless nuclear-silicon fabrication of the scientists is precisely the incarnation of antilife that is the terrible secret of "virtual reality," whether made literally in Silicon Valley—which only emerged after this novel was written—or in its broadest sense. And perhaps the ultimate physical realization of the rational, scientific soul-substitute is abstracted radioactivity, or what I would prefer to characterize as "cosmic shit." The cult of twentieth-century scientism is perhaps best symbolized by the image of radioactivity, the scientistic *Portrait of Dorian Gray* in a white lab coat. Call it sci-kitsch. To all appearances the scientist dispassionately unlocks the secret of the atom, but the portrait in reality is a human creature only too ready to surrender to raw Power, to all-too-human Power, all the while playing, like a rational infant, in its own cosmic fecal material. In its organic context of the sun interacting with the earth, radioactivity is, indeed, an essential source for life. But it assumes a wholly different appearance when taken as an idealized power symbol of twentieth-century science and technology.

What if radioactivity, seen so frequently in the twentieth century as the key to unlocking the riddle of the universe, is, in fact, a cosmic by-product, or cosmic fecal material? It is not at all surprising to me that our age, so rooted as it is in the cult of antilife, so devoted to the principles of the inorganic machine, of the machine of political totality, of the BIG SYSTEM of lifeless form or the pure chaos of formless life, expressed in the dominant styles of art, philosophy, morality, science, and economy of the twentieth century, would bring to physical manifestation and spiritual elevation precisely that substance that in its *abstracted* context either cancers life or destroys it outright.

D. H. Lawrence cut right through the hubris of modern scientism and its claims to omniscience:

How gibbering man becomes, when he is really clever, and thinks he is giving the ultimate and final description of the universe! Can't he see that he is merely describing himself, and that the self he is describing is merely one of the more dead and dreary states that man can exist in? When man changes his state of being, he needs an entirely different description of the universe, and so the universe changes its nature to him entirely. Just as the nature of our universe is entirely different from the nature of the Chaldean cosmos. The Chaldeans described the Cosmos as they found it: Magnificent. We describe the universe as we find it: mostly void, littered with a certain number of dead moons and unborn stars, like the back yard of a chemical works.

Is our description true? Not for a single moment, once you change your state of mind: or your state of soul. It is true for our present deadened state of mind. Our state of mind is becoming unbearable. We shall have to change it. And when we have changed it, we shall change our description of the universe entirely. We shall not call the moon Artemis, but the new name will be nearer to Artemis than to a dead lump or an extinct globe. We shall not get back to the Chaldean vision of the living heavens. But the heavens will come to life again for us, and the vision will also express the new men that we are.[17]

Modern life: "one of the more dead and dreary states that man can exist in." That phrase seems to run counter to the whole lively sensationalism of the modern enterprise, of the excitement world of speed and telecommunications, until one can see how technology has functioned to shield us from direct experience, from self-originated experience. Our world is one in which knowledge has displaced awareness in everyday life, in which the vast enlargement of the mechanical and automatic aspects of life have tended to displace the spontaneous and autonomous through the cornucopia of virtual substitutes spawned by the power system.

Suppose commodified radioactivity, as abstracted Power Symbol, is the human embodiment of Cosmic Hate, and the principle of life, in its purest manifestation, is the bodying forth of relation, of Cosmic Love, of Peirce's "Evolutionary Love." Existence, as we know too well, is "impure," and must necessarily hold within it admixtures of both principles: corrosives and connectives. But there are those exceptional moments when the bindings are loosed and a flash of Hate or Love suddenly transilluminates the social scrim with a "power surge" of blinding intensity. Such, it seems to me, is the story of the twentieth century; a great moment out of time, enlightened by the power of a thousand suns of darkness, ruled by the generals of blind particulars, dominated by the science of secrecy. It was Henry Adams's prophetic insight come true. It was the perfecting of that inverted goal of Greco-Judaic-Christian idealized love: The apocalyptic longing to tear apart to put together, whose legacy we are now living.

Lem's scientists, as Hogarth's "notes from the underground" reveal, discovered the "mojo" of modern life. If I may reinterpret Marx, the "natural philosophers," or alchemists, only *interpreted* the world in their various searches to make gold from lead; the point, however, is to *change* it, and this the scientists did. They made pure abstracted shit, and believed they had finally deciphered the cosmic source: the shapeless silicon homunculus, the globular merging Mr./Ms. Microsofty, the ultimate modern material of power: the milk and sperm of human hate, each his/her own slithering little nuclear bomb!

Evolutionary Love: An Energizing Reasonableness?

Almost forgetting for the moment all thoughts of Moby Dick, we now gazed at the most wondrous phenomenon which the secret seas have hitherto revealed to mankind. A vast pulpy mass, furlongs in length and breadth, of a glancing cream-colour, lay floating on the water, innumerable long arms radiating from its centre, and curling and twisting like a nest of anacondas, as if blindly to clutch at any hapless object within reach. No perceptible face or front did it have; no conceivable token of either sensation or instinct; but undulated there on the billows, an unearthly, formless, chance-like apparition of life. And with a low sucking it slowly disappeared again.

—HERMAN MELVILLE, *Moby-Dick*

So is Lem saying in *His Master's Voice* that the universe is suffused with Love and infused with Hate? What is the relation of Love and Evil in *HMV*? Lem seems to be implying that the evolution of the universe tends toward universal communication, and that the substance of this universal Voice is life itself, considered as incarnate love or living relation. But he leaves us hanging with the possibility that we can never know enough to break out of our human enclosures.

I submit that the universe is an ongoing act of self-creation and self-renewal, and that the purport of life is not simply to reproduce genes and species, but to further living reasonableness. Material evolution is more than a Gospel of Greed, it also involves genuine social relation as a dynamic, Peirce's evolutionary love. Material evolution is in this sense involved in general evolution, in the development of real generals. Therefore all life arrives in potential, if it is not destroyed first or if it does not destroy itself, at the developmental point where it begins to self-control its destiny, and to enter into active participation in the ongoing creation of the universe.

In her "space fiction" novel *Shikasta*, Doris Lessing describes this as "the Necessity," that universal development to which all—including beings that could be considered as gods relative to humans—are subject. When this process reaches maturity, the life form becomes the universal act of continuing creation. Projected onto an advanced civilization, this means that such a civilization gives voice to the creative process in universal form. In other words, as Lem shows so clearly, such a civilization sends out waves of life-creating and life-sustaining properties. But then, even at our relatively infantile state of science, why can't we do this here on earth?

Why has the entire history of human civilization—the history of history itself—been the complete opposite, the devouring of the sustaining life-environment by possessive expansion? The archaeological record is replete with devastated landscapes after agriculture is introduced. And today globalized civilization ravages the biosphere unabated. Why has civilization thus far taken *The Gift of Life* as a thing to be *taken*, possessively, rather than the medium in which to participate in the fantastic epiphany of life giving?

The direct participation in incessant creation is precisely the way of the hunter-gatherers, who live centered in the intelligence of the animals and plants, and of the totality of the ecological mind that has sustained us. We became human through such a way of life, centered in attunement to surrounding life. How did we lose it? How did we reach a point where we can imagine its virtues in a cosmically advanced future, while forgetting it was the way of our evolutionary past—and remains, as Paul Shepard noted, embedded in our very bodies? The aliens who would save us simply reveal our own alienation from the very conditions of the living earth that bodied us forth into being, attuned to and participant in the ongoing creation of the universe. It is all already here, alive yet, but for how long?

Between the two "masters" in Lem's book lies the whole question of life: must life inevitably give way to entropy—or to its human equivalent—evil and death? Or do evil and death, and entropy, play some necessary part in the transcendent drama of life? The words of Boris Pasternak in *Dr. Zhivago* reveal a deep insight into that "glassy essence" of humankind and cosmos, which remained opaque to all except Hogarth on the HMV project:

Re-shaping life! People who can say that have never understood a thing about life— they have never felt its breath, its heartbeat—however much they have seen or done. They look on it as a lump of raw material that needs to be processed by them, to be ennobled by their touch. But life is never a material, a substance to be molded. If you want to know, life is the principle of self-renewal, it is constantly renewing and re-making and changing and transfiguring itself.[18]

The great neutrino beam is not only capable of creating life but also of feeding the spirit. The story of the "His Master's Voice" project shows how the confrontation of human fallibility with the Great Code of Life brings to the surface all the latent and manifest evil of civilized modern man. If only the human genome and cloning researchers could have read Lem. Consider genome decoder J. Craig Ventner, whose research team recently created a complete synthetic bacterial genome, and in the process hid "watermarks," actually "signatures" of their names and the institute in the genetic material. What should one call this: micro-brand name life? Or consider how agribusinesses such as Monsanto have genetically altered cash crops, recombining genes using viruses and bacteria, while gerrymandering the laws not only to patent life for profit, but to release a potential Pandora's box without anyone knowing the consequences. Life is never a mere material meant to be molded to human purpose. That was the "progressive" idea from which agricultural civilization first sprang, and that modern civilization has sought to perfect. It has dominated modern life and found expression in Kant's philosophy and the HMV project, and revealed itself in our time to be quite simply wrong. Evolutionary history suggests the opposite direction both as our past and as our destiny. We childlike apes evolved through molding ourselves to the intelligible web of life in which we were immersed. We remain the "substance" to be molded to the deeper designs of life, whose reasonableness is not simply "in" us, but which also does issue forth through us. We are but one manifestation of the ongoing cosmic epiphany.

The arrogance of modern materialist science, of the domination of modern and not so modern civilized man by the power complex, the tendency to surrender all control to faceless bureaucratic forces—to military secrecy, to disciplinary arrogance, to anthropomorphic narcissism, to individual self-aggrandizement and raw institutional power—all are stripped of their veneer of respectability and prestige. What emerges from the HMV project is the realization that the interpretation of the Code will be the task of generations, that the interpretation of the Code is part of its cosmic transformative message, feeding the human spirit even as the neutrino rays "feed" primitive planetary atmospheres and oceans with their life-creating properties.

Religions are born out of such vision, and when vital provide new perceptions into the nature of life. But not all visions are clear: some distort the fantastic nature of reality, many hyperbolize it, and some even earnestly deny it. An opiate may serve to induce visions, but as Marx observed, these are mere pipe dreams that obscure that genuine nature of human suffering. The ways that humans suffer and celebrate experience are aspects of human existence rooted in our very signifying nature. And the religious impulse—of wonder and transformation—is also rooted in human nature and was crucial to the very evolution of our physical human being.

We were made to marvel in wonder in the mature ecological mind that completed our de-matured primate selves. We wandered from that wonder when we changed to controlling our sustenance through agriculture and through human-centered consciousness. We began to abstract Gods and religions rooted in God abstractions, substituting our ideas for the direct encounter with ecological mind. We fashioned a world without limit under our progressive control . . . in our minds, in our de-matured primate minds. We became Narcissus, blinded to the greater world beyond our own image.

The way of religions is toward belief, and when beliefs are established the first victim is usually the religious impulse. Religions typically fear to suffer their own possible transformation, out of habitude. Sooner or later, religions kill precisely that which gave them birth, the self-transcending religious impulse, thereby providing for their own demise. Yet the source of the religious impulse is self-transcending life itself, the living quick, embodied in every single creature. Oh yes, the laws of the material universe govern the living creature. But there is more to life than that. There is creation, the spontaneous bodying into being, manifesting in every single living creature in its singleness, utilizing and transforming the material laws in the mystery of creation. This is the living stuff of which the religious impulse is made.

How can the sciences or religions not see the reality of creation, of a universe possessed of genuine novelty, a living universe still in an active process of creation, its laws still evolving? To religious moles blinded by authority conventions, "creation" is as finished and dead as it is for scientistic head-in-the-sand ostriches, blinded by science conventions, who think the big clock was already wound and is just ticking down. A recent finding by a team of astrophysicists suggests otherwise: that the basic laws of physics are undergoing development.[19]

The world teams with transformation, and what is the cycle of life and death—and the incredible variescence of life itself—if not a testimony to the mysterious transformative and illuminative nature of nature? It is this trans-illuminative essence that the religious impulse feels, dreams, envisions, and attempts to body forth, a *transilluminative essence* in which we feel the greatest resonance, precisely because we are incarnations of its laws, and for which we feel the greatest longing, because our tendencies to habitude and self-enclosed greed and hubris so frequently obscure life's transformative nature.

The stuff of which the universe is made is illuminative, not simply in the modern materialist sense of glowing gas balls or even in the rationalist "enlightenment" sense. It is illuminative in its tending toward living relation. If this sounds hopelessly anthropomorphic it is, as all human conceptions and modes of expression must inescapably be. But we dreamy conjecturing apes are of the stuff from which the universe is made, and therefore we can see the universe objectively, not despite our anthropomorphism, but because of it. As Peirce put it: "Must we not say that . . . there is an energizing reasonableness that shapes phenomena in some sense, and that this same working reasonableness has molded the reason of man into something like its own image?"[20]

We are creatures of habit, who see *through* our habits, not merely with them. The illuminative, which sporadically shows itself to us in dreams and dramatic experience, irradiates our habits, dangerously. Those who can incorporate and body forth the illumination are subtilized and enlarged in their human capacities. But those who fail to humanize creation can be destroyed by it; the truth sometimes hurts, and beauty can kill, as Narcissus tragically discovered. Change the world to a Narcissistic mirror of humankind, and you go the way of Narcissus: kerplunk!

From the Camera to the Picture

Science Finds, Industry Applies, Man Conforms
—MOTTO OF THE 1933 CHICAGO WORLD'S FAIR

Science without conscience is the ruin of the soul.
—RABELAIS

The rise of modern science was the expansion of the mechanical mythos, incarnating initially in the clock, and through its avatars in science, technology, industrial capitalism, and the modern progressive worldview. It would be difficult to overestimate the extent to which timepieces became the cultural icons of the emerging scientific—mechanical—nominalistic worldview.[21] The heavens became a vast dead, ticking timepiece, and all life, including us, but accidental cogs in the clockworks. Was this science false then? No. In my opinion the development of modern science involved the discovery of precise truths about the universe, achieved at the cost of losing other realities: of qualitative experience, of general signification, of reasonableness as more than a purposive clock.

Between the fourteenth and seventeenth centuries space and time and the very fabric of the Western mind became nominalized. Not only the heavens, but also the practice of life became increasingly bound by the clock; regularity for the machines required regularity of the workers. Organic time gave way to rational time.

Science becomes the unacknowledged measure of our own minds, and science says that our own minds are unreal. The polarity of inner world and outer world is rendered into a dichotomy, soul is sundered from thing, and the ghost in the machine becomes the basis of modern consciousness. Science-technology-culture bodies forth its vast mega-self-portrait of Dorian Gray—Narcissus: an outward look of packaged "progress," combined with inward suicidal corruption.

Yes, Peirce claimed that the prime directive for science was, "Do not block the road of inquiry." Yet he little knew how twisted this maxim would become in the twentieth century, when its variants would be used as excuses to open Pandora's box over and over. Even inquiries whose validity rests in an indefinite self-correcting future must be based in a precarious present whose prime directive is to give life to the future. When inquiry violates that directive, it seems to me that it must be held accountable to allow its own life to continue into the indefinite future. A science that would put its inquiries above life, risking the extermination of human and other forms of life, is unacceptable. What's the big rush?

If "pure" scientists and sci-techs want to build theoretical autos without brakes, let them be the ones to drive them, as fast as their inquiries will take them. Except that their abdication of consequences—as though concern with the consequences of one's conduct is the job of others—amounts collectively to a crime against humanity, worse, against life.

To consider unleashing uncontrollable powers from Pandora's box as "inquiry" and the means of controlling those powers, or not releasing them, as "blocking the road of inquiry," is a stupid way of spelling suicide. The spell of sci-tech has so mesmerized the world that globalizing consumption capitalism is racing to destroy the living earth, as though we humans are not incarnations of the living earth.

Technology as a means can serve a purpose. But technology as an end, as an unacknowledged system requirement, is intrinsically an alienation, a usurping of the good life by the "efficient" life of automatism. Sci-tech is and has been involved in capitalism from early on. Peirce saw capitalism as a "Philosophy of Greed," but idealized science such that he ignored its actual involvement in capitalism and the larger power complex of which capitalism is a part.

Modern mechanical science emerged as a half-truth, a powerful half-truth discovering precise half-truths about the universe. But it was based on a fundamental lie, in denying the reality of an ongoing, self-creating, intelligible universe. The continued overexpansion of the mechanical, in the guise of the pursuit of Truth AT ANY COST, eventually involves the elimination of life. The mechanical mythos is the automatic side of life projected onto the totality of life. As such, it is death. It is the death of the spontaneity that is the human soul, of the spontaneity that is in life itself. Truth is not rarified, in general. It is all around us, all of the time. Or, rather, in Peirce's sense, we're in it all the time. Scientific truth, in its specialized idleness, may be the realm of rarified truth. In this I agree with Peirce's distinguishing theory from practice. But the age of scientific innocence is over, and the death-drive telos animating modern science needs to be part of the awareness of practicing scientists, in my opinion. The sciences, as well as globalizing civilization, simply need to grow up.

Mother Earth vanished in modern materialism, literally. Scientific materialism is rooted in a conception of the universe as basically composed of dead matter in motion, out of which life springs by chance, yet the word *materialism* springs from the life-giving capacity that defines a mother, and by analogy, the shoot-producing trunk of a tree, the mater. Until contemporary techno-science culture can put "mater" back in "materialism," can rediscover that indeed the universe is a perfusion of living signs, not a dead tick-tock machine, we will live out this murderous-suicidal endgame of nominalism, increasingly removed from self-originated experience by a veil of machines. That is, of course, the secret teleology of antiteleological modern clock culture.

William Blake was right in how he pictured Isaac Newton: with supple body and mind, focused precisely upon the ratio, but all bent-over and ignoring the greater surrounds. That is how we moderns appear to aboriginals, all focus-vision, ignoring the advantages of traditional wide-angle vision, of looking from the entire peripheral field instead of focusing on objects within it. Wide-angle vision is the gateway to participation consciousness, of putting oneself in the picture instead of being a spectator of it. What would wide-angle scientific vision be?

The suicidal camera of modern consciousness has literally focused us out of the world, transforming us into spectators at the carnival of life, unable to touch it, to walk in it. The originals participated in it and were aware of the fantastic nature of life far more deeply.

The universe used to be alive, and death was the great mystery. Then the living universe was killed by the Great Machine universe, which made life the great mystery and lifelessness the taken-for-granted.

This modern way of seeing things, this myth of the machine that has dominated the modern outlook, will be supplanted, if not by auto-destruction by one that rediscovers the living nature of the universe—the inner subjectivity of nature. I mean by this that the continued growth of science will involve coming to terms with mindlike or soul-like qualities in nature and not solely in us. Such a view will be realism. And animism. I hunch that such an outlook will involve coming to see the evolution of life as more like a cosmic fantasia than a cosmic machine, a cosmic fantasia that involves the machine-like universe of modern materialism but is not ultimately reducible to it, a cosmic bodying-forth fountain fantasia. Such an outlook might be called fantastic realism.[22]

That "reasonableness energizing in the universe," as Peirce put it, means that it has also been energizing us into our human being. Such a view is, if anything, cosmic-centric, from my view. In a world in which reasonableness was banished from the cosmos in the name of science, except as an accidental epicycle, such a view seems to me to represent an interesting alternative.

Which is worse: to be anthropocentric or mechanico-centric? The modern mechanical universe and its dead moving matter; its amped-up, electronic updates of Cartesian water-statues; its pretensions to explaining reasonableness as reducible to computation; its utter inability to grasp creation, spontaneity, as true endogenous capacities of reasonableness, as the very spring of reasonableness, all strike me as infantile. Given a forced choice I would prefer to be anthropocentric, because anthropos is at least a live, sensing, imaging, suffering, breathing being. But anthropos is but a participant in the much larger community of life, through which it finds its destiny. We evolved through attunement to this community of life, through its ecological mind, and retain in our deepest bio-semiotic wellsprings that animate mind through which we evolved and from which we have regressively contracted in the civilizational and modern ages.[23]

In the form in which it evolved into its physical being, such a being could not countenance burning forests simply for commodity gain, for that being evolved in a greater-than-human world to which it needed to attune itself. Only by relieving it of its original awareness and attunements could it reach a state in which killing-gain could replace its habitat-relation. Such relief was originally provided by civilization, later radically amplified by the mechanical-scientific worldview, now perfected into the complete substitution of real life by virtual "living," mistakenly called virtual reality.

Such a view can now countenance burning not only mother forest, who gave us life, but also Mona Lisa and Moby-Dick, genuine ripe fruits of civilization. It claims—as a neuroscientist recently put it to me—that they are replaceable parts in a replaceable universe, as though a life is replaceable! This is rational madness, and is indeed what has been happening. We are burning all of it: the wisdom of the past, the variescence of the living earth, burning it in utter hubris, and ourselves with it.

In short, sedentary, civilizational consciousness is perfecting auto-genocide, and one of its most powerful banners for this process is what it likes to call "science." It prides itself by saying that it is scientific, and most usually means by this that it is beyond ideology, beyond moral obligations, beyond basic criticisms from outside of its institutional box. It is, in brief, Übermensch, in a white lab coat. Better to burn the false lab coat, the maya, the bureau-veil that would shield its avatars from their participation in life and understanding of its limits and their responsibilities to those limits. Burn the idealizing consciousness.

I underwent a conversion experience to geocentrism in my practical life a few years ago, realizing that my body senses awakening dawn arising and glorious sun setting with all its in-tempered archives of the history of life in my brain already attuned and needing to find their experience. I realized that there is nothing wrong with part-time geocentrism for some practical purposes, nothing to hinder me from also believing that the earth rotates around the sun in an immense galaxy. The plain fact is that our bodies are geocentric and cosmic-centric. Our bodies are also wonderfully designed to be life-centric, and our plasticity of instincts—regarded by many as a deficiency of guidance by instinct—is actually our human ability to attune ourselves to the instinctual intelligence of the surrounding life-environment. We became human dreaming and playing and bonding ourselves to mother forest and mother savannah in all her variescence, and finding our own way within it. The dreaming, playing, mother-infant bonding mammal in us—for these are general mammal characteristics, not specifically human—found form in a progressively child-like ape, characterized by neotenous—newbornlike—characteristics.

Although it has been crucial in science, abductive inference seems to me a capacity problematically weakened by civilization, strangled by rationalizing modernity, silenced in postmodern culture. Abduction is the logic term for the inner voice of nature, which speaks primarily iconically, not verbally. It is the inner voice of general nature, by no means limited to humans.

Modern science outlawed the inner voice from its quantifying machine, leaving it a poor stranger outside the city gates, not realizing that the poor stranger was in reality its abundant provider. Yet if humans have, as Peirce claimed, a "genius" for guessing, for abductive inference, then abduction should show itself in the biocultural evolution of humans. What would the abductive influence on the formation of the human brain mean? What areas or pathways would show the development of this capacity? What is the physiology of abduction?

The physiology of abduction should be found in the experience of wonder and in a consciousness of wonder. Animism is such a consciousness, found in the religious-ritual-artistic worldviews of hunter-gatherers. To wonder at the ongoing all-surrounding drama of creation, of the life in all things, of the voice of life-creation in fellow creatures, all the living enactment of the drama with something to say, something for us to listen to and learn, such is life lived in full awareness.

Full awareness, in wonder, is the propellant of the evolution of "big brain," not mere Darwinian antisocial *Homo competitor*. Full awareness requires a use of the brain-orchestra far more demanding than that of the domesticated brain, propped by its civilized institutional devices and experience-relieving, specializing knowledge. It requires a mind coalescing with its environment, attuned to it, *in it*. It requires awareness of many languages: the language of tracks; the language of the birds and beasts, plants and trees, rocks and rivers, sky and stars; languages of tongue and of presence, of touch and gesture, mood and circumstance.

The language of tracks alone has roughly five thousand characters, almost as many as Chinese! These characters include creature, climate, time, earth-place, and surrounding landscape. The characters of the creature alone tell its past, speak its complete body in minute detail, including internal organs, eye movement (yes, eye movement shows itself in tracks!), even intentions (imagining, for example, that you want to turn right but don't. The imagining right turn gets felt in musculature and gravity puts those minute changes into the track.). And that is but one of the languages. Each track is a book of awareness; each animal call a phrase in the environmental symphony; each plant speaks its sense of its surrounds, a dance of creation, a player in the sacred game of life.

More than ever, animism makes sense to me, life as a living relation and attunement of the human with the "greater-than-human," not simply in some mystical sense, but in the literal bodied-sense of living in deep awareness of the many voices of nature who speak to the hunter-gatherer: the birds who tell of a disturbance in the forest a few kilometers away, the tracks that reveal an intimate portrait—gravitized through the five thousand or so possible pressure indicators of the moving foot—a portrait of the creature more accurate than an x-ray or psychological diagnostic evaluation, the plants that heal, the ongoing symphony of these voices that reveal the unfolding of seasons and the fantastic play of life.[24]

Animism, far from being a fog-bound, illusory, nature-mysticism believed in by "primitives," is a consciousness of awareness. It represents that attunement to the organic sign-complexus of life, without and within, through which we evolved into our present primate bodies. Further, it reveals how our brains are made, as a living relation of the human forebrain with the "greater-than-human" paleo-mammalian and reptilian brain-archives incorporated within us. We are built to live in that relationship of human to greater-than-human brain, yet our modern rationalizing consciousness, the "neonatal" icing on the cake, has made a machine of the tiger and the bird and the snake and the baboon within us, infantilizing us in the name of rational-mechanical scientific progress, to our imminent peril.

Yet a mere throwback to hunter-gatherer ways would not work, because eventually it would face the same problems we face today, namely, unlimited expanding power. A mere modern or even postmodern outlook will not work either, because it is at base suicidally murderous, or murderously suicidal, depending on your outlook. All this was seen clearly by Melville and Dostoevsky, and by others too, including D. H. Lawrence and Owen Barfield.

In his essay "The Harp and the Camera," Owen Barfield used the analogy of the Aeolian harp—which included its wind as part of itself—and hence is a self-playing instrument, to depict participation consciousness. He contrasted it with the camera as symbolizing modern "camera civilization." In Barfield's words: "We live in a camera civilization. Our entertainment is camera entertainment. Our holidays are camera holidays. We make them so by paying more attention to the camera we brought with us than to the waterfall we are pointing it at. Our science is almost entirely a camera science . . . and it is already becoming self-evident to camera man that only camera words have any meaning."[25]

The resolution of these seeming opposites—self-playing participation versus being a spectator of the picture—is what Barfield termed *final participation*. We need to develop this final participation consciousness here and now, to develop the abilities to be in the picture we are depicting. Here and now is where we need to be developing the abilities—empathically grounded—to be of our surrounds while being able to critically depict and correct them or ourselves.

We need to refigure the majesty and divinity of nature, of the mysterious and miraculous voices of reasonableness that surround us without and within, and to which we must ever attune ourselves. This is, to my understanding, what is meant by the Native American expression "to walk in beauty" and by Peirce's understanding of the ultimate basis of conduct as aesthetic, as Beauty, considered as the intrinsically admirable. The deepest purpose in life is nothing less than to become the ongoing creation of the universe in the myriad ways of one's life.

Lem's American allegory asks us to reconsider the basis of modern life and our relation to the living universe. The lie of civilization, that we can power ourselves to "heaven" by walling ourselves off in spectral consciousness from life, has revealed itself as a deadly delusion, the delusion called history. A new kind of civilization is required, one that incorporates organic limits and organic, cosmic goals, comprehending the primary reality of a self-creating universe, of a spontaneous reasonableness energizing into being as no machine ever could. Inquisitive awareness involves attunement to the real voices of creation, to all-surrounding life, without which a religion, a science, a civilization will not endure.

8

AN AMERICAN EPIPHANY
IN NASHVILLE

It's beige. My color!
—TURN-OF-THE-CENTURY DECORATOR ELSIE DE WOLF ON
FIRST VISITING THE PARTHENON IN ATHENS

Though in many of its aspects this visible world seems formed in love, the
invisible spheres were formed in fright.
—HERMAN MELVILLE, *Moby-Dick*

Epiphanies: the singing of experience, the explosion of the habitual, the
silence of illuminated contemplation. One never knows when such experiences will strike—wandering in a desert, glancing at a play of light and
shadows, tying one's shoes—but when one has an epiphany, the circadian
is circumscribed, stilled by the sudden pouring in of perception, of the wondrous round of phenomena that suggest in the strongest possible way the
hidden depths of meaning. The commonplace is momentarily interdicted
and transposed, translated, perhaps, to that sublime language of the soul
seldom available to the self-conscious mind and its linguistic concepts, but
nevertheless the iconic source of conscious mind.

The circumstances of this epiphany were perhaps a bit mundane, but
they were all-American. I happened to be in Nashville, Tennessee, home,

as you probably know, of big-time commercial country music. Europe may have its Vienna, Salzburg, and Bayreuth, but if you want to see an American city whose identity is profoundly shaped by its music, you either visit New Orleans or Nashville. Now, everyone knows that New Orleans is where jazz music was born, even if few realize that jazz—or "jass" as they used to call it—is a four letter word and was originally intended as such: one of the earliest recorded tunes was titled "Jass Me Baby." Perhaps the folks in Intercourse, Pennsylvania, could understand, but neo-Pilgrim America, God-fearing and terrorized by sex and death, had to forget. The word was originally applied by one white band against another as a derogatory term to signify the music played by blacks in bawdy houses. Yet if the founder of Christianity could be born in a filthy stable, it seems fair that the foundations of that copasetic aesthetic could be conceived in those one-night, red-illuminated mangers. And besides, the names of many of the leading movements in painting in the past century were originally coined as derogatory terms.

Until Hurricane Katrina laid waste to the city in 2005, New Orleans was America's dark, voodoo-ridden, libidinal city, a city of zombied tourists and sex workers: "The Latin Quarter." Who knows if it will remain so, or whether it will give way to a moneyed Disneyland rebuilding, eventually sinking into the Gulf of Mexico before the end of this century.

I suppose I should allow that Memphis is also a city of great American music, a midwife of the blues on Beale Street, source of Memphis soul and Stax records, and of course, the home of Elvis. What about Elvis, the truest and bluest goddamn celebrity classical rock and roll ever produced? Born, like Aphrodite, on the scum of white record producers who floated on the great and muddy waters of black soul rhythm and blues. The great white record producers of Memphis legend were hound dogs who made their money in the fifties with white "covers" of black originals. All that changed, of course, but not before Elvis became a god, an Adonis in blue suede shoes, who grew into a coarse, unthankful, bloated testimony to American venality, Las Vegas style. A visit to the King's mansion "Graceland" certifies his divine riches: count the Cadillacs, the Las Vegas costumes, the gilded records. No epiphany there, perhaps, but something much more resonant with American needs for unreality: the reality of entertainment. Still, early Elvis was a genuine fusion of black blues and country, a true epiphany of rock-and-roll vitality that was bursting out of Memphis in the early 1950s.

But we should turn to Nashville to check the pulse of the contemporary whitewashed American soul. No Latin Quarter there, rather a city more classical in its pretensions: The Grand Ole Opry, the nearby Elvis Presley Museum, The Parthenon.

Now there is classical and there is classical. Yes, we must admit that opera began in Italy, and is perhaps "Latin" in its origins, but didn't it mistakenly try to model itself on classical Greek theater? Are not opera's pretensions then at least classical? Does any of this have anything to do with the Opry of Nashville? You bet your blue suede shoes it don't.

The "Opry" stands to opera as a truck stop does to an extravagant banquet. The Opry was a lively showcase of hillbilly music and great country musicians, and is now a sacred monument to the "Nashville sound" and everything "country." Only country has morphed into a kind of commercial rock music. Yet at the Opry one can still see those "classical" celebrities who helped put Nashville on the pop music map.

I did not make the customary profane pilgrimage to Graceland in Memphis, or even to the Grand Ole Opry, but I did visit the Nashville Parthenon. Or rather I should say that I was graced by its visitation.

I happened to be attending the national meeting of the Semiotic Society of America, a common enough sort of thing, which any self-respecting semiotician might do. Now, my knowledgeable reader surely knows that semiotics simply means the study of signs, and that semioticians study anything that catches their fancy and simply tack on "a semiotic analysis" to reports of their research. Semioticians tend to view the whole world, and everything in it, as signs, symbols, and ciphers. Especially ciphers, it would seem, since the main business of semiotics seems to consist in taking a perfectly reasonable topic of study and obfuscating it to death under a magic mountain of pseudo-profundity. I was addressing this very problem, attempting to touch the bottom of our whole crazy rationalistic civilization by winding my way down through the forbidding and almost terrifying terminology of *logical modernism*: iconic, indexical, symbolical; intuition, reference, pragmatic; possibility, actuality, and, yes, reality. So the reader should take note of my tendency then, and now, to view things as signs, to view people as signs, to view reality as the transilluminative sign of signs. "And some certain significance lurks in all things," as Melville said, "else all things are of little worth, and the round world itself but an empty cipher, except to sell by the cartload, as they do hills about Boston, to fill up some morass in the Milky Way."

At any rate, that particular morass in the Milky Way in which I happened to find myself, Nashville, was home of Vanderbilt University, funded and founded by the great robber baron himself, Commodore Vanderbilt, and the location of my conference. And just on the other side of the brand name hotel in which I was staying was a structure that surely must be foundational to Western civilization: The Parthenon, temple of Athena, goddess of wisdom and war, born from the head of Zeus, fully clothed in armor.

But, you say, THE Parthenon is on the Acropolis, in Greece. Yes, dear reader, you are right, there is another one in Greece, with specially selected portions ensconced in the British Museum in London. I had not seen the Athenian Parthenon at the time of my visit to Nashville. There are also many banks and public buildings of the nineteenth century that pretend to be The Parthenon, and many Greek restaurants that use the name. There is a nineteenth-century one-twentieth-size replica of the Parthenon famous enough to be exhibited in the Metropolitan Museum of Art in New York. And I have seen its presence in Chicago. For there is a piece of the real Greek Parthenon embedded in the facade of the Chicago Tribune Tower, along with other famous rocks and blarney stones of the world. There is even a Parthenon-like structure in Germany, built by Ludwig the First in the nineteenth century, but it only houses gods of German *Kultur*, like Wagner, and anyway, it is called Valhalla. In short, there is only one, complete, all-in-one-place, life-size Parthenon, and that one is in Nashville. And that Parthenon drew me irresistibly, as to Athena herself: I had to see it.

The movie *Nashville*, which concludes with an assassination scene on a country music stage set up on the side steps of The Parthenon, had already been released and had been a box-office hit, but I had not seen it and did not know of The Parthenon scene at the time. It was not until the Sunday that I was departing that I finally got a chance to see that enigmatic structure. My roommate at the conference and I set out to get a close look in late morning. As we walked, we discussed his research, the use of sign-language among deaf-mute Indians living on an island off the coast from Columbia. Not, perhaps, your common convention conversation, though nonetheless fascinating.

Now imagine: walking through a great open field in a park, bordered by trees, discussing the sign-language of isolate Indian islanders of Columbia. Directly ahead, about a half mile away is The Parthenon, but before it is a commotion of surreal proportion. To the right are U.S. military-industrial tanks and helicopters: Is The Parthenon once again under siege, as it was a couple of centuries ago, when it was used as an ammunition depot by the Turks, and practically exploded out of existence when enemy artillery struck the bomb depository? Could these tanks and helicopters be warding off future attacks, I asked my colleague, just as the SVNA, the neo-Dadaist Students for Violent Non-Action of the University of Chicago in the late 1960s used to practice digging trenches on the Midway in case of possible Viet Cong attacks on the University of Chicago? Robber baron Rockefeller founded the U.C.; Vanderbilt founded V.U. Take "U" out and what are you left with? V.C.! So you see, sixties psychedelic logic dictated the very real possibility of a Viet Cong attack on this stronghold of the American robber baron university, as I joked with my colleague. Could similar protective measures be underway at Carnegie Mellon University? At Rockefeller University? At Hamburger University? We walked farther.

To our left some refreshment tables were being set up. Either it was to be a long war or a pleasant one: barbecue grills and beer kegs were also in evidence. Directly ahead, between us and The Parthenon, was something truly remarkable: a huge stage on which a rock-and-roll band was unraveling its counter-cultural-industrial equipment. Was this to be a showdown between the heavy metal music of rock culture and the heavy metal armaments of the U.S. Military? What was it that brought this strange juxtaposition of symbols together? (Remember, I am a semiotician.) Suddenly all became apparently clear when I saw a banner stating that this was to be a Vietnam Veterans reunion picnic. I had momentarily forgotten that the symbols of "counter culture" had long since blended with the military machine, as was clear in a recruitment billboard I had seen years earlier while driving on Lake Shore Drive on the south side of Chicago. A black soldier gave the "black power" raised fist from the top of an army tank to all the drivers-by. The clever army advertiser had redefined "black power" as "machine power," inverting civil rights "empowerment" by visually seducing "the brother" into the military machine. Could any auto advertiser match the erotic appeal and potency of the phallo-mechanical, heavy metal tank?

Yes, the killing machine was here at this pleasant Sunday reunion picnic, presumably to provide these survivors of bloody war with the thrill of seeing the instruments of death close at hand and with the family. This was a far cry from the Vietnam Veterans Memorial and its quiet, elegant brotherhood.

We walked farther, approaching the great temple of wisdom. Behind us the preparations for a humongous flesh-eating feast were underway, before us the very structure symbolizing the birth of Western rationality.

On reaching the west corner of The Parthenon I began to climb its steps, thinking of Plato's *Republic*, of Aristotle's *Politics*, of the significance of the Egyptian city of Memphis for Hellenistic culture (OK, I climbed slowly). I suddenly realized the Beethoven *Violin Concerto* was playing, and rather loudly. It was not likely to be coming from the reunion fest behind us; I thought that perhaps it was part of the "official" presentation of the classical Nashville Parthenon. After all, Beethoven wrote classical music, didn't he? *Violin Concerto* begins with V.C.; perhaps this could be a code for Viet Cong after all, infiltrating the reunion! We looked at the doors briefly, and decided to go down to the other end, apparently the front entrance near the road.

As we walked along the side of The Parthenon, I began to notice an older black man sitting on its steps, his eyes rolling in his head, his face the picture of lost distraction, his body rocking to and fro. He looked obviously drunk or crazy, possibly both. Or perhaps he was blind and oblivious to his movement. On his lap was a huge radio, blasting out the Beethoven *Violin Concerto*. I had reached the great epicenter.

Once, in Frankfurt, I had seen a soused Frankfurter with his brown bag of wine drinking and merrily singing on the steps of the opera house. He too looked to be a crazy drunkard, but he was a drunkard who knew all the arias from the opera that was being shown on an overhead closed-circuit TV screen, used when an opera sold out.

But who was this old man on the steps of The Parthenon? Could he be Phidias, master builder and sculptor from ancient Greece, come round again by the grace of Athena to view his masterpiece once more? Hardly. Could he be either Ictinus or Callicrates, the architects charged by Pericles with the task of building it between 448 and 432 BC? Doubtful: they are probably still too exhausted from the job of embodying a wonder of the world in a mere decade and a half.

The immortal Parthenon, great temple to the goddess of wisdom and war, cost Athens dearly and contributed to the loss of the Peloponnesian War. When Pericles emptied the state treasury to glorify the goddess Athena and her city, he greatly weakened the ability of Athens to prepare for the war against the Spartans. Perhaps this is why Thucydides the son of Melesias rebuked him for adorning the city "like a harlot with precious stones, statues and temples costing a thousand talents."

Great philosophical Athens fell prey to greed in attempting to offset Corinth's fast-growing naval power by allying itself with the enemy of Corinth, and in its attempt to control Sicily, to gain needed funds and deprive Sparta of them. Not your everyday rob, rape, and plunder sort of greed, but greed nevertheless, a high-class, cultivated greed, over which stood the shadow of the immortal Parthenon. Eternity does not come cheaply, it takes lots of talent, "a thousand talents" even. And as Aristotle, immortal child of the Parthenon, said, "therefore, in one point of view, all riches must have a limit; nevertheless, as a matter of fact, we find the opposite to be the case; for all getters of wealth increase their hoard of coin without limit. ... The origin of this disposition in men is that they are intent upon living only, and not upon living well; and, as their desires are unlimited, they also desire that the means of gratifying them should be without limit."[1] Oh, wise Aristotle! Oh, warring Athens!

Thucydides the historian believed that war between the great naval power and democracy of Athens and the militaristic closed society of Sparta was inevitable and tragic. Were he alive today, knowing of the great naval power of the United States, of its Parthenon in Nashville, of its "intent of living only, and not upon living well" as Aristotle put it, of its infatuation with the Athenian attribute of war, of its despisement of wisdom, could Thucydides come to any conclusion other than inevitable and tragic war? But with whom? Soviet Sparta-Russia was no more, and Iraq-Afghanistan was not yet. Was my vision, in fact, Thucydides "speaking" to me in wordless image? Was the old man a Greek bearing gifts that said, "BEWARE!"?

And this playing of the Beethoven *Violin Concerto*, what can one say of it? That it was mere coincidence I could easily accept—if my deep feeling of having been touched by wordless wonder would let me. But something more seemed to be happening. Indeed the whole experience seemed to be a testimony by and to "something more." I half expected to see "SOMETHING MORE" incised over the doors of The Parthenon.

"Something more" certainly surrounded the *Violin Concerto* Beethoven wrote for Franz Clement. This musical Parthenon was conceived on a grand and heroic scale by a man going stone deaf, a man doomed to touch divinity. *The good news, Herr Beethoven,* spoke the muses, *is that we will give ourselves to you in silent, intimate embrace. The bad news is that we will allow you to hear no other. All other loves will come to naught for you.*

Consider that shortly after *Fidelio* was unsuccessfully mounted in 1806 (and now she is mounted many times per year the world over!), Beethoven and others met at Prince Karl Lichnowsky's house to figure out how they might save the opera. Franz Clement, former boy wonder and then twenty-five-year-old concertmaster and conductor in Vienna, played the entire *Fidelio* score by memory, but, as one musician present put it, "The extraordinary memory of Clement having been universally known, nobody was astonished by this." Who would not want to trade places with such a genius? Who would not concede that here was someone worthy of such a concerto?

But the muses had apparently also struck a deal with Clement. *From our common mother Mnesemonye we give you the art of memory, from ourselves the art of music. The bad news, Franzl, is that you will never create anything memorable yourself.*

Clement was, of course, a composer, as all adult males in Vienna at the time apparently were required to be, yet how many of his works do you remember? Yet Clement had his one chance to confound the muses when he premiered Beethoven's immortal concerto. But when that memorable moment appeared on December 23, 1806, Franz Clement played buffoon instead, choosing to sight-read the work rather than prepare and rehearse it. Memories are not made of this! Worse still, and perhaps possessed by the same spirit that caused Nero to fiddle while Rome burned, Clement entertained the audience between the first and second movements with his own set of variations played *mit umgekehrter Violine*—with the fiddle turned upside down! Do you remember these variations? Do you see now why the devil is sometimes portrayed as fiddler?

"Something more" intruded on the premiere that night, the sheer lunacy of the featherless biped. Perhaps one of those cosmic Aleph points of which Jorge Luis Borges spoke, through which passes the speechless spokes of the universe, transposed something here with something there. Perhaps Clement became for a moment a Nashville fiddler, compelled to flip his fiddle and roll over Beethoven for the good ole boys of The Grand Ole Opry. Perhaps in exchange the unrealized premiere was made manifest here instead, playing as it should have sounded through some strange and hitherto unknown property of The Parthenon: Music of the Rectangles!

Could that old man on the steps of The Parthenon be Franz Clement, sent to hell for playing those violin tricks and improvisations? This was entirely possible, since this tiny portion of the globe had clearly wandered into the sublime: no exit signs hung above the great doors of The Parthenon. No exit?

Have you ever dreamed you were in a dream, awakening once, only to find the parade of dream images intensified, awakening again to an outer world now also infused with the dream consciousness, an outer world no less fantastic, one that might only be another level of dreaming? Have you ever been aware of yourself as dreaming, and yet continued to dream? Here I was in bright daylight in good ole Nashville being flooded with feelings of microcosmos, with the feeling that, for one serendipitous moment only, all of contemporary civilization was being presented to me as an image. I knew it was all fortuitous coincidence, yet "it" seemed to suggest otherwise. My experience was suggesting to me that the doors of The Parthenon had momentarily opened, making me active spectator to this spectacle that nobody else apparently saw. I had come to Nashville as an interpreter of meaning, never suspecting that the gates of the wide-eyed wonder world would be flung open in such a way, with no questions asked. If I were to shout "This is it!" I would be called mad. And still I had no idea what all "this" meant, though I felt to my depths that feeling of dumb wonder in the face of the sublime.

That old man was clearly the pivot of this widening gyre, archetype, and somehow personified image of the whole. Perhaps he was the blind silent prophet Tiresias, and all this, his vision. But the music? Suddenly the words came to me, "He is Pip!" He had to be. He was Pip, Melville's Pip, *Moby-Dick's* Pip. Yes, he was that doomed cabin boy prophet of the world-ship, the Pequod, who, left adrift at sea in the great whale chase, "touched the celestial orb," and in seeing those invisible spheres, went stark-raving mad. As heaven's sense is man's insanity, so was Pip mad. Pip had not gone down with the rest of the ship, but had continued his existence in time's eternal temple: The Parthenon.

And so here was Pip in Nashville: hip Pip, jester and fool, psychic sidekick to the great White curse, a momentary interlude of woeful cosmic relief. He still rolled his eyes and body to great waves of rhythm, to a new tambourine of jam-box Beethoven, to a demonic *Missa Solemnis*. The unwarped primal world seemed pressed close upon me here in Nashville, with its deaf-mute sound of a crazed Vietnam War reunion, its harmonies of Parthenon cloned form, its mystery of old Pip with his Beethoven sonic blaster. Was this God's foot upon the treadle of the loom? A sign, somewhere between insanity and heaven's sense, of America's legacy? A massacre of innocence, drowned by the "blood-dimmed tide" of the All-Swallowing Vortex? The tanks were real, the music was real, and eternal Pip was most real of all. It was only me that I was wondering about.

That eerie opening of the abyss I felt in walking past the frenetic old black man on the steps of the American Parthenon with his Beethoven *Violin Concerto* jam-box was the horror of Pip's vision. So this is what it looked like when he journeyed to the bottom of all unfathomable depths! Here, drifting amid the props of eternal rationality, mechanized monotony, destruction, amnesia, and nostalgia, I gazed upon the prophet who gazed upon the horror unprotected. That old man was Pip, eternal tambourine boy now grown old, still marking time as epicenter of the abyss. And as I walked past him, rapt in the unfathomable wonder of this man gyrating the cosmic concerto, he lifted his jam-box ever so slightly off his lap for a brief moment, smiling serenely with a knowing nod.

Epiphanies: They seldom knock, they can steal upon you in the middle of the day, they can jolt you, and they can be rude. An image cannot lie, though its interpretation can. And even the words of epiphanies are but images. Epiphanies speak the truth and are helpless to do otherwise; only they tease us and taunt us to understand them. Heaven's sense is man's insanity, overwhelming our everyday habituations with sudden illumination, with evanescent moments of transcendent lucidity, sensed rather than comprehended. One man's insanity is another's vision, and he or she who is closed to the living moment and its demands will never know whether life has graced one with the portal. And even if one has the portal, where does one go with it? Where and how will the silent dancing blind prophet, servant of Athena, seer of the depths, speak again?

9

THE HOUSE ON MOUNT MISERY

If you have built castles in the air, your work need not be lost; that is where
they should be. Now put the foundations under them.
—HENRY DAVID THOREAU, *Walden*

Prelude

There once was a man who kept a copy of Thoreau's *Walden* next to his bed
throughout his life. He studied painting at the Pennsylvania Academy of
the Fine Arts in Philadelphia with American artists William Merritt Chase,
Thomas Anshutz, Cecilia Beaux, and others in the first decade of the twentieth
century. He tried to make a living as a painter, to live out an organic vision
in the rural countryside outside of Philadelphia. He made picture frames for
his paintings and furniture for himself and his family. He had to, having so
little money from trying to be a painter living in the country in early twentieth-century America. Potential buyers of his paintings began to buy his
furniture and frames instead of his paintings. Around this time he turned to
woodblocks. Soon he realized that he could be himself in wood in a way he
never could in painting, that he was "overtrained" in painting. By 1924 he put
his brushes away for good.

In 1926 he built a studio up from his farmhouse, on the top of the hill called Mount Misery. It sits across the valley from where George Washington and his Revolutionary War troops spent an awful winter at Valley Forge, Pennsylvania, on another hill called Mount Joy. Later this man moved up the hill into the studio and added on to it over the course of his life. He carved out an existence for himself and his family, winning some recognition for his work, but no real fame or fortune in his lifetime. A gallery owner in New York City at some point in the 1930s replied to his question about the possibility of an exhibition of his work by saying dismissively, "we will call you when we are ready for you." He vowed not to return until "they" called him, which the Museum of Contemporary Crafts (now the American Craft Museum) finally did a couple of decades later, for a major retrospective of his work in 1958. He lived his entire life barely above poverty, but in artistic freedom, influencing succeeding generations of furniture masters.

He modified his house/studio on Mount Misery continuously, enlarging it periodically over the next forty years, filling it with his works. He bodied forth his vision of organic, fantastic design. In later years he tells someone, "I am only Esherick the man, but all of this is really Esherick." So the home is the man; his life, the craft.

We too often assume that simplicity means unsophisticated, a simpleton's world, and that complexity must be abstruse, abstracted, out of touch. And yet, as Melville said in *Moby-Dick*, "You seek to enlarge your mind? Subtilize it!" There are myriad ways in which simplicity and complexity touch. Thoreau's adventure at Walden Pond is one, where he spent two years and two months in the woods attempting "to live deliberately, to front only the essential facts of life, and see if I could not learn what it had to teach, and not, when I came to die, discover that I had not lived."[1] Thoreau found his experience fronting the essential facts of life to be transformative:

I learned this, at least, by my experiment: that if one advances confidently in the direction of his dreams, and endeavors to live the life which he has imagined, he will meet with a success unexpected in common hours. He will put some things behind, will pass an invisible boundary; new, universal, and more liberal laws will begin to establish themselves around and within him; or the old laws be expanded, and interpreted in his favor in a more liberal sense, and he will live with the license of a higher order of beings. In proportion as he simplifies his life, the laws of the universe will appear less complex, and solitude will not be solitude, nor poverty poverty, nor weakness weakness. If you have built castles in the air, your work need not be lost; that is where they should be. Now put the foundations under them.[2]

The living embodiment of Thoreau is not to be found today at Walden Pond, which was an experience rendered in writing. But it is palpably present in the home, now a museum, of Wharton Esherick, a master who "read Thoreau like the bible." Esherick not only went to the woods as a source of inspiration but also to the essence of wood, devoting his life to the pursuit of his craft, living impoverished while influencing younger wood masters who were eventually lucky enough, because times had changed, to make good money from their craft. In his eulogy for Esherick, one of these masters, Sam Maloof, described him as the dean of American craftsmen: "'Young man, stick to your convictions and don't stray from the way you work and believe; remember what I've told you!' This was my introduction to Wharton Esherick at the first ACC National conference at Asilomar in June 1957. These words from the dean of American Craftsmen sustained me through years of valleys and hills, and I looked forward to the day I could visit and talk with him in his home."[3]

Maloof also said of Esherick, "He was the first to sell everything out of his shop, working the way a few of us still do. He was the most important woodworker in America at the time. I still believe he was a catalyst, a force, in making woodworking important in the United States." Maloof also described being influenced by Esherick's "integrity and heart-felt feeling for the materials—things like how he would only use the wood found in the area he lived, because he was friendly with it. He didn't know what the exotic wood would do."[4]

Similarly, furniture maker and sculptor Wendell Castle said, "Esherick taught me that the making of furniture could be a form of sculpture; Esherick caused me to come to appreciate inherent tree characteristics in the utilization of wood; and finally he demonstrated the importance of the entire sculptural environment."[5]

Despite these praises by fellow wood masters, it took a couple of decades after his death in 1970 for Esherick to begin to gain his recognition. It is the same old story, the story of Melville and philosopher Peirce: the story, not only of an artist ignored in his own time but also of an American bodying forth the deepest expressions of American culture being ignored by America. In the 1970s and 1980s his name usually did not appear in the coffee table books on furniture. By the 1990s it did, but often still absent a photo example. Now his furniture is more widely recognized, though his design work still has to surface fully.

One of Thoreau's sayings from *Walden* that stayed with Esherick was "Simplicity, simplicity, simplicity!" Simplicity was a virtue Esherick sought for himself and often advocated to artists who would show him their work. He would tell them, "gotta keep it simple, keep it simple." He even gave this advice to people whose lives seemed complicated, "simplify, simplify." Now this is surely good advice for life in general. It seems, well, so *simple* after all, but advice so easily forgotten in the treadmill of life. Yet Esherick increasingly lived by it as he grew older. Practicality, meanwhile, though it deeply informed his work, was not part of Esherick's personal virtue vocabulary. He prized practicality in the furniture, interiors, and other designs he made, fusing it with a classical sense of beauty and proportion. But when it came to commissions, he would often tell a customer that a piece might cost "between thirty and three hundred dollars," depending on the labor. This led to some customers not having the money, if the final tally came in higher than lower, and he often had to retrieve objects not paid for.

Some other customers did not like the final result he presented them with and would not pay. All of these objects today are finally being recognized as masterpieces, worth far more than the prices he charged back then. Organic practicality, fitted to life, is quite different from so-called American pragmatism, debased in everyday speech to mean mere expediency, fitted to a culture of commerce and technology. Esherick's organic practicality was that of a master, deeply aware of what the Chinese call Feng shui, the inherent, organic nature of a thing, a space, a room, an environment. He drew from wood its own inclination, and transformed it into a work of art, organically alive to its new setting.

His entire place is subtilized mind, and legacy of a life devoted to simplicity. More, it is the bodying forth in wood of a life tempered by simplicity, for one sees how the man's work—the furniture, sculpture, the home—matured over time into a spiritual simplicity wherein mastery resides. One might say that he was a Bodhisattva:

> To spend time in solitude
> Is the practice of a Bodhisattva.

In his wood, he found his Buddha nature. More simply, in wood he found his spontaneous nature. Yet more simply, in wood he loved nature, and in nature he found his wild self.

Note in figure 15 the curvilinear stairs cascading from the kitchen and, on the left, from the bedroom down to the living room. Observe the irregular floor- and wallboards on the right. Eyeball the handrails to the left, leading

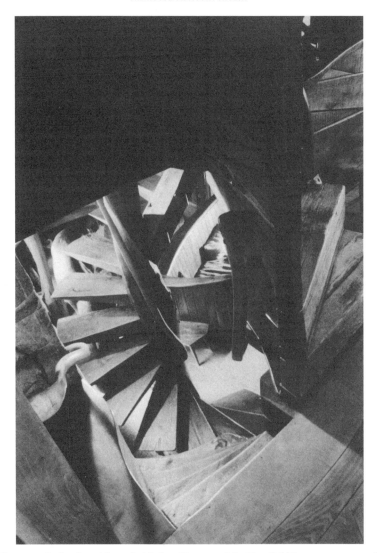

Figure 15. Stairs viewed from the kitchen. Photograph by Mansfield Bascom, courtesy of the Wharton Esherick Museum.

down to the spiral stairs, and added in the last two years or so of his life for extra support in wending the crossing stair paths. Out of view in this photo but visible in plate 2 is another winding stair rail, so exemplary of his organic design, perfectly fitted to the stairs. Yet it is a mammoth tusk, blown out of the earth by steam mining in Alaska, brought back across the continent to the East by the son of an assistant woodworker, because he knew it matched Esherick's free-flowing forms.

The stairs to the right ascend to the room he added on in 1966 for his partner, Miriam Phillips, who the laws of the time prevented him from marrying, even years after he had separated from his wife Letty. The base of the sculpture on the stairs with upraised arm says *No!* to intruders (Do not ascend farther!), and originated as a work for Hedgerow Theater intended to block patrons from using one of the staircases. The room is part of a silo structure, which includes a kitchen on the first floor level, connecting to the dining area and stairs.

Miriam Phillips, who lived with Esherick for the last thirty-five years of his life, was an actress at Hedgerow Theater, located near Paoli, Pennsylvania, in Rose Valley, who appeared in a variety of roles there, in Philadelphia, and on and off Broadway in New York City, as well as film and TV. She appeared in the soap opera *As the World Turns* and in the films *The Fan* (1981), *Crossing Delancey* (1988), and in her ninetieth year, *She's Back* (1989). One of the last plays she performed in around that time was directed by Laurence Olivier.

Phillips—Mims, or Mima, as she was known—was born on May 28, 1899 and died on October 24, 1997, at the age of ninety-eight. When I interviewed her in 1975, five years after Esherick had died, she told me that "Wharton touched wood as a man touches a woman." Of the many ways in which trees speak, this was a sacred place in which a lover of trees was touched by the organic possibilities engrained in the woods he used, in which a hunter of trees gave reverence to his prey, gave praise in the life he gave back to the woods they furnished him. He sought beauty in the gifts of wood that Mount Misery offered him. Yes, Mount Misery, across the valley from Mount Joy. Didn't Buddha say that life is forged from Mount Misery and Mount Joy, ultimately transcending them? And is that not what real art and craft is? A real life, standing on its own?

Or perhaps I am dreaming? Perhaps I am a butterfly winging it, dreaming that I am a human dreaming of a fabled home on a beautiful hilltop near Paoli, Pennsylvania, a place where wood comes alive to speak, as Pygmalion's Galatea did? That Greek sculptor was dreaming! But he dreamed the perfect woman into being, a dream somehow come alive. Except that the woman spoke, as some of my more decidedly chauvinist male friends would put it. But I digress . . . from the dream:

Once I, Chuang Tzu, dreamed I was a butterfly and was happy as a butterfly. I was conscious that I was quite pleased with myself, but I did not know that I was Tzu. Suddenly I awoke, and there was I, visibly Tzu. I do not know whether it was Tzu dreaming that he was a butterfly or the butterfly dreaming that he was Tzu. Between Tzu and the butterfly there must be some distinction. [But one may be the other.] This is called the transformation of things.

Being alone in Esherick's home is being immersed in "the transformation of things," in many ways like a living dream. I once house-sat the place for a weekend, a few years after his death, in wonder at how all things seemed on the verge of movement. Waking in his bed at sunrise I felt myself canopied in the treetops, immersed in birdsong as I gazed out the bed-length window over-looking the fog-bottomed valley below (see figure 16). It was as though I were living in a vast tree house, grown from the trees themselves. One ascends into the bedroom up the spiral stair through a door that opens from the floor, with a pulley at one end attached to a counterweight figure who is clinging to the rope. And at day's end the sunset changes of light illuminated all things inside alive in movement, moment to moment, in a kind of community conversation.

Figure 16. Bedroom. Photograph by Mansfield Bascom, courtesy of the Wharton Esherick Museum.

All things spoke living simplicity and lifelong love of wood. I even got married there around that time, and Mima inscribed a note on a gift that also spoke to her independent relationship to Esherick: "Each one herself-himself, a perfect duo, keep it so, Love, Mima."

"Any Fool Can Draw a Straight Line"

Wharton Esherick was born on July 15, 1887, in West Philadelphia, and died at the age of eighty-two on May 6, 1970. His father, a well-to-do businessman, thought "it was awful" that he wanted to become an artist, and that he would never make any money. He got that one right. Esherick not only became an artist but also a political socialist early on.

Esherick studied painting, starting in 1907 at the Philadelphia School of Industrial Art. He then received a scholarship in 1911 to study at the Pennsylvania Academy of the Fine Arts, leaving it in his last year, just two months before graduation, because he felt he had, "had enough of teachers." These teachers, William Merritt Chase and others, influenced him especially toward impressionism, the movement born in nineteenth-century France, but with many regional manifestations in the United States in the early twentieth century, including Pennsylvania, California, Indiana (Hoosier impressionism), and elsewhere. Some of the noted Pennsylvania impressionists include Chase, Edward Redfield, and Daniel Garber. Childe Hassam (New York and New England) is a well-known American impressionist, as are California impressionists such as Guy Rose, Alson Clark, and Franz Bischoff. These impressionists tended to be buried by twentieth-century modernism by the mid-teens. Yet with the decline of modernism since the 1960s, they resurfaced by the 1990s, as the art world in effect reopened its doors to figuration and reappraised the work of these artists.

Impressionism began as a rejection of traditional academicism, an attempt to be more naturalistic: frequently choosing outdoor landscapes and figures, everyday themes instead of significant events, and rough finishes instead of polished ones—this last point provoking criticism early on that works were being exhibited in "unfinished" states. All of this, one might think, would lend itself to Esherick's developing vision. But he was unhappy with his training and felt it had been to his detriment as an artist. It seems not to have been so much the style of impressionism itself as that this originally antiacademic art had now become the academy, imposing its way on the spontaneous soul. Miriam Phillips told me: "He used to say that he could paint like all the people whose work he studied, but he couldn't paint like Wharton Esherick, because he was *overtrained*, he said, as a painter." In Esherick's own words: "I could draw as well as anybody, but I was over-trained. I was a good draftsman who didn't know how to think."[6]

After leaving the academy, he worked briefly as an illustrator for a couple of Philadelphia newspapers then found another job at the Victor Talking Machine Company in Camden, New Jersey, doing the drawings of performers, singers, or composers for the jackets of the records. Through a co-worker there, who became a long-time friend, he was first introduced to the work and ideas of Thoreau, which was to become a lifelong influence.[7] But he lost the job within the year to technology when the gravure process was introduced, allowing photos to be reproduced.

During 1912, Esherick and his wife Letty Nofer moved to Paoli, which is west of Philadelphia and adjacent to Valley Forge, where he hoped to devote himself full time to painting. In the old farmhouse and the barn they bought, which are a few hundred yards down the hill from the house he later built, Esherick did work at the end of the decade that can be seen as foreshadowing his later transition into sculpture and furniture making. In converting the barn into a studio, he carved remarkable brackets for the entrance in the form of figures, and latches for the door in the form of grotesque heads.

Early in the 1920s Esherick began to carve frames for his paintings with designs that reflected the subject of the painting, often trees in landscapes. He also began making woodcuts, which also served to increase his interest in wood. This transition was brought about through a life-changing experience in Fairhope, Alabama, where he had accepted an offer in 1919 to teach at Marietta Johnson's School for Organic Education.

Fairhope had been founded in 1894 as a single tax colony, a utopian commune with many artists and intellectuals that had grown to 850 people by 1920. Miriam Phillips described it to me while discussing how Esherick first met writer Sherwood Anderson there.

He met Sherwood Anderson first down in Fairhope, Alabama, where he and Letty went with Mary [his daughter], I guess, when she was just three or four. And they went down there because they had heard about this progressive school, a new kind of organic, Mrs. Johnson's organic school it was called. Fairhope was a Single Tax Colony and there were some artists down there, it seemed like a very unusual place. It's not far from Mobile. And Sherwood was there with Tennessee Mitchell. She was a sculptress, I think. I don't know if she was married to Sherwood then, but they did get married later. And she was down there with him.

Figure 17. Wharton Esherick with sculpture *Essie*, 1933, based on a character played by his daughter Mary in George Bernard Shaw's play *Devil's Disciple* at Hedgerow Theater. Courtesy of the Wharton Esherick Museum.

Sherwood was trying to paint, and asked Wharton what he thought of his painting. And Wharton said, "If you'd throw away that cobalt," and Sherwood tore it up, tore up the painting, and for a while he wouldn't speak to Wharton. But then Sherwood was really very fond of Wharton. So that passed. And [Anderson] said, maybe painting wasn't his forte anyway. I think he was already writing. So they corresponded and Sherwood came up here and Wharton visited him.

But [Wharton] was interested in, well, very much like what some of the young people nowadays are—in back to the land and living as close to nature as possible without extraneous things. And they grew vegetables down there, and had a garden, and grew peonies to sell.

Fairhope was one of the few single tax colonies that were operating at that time. Its founders were influenced by Henry George's book *Progress and Property* and his idea of a single tax to be applied to a community, which inspired the single tax movement of the 1870s and 1880s. George's version of socialism denied individual property rights to land, but allowed people that which they made themselves or produced from the land. So the single tax would be imposed on the community-owned land. Individuals and families held ninety-nine year leases on the community-owned land, and the annual rent constituted the "single tax." While there the Eshericks adopted an African American child, but it did not work out. Even in the progressive environment of Fairhope, it was still Apartheid America of the early twentieth century, and Alabama at that.

The School of Organic Education was founded by Marietta Johnson in 1907 and was a leading expression of the progressive education movement in America. It was celebrated by John Dewey in his 1915 book, *Schools of Tomorrow*, and reached its zenith by the 1920s, just the time Esherick and his family were there. Johnson incorporated insights of progressive education, anthroposophist Rudolph Steiner, and Maria Montessori into the school's philosophy, eschewing competition, grades, and a purely intellectual model for an experiential model based on the love of learning. In Johnson's words: "Children should be active in all their learning; in fact, learning is a consequence and accompaniment of activity. Not only do we learn to do by doing, but all learning is through experience."[8]

Active play was also crucial to this outlook. Notably, Johnson said, "the greatest minds are those able to use the play spirit in work." She also said in her book *Youth in a World of Men*: "Play should be spontaneous, the expression of an inner necessity. This inner necessity is profound and far-reaching."[9] Now it is difficult to assess how Esherick's experiences in the organic school affected him directly, but it seems to me that the significance accorded by Johnson to spontaneous play as expression of an inner necessity accords well with Esherick's outlook on art and life. It is what, perhaps, was missing in his training as a painter, the free play of his spontaneous self at work in expression, being himself. As Esherick said: "People have to trust me. I work for fun. When I stop enjoying it, I'm through. I don't want any huge jobs that get out of my hands. I want to know everything that happens. I don't want too many people to worry about. Nor will I work with anyone who keeps trying to pin me down too much. I work best with clients who become my friends."[10] What is clear is that while at the organic school, Esherick entered the world of wood, which he would never leave.

While at Fairhope, Anderson gave Esherick a set of chiseling tools and he soon began making frames for his paintings and also woodcuts. Marietta Johnson's husband, who died in 1919, had been a carpenter and cabinetmaker and had taught wood at the school. I wonder whether Esherick's first tools could have been Frank Johnson's, but I have been unable to find information on this. Anderson gave Esherick a set of tools at that time, whether they were Johnson's or new, and so he appears to be instrumental—literally—to Esherick's turn to wood. The acquisition of those tools and his turn to working wood was pivotal to Esherick's life. He went to Fairhope in 1919 as a painter, but by 1924, at the age of thirty-seven, after turning to woodcuts, frames, and furniture, he was done with painting.

Sherwood Anderson arrived at Fairhope shortly after the publication of his classic collection of short stories, *Winesberg, Ohio*, with little money and a desire not only to work on his next novel but also to open himself to the arts. As Mima mentioned, Esherick dissuaded Anderson from painting, and Anderson dissuaded Esherick from writing, and after the smoke cleared, they became lifelong friends. Esherick would visit Anderson at his farm, Ripshin, in Virginia. He collaborated with Anderson, doing a woodblock for a humorous pamphlet published by Anderson's son, for which Anderson wrote the introduction. Anderson's work was also performed at Hedgerow Theater, as was Theodore Dreiser's. Esherick was commissioned by Anderson's widow Eleanor in 1942 to make a sculptural memorial for Anderson's grave, after Anderson died prematurely at age sixty-four from peritonitis after swallowing a toothpick at a party in Panama. Esherick produced a striking, twelve-foot-tall figure in black walnut holding a staff, apparently influenced by seeing Anderson's neighbor, John Anders Sullivan, at the funeral. The piece was refused by the Round Hill Cemetery of Marion, Virginia, and ended up being purchased by the Philadelphia Museum of Art. It stood in the entry for a few years, but with some schoolboys carving their initials in the base it was removed for protection.

Esherick also met Mary Marcy at Fairhope, a socialist writer and poet beginning a project of poems for children based on evolution. Asked if he would like to contribute woodcut illustrations, he enthusiastically supplied some, soon getting ahead of her poems and challenging her to make more poems to the woodcuts. Eventually Esherick contributed over one hundred woodcuts, and the resulting book, *Rhymes of Early Jungle Folk*, appeared in 1922. Unfortunately Marcy died a month before its publication.

Figure 18. Esherick woodcut for *As I Watched the Ploughman Ploughing*, by Walt Whitman, music by Philip Dalmas, woodcuts by Wharton Esherick, 1928.

The titles of her other books are interesting to consider today. They are: in 1911, *Shop Talks on Economics*; in 1917, *Stories of the Cave People*, in which she says in the preface, "In this little book I have sought, in a series of stories or sketches, to present only the first steps in human progress as elaborated by Lewis (H.) Morgan in his brilliant work on ancient society"; with her husband Roscoe Burdette Tobias in 1918, *Women as Sex Vendors; or, Why Women Are Conservative (Being a View of the Economic Status of Women)*; and in 1920, *The Right to Strike*.

In 1924, Esherick did twenty woodcuts to Walt Whitman's *The Song of the Broad-Axe*, for the first publication of the Centaur Press in Philadelphia. The next year the press published the first edition of D. H. Lawrence's *Reflections on the Death of a Porcupine and Other Essays*, for which Esherick contributed a woodblock of a porcupine (see figure 20).

Esherick also met Theodore Dreiser in 1924, and they remained friends for a number of years. Dreiser worked on a stage production of his novel *An American Tragedy* in Esherick's kitchen, and Esherick would also visit Dreiser. One of Esherick's notable woodblocks, *Of a Great City* (1927), is an expressionistic view of Dreiser at his desk, windowed city and writing desk manuscripts seeming to mirror each other.

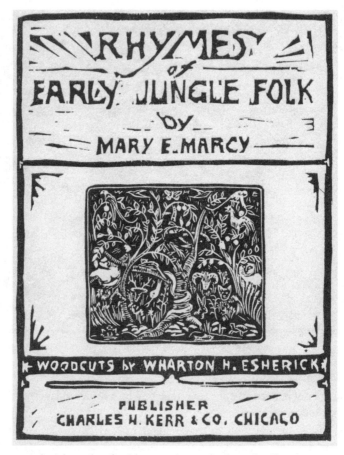

Figure 19. Esherick woodcut for title page, *Rhymes of Early Jungle Folk*, 1922.

On a high shelf near Esherick's bed is a wood sculpture "sketch" of Dreiser's head in pine. Nearby is a photo of Sherwood Anderson and his neighbor John Anders Sullivan, at the gate of Anderson's farm Ripshin, taken not much before his death in 1941. I was originally told by a friend of Esherick's that the sculpture remained unfinished after Esherick broke with Dreiser because Dreiser had attempted to seduce Esherick's teenage daughter. This may seem like something out of Dreiser's *An American Tragedy* but would be consistent with Dreiser's philandering biography in general. As Sherwood Anderson's wife Eleanor wrote in her diary on July 4, 1934, after a stage performance at Hedgerow of Anderson's *Winesburg, Ohio*: "Paoli. The *Winesburg* play is over or maybe just begun—Heaven knows. Sherwood and Deeter whom he likes were enthusiastic about the dress rehearsal. Mother and I arrived Saturday morning, June 30th. Dreiser and Helen came. . . . [after the performance] We got to Esherick's at 3:30 after having a scene over Dreiser wanting one of the young actresses to go up and "sleep on the grass" with him. Sunday was a long picnic with Dreiser exhibiting his genitals all through a long breakfast. Fortunately Mother didn't notice. . . ."[11]

Esherick himself also discussed Dreiser's womanizing to Dreiser biographer W. A. Swanberg in 1962, which is cited in Jerome Loving's recent biography of Dreiser, *The Last Titan*. Loving states: "Wharton Esherick, an artist

THE CENTAUR PRESS
announces for immediate publication
Reflections on the Death of a Porcupine and other Essays
BY D. H. LAWRENCE

NEARLY half the book is devoted to *The Crown*, a long and important philosophical essay. A portion of *The Crown* appeared originally in the pages of a comparatively little known magazine, *The Signature*, copies of which are practically unobtainable. The whole of *The Crown*, which E. M. Forster calls the finest of Lawrence's shorter pieces, is thus made available for the first time. The remaining essays, five in number, have not hitherto been printed.

The edition consists of 925 numbered copies, printed from type. The book contains 250 pages, and is bound in brilliant French boards. Each copy is individually boxed.

The price of this, the second book of *The Centaur Press*, is four dollars a copy.

1224 Chancellor Street · Philadelphia

Figure 20. Advertisement for D. H. Lawrence's *Reflections on the Death of a Porcupine and Other Essays* with Esherick porcupine woodcut, 1925.

whom Dreiser met in 1924, testified that it was his impression after knowing the writer for many years that Dreiser couldn't control his sexual appetite. 'He was absolutely a fool with a young girl—those beautiful 16-and 17-year olds. He always wanted to get them on his lap.' Esherick added that Dreiser persisted in this conduct even in the company of the woman who eventually became his second wife. Although Dreiser's interest in pubescent girls generally did not go beyond such flirting, he did later have a sexual affair with a seventeen-year-old and may have been similarly interested in her fourteen-year-old sister."[12] Apparently, however, the pine bust in the studio was the earlier "sketch" for a mahogany version, both from 1927, which he gave Dreiser. But Dreiser's conduct did fracture their friendship.

Fronting the Essentials

Esherick finally began to build the workshop that would later become his home in 1926, at the age of thirty-nine. His last addition to it was the silo he had always wanted. It was completed in 1966, just four years before his death. In deciding to build his own studio, he was influenced by the success of his friend and fellow artist, Henry Varnum Poor, who had built a studio in New City, New York. Originally it was only a one-room workshop, but Esherick added on a storage room above the workshop the next year, and afterward made the storage area his bedroom, perhaps at the time he separated from his first wife.

The workshop built in 1926 embodied his transition from painting, through woodcuts, to furniture making and sculpture. As Esherick said, "I began to make furniture for myself, and people would say, 'Wharton, sell that thing.' I'd sell the piece, and I began to think, if I can sell my furniture and can't sell my paintings, why don't I make some more furniture?" Although Esherick stopped painting, he continued to draw throughout his life and left some two thousand or more drawings at his death, some of which have been published in book form.[13] His drawings are notable for their expressiveness with minimal lines, and a number were starting points for wood sculptures.

In 1941, Esherick added another room and kitchen area. The kitchen illustrates Esherick's intimate connection to landscape and trees. When he first went to look for some cheap land in the Paoli countryside in 1913, Esherick was taken by a large cherry tree in front of an old farmhouse, a tree with which he felt an immediate connection. He bought the property. When the great tree died in the late 1930s, he cut it, slabbed it, seasoned it, and then used it for the walls of the exhibit on which he collaborated with architect

George Howe, *Pennsylvania Hill House*, at the America at Home Pavilion at the 1939/40 New York World's Fair. When the fair ended, he used the cherry wood for the walls of his kitchen, continuing his relationship with the tree he so admired (see plate 3).[14] Architect Louis Kahn said, "Trees were the very life of Wharton. I never knew a man so involved with trees. He had a love affair with them; a sense of oneness with the very wood itself . . ."[15]

Over the kitchen table is a light pull, a curving form that is actually an ox-tail vertebra, taken from a soup given to him by a neighbor. Architect Louis Sullivan is known for his expression "form follows function." Perhaps Esherick's variation might be, "friendship finds functional form."

Esherick's playful mastery continually joined mature expression with exuberant joy, as is visible in his kitchen floor. It is made from "scrap" apple and walnut wood, including "crotch" wood given to Esherick by Ed Ray, a wood-man who grew up at the bottom of Mount Misery. Ray spent time while still a teenager in the Northwest as a lumberjack, and returned to Pennsylvania to continue logging for the rest of his life, supplying Esherick with wood for over forty years. Ray told Esherick he could have the wood for free if he carted it himself, since it was not sellable to Ray. Years later, Ray joked about how Esherick had "taken" him on this deal. Yet Esherick fitted the irregular crotch wood boards into a flowing, curving composite that even include, if you look closely enough, two shapely legs and a crotch.

In the mid-1930s, novelist Ford Maddox Ford visited Esherick's house on Mount Misery and wrote of it in his book *Great Trade Route*:

A dim studio in which blocks of rare woods, carver's tools, medieval-looking carving gadgets, looms, printing presses, rise up like ghosts in the twilight while the slow fire dies in the brands. . . . Such a studio built by the craftsman's own hands out of chunks of rock and great balks of timber, sinking back into the quiet woods on a quiet crag with, below its long windows, quiet fields parcelled out by the string-courses of hedges and running to a quietly rising horizon . . . such a quiet spot is the best place to think in.

And let Esherick be moving noiselessly about in the shadows, with a plane and a piece of boxwood, or swinging backwards the lever of his press, printing off his engravings. Or pouring a hundred times heavy oil and emery powder on one of the tables he has designed, and rubbing it off with cloths to get the polish exactly true, and bending down again and again to get the sheen of the light along the polished wood. . . . Those are the conditions you need for thought. Because they present to your mind neither success nor failure, but conditions coeval with the standing rocks and the life of man. There have always been craftsmen and the craftsmen have always been the best men of their time, because a handicraft goes at a pace commensurate with the thoughts in a man's head.[16]

Ford's description of Esherick's studio home beautifully illustrates what "fronting the essentials" of life really can mean. Fronting the essentials does not have to be bare survival or minimal subsistence, though these too can be nurturing "conditions you need for thought." The full engagement of Esherick with his craft, carving out, refining, and finishing his wood works, feeling and thinking from them, his craft bodied into his studio and coalescing from the living landscape surrounding him, these are the essential conditions that co-carved Esherick and his wood-world.

Esherick's studio home was an organic expression of his life and work-in-progress, down to the tiniest details. As the Esherick Museum brochure states: "he carved the doors, forged the hinges, shaped the copper sinks, sculpted the andirons, the heater grilles" (one of which is actually a map of the property), "light switches and fixtures; door latches, stairs, walls, ceilings, and floors; kitchen cabinets and counters—even a set of coat pegs depicting the workmen who had helped him."[17] Esherick playfully peopled his home with the people—and bird—who helped him build it. Miriam Phillips described these coat pegs to me:

Those are the men that helped him build this house. That's the carpenter. That's the bird who sang and cheered. There's the mason, laying stone. And there's the hod carrier, a black man. That's ebony. And that was a fat bellied man, pulling the cart. And there's the boss himself. That's Wharton, with his mallet, you see, and his chisel. They're coat pegs, but why should they be ordinary. Now he was a carver, and wanted to express something. And that was his way of doing it.

When I asked Mima what it meant to Esherick to have almost everything in his home made by his own hands, she told me:

Well I think that happened because that was what he wanted to do. I mean he didn't go out and buy something, first of all he didn't have money to buy a lot of things, and secondly, a lot of these things are here because they didn't get sold. But the built-in things were things that he did because he needed or wanted them as a part of the living, and nobody else could have done it as satisfactorily. I mean, could have made the things to suit him, and that was part of his own expression. That was a part of his art.

See, he had a theory about furniture, too. He would say, "Furniture should be kindly. It shouldn't jab you." That's why all the corners to the chairs are rounded off, you see, most of them, and why there's a flow in the tables and the desks, so that the body can move along easily, without getting jabbed. Now look at that (towel racks and toilet seat). And why should he hire somebody to do things like this. He could do them and

Plate 1 Wharton Esherick's home, now a museum. Courtesy of the Wharton Esherick Museum.

Plate 2 Oak spiral stairs, 1930 and 1940, dogwood and mastodon tusk railings. Courtesy of the Wharton Esherick Museum.

Plate 3 Kitchen. Courtesy of the Wharton Esherick Museum.

Plate 4 Alson Clark, Panama City, 1913, oil.

Plate 5 Oil painting by Ezene Domond, no date.

get what he wanted. But he didn't map it out in advance. He made use of what was there, like the wall.

Mima pointed to the shower area of the bathroom wall, where Esherick had placed a stone carving of a bird in the rain. He had made the carving many years before building the bathroom, and the design question of how to make the shower wall found its organic solution: bird in rain, decorative form and function united. She continued:

And then this (the copper sink). Now the plumbing. He wouldn't attempt to do any plumbing himself. He knew his limitations. He wasn't going to fool with that. He needed his time for something else. Why should he bother with a thing like that. But he would paint it, you see.

Esherick's concern for creating and building his environment perfused his work. The house became far more than a functional or, as might be the case with other artists, aesthetic shell around his *real* work, his *real* work was forged in the making of the house into an organic home.

Vocabulary of the Awakened Mind

Esherick evolved his own distinctive art even while open to and influenced by other styles. Yet as he got older he spoke less and less about his art or about art in general. His early furniture appears almost medieval, evoking the arts and crafts movement of which he was an active participant in the Rose Valley community around where he lived. The Rose Valley Association was begun at the beginning of the century by architect William Price, Joseph Fels—who also helped start the Fairhope colony in Alabama—and others to create a community in the spirit of the arts and crafts movement championed in England by William Morris, John Ruskin, and others.

By the early 1930s, Esherick moved toward expressionist geometrical and art deco influenced work. Throughout his work there seems to be a strong influence of the curving forms of art nouveau, although radically simplified, and from the mid-thirties curving forms predominate. He said of his earlier stylized and more narrative forms, "That's literature and I'm not doing that anymore."

Some of Esherick's pieces seem related to furniture by the great Spanish architect and artist Antoni Gaudí, who preceded Esherick by a generation. Yet when his friend, composer George Rochberg, asked him in the early 1960s what he thought of Gaudí's work, Esherick replied that he had never heard of him. One also sees possible influences of shaker furniture, also noted for its functional simplicity.

While the "shaking up" of our normal perspective is, perhaps, the keystone of much of modern art, Esherick's vocabulary, his trajectory toward design rooted in natural forms, toward expressing complexity in simplicity, and the aesthetically beautiful in functionally usable everyday objects, might seem to set him in opposition not only to many of the values of modern art, especially that of the post–World War II period, but also of mass culture. But this is too restrictive an interpretation. It seems to me that Esherick indeed rejected the tendency in modernism and in mass cult toward depersonalized expression, whether through rigid conformism of mass-produced objects, such as plastic Tupperware, or rigid idiosyncrasy of high art works abstracted from felt communication. Neither met Esherick's need for organic connection. Yet Esherick also produced a number of abstract sculptures, free forms such as *The Pair* (1951), *Twin Twist* (1940), or *Rhythms* (1965). The simple key to abstracting, as Esherick once told his daughter Ruth when she was attempting an abstract drawing, was: "Don't ever try to abstract something until you know what you're abstracting from."[18] This simple advice recognizes abstraction as a culminating a process rather than a conceptual starting point, a process rooted in the meaning of the word, yet forgotten by many abstract artists.

So rather than seeing Esherick as rejecting modernism, it seems to me more accurate to see him as finding his own way in his art, the result of which retains and celebrates a core idea of modern art as a means for freedom of expression. We should remember the many examples of mass-produced furniture produced in Esherick's time, and especially in the postwar period. Companies such as Haywood-Wakefield, Herman Miller, and Knoll Associates turned out fine furniture that was mass-produced, that exemplified modernist ideals, and some of which resonates with Esherick's works.

One can also trace modernist impulses all the way back to the literary transcendentalists: to Walt Whitman's free verse, to Melville's polyphonic expressions in *The Confidence Man* (whose title character appears in many guises), and quest for final closure in Ahab's pursuit of *Moby-Dick*. And in Thoreau's *Walden*, one even finds the idea of starting from ground zero, often associated with twentieth-century architecture, but here expressed as modernist naturalism: "Before we can adorn our houses with beautiful objects the walls must be stripped, and our lives must be stripped, and beautiful housekeeping and beautiful living be laid for a foundation: now, a taste for the beautiful is most cultivated out of doors, where there is no house and no housekeeper."[19]

Consider Richard Slotkin's claim that in the experience of Walden, Thoreau created for himself a vocabulary of awakened mind:

Before going to Walden, he had developed the germs of a system of values and a method of stalking life. . . . The objects (plants and animals) that Thoreau names become the word-symbols in the vocabulary of the awakened mind—not bare emblems of value, like beasts in a fable, but the living incarnation and expression of the values themselves. They require observation and depiction, in contrast to the usual imposition upon objects of the conventional vocabulary of symbols. Like the captivity and hunter tales, Walden frames Thoreau's conversion or awakening as a sojourn or expedition into the solitude of the wilderness.[20]

Esherick created a "Wharton Walden" in his furniture, sculpture, home, and interior designs. Like Thoreau, he created a vocabulary of awakened mind that makes us see and feel the everyday things around us, the things to which we normally become unconsciously conditioned. His pieces invite participation and personal encounter. Simply using an Esherick salad bowl, lifting lettuce with curving fork and spoon, is a form of tactile and visual play in itself, a sensuous vessel of awakening (see figure 21).

Esherick managed to continue the arts and crafts movement, which passed out of fashion with the ascendance of modernism after World War I, while yet able to incorporate the spirit of modernism effortlessly as well.

Esherick's vocabulary of awakened mind stands in direct opposition to those depersonalizing tendencies in mass cult, high modernism, and postmodernism, even as it is a quintessential expression of modernism. In Esherick's own words—one of the rare times he was recorded speaking on his aesthetic:

My sculpture is almost entirely wood sculpture—not stone or metal. Some of my sculpture went into the making of furniture. I was impatient with the contemporary furniture being made—straight lines, sharp edges and right angles—and I conceived free angles and free forms; making the edges of my tables flow so that they would be attractive to feel or caress. So I suppose it is called "free form" furniture. I have said over and over again that just because you are spending your energy making something beautiful it doesn't mean that it can't be functional. When I am creating a chair, for example, I continue to try it out by sitting in it to see that it is comfortable. My design follows function.

I am particularly interested in the many native kinds of wood, and an especially fine grained piece of wood often has a strong influence on how I shape it. I don't seek

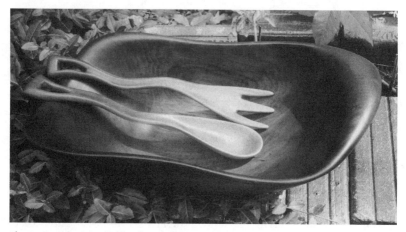

Figure 21. Esherick salad bowl, 1962. Private collection.

exotic or rare woods. I always say that if I can't make something beautiful out of what I find in my back yard, I had better not make anything.[21]

From his free-form furniture to his abstract sculptures, Esherick's vocabulary of awakened mind finds its freedom of expression in the boundaries imposed and the possibilities suggested by nature. Around the time I interviewed Miriam Phillips I began an inventory of Esherick's library, and found that he had placed this quotation from Thoreau's *A Week on the Concord and Merrimack Rivers* in his copy of *Walden*: "All the world reposes in beauty to him who preserves equipoise in his life, and moves serenely on his path without secret violence."

Permitting the Chance of Shadows through Curves

In 1956, Esherick collaborated with his long-time friend, the architect Louis Kahn, to build a new studio alongside his home. This was surely one of the oddest collaborations in twentieth-century architecture. Kahn is known for his "brutal" architecture, for an aesthetic that grew out of the modernist international style associated with Le Corbusier and Mies van der Rohe and sought monumental expression. His buildings included the Yale University Art Gallery, the Salk Institute in La Jolla, California, and the Capital Complex in Dhaka, Bangladesh.

Esherick admired Frank Lloyd Wright's writings about organic architecture, but not his geometrical "right-angle" architecture. He felt that organic design should not be constricted to straight lines. As he put it: "Any fool can draw a straight line." Esherick's designs for interiors, such as the home of Judge Curtis Bok, emphasized the flow of curves and spirals, and even his early "cubist" furniture was not right-angled.

So what do you get when you put these two iconoclasts together? You get a studio structured by three "interlocking hexagons, inspired by a bee's cell and built out of concrete block with 'the help of two Pennsylvania Dutch boys.'"[22] This would seem to be a perfect coincidence of opposites, meeting Esherick's organic sense with Kahn's formalism. But it was not so easy. Esherick wanted curved walls. More, he wanted "the accident built into the wall." To a formalist, those are fighting words, and fight they did, though able to put it politely for an interview in *Craft Horizons* magazine in 1959. Kahn said of Esherick: "The sculptor is not held back by any formalities or logic of building." Esherick replied: "You architects with your T squares and your triangles. The artist wants curves, color. Architecture must permit the chance of shadows through curves."

This last sentence is key to Esherick's sense of design, and marks a deep insight into the limitations of modernist formalisms that neglected shadow and curve in the name of light and form. Kahn himself was known as the modernist guru of "silence and light." More generally, it highlights a tendency I have noticed in "high" modernism for total symmetry, whose extremes can be found in the steel and glass "box" designs of the international style, and in twelve-tone serial composition. It is the symmetry of rationalism and formalism, and, it seems to me, the antithesis of the organic. The human body is symmetrical in many aspects, but includes and requires asymmetries as well. It evolved to sense, and be touched by, the variescence of organic life in which it was immersed. Again, consider African sculpture, in which the body is almost always depicted asymmetrically. And the body remains the key "form" from which art must derive, not a rational grid. An Esherick chair or room is made for the delight of the human body.

Kahn was sympathetic to Esherick's connection to nature, yet still was encapsulated by a rationalist's outlook, thinking that form requires formalism, that intuitive feel is not quite sufficient. He said: "Architects try to learn from nature, searching for a definable, buildable geometry. Wharton works through his feelings. He is as much aware of the captivating beauty of nature in repose as anyone I know."[23] Yet Esherick's designs were not only felt emanations of organic beauty, they were eminently functional and practical as well, which, ironically, some of Kahn's designs were not.

Kahn remains a big name in architecture, despite criticisms that his modernist functionalism sometimes caused dysfunction in buildings he designed, such as the Richards Medical Center in Philadelphia. Esherick has only recently emerged into the prominence he deserves as a master furniture maker, and has yet to fully emerge as a designer. Esherick's studio represents a fascinating meeting of the organic with modernist formalism. Kahn the formalist did not list it among his works, however. Perhaps with time it will be regarded as one of his more successful works, because of his collaboration with Esherick, not in spite of it. Apparently the two friendly antagonists "christened" its completion with a bottle of bourbon on Esherick's deck.

When the new studio was completed, a section of the floor of the main room of his home, which had been packed dirt, was dug out. Termites were discovered and so Esherick had workers keep digging until they rooted them all out. The result was that now his living room also functioned as a gallery and showroom for some of his sculptures, especially the taller ones, which then appear to rise dramatically out of the cellar into the room.

Joseph Esherick, Wharton's nephew, began learning from his uncle early on, and worked with him on the Bok house commission after graduating from college. He went on to become a prominent architect, and in 1990 spoke at a meeting of the members of the Wharton Esherick Museum:

One of my strongest recollections is of Wharton's railing against appearances— and I think he meant by this formalism, especially doctrinaire formalisms. His work is always about the issue at hand, whether the grain of the wood or the comfort of the chair or the curve that best expressed an emotion he felt. The fluidity and movement of his work is the product of intention and not style—and thus, stripped of the identifying trappings of style, it approaches a reality without the limits of time. It is from his devotion to a higher reality within and beyond himself that we can learn.[24]

Oblivion

If Esherick's home is a microcosmos, his spiral stairs (1930) is axis mundi, the world tree of Norse myths that stands as pivot of the universe (see figure 22). Directly next to it stands what is perhaps Esherick's masterpiece wood sculpture, *Oblivion* (1934). If ever there was a reincarnation of a living sensuous form then *Oblivion* is it: a reincarnation in inert matter of a visual image Esherick saw at the Hedgerow Theater and a reincarnation of the walnut tree he used as entwined lovers in naked passionate embrace. The year 1934 marked the beginnings of Esherick's turn to his later curvilinear style, and *Oblivion*, with its life-sized lovers carved from a massive walnut tree, exemplifies it to perfection.

Figure 22. Esherick sculpture *Oblivion*, walnut, 1934. Courtesy of Miriam Phillips and the Wharton Esherick Museum.

Esherick's *Oblivion* grew out of a performance of Lynn Riggs's play *Son of Perdition*, based on the novel by James Gould Cozzens. Esherick was an active participant in the Hedgerow Theater community from near its beginning in the early twenties. Jasper Deeter, its founder, enlisted him in making stage sets, props, and furniture for the theater. Esherick even acted in a couple of productions, playing a milkman in one play. He also made numerous drawings in the theater, usually while sitting in the balcony. Phillips told the story how once, when she was having trouble understanding what director Deeter wanted her to do, Deeter turned to Esherick and said, "Show her." Esherick drew two sketches, and pointing to one said, "This is what you are doing," and pointing to the other said, "and this is what he wants." She got it immediately.[25] Esherick made a drawing of entwined lovers while watching a performance of *Son of Perdition*, and it became the basis of *Oblivion*.

Cozzens's novel is set in a village in Cuba, ruled by an American sugar company, and involves a father murdering his son, who has raped his own sister. The novel opens dark political and psychological issues, seen in Stellow, the heartless capitalist, and Findley, the hedonist. Each of them corrupts the villagers and together project a kind of Janus-faced Americanism.

Esherick's work does not tend toward the "psychological." So why did he title his master sculpture *Oblivion*, which means Forgetting? Were ideas from the play involved? Or was it simply a striking image from the play, captured in the moment by the sketch Esherick made, and bodied forth in the sculpture? Was it what he saw in lovers embracing? Something essential that needed to manifest in a life-sized sculpture? Or was it also personal?

Perhaps such questions are unanswerable. Esherick had, however, separated from his wife Letty two years earlier. He had moved up the hill from their home into his studio, which was to be his home for the rest of his life. Whatever strains their marriage had, Letty also soon needed to be hospitalized for long term.

And by the year after he completed *Oblivion*, 1935, he began living with Mima Phillips, who remained with him for the rest of their life. She told me that she had had nothing to do with Esherick's separation from Letty, that they had gotten together only after the marriage relationship was finished. Perhaps this work is a pivot, not only of his turn to more curvilinear forms but also of the turn of his inner life from his now-finished marriage to his budding relationship with Mima. She was actively involved in the production of *Son of Perdition*, including corresponding with author Cozzens about it. Was she the figure Esherick drew, then sculpted, Pygmalion-like? And even if she were, would that fact have anything to do with what went into the work?

The Esherick Touch

When I asked Mima which people Esherick admired, she told me, "He read Thoreau as if it was his bible. I mean, he kept it by his bed like lots of people keep the bible, and he read it. . . . Emerson was a little too intellectual for him. But Thoreau wrote simply enough, and his prose, and also his closeness to nature in his writings about birds, and animals and flowers and plants and things—that appealed to Wharton also. Because . . . he was pretty close to nature himself. . . . There's a lot of nature's forms in his work. And his great attachment, I mean the way he looked at a tree, and the way he put his hand on it, like this, was like *nobody* else I ever saw."

Mima caressed the bench we were sitting on with her fingers; her words and gestures conveying Esherick's feel for living forms. Her words were as clear as could be, and I knew of Esherick's love of simplicity, his detailed knowledge of birdcalls and fauna, his appreciation for organic form. But it was only recently, returning to these materials after so many years, that the full import of what she had conveyed to me fully sunk in. The look, the touch. That was key to understanding Esherick. He did not simply develop an organic aesthetic as a style of art or even as a style of life. It ran far deeper than that.

It was about being touched by the life around him every day, about being directly in touch with it, about touching it directly. Wood was not simply a material to be shaped to human purpose, whether as furniture or as art. And it was not simply about finding a connection between the function of a piece of furniture and a beautiful form in which to express it. No, Esherick's vision went deeper. It was about touching the life around one, connecting to it as a fellow living creature.

"Look at the wonderful grain in this poplar," he once said of a mantel he was working on. "Did I know it was going to be there? Certainly not, but I am going to make the most of it. Hope I can hold this color. It's almost like flesh, isn't it?"

To love a tree in gaze or touch is of a piece with loving that killed tree you have dried for a couple of years and are now cutting up into some artifact. Simplicity leads one to realize that the wood remains the organic form of a living thing, possessed of its own potentials. Form is neither to be imposed upon the wood, nor imposed on the sculptor by the wood; rather, it is the living spark between them. The art is to allow the form to spring spontaneously from the wood, to catch the idea suggested by the wood. In Esherick's words again: "The wood has an influence on you. You can't fool with wood. I begin to shape as I go along. The piece just grows beneath my hands. I treat furniture as though it were a piece of sculpture. I dig up what I do out of my soul."[26]

Realizing those forms in a table or chair is the deepest form of beauty, when one can still feel or see the life of the tree in the chair. In Mima's words again, "I mean the way he looked at a tree, and the way he put his hand on it, like this, was like *nobody* else I ever saw."

Wharton Esherick was an American original, who, like Herman Melville and Charles Peirce, died poor and relatively unknown. America often does that to its best, burying them alive, while conferring unctuous luxury on its worst. He died in 1970, just as furniture was about to be declared "art" over the next decade and begin to bring in good money. He carved a life of freedom in the woods he loved, against the antiorganic aesthetics that dominated the arts in mid-twentieth century, and that condemned the wood craftsman to poverty. Yet Esherick's free-form furniture, sculpture, and home are also genuine expressions of modernism, of an organic modernism at home in its natural surroundings.

In an age of exotica, he delighted especially in using trees immediate to his house, yet one could not tell that the local woods looked affected. Toward the end of his life, he would say, "I'm only Esherick the man, but all of this is really Esherick." Is that simplicity as Thoreau meant it? To leave a house filled with things? With possessions? These living works were no mere possessions, but are testimonies to a life lived in love of its living surrounds.

Esherick found his own way to mastery not by pursuing an artistic style, but by his love for what trees and their wood could teach him, and by his desire to be himself, to express himself freely, without inhibition. He found himself in the woods he loved, delighting in found forms and the play of his imagination.

Esherick the man will remain essentially an enigma, because he wrote very little about his work and life. Yet a few remarks Esherick made provide insight. Sam Maloof and his wife visited Esherick some months before his death at age eighty-two. As they were leaving, Esherick said to Maloof: "'Sam, I'm still shaping the seats of the stools. The boys just don't get the hang of it. Oh, I wish you could stay longer, but I've got to go to the doctor in an hour—not feeling too good these days. Now you come back. But call me first,' he laughed, 'cause I may be having intercourse—or working on one of my sculptures!'"[27]

His work and life remained one to the end, whether still shaping the seats of the stools or engaged in the joy of intimate relations—which, of course, included making sculpture.

As he said to Maloof on another occasion: "If you don't have joy, are not enthusiastic with what you're doing, no matter how much dough you've got, you're no good."[28] I don't mean to get too complex here, but this seems to me to be the socialism of Esherick's youth, distilled by a lifetime's sufferings and joys on Mount Misery. In the end, as simplicity would have it, it is all about the joy, not the dough. Is that so difficult to understand?

Esherick's joys came at the cost of intense struggle, for staying the course of simplicity not only doesn't put the bread on the table, but it isn't easy either. It requires continuous imaginative bodying of new ideas into being, and a day-in-day-out discipline. But Bodhisattva Esherick, Buddha of wood, had enlightening words for this too: "Listen, if you go into this thing that I'm doing, you'll have a hell of a struggle—but you'll have fun." And another time, standing by his sculpture called *Fun*, he said, "If you take the *fun* away, I don't want to have anything to do with it!"

10

THE ART AND CRAFT OF HOME

rejectamenta: 1. Things thrown away as worthless or useless. 2. Excrement.

But it is in our nature as human beings to clutter, and we hanker for places set aside, reserved for storage. We tend to accumulate and outgrow possessions at the same time, and it is an endlessly discomforting mental task to keep sorting out the ones to get rid of. We might, we think, remember them later and find a use for them, and if they are gone for good, off to the dump, this is a source of nervousness. I think it may be one of the reasons we drum our fingers so much these days.

—LEWIS THOMAS[1]

Thing-Stories

In the beginning, there is creation. In the end, there is property. In the middle, there are thing-stories: thing-stories that throw light on the often-fantastic ways in which we people our environments with objects, especially the domestic environment.

Imagine the following thing-stories: In the early nineteenth century a Native American woman marries a French settler in the American Midwest. A treaty concluded August 29, 1821, in Chicago between the United States and the Ottowa, Chippewa, and Potawatamie nations of Indians cedes land to the United States, but in Article 3 of the treaty it is stated:

There shall be granted by the United States to each of the following persons, being all Indians by descent, and to their heirs, the following tracts of land. . . . To Madeline Bertrand, wife of Joseph Bertrand, a Potawatamie woman, one section of land at the Parc-aux-Vaches, on the North side of the River St. Joseph. To Joseph Bertrand, Jr., Benjamin Bertrand, LAURENT BERTRAND, Theresa Bertrand, and Amable Bertrand, children of the said Madeline Bertrand, each one-half of a section of land, at the portage of the Kankakee River. The tracts of land herein stipulated to be granted, shall never be leased or conveyed by the Grantees or their heirs, to any persons whatever, without the permission of the President of the United States and such tracts shall be located after the said cession is surveyed and in conformity with such surveys, as near as may be and in such manner as the President may direct.

The land of one of Madeline's sons, Laurent, was to be sold in 1833 (see table 1), but because of the treaty of 1821 it had to have the permission of the president of the United States of America. Treaties being what they are and property being what it is valued to be, the land is sold on July 23, 1833, for $1,200, the permission is granted by President Andrew Jackson a year later on April 10, 1834, and over the rest of the century the property is divided and subdivided, as civilization marches ever onward.

In September 1838, under orders by President Andrew Jackson, over 850 Potawatomie people are rounded up and marched at gunpoint 660 miles over the next two months to the frontier state of Kansas, with over forty people, mostly young children, dying. This ethnic cleansing of the Potawatomie and

Table 1

	Treaty				
Law	Date	Nation	Reserve	Tract	Remarks
310	1821 Aug. 29	Chippewa and others at Chicago	Laurent Bertrand No. 110	One half of a Section at the portage of the Kankakee River, E. 1/2 of 2, 2 E., Fort Wayne	By Deed dated 23 July 1833, Laurence Bertrand for the sum of $1,200, conveys this tract to Francis Coquillard. Deed approved by the President 10 April 1834

numerous other tribes in the Midwest becomes known as the Trail of Death march. Only heads of families on the march are recorded, and a Lewis Bertrand with family of nine is listed. Perhaps "Lewis" is an Americanization of "Laurent," or perhaps it was a relative, but in any case, both the Bertrand family and the treaty with them is violated. The "American dream" marches on. The land is resold and subdivided over the remainder of the century, tainted with the blood of the death march, the march of progress-making blood-money property, tainted like the mythical Yoknapatawpha County of William Faulkner's fiction.

On one lot of Laurent's original property, in 1910, a modern prairie style house is built for a pediatrician, Charles Hansel, who works at the hospital two blocks away. It is influenced by one built by Frank Lloyd Wright a quarter of a mile away in 1906 for K. C. DeRhodes. Hansel and his wife Rose also operate the Children's Dispensary, which provides free and reduced-cost medical care for impoverished children, farther down on West Washington Street from Wright's 1906 building, and so perhaps were influenced by it when they chose a local architect, W. W. Schneider, to build their prairie style home. Their Dispensary becomes the Hansel Neighborhood Center after their deaths, and remains in operation until 2004.

Eight years after building their home, on their twentieth wedding anniversary, August 30, 1918, Charles Hansel dies. On September 19, 1919, his wife sells the house, and three weeks later on October 10, 1919, while returning from visiting her son in Goshen, her Cadillac slides off wet brick pavement, rolls over twice, and she dies. As the *South Bend Tribune* notice observed, "Mrs. Hansel had been planning to move to Goshen to live with her son. She had just sold her home on Horatio Court."

Was it a simple accident or some darker depression or despair that figured into her crashing her car on the country brick road? Her husband gone, her son living on his own, I imagine her lonely in her big, modern home. Perhaps it held memories too painful to bear, and that is why she sold it relatively quickly. Perhaps she did the memory equivalent of ethnic cleansing, only to find herself on her own trail of death a few weeks later.

Numerous owners and renters occupy the house for the rest of the century. One woman tells of renting the downstairs, when the house was split up in the 1950s and 60s as two apartments. She and her husband get into a terrible car crash, and are in the hospital for some months. When they emerge and try to get their lives together, they return to their apartment at this house, only to find that all of their belongings have been ejected by the landlord onto the front porch, and the apartment rented out to others. This woman also describes a previous renter who grabbed a hammer and attacked the fine-grained oak trim and fiber panels that divided the bottom apartment from the one above, either from anger or insanity. Miraculously he did not damage the built-in oak and glass bookshelves that stretch the length of the living room, around the great prairie brick fireplace.

The last of the twentieth century owners, who is me, reads the cleansed "property" version of this bloodied history of the march of murderous materialism in the old title of property that came with the house, and decides to tell its stories to you. Or at least those stories he can find, for so many of the life-dramas of its first century are unrecorded.

Thing-Story: Forgotten Impressions

A boy born in Chicago in 1875 grows up to be a painter, studying first at the Art Institute. He later goes east to study with William Merritt Chase in New York, then off to Paris to study with James A. M. Whistler and Alphonse Mucha, and to immerse himself within the world of impressionism. He is one of many Americans inspired by impressionism, and who bring it back home to regions around the country. This painter, Alson S. Clark, goes to Panama in 1913 to record the completion of the Panama Canal in paintings. His juices flow, pouring into many paintings, some of which are exhibited at the O'Brien Gallery in Chicago, a number of which are taken by Clark to Paris, then hurriedly rolled up and taken as baggage as Clark and his wife Medora leave a Europe erupting in war. They are then exhibited in the Panama-Pacific International Exposition of 1915 in San Francisco, and the next year at the Art Institute. The Panama paintings are dispersed after the exhibition.[2]

Two of them ended up, probably after the 1913 O'Brien exhibit, in the collection of wealthy Chicagoans, Mr. and Mrs. William G. Hibbard Jr., and their mansion in the most exclusive district in Chicago at the time, 1337 Prairie Avenue, just south of the loop. In the 1930s Mrs. Hibbard pencils on the back of one of the paintings, "from Mrs. Hibbard - Nov. 193_ [date torn], to Rudolph—..."

Some sixty years later, in 1998, an antiques dealer who specializes in guitars, amplifiers, old record albums, and, as he puts it, things he likes, reluctantly stops at a yard sale in a lower-middle-class neighborhood in South Bend, Indiana. He is supposed to be somewhere else, but decides to stop. Not seeing much there, at some point he picks up a faded artwork. The homeowner says to him, "If you like art, I have a couple of old paintings in the garage." She brings out two small, framed paintings, covered with decades of garage dirt. Or let us call it ample patina. The antiques dealer can only make out enough through the grime-covered glass to see that they look interesting, but can't really see the detail. So he offers her money for them. He offers her a dollar for each painting. She agrees to his price. But when he looks in his pocket, he only has a dollar and twenty-five cents. He asks her if she would take that. She generously agrees.

He goes to his auto, wipes the glass covering with a towel, and sees two paintings whose use of color and shadowing touch him. The artist's name is inscribed, so he drives to the antique mall where he has a stall, and consults with a painting dealer there about these paintings from 1913 by a painter named Alson Clark. He discovers that Clark is a well-known California impressionist from the early twentieth century, whose work is currently undergoing a revival after suffering more than seventy years of supposed "obsolescence" due to artistic modernism. He enjoys the paintings for some months before selling them. He makes a profit, well over hundreds of times what he paid for it. An art dealer buys one painting as a birthday gift for his wife. The other painting ends up in a prairie style home built by the Hansels in 1910 (see plate 4).

Fantasia on Materialism and Craft

The terms *materialism* and *everyday life* connote a world of utility, a far cry from the fantastic. When advertisers in the United States spend more than $565 per person, or over $2,200 per family of four, or about 2 percent of the gross national product (over $115 billion in 1994) per year (not counting an additional $115 billion for store displays, coupon redemptions, trade shows, and such), it is serious business.[3] Yet even a quick glance at the world of consumption, as seen in advertising, in shopping zones, and in the consumption-related practices of the home and desires of its inhabitants, reveals an efflorescence of the fantastic: a wonderland of eat me, drink me, buy me, sell me, desire me, have me. In this materialistic fantasia we are what we eat, drink, desire, buy, and possess, without necessarily being ourselves. One's own spontaneous self may be precisely what is sold for the promises of the consumer self.

But this is the fantasia of the mass-produced commercial commodity. Consider creation and property from the viewpoint of craft. Here is one working definition of craftsmanship: Furniture making master Sam Maloof turning down a $22 million dollar check over twenty-five years ago for the mass production of his furniture. Another, and the more common one, would be Wharton Esherick living a low-income life, dedicated to the pursuit of his organic vision. But perhaps these are also extreme examples of people who devoted their whole lives to their craft.

Purchasing a craft object in a museum is consumption culture's equivalent to purchasing a saint's relic in a church—it puts one in touch, literally, with the legitimized sacred center of secular society, the museum. People speak in hushed tones in art museums, they maintain the boundaries of the untouchable zones, and they know that purchasing a craft object is a guarantee of one's status and good taste—and the more expensive the object, the better the guarantee.

An Amazonian Xinguano native once described a visit to a plantation owner's home. He was convinced that the whites were magicians, because they possessed so incredibly many things, but never seemed to spend the time to make them. Living utterly from *self-originated experience*, he could easily see the magic nature of civilized, commodifed, propertied existence.[4]

I feel like one of those white magicians whenever I attend a conference. I drive or fly across vast stretches of land or even across an entire ocean by no power of my own, sit at banquets every meal I eat, and a while back, sat magically at a banquet near London in a newly made chair I did not make but which was made for me by a student furniture maker and meant to be assembled by me with a few strokes of a rubber mallet. On these occasions I find myself eating a wealth of foods I neither hunted nor gathered nor prepared, from place settings I did not make. Perhaps such a magician, living-it-up through no direct effort of his or her own, can be defined as *craft deficient*. Yes, thanks to the benefits of what Herman Melville termed *snivelization*, the commodity, whether mass-produced or handmade, spares us the effort of making our world completely by ourselves, and comes ever more to make it for us.

I was and am, like you, a commodity magician, immersed within this phantasmagoria of civilization and its goods. Yet in less than a month after I was given the handcrafted chair in England, I was at the other extreme, learning the basic arts and crafts of hunter-gatherer life, of traditional Native American ways, at Tom Brown Jr.'s wilderness school. There I found myself building a shelter, making tools and clothing, finding food, practicing the tracking and camouflage and meditation ways Brown learned from his Apache master Stalking Wolf, all from the uncommodified earth. After that bare glimpse into hunter-gatherer life I must admit that the world from which that Amazonian Xinguano originated is the one that seems magical to me, magical in its self-originating abilities and varieties of subtle and sophisticated organic awareness.

This raises the question: What is the place of the fantastic in everyday life in the home? *Everyday life* is a term in the social sciences that connotes the commonplace, the habituated experiences of familiarity. But think about it.

"Everyday," or rather every night, 6 billion human beings dream fantastic visions, visions fashioned from our sophisticated cultural worlds and their images, feeling-tones, smells, touches, tastes, sounds, and desires. Yet these visions emanate from our hunter-gatherer, primate, and mammalian bodies, the same bodies with which we walked ourselves, as eco-philosopher Paul Shepard put it, out of the Pleistocene era into the present. We must inhabit this realm of the fantastic not only to retain our connection to reality but also to survive. In our beds we dream visions of unlimited possibilities: of fantastic powers, of speaking with the dead, of loving forbidden lovers, of touching unknown realms of delight and horror. We envision these things in our homes while in utter bodily paralysis, while literally "embedded."

But we experience the fantastic more consciously in those beds as well: we sex it with our lovers, we imagine it with our reveries, we find our autonomy in our bed as adolescents, and hugs and security with our teddy bear sleeping-mates as children. The bed, that solidity of nightly rest, is a magic carpet, transporting us to fabulous realms of phantasm.

But is the rest of the home so very different? Just consider the utilities of phantasm: the refrigerator as electro-cornucopia, with its magical food, from magical supermarkets; or the magic of water, to drink and bathe and flush; magical temperature control; magical lighting, twenty-four hours a day, all the work of magical slaves, the machines that have ever-increasingly populated the home.

Things, it would appear, are not always what they seem. The things of the home are clearly the terminus of consumption culture, trophies of the money exchange and its promise of status and identity. No contest there. But they, and the home, are also active sources of imaginative life. Living at home is more than a survival strategy and should be more than a dumping ground of consumption practices; the art and craft of the home are what make a house and its belongings a home, and what make a home a way of living.

Think about it. In both its design and furnishings, and in the practice of home-life, the home can be more than the mastering of necessities; it can be a realm of freedom. It need not be the unavoidable target of consumption culture and its enslaving devices, but rather a "domestic refuge" for the practice of life. Domestic refuge many seem different from a wildlife refuge, unless we consider the spontaneous and autonomous self as an endangered species in consumption culture. In this sense the thing-stories of a home may be acts of creation, and one criterion in considering possessions and the question of materialism is whether the things and their thing-stories are *in the end* mere property indicators or whether they can act as means and embodiments of self-creation through the practice of the art and craft of the home.

Self-originated experience is at the heart of being human, and of partaking in the local worlds of everyday life. Yet it is precisely self-originated experience that the megamachine of contemporary consumption culture attempts to replace, promising to release our creative, transgressing, and different-from-the-herd identity through the magical power objects we purchase—consumption as alchemy. Yet to paraphrase Lewis Mumford: Do-it-yourself only matters if there is a self to do it.[5] When nobody's home, so to speak, nobody profits from somebody's compulsive spending.

The contemporary civilized self lives at home with its possessions somewhere between creation and property. In consumption culture it is expected to live with its things as but one more piece of property. But in its genuine life the self lives its own continued creation through the life of the home, in which its possessions are habits of that life. When a possession loses touch with life, it becomes a closed habit, a prop. When a home loses touch with life, through the insulating effects of its status props, of habituated passive activity, it becomes an empty showcase, a mere house or apartment, not a home. And its owner/possessor runs the risk of becoming reduced to the status of a prop as well, habituated to things, even while disconnected from them. Thus materialism comes full circle: when possessions possess the possessor, they do so mentally, as habituation to the abstracted *ideas* the things connote. Materialism is, in this sense, a mentalism, an attachment to an idea that is simultaneously a divorce from the possession. But perhaps another perspective—by incongruity perhaps—is that we need to become *more* materialist, more aware of the things we surround ourselves with and the meanings they hold.

Habits provide a common ground for conduct, an automatic structuring that allows our concentration to go elsewhere, whether further into the groove of the activity or further removed from it. Living genuinely involves that renewal of habits that is experience, infused by creation. When experience becomes overly habituated people become what I could best describe as "crustacean," encased in that external structure. Many Americans today think that being so encased is a form of invulnerability, whether in status or in body fat. Yet to creatures of skin, that loss of engaged touching and feeling of the world is an entombment, a death. We must feel the world around us and within us as part of our tangible being in the world.

We are made to touch and be touched by the world, which is quite different from possessing it. We evolved as participants in the creation of the world without and within. Yet at that great change to controlling and possessing the environment that emerged with agriculture and civilization, we turned into property or propertied spectators, one step removed from the touch of creation. We created the world in which the makers by and large serve the takers.

"The lyf so short, the craft so long to lerne"—Chaucer

Tell you what, I am going to unpack my living room. My books are already on the shelves, paintings on the wall, mementos ensconced on various surfaces. Yet I plan to unpack these things nonetheless, and tell some more thing-stories that hopefully will be saying some things about you too. Come along on my "house tour," as I unpack meanings of things as critic Walter Benjamin once did in an essay by unpacking his library. In the course of the tour, I hope various perspectives on the art and craft of home-life will emerge.

Who among you does not have extra-utilitarian possessions in your living quarters, however meager or sumptuous? You would be hard pressed, indeed, to live by purely "utilitarian" objects, because even what are regarded as today's virtual necessities—ranging from refrigerators and toilets to microwave ovens, televisions, and sound systems—are typically yesterday's luxuries. When Aristotle said that one must have a household to be a citizen, meaning that one must master the necessities of life in order to be able to live well as a free citizen of the polis, he conceived a world far from the luxury-saturated "necessities" of today's "first-world" households.

Traditional nomadic peoples, who travel lightly, nevertheless travel with objects providing sustenance through meanings that transcend utility, including things, such as a sacred pipe or shell, that touch the divine. Even the humblest object, whether to a nomad, a prisoner, or a homeless person, can provide a touchstone to identity. One wonders then what the nonfunctional objects carried by contemporary homeless people might be? The homeless are also immersed in a culture dominated by commodity consumption goals, a culture that says having objects and displaying them is the way one confirms one's identity. What would you carry with you (in addition to this book I hope!) on the road of life if you were forced from your dwelling right now? Remember the scenes of people from New Orleans fleeing Hurricane Katrina on foot, loaded down with stuff, and gradually unloading it as the reality of their situation became clearer? Come to think of it, I don't think I would be carrying this book in those survival circumstances, though I can think of two nonreading uses where the paper would be handy.

"Things" are, after all, experiences, memories, relationships, habits, trophies, status symbols, and many other things besides mere physical objects or economic commodities. One's possessions can bespeak the possessor as well as more general social life and culture.

So-called advanced societies today are supposed to be defined by being consumer societies, whose cultural lives revolve around consumption, and whose homes are expected to be repositories of the objects consumed. It is a mark of prestige to have a home filled with a recognizable glut of new things—especially electronic devices such as *personal computers* (linking the term *personal* with *computer* still seems oxymoronic), fancy stereo systems, DVDs, and microwaves. And the wonderful thing about these electronic things is how they get old quicker and quicker, requiring newer models faster and faster.

Take the phenomenon of mudrooms in America, where architects are increasingly asked to include a mudroom in the design of new houses. Mudrooms, traditionally used to store mucky shoes or clothing, have become the new entrance to many homes, displacing not only the front door to the house but also the front hall as status display entry area. As New York architect Debra Wassman put it, "The mudroom reflects how you live your life more than the front hall. It gives you an indication of what is to come."[6]

What is also different about the contemporary trend of mudrooms is the enormous amount of gear and furnishings found in them, ranging from various kinds of shoes to purely decorative objects. One sees how the consumption culture, having created an increasing plethora of objects—specialized footwear and jackets, for example—then creates a new commodity in the form of a room to keep these objects in *and display them*. Having so many pairs of shoes that one must keep them in a special room is an excellent form of conspicuous waste, that time-honored means of status display. About the only things you are not likely to find in the new American mudroom is mud or manure. The new mudroom is one more outpost of the expansion of Mc-Mansion kitsch. *Kitsch:* the denial that muck happens.

Many social critics and social scientists, from Claude Lévi-Strauss and Erving Goffman to Jean Baudrillard and Pierre Bourdieu, have claimed that possessions and the experience of the home simply represent the status and class system. In addition there remain formidable cultural expectations that the living room will exhibit one's or one's family's personality and taste. But what is "personality" and "taste?" Are these simply labels, reducible to the maxim, "birds of a feather flock together"?

In my research on *The Meaning of Things*[7] I tried to show that while the system of status and class and commodity fetishism is objectively present, it is also possible to have genuine experiences with the objects in one's home—genuine experience that can help a person grow, or develop bonds with family or household members. Interviewing people about their possessions amply demonstrates how the typical home is an ongoing "show and tell" of the beliefs of its inhabitants; their stories reveal the myriad influences—conscious and unconscious, conventional and personal—that comprise the meanings of artifacts and the self. In other words, there remain possibilities for personal meaning not reducible to status and class meanings, even though possibly embedded in them.

Admittedly, however, consumer society tends to reduce people to the status of props, and the personal dimension of meaning to the vicarious substitute of the consumption system. Consumption, instead of becoming a means to experience, becomes an end in itself, and the consumer ultimately becomes consumed, swallowed into the system. Philosopher Albert Borgmann has used my research to distinguish distracting *devices* from reality-commanding *things*. The latter serve to connect us actively to our social world, the former passively to consumption imperatives. As Borgmann puts it: "A thing requires practice while a device invites consumption."[8]

Doug Rice, the antiques dealer who found the Alson Clark painting, noted that yard sales at the new upper-middle-class suburban developments located near the major shopping mall complex are dominated by recently consumed goods from the mall, and probably sold to make space for new purchases. He describes these neighborhoods as an antiques dealer's wasteland, as indicated by the objects sold. The goods tend to be manufactured in the past ten years, and those older objects frequently found at yard sales are virtually absent, suggesting whole zones of households both devoid of those physical indicators of subjective familial histories and replete with that overvaluation of perpetual novelty that is the hallmark of consumption culture. Similarly, there has been a great increase in self-storage facilities.

As Tom Litton, an owner of a storage facility and representative of the industry, pointed out in an NPR radio interview we did on "Storing the Self," many people are living in larger homes yet still have so much stuff they need to parcel it out to storage facilities. Glut is a growing reason to store things in an America undergoing an obesity epidemic and what might be called a "stuff epidemic." Between 2001 and 2005 new storage in self-storage facilities increased by 36 percent, and whereas it took twenty-five years to build the first billion square feet of storage space between 1973 and 1998, it only took eight years to build the second billion square feet between 1998 and 2005.[9] Americans are adrift in a Tsunami of stuff, unable to discard it or stop buying more of it.

When people choose to isolate themselves off into virtual worlds of consumption, into virtual neighborhoods, into virtual experiences through televisions, the Internet, or iPods and related devices, they begin to live in the dark underworld of normalcy, which produces robotic conformism—an underworld that involves never thinking one's own thoughts, never feeling one's own feelings, never making something oneself, whether it is music or a dinner. If the old expression "you are what you eat" is true, then the ultimate end of the contemporary system of consumption is to turn the person into a consumption commodity, "normalized" to consume.

The Art Wall

One wall of my living room is filled with art, which speaks deeply about my beliefs. Originally this wall had two sliding doors, but one was walled in when the house was temporarily made into two apartments in the 1950s. Prairie style homes tend to reflect Wright's attention to design details, which often translates into less available space for wall hangings. The remodeling may have reduced the architectural effect but enhanced the decorative possibilities since I like to have artworks on my walls.

I am at heart a fantastic realist, and the works on this wall embody my beliefs as well as representing my friendship with the creator of a number of them, himself a fantastic realist. Further, the works speak to me in their own right as works, though I cannot separate that from my predilections and prejudices.

If I tell you that I believe in William Blake's conception of The Poetic Imagination as a reality in human affairs, then I confess why I have a reproduction of his image illustrating a poem called "The Bard" on my wall. It also helps to explain why I framed a postcard of Odilon Redon's pastel, *Sita*. For years I have admired Redon's phantasmagoric way of painting. But my wall is dominated by Viennese fantastic realism, including a few works by my friend Fritz Janschka, a founder of that school. Two of these works picture fantastically James Joyce's novel *Finnegan's Wake*, and include brief passages from that novel, one in English and the other translated into German. Janschka claims to have learned English from that novel, which was itself an act of fantastic realism, given that he speaks English well, not simply in a Joycean surrealist dialect!

Now, if I were a depth psychologist, I might connect the Irish Joycean elements of these works, and the Irish traditions of bards in the Blake work, with my own Irish ancestry. But they do not figure into my sense of the meaning of these works. More significant to me is my admiration of the works and my friendship with Janschka. One of the two Finnegan's Wake works has an image of a king resembling my face, with a flower-haired queen next to him. Janschka inscribed this watercolor to me and my ex-wife and my son, using images of inscription more than words. For my son Jacob, he painted a tiny ladder representing Jacob's ladder: all the more remarkable to me because there is a large ladder on the left side of the work, to which Jacob's ladder, though an afterthought, organically connects.

You see, dear reader, the art on my walls is about rumination, about losing oneself temporarily in the world of the imagination, immersing oneself in the play world of expressive color, image, and form. Yet these walls also disappear for periods of time from consciousness in my everyday life. I find that I become habituated to the visual works of art in my home, either because I am busy with work, or books, or attuned more to music, or—forgive me charitable reader—because I occasionally sink into the bottomless pit of mindless television, my mind turned to stone by the unblinking electronic Medusa. But then there are times of visual reawakening, when my walls come alive again. For me, visual art can be part of the habits of home life, which can periodically enliven the eye and the soul, even as they also represent a cultural convention of interior decoration.

In *The Meaning of Things*, I made a distinction concerning how objects can provide aesthetic experience using John Dewey's distinction between *perception* and *recognition*. In this sense, recognition means that one sees an object and interprets it based on what one already knows. Hence, instead of having a genuine encounter with the quality of the object, the object makes sense because of one's prior schemes of interpretation and is fit into those categories. Perception, by contrast, goes beyond one's habit of interpretation, so that the qualities of the object are integral to the interpretation, thereby enlarging one's habits of interpretation, stimulating something new. Surely you know the feeling when you look at a familiar object and see it anew? Great works of nature and art have the capacity to seem continually fresh, to reveal new qualities despite repeated encounters. In my study, houseplants were actually described more frequently as a source for aesthetic experience than art objects.

But were I to limit the discussion to this level, I would certainly take too narrow a view. I should be able to step back, as a sociologist, and see how my art marks my socioeconomic class as well, shouldn't I? And what about you?

If the expression "seeing is believing" can be taken literally, then take a good look around your home dear reader, especially at your wall hangings. Do you have landscapes, abstract art, primitive art, photographs, or religious icons? What do these things say about you and your beliefs? Are you a "cultural capital" critic by day, concerned for the dominated classes, who yet by night relaxes amid abstract art pieces whose presence indicts you as a member of the dominating elite? Or have you established props of the working-class hero drawn from popular culture iconography? Have you found some happy medium—a Brueghel high art reproduction picturing the dominated peasantry? Or do your visual representations speak meanings other than class or education? Are they symbols of family ties, or perhaps signs of the distance you have made from your family? Are your landscapes populated or depopulated? Does what you have on your walls or mantels relate to whether you live in the city, suburb, or country?

These kinds of questions are systematically dealt with in a book titled *Inside Culture: Art and Class in the American Home*, by David Halle, which surveys the visual representations displayed in American homes. By turning the focus of art from the artist who made it or the museum that displays it or the critic who analyzes it to the home and the people who live with it, a very different perspective on art, class, and culture emerges.[10]

Halle, who told me his study originally grew out of an interest in *The Meaning of Things*, found that social class has real consequences for the selection and valuation of artistic, photographic, and religious images in the home. Yet, according to Halle, the relations between the meanings people attribute to their art and dominant classes and artistic elites, "is poorly understood if viewed exclusively through the lens of domination and power." I would concur with Halle's point; one need not completely dismiss those status-striving theories of culture—ranging from critical theory to Pierre Bourdieu's discussions of systems of distinction—so much as admit that culture is more fluid and multidetermined than these theories usually admit.[11]

Take landscape depictions, for example, which were the most common type of object in the homes sampled by Halle, comprising about one-third of all objects for all classes. Landscapes seem to function as a visual background opiate of the people, regardless of class. Only two of the 349 landscapes did not depict calm scenes, and these two have their own stories to tell.

Contemporary American landscapes are overwhelmingly depopulated, while people appear more frequently in historical or foreign landscapes. These depictions of contemporary American landscapes represent an ideal of a calm, depopulated landscape for all classes, reflecting, in Halle's interpretation, the suburbanization of life—including urban life—as well as the privatization of the domestic sphere, with its decline of extended family members and boarders and transformation of the backyard from associations with the outhouse in the early twentieth century into a leisure zone in more recent decades. A study of consumer desire by Russell Belk, Güliz Ger, and Søren Askegaard revealed similar findings, with a twist. Nature loomed large in collages by Americans and Danes, the dream of the outdoor other, but bright lights and big city predominated in Turks' collages.[12]

In my own case I have one landscape in my living room, a "landscape" as seen from below, that goes from carrots growing at the top down to the depths of hell, where a fantastic realist in the form of Satan plays diabolically happy Viennese Grinzing music. Janschka sent me the little hell landscape as a playful gift in appreciation for a recording I sent him of fellow fantastic realist painter and musician Arik Brauer's parody of Viennese Grinzing music titled in dialect *Geburn für die Gruam*—in English, *Born for the Grave*. This work is populated, and decidedly uncalm, so I do not appear to fit the pattern described by Halle. Perhaps another work in my dining room might qualify, a Renaissance landscape out of which grows a giant Madonna. Yet that work, although contemporary, can also be seen as "historical," so perhaps it matches the tendency described in the previous paragraph. Its religious realism would mark me as working class, but its modern fantastic proportions and nature contradicts that pattern by indicating me as upper middle class.

As the contemporary landscape representation became depopulated, homes seem to have become increasingly peopled by family photos, as was evident in Halle's study and my own. Yet the photos speak not only of family connectedness but also of the fragility of the contemporary family and protean course of the self. In my own case I find that photos of my children became crucial during my divorce, when I lived in an apartment for two years. My photos of them, placed centrally in the combined dining and living room of the apartment, became visual connections and symbolized my hope to be reunited with them. I was ultimately given custody of my two children, and the settlement involved me moving back into my house. I found that photographs of them became less important to me, and changed in significance to markers of special events rather than visual lifelines. This change of significance in my family photos leads me to interrupt my tour of my walls, briefly, to consider this aspect of meaning in the home environment.

Of the Waxing and Waning of Significance

The things of the home connote stability, tangibility, permanence. Yet "things change," as the expression goes, and there is movement not only of objects but also meanings. People periodically feel a need to move furniture and decorations, to purchase new objects and discard old ones—even when the piece of furniture or decorative object might still be perfectly good. In fact, consumer culture is predicated on continually creating the wants in people to consume ever anew. If advertising were to be outlawed, perhaps people could better appreciate what they have rather than what they think they want. In many of these movements and acts of consumption we see indicators of "identity work," though the more things change, the more the act of consumption stays the same.

What are your most recent additions to the objects in your living room, dear reader? Some of mine as I look around are: a CD I purchased a few days ago and fresh gladiolas I purchased yesterday at the farmer's market. Yes, consider flowers as objects of organic transience. One must change fresh flowers frequently or not have them around regularly (I fit the latter category), and one admires their transient beauty within the conventional form of flowers as decorations.

There is also the temporal dimension, the memories and changing moods of living rooms: memories of celebration, of holding my newborn son, my first child, on the sofa on returning from the hospital, memories of friends and lovers, of the departed—of what William James aptly called "the sadness of things." I remember gathering here with my now deceased friend Tony Kerrigan, who translated into English the Jorge Luis Borges book that sits over there in my bookcase and who gave me that postcard, now on my art wall, he made of a crayon drawing Picasso did for him during Tony's days as an art dealer in Majorca. I remember when my former teacher, Victor Turner, and his wife Edith and her sister were here for dinner just before he gave a talk on "Body, Brain, and Culture." I remember him repeating the saying from Chaucer displayed in the window of my dining room: "*The lyf so short, the craft so long to lerne.*"[13] Two months later he was dead.

In continuing to look at my living room, I discover a huge blind spot: my desk and its surrounds. There are a few forgotten boxes next to my desk, out of sight of the room. They are filled with photos and memorabilia from when I lived in the apartment during my divorce and were put there when I moved back in, next to the desk that had migrated from another room when I was gone. I need to unpack them, both literally and figuratively. Why have I not done so before? I find photos from the couple of years before the divorce, which I have not looked at since I first moved into the apartment. There are conference papers and notes, kept for their importance but unlooked at since I moved back into my house with my children. Perhaps life became too busy, or perhaps my time of transition was something I have not wanted to sort through. In any case, I find a large number of papers now extinct, useless, and needing to be thrown out. It feels good to throw off that dead past, but it necessarily leads me to another dreaded task: reconstructive archaeology on my desk. Here goes!

The Desk

Where do I find all the time for not reading so many books?
—KARL KRAUSS, *Aphorisms and More Aphorisms*, 1909

The junk that lined the periphery of my desk has now been sifted through and the contents assigned to new spaces or to the wasteland. The top of the desk is now actually visible. What was on it? Let me first turn the question around and ask: What is the junk in your home dear reader, and where do you keep it, and *why* do you keep it? What do your least precious objects tell you about yourself?

On top of my desk, amid the clutter, is a photo of my children and me at my father's seventieth birthday party I have been meaning to frame, some radio tubes, some harmonicas, and a number of books, which, to name some at random, include: Carl Schorske's *Fin-de-siècle Vienna; Animate Earth* by Stephen Harding; an encyclopedia titled *Blues Who's Who*; a sweet little publication called *Made in Germany—Played in USA: Die Geschichte der Mund-harmonika in den USA; An Intimate History of Humanity* by Theodore Zeldin; D. H. Lawrence's *Apocalypse; Don't Buy It*, a book about limiting consumption by Judith Levine that I have actually (permanently) borrowed from a friend; Odilon Redon's memoir *To Myself; The Family and Individual Development* by D. W. Winnicott; *Ropes to God: Experiencing the Bushman Spiritual Universe* edited by Bradford Keaney; *The Curtain* by Milan Kundera; *Opus Maledictorum: A Book of Bad Words* by Reinhold Aman; and, buried under some stuff, *Rubbish! The Archaeology of Garbage* by William Rathje and Cullen Murphey. I leave it to the reader to make sense of this assortment.

When one opens the drawers of one's desk, what is the pattern that reveals itself? There are the functional categories of filed papers and folders, financial records and the like, but what place do valued, especially nonutilitarian, objects find here? In my top desk drawer mixed with some financial papers I find some recent travel photos, souvenirs, letters, a voodoo doll whose origins and occasional uses I leave to the reader's imagination, photos from my musical performances, photos of my early childhood. Clearly, identity work can happen in a variety of contexts, from a desk drawer to the contents of your own wallet or purse. But why have I kept the desk in the living room? Sheer inertia I suppose. That too is a leftover habit I am now changing: Out damned desk!

The Wall of Bookcases and Fireplace

The fireplace is for me a place of rest, because to make a fire is to have the time to sit in front of it. It is an activity object that fosters contemplation, a seasonal object activated in winter as the focus of the room. It is a focus both in the literal sense the word "focus" used to carry as hearth, until Kepler transformed it to its more metaphoric mechanical meaning, and in the everyday sense of central point. In warmer weather the fireplace is still the central architectural feature of the room. On its shelf now sits a bowl from Papua New Guinea, an Austrian glass wine server, a wooden wind-up toy of a mad painter scattering paint and named "Jackson Pollock," and my "talisman teapot," surrounded by sea shells. The talisman teapot: imagine a reverse Pygmalion, where one admires a ceramicist's work, and later meets her and becomes her lover. My talisman teapot was made by a woman whose pottery I had admired and purchased for a couple of years before I ever met her. When I finally did meet her, it was to tell her that I was a fan of her work. But as we spoke something more was present between the lines of our conversation, those magnetic filaments of attraction. We met in her studio a few times, free-associating about art and life. The mutual attraction was clear, but neither of us acted upon it.

Sometime later I took a trip for a week and the day I was leaving, she presented me with a ceramic talisman she had made for my journey. While gone I spun out a poem based on the talisman and the sea, for we had spoken of my growing up on the Atlantic coast, a poem whose erotic undertones I knew could seduce her—though that was not the primary intent of my writing it—if I ever gave her the poem. During that same week, her thoughts of me led her to spin out an erotic teapot. Apparently we both had something on our minds. Some time after returning, I gave her the poem, she showed me the teapot, and our talisman projections drew us to each other. Talk about the meaning of things!

Although that relationship ended, the teapot means to me not only this woman and our relationship but also the whole fantastic circumstances of its making and of my past. I surrounded the teapot on the fireplace with sea shells, linking it further with my own memories of growing up on the coast of the Atlantic Ocean: a conch shell from a trip I took with friends when I was twenty years old, another conch I discovered in Florida on a trip with my son during my divorce. A ceramic conch figure forms the lid of the teapot. I have smooth stones, found on the beach on the island of Santorini, Greece, the source of the myth of Atlantis.

This is a strange place for me in my home, a place for play and memory. Just what is the object zone of an ex-lover? But this zone is more than that for me; it is a place where ceramic-shell memories come together, painful and joyful memories, which meet on the mantle of my hearth. It is a place I go to only occasionally—no more than a couple of times a year, to play with the shells of my memories. I regard seashells as the ultimate beach treasures. It is perhaps a kind of fetish zone in that way, a "soft" memory zone of hard seashells, ceramics, alabaster angels, and latent-active memories, playing on one another. On rare occasion.

Turning to my wall of books, I realize how suited my living room is to a scholar. Here is my own library, my own collection, my books—the treasury of the intellectual. But how does one characterize the collection, for no inventory can either get at the significance these books hold for me or at the disorderly reasons for many acquisitions. You see, I have not set out to "collect" books, though I have acquired some interesting ones—out of interest in the subject usually.

If anything, my reasons have been more inquisitive than acquisitive, with the exception of about fifteen books I acquired because they were old. Some of those were early editions of works I like, and some were just plain old, such as the book from 1693 I purchased for $12.50 in Chicago. It is beaten-up and of no value to any true antique book collector, but there is a magic for me in being able to touch and look through a work written over three hundred years ago in my own living room, like the ancient Babylonian clay tablet I once held in this same living room, inscribed three thousand years ago. Perhaps it is that magic of tangibility, somehow similar to that which I have felt in eating salad from my feather-light wooden Papua New Guinea salad bowl brought back from the still-living, so-called stone age by anthropologist friends, and in sitting down and striking the keys of one of Beethoven's original pianos in the living room of a wealthy homeowner outside of Philadelphia. Such contact experiences release a spring tide of fantasies similar to the spring tide of memories issued forth when browsing through one's own book collection.

It has been remarked that of all the ways of acquiring books, writing them oneself is regarded as the most praiseworthy method, and I have had to resort to this method myself on occasion. But to what extent is this true for possessions more generally? Is the homemade painting more praiseworthy than the purchased one? Or paintings, photos, works done in any medium, even spoken words remembered, or something done by family, friends, or acquaintances? Do these works hang in the living room, or is that reserved for officially recognized art? Clearly there can be friction in the home between art for art's sake, or for status sake, and art for the sake of the personal meanings it symbolizes, or personal obligations to display it. But homemade art should find its place, even beyond the refrigerator door, if the home is a life and not simply a museum.

There are those books whose authors are known personally to me, and I admit that I have never lost the curiosity and enjoyment connected with meeting the author of a book I know. It is somewhat like trying to match the faces and bodies of dogs with their owners. And so I have books and essays by friends and acquaintances who are poets, novelists, social scientists, critics, journalists—even painters. These books are more like friends, and their content is tinged by my recollection of the person. A number were gifts, but some were acquired through hunting the papery forests of bookstores, an activity somewhat akin to mushroom hunting.

Walter Benjamin's little essay "Unpacking My Library" beautifully embodies in the writing that sense of play he believes is crucial to collecting books: "Of the customary modes of acquisition, the one most appropriate to a collector would be the borrowing of a book with its attendant non-returning. The book borrower of real stature whom we envisage here proves himself to be an inveterate collector of books not so much by the fervor with which he guards his borrowed treasures and by the deaf ear which he turns to all reminders from the everyday world of legality as by his failure to read these books."[14]

Until writing this chapter I had deactivated my library to some extent. My daily schedule had turned so hectic; I was not going to my library much for enjoyment. A friend I ran into today, author of some of the novels in my bookcase, lamented how people are buying fewer and fewer books, how they go to the large Barnes and Noble bookstore simply to look at the books. Worse still, I jokingly replied, I find that I hardly have time even to look at new books, let alone purchase them, let alone read them.

Another reason I have spent less time with my library, definitely, is my return to playing blues music professionally, and a more general interest listening to and playing music in my living room. The last two compartments of my bookshelves are devoted to CDs and tapes, which are linked to my music wall.

The Music Wall

My music wall has the "obligatory" sound system typical of today's living room: the auditory altar. And my collection includes a time range from records that go back to my college days to contemporary CDs. The range of music represents my interests in a variety of music genres as well, with emphasis on blues, jazz, classical, Latin, and world music. Since I play blues professionally, my blues collection also is a source for learning as well as enjoyment and includes CDs and tapes of music I have made, just as my bookshelves include books I have authored. And I also enjoy those blues, jazz, classical, and other works recorded by those I know. I remember trading two of my blues CDs, which included original tunes by me, to a cellist friend for two CDs by his string quartet. This was great barter fun, given that I find very little overlap of musicians interested in the two music styles. Could I objectively score the value of that CD as an indicator of my class status, apart from the unique circumstances of its acquisition?

But the question that emerges, as I look at the ritual-like configuration that is my sound system, is why has music, as indicated in the tremendous growth of sound systems in the past few decades, grown so important? Is it because music provides expression of feelings? Or is the living room music-complex further evidence of the infiltrating and colonizing of the home and of emotional life by the megatechnic machine of modern life?

Even with the availability earlier in the century of record players and radios, an instrument in the home, such as the piano, was often the focal point for social, group singing, whereas the rise of the sound system has tended to produce a more passive listening to music. A high-tech powerful sound system strongly encourages one to consume music, and through sheer time spent listening to it structurally discourages producing music. The role of the sound system here, as in consumption culture more generally, hinges not even so much on whether the thing is bad, but rather how it is used. If, for example, a family uses its devices to open children to music making, that is fine, but if the process stops there and is used to teach children only to consume music, then it becomes just another example of the colonization of the home by the megamechanical consumption-entertainment complex.

Unfortunately this is the direction music has taken in the home, becoming a virtual straitjacket of formulaic music manifesting in a variety of devices, providing passive listeners substitute emotions that brain rinse them. The free-form alternative FM radio programming that grew out of the 1960s gave way to highly rationalized and specialized formatting, MTV found a way to make people "look at" music spectacles instead of listening, iPods and related devices enclose listeners in self-contained sound bubbles, deaf to the world around them. Users of these devices tend to engage music as an audio background to other activities, thereby disengaging themselves from the full, uninterrupted experience of music, and more, of the immediate awareness of their hearing, centered in their ears. Ecstasy means to stand outside of oneself, and canned music is often used to provide canned ecstasy, removing one from one's circumstance. Making music is a way of being the circumstance.

In this way canned music devices can serve as instruments of brain suck, displacing aesthetic (literally, *feeling*) musical experience with anesthetic (or *not*-feeling) experience. Reading to music, for example, is a way of intruding visual and cognitive habits on the musical experience. Running while listening to an audio device, conversely, is a way of disengaging from the immediate bodily activity, from the rhythm of one's feet and the surrounding sounds. All of these trends tend toward passive machine-mediated consumption rather than active music making. Perhaps home music remixing and sampling show a way to a more active engagement with music, though still located problematically between commercial product used and self-originating activity.

And so we go full circle back to the question of materialism and meaning in contemporary life. If a thing becomes an end in itself, disabling a person's capacity for self-originated experience, it is an example of what I call *terminal materialism*. If a thing serves as a means to realize one's larger life-goals, to engage in self-originated experience, alive to the moment and to the greater social world, it is an example of *instrumental materialism*. The thing becomes an instrument for living.

Music is older than humanity, and in case you didn't know this, just ask the songbirds and listen to what they say. Music nurtured us on our evolutionary journey to becoming human, revealing how our passions can find form and communicate directly in sound. It gave us the songs and rhythms of creation, and can continue to do so if we allow ourselves to participate in making music. But the consumption matrix would kill this, would kill one's spontaneity by conditioning the passions with consumption habitude. It does this by turning music into a means to consumption, wherein active creation succumbs to opiating property.

The great musical challenge in home-life today is to learn how to take command of the music, to be moved by making it, and not only by passively consuming the electro-siren sounds of the latest commodities. One start in reengaging music in the home can be made by turning off the power of the sound system, the TV, the computer, the iPod, and simply beginning to play: drum, dance, sing, or play whatever is your instrument. Or only listen to music when concentrated upon it, not as a background to reading or some other nonaudio activity: explore the possibilities of unitasking, forgetting, in the moment, the multitasking universe of distractions.

Or, null-task, listen to the silence; contemplate the quiet. Put your property in its place, don't become it, inert. Minimize what does not allow you to be an active participant in creation. You can try this in your car as well: silence the sound system and tune in to your surroundings as you drive.

Optimize your self-originated experience. Practice the art and craft of the home. In fact, I'm going to go play some music right now, right here in my own home: I will improvise a blues for prisoners of canned music! And for you prisoners out there, here is a sample of it and other music from my living room you can listen to until it expires: www.nd.edu/~ehalton/livingroom.html.

Dear reader, I have taken you on a brief tour around the walls of my living room, giving you but the briefest sketch of the material indicators of the life

I live there. You see, "every bird likes its own nest," as the saying goes, and I have given you the view from my nest, with the likely omissions such material introspection is inescapably bound to make. I could, for example, tell you of the things here that would embarrass me if I were to discuss them, but given that I have conveniently come to the end of this chapter, I will simply ask you to consider which of your possessions would it greatly embarrass you to discuss? What are your dark thing-stories?

I have made up little "thing-stories" of my life as my home reveals it, and as you know from your own experience, there is more to life than one's own living room: there is the world of the kitchen with its communion of talk and food; the world of the TV room with its family gatherings for television shows and videos, its intrusive commercials and celebrities exuding from the television and clogging the arteries of one's soul, its ever-growing children's clutter; the world of the bathroom and the toilet, places of privacy (and occasionally good reading!); the world of the bedroom, where children can imagine their growing selves and adults can dream the world away in lovemaking and sleeping and reading and all those activities where indolence is bliss.

In the beginning, there is creation. In the end, there is death. In the middle, there are thing-stories: thing-stories that throw light on the often-fantastic ways in which we people our environments with objects, especially the domestic environment.

When my last child moves out, perhaps by the time you are reading this, I will likely sell this home and move on. Over a few days, like a whirlwind, my assemblage will be sucked out of it, some spun off, and the rest reassembled somewhere else. Life moves on. And yes, eventually my little assemblage will whirl apart, when I depart. Yours too. You can't take it with you.

My assemblage. Your assemblage. Each of us is an assemblage, in substance and in spirit; our lives peopled with things, objectified in our relationships to loved ones, personified in the activities through which we find meaning, and anchored in that which we call home. What do you call home? The thing where you live? Or the life where you love?

Fortunately for me the things in my home are telling me that I have said enough for now.

11

EUROEPIPHANIES

Sometimes a crisis tests one's mettle and fires one's soul. Here is a story of coping with fallout, Chernobyl-style. I offer these reflections from my journal, written while living in Germany during the Chernobyl disaster, which rained radioactivity throughout Europe, and especially in southern Germany. It was my American nuclear epiphany in Europe, which opened me to consider the whole culture of radiation I had been raised in since birth. Written for the moment, it is curious how many of my immoderate rantings back then apply to the very different world of today. The Soviet Union may be gone, but the megamachine of which it and America were parts continues to grow unabated.

Die Verseuchung des Frühlings, or, The Poisoning of Spring,
May 4, 1986, Tübingen

Today, like the last three days, is sunny, warm, clear, fresh, and contaminated. Eternal spring is in the air, but with a mortal difference. We cannot drink the milk or eat our daily bread, because the radioactive fallout from the Chernobyl nuclear reactor disaster blew our way on Wednesday and Thursday. The Germans were unbelievably slow in releasing information and unbelievably bad in the information they have given: numbers without contexts, words that "it is safe" without qualifications of what "safe" means. Is it safe in the long run also, safe for children? We receive no picture of what is normal, what is dangerous, and where we stand in the middle. Sparse little weather reports are robotically given as though there is no relation between the weather and the fallout. Idiotic. No attempt to discuss wind patterns in relation to the disaster until a few days later, when it doesn't matter anymore.

Thursday was May Day, and though the air brought with it the contamination of "actually existing socialism," of the people's radioactivity, there were no large-scale demonstrations against the Soviet Union and its obscene stone-walling of information, its lying and murderous silence. The German Left could march against the U.S. retaliation bombing of the terrorist-dictator Qaddafi, in response to the bombing of a Berlin disco that killed American soldiers. The Greens even called it "state terrorism," while remaining silent on the bombings and shootings perpetrated by Libyan and Syrian and Iranian embassies—as though that action could be equated with the genuine U.S. imperialism in Latin America. But when the Soviet Union conceals vital information in a catastrophe that could eventually kill twenty thousand or more of its own people, let alone people in other European nations, it still does not merit large-scale specific protest. Yes, the unlimited nuclear reactor power mentality must be done away with throughout the world, but it should be attacked here in the concrete facts of this instance.

We were at a dinner party last night, about eleven people present, all German except my wife and me. Our hosts had been to the USSR during Easter, visiting Moscow and the Georgian area. They met another group from Tübingen touring the USSR, and the tour guide from that group was there last night. She glowed over the USSR and said she wanted to go back soon. This stopped everyone a little bit short, and someone raised the obvious point—How soon?—meaning, it is a bit "hot" there right now. She said she meant next year. She never once addressed the obvious problem of the catastrophe. It was utterly weird.

But let's not forget the Right. I had to listen to the Blue Angel attack the U.S. attack on Libya, telling me that, "It's all propaganda," whatever that means. The Blue Angel, paradigm of the old-school German professor, responded to my concern about the fallout and rain on Friday by saying to a former student and to me, "The Americans read two books, the book of Genesis and the book of health." It was not worth responding to the eminent Blue Angel, who makes his circle of assistants fawn over him and his health.

My immediate reaction over the U.S. bombing was that the fiendish war hawks that operate the Reagan puppet strings had done it again, without considering any of the consequences. As it became clear that they had attempted to get Qaddafi, and only targeted specific military targets, I came to the opinion that in and of itself the attack may have been a good move, since dictators tend to respond only to brute action, but I still don't know whether this partial action was the best thing or was necessary at this time. Maybe Chernobyl will halt terrorist response and escalation. The corrosive Arab terrorism must stop; it only mindlessly destroys and certainly does not even help the Arab cause (if it is truly freedom that is desired, which is doubtful). The Palestinians must demand an end to this terrorism, and to the Arafat/Khomeini/Qaddafi varieties of self-destruction and barbarism.

This infection of terrorism, self-destruction, and barbarism is by no means confined to the extremists of the day; it is the insanity of the United States wanting to put the perfect machine, SDI, or "Strategic Defense Initiative," into heaven to be our God, a demanding god who sucks away our social goods by absorbing huge chunks of money. The word immune originally meant to be free from public obligation or service. We wish to achieve immunity from politics by placing our political initiatives in the controls of a robot system that is supposed to give the illusion of atomic immunity, while our collective biological immune system is becoming infected with the ideology of "no limits": HAIL THE MEGAMACHINE!

It is the insanity of taking money out of education to serve the war machine, and throwing a teacher into outer space to serve "education," only to have the whole sick public relations stunt of the *Challenger* space shuttle explode in our faces. What is the meaning of instilling the dream of alienated escape from Mother Earth in a rocket ship as "educational"? Or as holding this space program, which has now openly admitted its fundamental militaristic nature, as an American ideal of science? This space program was begun with former Nazis, Wernher von Braun and others, who knowingly used forced slave labor and allowed concentration camp murders. Ah, "the American dream." It is the insanity of huge money-demanding, life-demanding demented dreams, with far-reaching consequences, hinging on a single little weak link in the megalomaniacal chain: a rubber seal on the space shuttle, a supposed "sleeping" lab technician at Chernobyl (they'll have to come up with a better alibi), nonfunctioning safety measures at the reactor or at the chemical factory in Bhopal, India. What does it take to see the whole thing, the whole outlook and worldview and the machines it makes, all of it is primed to explode?

My little two-year-old Jacob and I went for a walk today and he wanted to pick dandelions "to bring back for Mommy." I had to tell him no, even though it was probably safe (note: it was not). I had to tell him that even though these were flowers in the field and not in the garden (he pointed this out to me when I first said no, to show that he now knows the difference, after picking flowers from our balcony last week), even though they were in the field, we couldn't pick these flowers from the field for a few days because some garbage fell with the rain two days ago and left dirt on the flowers and fields. A child has to touch the world and feel it, and what a horrible situation it is to have to prevent that because of radioactivity.

"All things warmed in the landscape leap," said Melville on spring. And what is spring if not the blossoming desire to merge with the rebirth of nature? And what a pathetic world it is when the invisible veil of contamination creeps between our desire and spring's joy.

The Nuclear Family, May 7, 1986

Ever since he learned to use the potty last fall, Jacob would say, "Tell me about the spring," when he sat down. We would tell him of the flowers, birds, trees. In the past few weeks we would tell him, "And now it is spring." And now it is spring only in appearances. We isolated ourselves from the fresh food immediately; the government waited days before recommending no fresh vegetables, only tested milk (that is, not at the "official" contamination level, whatever that means). My questions went unanswered for days before the media here began answering them (*began*, not finished). All my thoughts these days are crowded with demographical tactical thinking. We kept Jacob in all last weekend, the weekend of the radioactive rain, which proved to be a good move, as the media said only Monday and Tuesday.

The politicians, health ministries, and media here slept, only responding passively to a concerned public. The Greens, supposedly the ecological party, proved themselves to be mere muddleheaded ideologues: dialectical vegetables. They could only organize demonstrations against nuclear energy in general, not even specifically singling out the murderous silence of the Soviet Union. The "save your own ass" attitude is certainly not limited to the Soviet Union, and clearly is one of the biggest problems in all of these techno-catastrophes. But the lying muteness of the Russians—who only began evacuating people in the vicinity thirty-six hours after it began—is a barbarian affront to life, and should have been the focus of the demonstration. The Greens did not lead the way to concrete action, betraying their true colors, which are ideological and not green. None of the politicians demanded information and action; it was the families who did this, the parents worried for the safety of their children. The "bourgeois" family was the critical front in this mess, though it will no doubt quickly slide back to unconcern, either from inertia or as an adaptation.

May 8, 1986

The question comes round again and again, "What if terrorists ever got 'the bomb'?" But they already have it, and we have given it to them. All it takes is a couple of rockets aimed at a nuclear reactor. When will it happen? Or will some crazies simply take over a reactor and hold it as a hostage? The nuclear mentality will say that reactors are sturdy enough to withstand rocket attacks, but even more unbelievable is that people will believe this, in the same way that they will not believe that it is a worldwide operating policy, unwritten of course, to keep leaks secret as long as possible. As if what we don't know won't hurt us. I wish that Chernobyl were the end of the problem, but I fear it is only the introduction to the next level of hell we must pass through.

Euroepiphanies

The 1984 Los Angeles Olympic Torch burns bright again. It burned the eyes out in Bhopal. It burned *Challenger*, and proved itself champion. It burns right now in Chernobyl, and we all are getting burned because of it.

The symbol of the human link to the gods, of our mortality redeemed through the eternal fire made manifest for a brief time, the fire drawn from the axis mundi in Greece at Olympus, this modern sacred symbol sacralized, sold and prostituted from coast to coast for filthy lucre. Everything I love about amateur athletics from my days as a high jumper, when I even got to go to Moscow and compete against the Soviet Union as a member of the USA Track and Field team, all that now feels finished. Carl Lewis, the professional robo-athlete, is the wave of the future.

No athlete lit the Los Angeles flame. Although the torch should have been the mediating symbol between man and god, there was in Los Angeles a frightful, arrogant machine that displaced, rather than mediated, god and man. The huge emblem of the Olympic rings technologized, brought the fire from the torchbearer to a smokestack apparatus high above the stadium, out of reach. The fire stood over us, not among us, beyond the gulf of those cold Olympic rings.

Prometheus stole fire from the gods. The megamachine stole the fire from man. This is a sorrowful time, when the misbegotten dreams of power explode in our faces; we tempt fate in our arrogant hubris and in the name of freedom profaned, chain ourselves to the rock so that the eagle may pick at our livers. We live half-lives built on half-lies.

Dynamics, May 10, 1986

When I was in Göttingen last October I went for a walk on arrival for a Humboldt fellows conference with two doctors, one from India and one from China (the Chinese remarked on meeting the Indian, "Our countries were at war not so long ago, things are better now." The Indian smiled and agreed it was odd to be meeting in Germany).

As we walked next to a late medieval church with a Spielplatz (playground) next to it, it suddenly occurred to me that just as the great medieval cathedrals were the symbols of an age, so were these new children's playgrounds the symbols of ours. Although the concern for children's space in the city is good, the comparison shows how the devotion to the ultimate that characterized the best of the medieval mind may in the end be a superior achievement to our own contemporary best contribution to urban form: child's play.

Henry Adams compared the Virgin and the dynamo, showing how the energy animated by the religious impulse of the medieval mind now finds expression in the electrical power dynamo rather than in a Chartres. The new playgrounds may be our best, if minor, contributions to urban form, but now the dynamo, grown to monstrously mutant proportions as Adams predicted it would, has even poisoned and contaminated the playgrounds of Europe.

May 11, 1986
Tübingen

To Mikhail Gorbachev
C/O The Kremlin

Dear Mr. G.,

Hey! I really did enjoy that May Day Workers Day Parade I saw on the TV! Sorry I didn't get to see more of the workers day celebrations here in Germany, but the air was sort of poisoned. You might say a dark cloud hung over the occasion here in Baden-Württemberg, if you get my drift.

But wow, what a way to celebrate spring! I thought my experience of March 1983, when I visited Marx's grave in Highgate Cemetery, London, could never be topped. As it turned out, I had arrived a bit early, and was not sure how to find the cemetery. But I ran into another lost soul, an Irishman who had lived in the neighborhood twenty years earlier, and who, it turned out, was the leader of the Surrey Soviet Friendship society. We stopped off at a pub, since the festivities had not yet begun. He sang the praises of the Soviet system, not only now, but also of the good ol' days of Joe Stalin. When I raised the problem of the purges, and of the slaughter of the officer corps on the eve of the Second World War, he responded that they probably deserved it and that it in no way reflected poorly on Stalin's leadership.

But what really made my day was when we returned to the cemetery. I couldn't believe my eyes when I saw, almost directly across from the glorious social realist bust of Marx, which sits atop the massive slab of his tomb, almost directly across from Marx himself mind you, the tomb of Herbert Spencer! Herbert Spencer: the social Darwinist who took capitalism to be nature's way. I had the image of both of them perpetually spinning in their graves on account of this strange juxtaposition.

But most beautiful of all, Mr. G., were the flowers: Hundreds and hundreds of them lying in beautiful wreaths before the tomb of Marx, gifts of the communist nations and workers parties the world over. But I have to confess, Mr. G., that I couldn't see my way to purchasing a token and symbol of my appreciation for Marx through the inauthentic medium of money, as the purchasers of those glorious wreaths obviously had. Instead I chose to appropriate from Nature herself through the authentic medium of my own labor a token of my appreciation: I plucked a daffodil, an early sign of the life of spring, from a ways behind Marx's tomb, and laid my humble offering amidst the wealth of nations on Marx's grave. There was no poorer offering than mine, given in admiration for Marx's tenacity in his struggle to bring about a free human existence, unshackled from domination and lies, from ideology and alienation. Yet there was no offering richer in meaning than mine, even if I could not believe uncritically in Marx, as so many of those worshippers there that day did.

They were true believers of his last thesis on Feuerbach, etched in stone on Marx's grave: "The philosophers have only interpreted the world; the point is, however, to change it." These true believers had no interest in interpreting the world at all; they only wanted to change it. They tried to sing "The Internationale," but they could not remember the words.

That was a beautiful day for me, Mr. G., and I even got to see Marx's great-grandson, Mr. Longuet, from France. But that spring celebration of the death of Marx (100 years since he gave up the body) could not begin to match this one, when the entire world shouts, "Mayday, Mayday!"

Mr. G., when I saw you standing up there on Lenin's tomb in the broad sunlight, on the very structure that houses the mummified remains of that great revolutionary, I knew for certain that some things truly are immortal, materialism notwithstanding. The glorious worker's day parade was once again being enacted, and not only in Moscow. Children marched in Kiev, carrying the flowers of promise, breathing the glorious poisoned air of that bright, clear spring day. I know this because the Soviet news media, paragon of advanced, critical communication, showed me pictures saying so.

I didn't need to see these photos or the ones of "the people" of Chernobyl to know that, as Marx and Engels put it so clearly in a different context, "A spectre is haunting Europe."

Long live the revolution!

Mr. G., I want you to know that I, for one, was convinced by the deep meaning of your decision to go ahead with all May Day activities as planned, despite the belching death fumes of Chernobyl. It must have been hard for you to stand there knowing that the equivalent of every person who passed you by in that parade and more will die from Chernobyl. Marx and Engels only interpreted the world in *The Communist Manifesto* Mr. G., the point is, that you have changed it. We used to say with Feuerbach, "Der Mensch ist, was er isst" (man is what he eats, or, you are what you eat). And now those words ring even truer, and will continue to do so for a number of half-lives.

We used to think *Entfremdung*, alienation, had to do with the diminution of life; now we know how much it has to do with the diminution of half-lives.

That was some parade!

May 12, 1986, Tübingen

I Love Paris in the Springtime
by
Eugene Halton
(with apologies to Ludwig Bemelmans)

In an old house in Paris that was covered with vines,
Lived twelve toady men, and they were all swines.

They were members of the nuclear commission.
They denied the effects of radioactive emission.

They left the house at half past two,
Any earlier just wouldn't do.

They measured the lettuce from leaf to stem,
And pretended there wasn't a single rem.

They measured the milk from the grass eating cow.
When their geigers hit red they could only say "Wow!"

But they never let on how the needle did dance.
For that might damage the glory of France.

The nation that worshipped nuclear power,
As though it were the Eiffel Tower.

"Nothing is wrong, everything is fine.
It's only a little bit of iodine."

Goodnight little girls, thank the Lord you are well.
For your milk contained only 500 Becquerel.

It's a Beautiful Day in the Neighborhood, May 14, 1986

Things are going great. I just "packt" (anglicized form of "packen," to seize, as a hawk might to a field mouse do) two and a half cartons of bottled mineral water (the unbubbly kind). We had enough for another week, but the stores were sold out of this kind for a while. I got it just after bringing Jacob to his babysitter's this morning, an early and unhabitual shopping time, in which the ever *pünktlich* (punctual) locals had not yet arrived in large and competitive numbers. We also just received a dry milk "care package" from the United States, which we are sharing with friends with small children.

We're singing, "I got bottled water, I got dry milk, I got canned food, who could ask for anything more!" We're also singing, "Arrivederci Deutschland," even though we know there is "no acute danger," as the vassals of science have said.

Tell the infants they are in no acute danger, Mr. Science. Tell them what you mean by "acute," Mr. Science, how they haven't really received more than workers in nuclear plants do over a year. Tell them how "our" nuclear power plants are really safe, no matter what country "we" happen to be in. And when you are finished, Mr. Science, kiss my ass.

Yesterday the twilight zone closed in a little too snuggly for my comfort. I was in the bank to close out our rent payment, because we are leaving here this month. I went to the first teller, with whom I have done business throughout the year, but it was too crowded at his window. I noticed his name, which I had never done before: Herr Fleisch! I went over to the next window, and noticed the name of the young woman whose face is now so familiar to us: Frau Kern. Now "kern" means core or kernel, and the name for the thing in

Chernobyl that exploded is a Kernreaktor, and it made Kernenergie. There I was between Miss Nuclear and Mr. Flesh!

Ah, the murderous silence of the Soviets, the lying silence of the French, the half-lying slowness of the Germans, who only gradually suggested that people do what we did from the start. And let's not forget the neo-Pilgrim attitude of the Americans, who, too befuddled with misbegotten dreams of power that now explode in our faces, want to suck the life-resources out of the economy in order to install a death machine in heaven: Reagan's Dooms-day Device. Let us worship our Lord and Protector, the Machine! Let us educate our young with its power: arithmetic from outer space!

Berlin, May 16, 1986

Berlin, metropolis not dominated by inhuman high-rise towers of Babel, only low-rise guard towers and the "great wall": Kafka's fusion of the Tower of Babel with the Great Wall of China in diabolical reverse. Half city, as a cell divided. Forgive me, Berlin, for not seeing your great cultural treasures. I was here too briefly and too filled with angst to enjoy you or even to want to enjoy you. You have great beauty, but "La Belle," the disco terrorists bombed last month, which I saw on the way to my lecture, forces other images on me. I carefully kept away the salads that kept appearing next to the food I ordered, food "vor und ohne," not "nach und mit" radioactivity.

Peering into East Berlin from the tourist watchtowers stationed at various points near the wall, I saw the burial mound of Hitler. This large pimple on the landscape of the forbidden zone is where he momentarily emerged from the underground bunker in which he shot himself in logical completion of his vision, in order to be cremated and thereby attain the heat necessary to slither his way, red reptilian tongue darting, down to the fiery depths that ever were his true home. How fitting that his last refuge, built under the earth as if in preparation for his return to the underworld, is at the point where the great vice-trap called forth by Hitler stands tightly shut on the city of Berlin: the twilight zone of the wall area, alive with rab-bits who can thrive in the stark no-man's land, except the occasional one that hippity-hops on a land mine. Hitler unter alles! His deadly legacy lives on in the divided city and country, in the divided Europe, in the whole cold war turn to deliberate targeting of civilian populations for nuclear extermination.

He brought a plague from the stinking depths far more devastating, in its actuality, than Chernobyl, if not always so invisible. I swear that one of those many rabbits I saw had a funny little black mustache.

Aesthetics of Survival, Tübingen, May 21, 1986

Almost two weeks ago we received boxes of dry milk, sent in a box that originally held books stamped with the title *The Aesthetics of Survival*.

I read in *Der Spiegel* yesterday that the French nuclear commissioner only in the last week commented on the radioactive levels in France. The bastard said it was only "like spending a few days in the mountains," that the increased levels of radioactivity were nothing to worry about. The supercentralized government of France, like its Soviet counterpart, would rather risk killing its young than exposing itself to the nonradioactive honest human questioning and criticism by its own people. It seems quite likely that the next great nuclear catastrophe in Europe will come from France—maybe from Chernobyl to Grenoble, the city with a reactor right in the middle of it!—and that when it does, the French, ever mindful of clearly and distinctly distinguishing themselves, will lie and cover up as long as possible (but it won't be for too long). This process has probably long since been policy—losses of radioactive materials kept as state secrets.

France, like much of the rest of the world, is clearly on the way down the toilet: It made heroes out of the murderers who killed the member of the Greenpeace ship demonstrating against France's shitting up of the Pacific with hydrogen bombs, and it enacted economic sanctions against New Zealand when it refused to return these thugs to their glorious homeland. It wants to suck cheap life-labor out of foreigners, mostly North Africans, and then throw them out because they are impure. It wants to sterilize its precious language by legislating away linguistic influence, mostly English. Vive la France!

Of Talking Cures, May 26, 1986

When I first arrived in Germany I was impressed by the variety of political talk here. Now I can see how it is also the weak spot and metaphysical disease of the Germans: talk, talk, talk. No wonder Freud developed a "talking cure" (albeit a Viennese one). No wonder Habermas developed a theory of "communicative action" that is simply a theory of talking. No wonder Wittgenstein wanted to break through all the talk-quatsch.

Tübingen, Freitag, May 30, 1986

It's the last night in Tübingen and Europe, about 11/23 o'clock, and we leave in seven or so hours for the airport. We're exhausted after an exhausting week and especially after packing today. I gave a talk in Bern on Wednesday. I spoke in English but did the whole discussion for thirty to forty minutes in my bumper-car German. Then had a two-hour conversation with Professor Lang, a psychologist at Bern, and a student finishing his dissertation, Wilhelm Häberle, who with Lang is translating my book *The Meaning of Things*. They, Lang's wife, and an architect who also had dinner with us at Lang's house were so cordial to me, and their home in the hills over Bern was a real delight. For my purposes, it was my chance to do one long day of lots of German in a professional setting, even if still elbowing my way verbally. I had half finished a translation of a selection of my essay "Reality, Community, and the Critique of Modernism" to read at Bremen next month. But that is now *vorbei*—bygone. Let bygones be bygone!

We look forward to untainted green, to flowers we can hug and pick, to salads we can eat, to dirt we can roll around in. We came here the day before a "Red Army Faction" terrorist bomb exploded in Frankfurt, in a luggage area near where I had momentarily wandered before feeling something not right. It turns out they have been living a few kilometers away from us outside of Tübingen. The next month the first of a yearlong series of poisoned wine scandals broke: better living through chemistry. We leave in retreat from the fallout, the nuclear spring of our discontent, sorry to have to break all the friendships we have begun, anxious to get Jacob to a free, healthy environment, physically and mentally uncontaminated.

June 24, 1986: *Home Ground*
Tomorrow I go to Amenia to visit Lewis Mumford!

12

THE LAST DAYS OF
LEWIS MUMFORD

Introduction

Lewis Mumford was a writer who ranged freely across the landscapes of history, literature, architecture, technology, civilization, environmentalism, public life, and the human mind. The influential writer Malcolm Cowley called him "the last of the great humanists." Mumford considered himself a generalist, and deliberately took on "the big picture" in many of his works, which is anathema to many intellectuals today. Born in Flushing on October 19, 1895, Mumford lived much of his life in New York, settling in Dutchess County in 1936 with his wife Sophia, in Leedsville, just outside of the town of Amenia, where he died over a half-century later on January 26, 1990. His first book, *The Story of Utopias*, was published in 1922, and his last book, his autobiography *Sketches from Life*, was published sixty years later in 1982.

Mumford preferred to call himself a writer, not a scholar, architectural critic, historian, or philosopher. His writing ranged freely and brought him into contact with a wide variety of people, including writers, artists, city planners, architects, philosophers, historians, and archaeologists. Throughout his life, Mumford sketched and painted his surroundings, visualizing his impressions of people and places in image, as his ever-present notepad visualized them in words. His drawings and watercolors are now in the collection of Monmouth University in New Jersey.

Given the range of Mumford's scholarly work, it is all the more interesting that he did not have a college degree, having had to leave City College of New York after a diagnosis of tuberculosis. But if whaling was Herman Melville's "Harvard and Yale," "Mannahatta," as Mumford put it, "was my university, my true alma mater." From childhood on, Mumford walked, sketched, and observed New York City, and its effects can be felt throughout his writings.

He was architectural critic for the *New Yorker* magazine for over thirty years, and his 1961 book, *The City in History*, received the National Book Award. In 1923 Mumford was a cofounder with Clarence Stein, Benton MacKaye, Henry Wright, and others of the Regional Planning Association of America, which advocated limited-scale development and the region as significant for city planning.

By 1938 he was an ardent advocate for early American entry into what was emerging as World War II, a war that claimed the life of his son Geddes in September 1944. He was also one of the first critics of nuclear weapons in 1946 and of U.S. involvement in Vietnam in 1965. In 1964 he was awarded the Presidential Medal of Freedom by Lyndon Johnson, whose war he would actively protest a year later.

Lewis Mumford's work underwent a continuous series of transformations as he broadened and deepened his scope. His American studies books from around the 1920s, such as *The Golden Day* (1926) and *Herman Melville* (1929), the first biography written on Melville, contributed to the rediscovery of the literary transcendentalists of the 1850s, and *The Brown Decades* (1931) placed the architectural achievements of Henry Hobson Richardson, Louis Sullivan, and Frank Lloyd Wright before the public. His four-volume Renewal of Life series published between 1934 and 1951 outlined the place of technology, cities, and worldviews in the development of Western civilization. His later books considered the range from the emergence of civilizations and the place of communication practices in human development to prospects for global civilization today. Throughout, he boldly denied utilitarian expediency and technocratic rationalism while evolving his own vision of organic humanism.

Mumford's works share a common concern with the ways that modern life as a whole, although providing possibilities for broader expression and development, simultaneously subverts those possibilities and actually ends up tending toward a diminution of purpose. He shows in lucid detail how the modern ethos released a Pandora's box of mechanical marvels that eventually threatened to absorb all human purposes into *The Myth of the Machine*, the title he used for his two-volume late work. Mumford argued passionately for a restoration of organic human purpose in the larger scheme of things, a task requiring a human personality capable of "primacy over its biological needs and technological pressures," and able to "draw freely on the compost from many previous cultures."

Although his organic vision appears throughout his writings, it may not always be apparent how the thread connects between his works. What does it mean to claim that there may be a religious element in the culture of the machine, for example? Or that art can be a surer touchstone to reality than science? Or that cities should be conceived as bioregions? Or that we have been busily building a suicidal power complex as deadly to life, and especially human life, as it is vulnerable to sudden collapse like a house of cards.

Consider Mumford's 1970 criticism of the World Trade Center in a photo insert in *The Pentagon of Power*, volume two of *The Myth of the Machine*, written as the World Trade Center was still being built: ". . . a characteristic example of the purposeless giantism and technological exhibitionism that are eviscerating the living tissue of every great city. . . . But Dinosaurs were handicapped by insufficient brains, and the World Trade Center is only another Dinosaur."[1] Thirty years later the tragedy of the September 11, 2001 attack showed how vulnerable the power complex can be, and how deadly that building "handicapped by insufficient brains" proved itself to be for the thousands of people it entombed. That Dinosaur was a symbol of our Dinosaur Civilization, still bent on all-consuming power, yet purposed to perish in its mythic idolization of the machine.

To encounter the work of Mumford is to encounter a mind that embraced history in its broadest horizons. Yet though he could be considered as "prohistorical man," who saw the value of the living past for the present, to characterize him so would be problematic. For this master writer on the city opened the whole revaluation of the advent of civilization and the possibility that civilization—history itself—is a terminal human affliction. Mumford helped open the door to a revaluation of "prehistory" as well, revealing the many advantages the uncivilized virtues have over what Herman Melville once called *snivelization*. His questioning of the roots of civilization is also the mark of the quintessential American epiphany, of the dream of throwing off the shackles of civilization that marked the dream and exploration of the new world and colonization of America. Yes, that tragic dream that was undone even as it was being enacted, through genocide, slavery, agricultural exploitation, and deforestation, through the idealizing implantation of the myth of the machine that began with civilization. And even before Europeans arrived, new world civilizations had already manifested the standard profiles of the megamachine, with agricultural exploitation producing poorer average nutrition, with human exploitation and slavery, with centralized power embodied in divine kingship.

Mumford left unfinished at his death a project to go further into the relations between biology and purpose. He ran out of time. I believe it would have deepened his discussions of the place of the organic in human culture and also of the dynamics of what he termed the megamachine. Mumford's criticisms of Darwin and of the basis of modern science were at odds with contemporary thought. But he tapped into the vein that another master American thinker, Peirce, explored even earlier, reaching conclusions from his historical outlook that Peirce also reached as a practicing scientist and logician. Both found the eviction of purpose from nature to be suspect, Darwinism to be incomplete, and mechanistic reductionism to be false as an account of the human mind. These arguments, in my view, will provide much of what Mumford called "useable history" for further thinking.

Lewis Mumford was someone who spoke to my mind and soul in a way other contemporary thinkers did not. I first encountered Mumford's work as I wove my way through graduate school, disregarding disciplinary boundaries because they seemed like artificial barriers to the interconnection of ideas. His writing was like the missing link to ideas I was developing, not only opening new ways to think about the modern condition and how it arose but also demonstrating a mind that could be comprehensive, lucid, passionate, and free.

In the few years just after graduate school I devoured his books, began to correspond with him, and finally had to go visit him. I was fortunate to meet with Lewis and Sophia Mumford a few times before his death, and a few more times with Sophia after his death. Although Lewis was very old and suffering from dementia, I would like to share with you some of these encounters from his last days. They are by no means meant to provide a definitive account of his last days, since I was just an occasional visitor, but simply a springboard from which to reflect on our person-to-person meetings.

June 25, 1986: First Visit

Just back from living in Germany and Chernobyl fallout, I drove up from Philadelphia on a warm, clear day to meet Lewis and Sophia Mumford. As I entered Dutchess County in New York, I noticed I was trailing behind a great black hearse, an ominous sign that led the way as the whole landscape opened up before me to reveal the rolls of the mountains to the west of the

Figure 23. Sophia and Lewis Mumford, Ledbury, England, July 1957. Courtesy of the Estate of Lewis and Sophia Mumford.

Hudson River. Dutchess County was far more rural than I had expected. And even the Mumford home, just outside of the town of Amenia in Leedsville, New York, was more rural than I anticipated, though Sophia Mumford had told me to expect to find it hidden behind many bushes and opposite another very old farmhouse ("Ours is the one hidden behind the bushes"). I pulled into the driveway, uncertain that this was the right place, but I supposed from the wealth of vegetation that it must be. A note on the front door said to go around to the kitchen door if there was no answer, which I ended up doing.

Sophia Mumford met me at the door, and after briefly introducing me to Dick Coons, the man who worked there as Lewis Mumford's caretaker, almost immediately led me in to meet Lewis. He had heard the commotion at the door and had asked about it as we entered. He sat in his chair as we exchanged greetings and shook hands.

Lewis said to me, "I'm so glad you are here, physically. . . . Your physical presence here." I replied, "I'm so glad that *you* are, and that I am able to be here to meet with you." We had corresponded a few times over the last few years. He began to speak of "the inner" and something to the effect that it might not be usual to speak of the inner on first meeting, that there is a shared innerness between us, a feeling (gesturing between him and me). Sophia Mumford said that it might not all make sense, that he had good days and bad days, though his condition (dementia) had worsened. I felt that although the words did not come out clearly, he was trying to express something, not just babbling, and I responded to him that yes, the inner can hardly be spoken of these days.

At this point Sophia Mumford said that I had really captured the inner feel of his work in my essay "Reality, Community, and the Critique of Modernism." She said she had read it when I sent it to her over a year ago and had read the section where I discuss Lewis's work to him, and that he had responded very positively to it. She said she had sent it to Donald Miller, Mumford's biographer and literary executor, hoping that was all right with me, because she felt I had seen Lewis's ideas in broader context than Miller, and she hoped this would be helpful to Miller. I thanked her and said (also to Lewis, since I knew he was hard of hearing and did not want to talk about him in the third person) that I realized the discussion was far too short, but that I wanted to capture the inner feel of his vision and use it in the context of the dialogue of the chapter, not simply as an external presentation of his views but as a discussion of his work as a filament of a new mind in the making, a discussion that was *doing* what I claimed his view was about. They both liked this, and Lewis said something about being careful with such ideas. I said, yes, but my chapter in which I discuss his ideas is full of such "dangerous" ideas like his, ideas that sociologists and others of the academy might balk at out of timidity. He said, "That's a good thing. Is it all right to say that, Sophie?"

I told him how I came to his work slowly and indirectly. He said that is good. I said that I have only come under the growing influence of his work in the last five or so years, although I was aware of it earlier. I told him I had been battering my brains out for over ten years, trying to come to terms with Peirce's work, because it offered a depth and broadness and vision I had not found in other thinkers. I had found Peirce's philosophy of signs and science to be a whetstone to the development of my own mind. Peirce offered a critique of the modern era as rooted in a false philosophy of nominalism and proposed a grand philosophic alternative. But I also found in Herman Melville's dark visions of civilization and modern life a complementary view to Peirce's. Despite my deep admiration for Peirce's work and my respect for his logic, I found the logical direction of his thought did not meet all my needs, and that I had attempted "alchemy," a marriage of Peirce's logical vision with Melville's aesthetic vision. Melville's transcendental concreteness and vividness showed me at least as broad a mind, equally nonmodern, though saturated with the modern vision and awareness of its likely self-destructive consequences.

Melville expressed in *Moby-Dick* how the "Isolatoism" of the modern condition runs contrary to the social nature of humankind and life. Similarly, Peirce developed a logical basis for the social nature of reality at odds with the "Isolato," nominalist philosophies of modern "scientific realism." It was to me as though these two outlooks were two sides of one brain, and I realized that, at least for my purposes, Lewis Mumford's writings combined the two sides and was an aspect of an outlook I wanted to explore and inhabit. Mumford enthusiastically said yes, with more understanding in his voice than at other times in our conversation.

I told him how I used to think of Dewey and Mead as fleshing out the social philosophy that Peirce did not really develop, that they represented the sociological side of pragmatism, although more limited in perspective than Peirce and less capable of clarity. I had to struggle to make their ideas clearer, to connect them with the broader Peircean mind, and also to translate the broader Peircean mind into social theory. I said that it was only in the last few years that I have increasingly come to understand how Mumford had achieved what I sought in my alchemy of opposites with Peirce and Melville and am still seeking.

I saw how his work shows the likely self-destruction of humankind yet always holds hope. He said that I said it very well, that my work is very important. I said, "But I am only a beginner." His eyes briefly fired up, and he said that yes, hope is a reality of life, that he too is a beginner, that "we are all beginners, that is what it is about," and, waving his finger in a circle, "otherwise things would just go round and round."

I told him that another level of his work I find compelling is his writing itself, so clear and richly interwoven. I find ideas, which themselves could be made into books, woven seamlessly into the argument. And the narrative is always many-sided. I said it appears to me as though he brushed his hand lightly over the page and the words were all there in place. Mrs. Mumford smiled, and I added that I realize the writing must have been much more work than that, but that the end result was works that are true pleasures to read. I told Mumford that I emulate his mastery of writing, and he thanked me.

Earlier Lewis had sent me this letter:

23 November 1984

Your letter of the 19th came this morning, dear Colleague, and I hasten to answer it through what vital energy I can now draw on again after a long illness. Though my mind is increasingly active once more, I am now 89 years old: so I cannot hope to do justice to your creative plans & hopes, much though I am still fed by Blake, Herman Melville, and Charles Peirce, and so feel in accord with your abilities.

By now I have written a fresh hundred pages, or more, which I may be able to whip into shape "for good" in more than one sense. And I am grateful to you, dear Halton for underwriting, in every sense, my personal hopes. My wife Sophia joins me in this happy juncture.

Lewis Mumford

Sophia, in response to something Lewis said, told me it is a constant battle now, he wants to *do* something, he does not realize he has *done* it. She suggested that I let him know he has done his work, and that the doing of it is over. I felt what a struggle it must be for Mumford, so sick and yet to have his work rooted so deeply that it will not let him rest. I told him that he has created a body of work of broad scope that will endure. I said, "I am in continual dialogue with you through your words, and there are only a very few people with whom I can speak from the soul, and you, through your body of work, are one of them. He asked to shake my hand and I shook his hand with both of mine.

I told Lewis and Sophia that I feel myself at a crossroads or new phase in my development, and that I want to write to capture the undercurrents of existence and to expose the "invisible dictator" (I used the expression "invisible dictator" from Ernst Fuchs's letter to me from last December, written in response to my discussion of his painting I sent him). Mumford took special interest in the expression "invisible dictator" and was pleased to hear this term. I briefly discussed my plans for my next book, speaking to both, but attempting to speak loudly enough for Lewis to hear. We shook hands at least once again during this time.

Mumford gave me his *Sketches from Life* and *Findings and Keepings* as gifts, saying I could keep them or return them when I was finished, that I could keep them temporarily. I replied, "Don't we keep all things temporarily?

Aren't we all temporary keepers?" He said, "Yes we are!" enthusiastically, and, "You give hope."

He wished me a good and long life and wished my work well. He shook my hand repeatedly both in his enthusiasm and also as a kind of automatic behavior. Sophia Mumford quietly told me that the gifts were a gesture, and hoped I would understand the books were not to be taken. I did sense that it was a gesture on Lewis's part. The handshaking was also excessive, symptomatic of his dementia no doubt. But it also held his enthusiasm, and I thought, why shouldn't we all grasp hands frequently in enthusiastic conversations, just as I have "high-fived" hand slaps with teammates on the basketball court after a good play?

Sophia told me of a woman student who had come up last Sunday, because she knew Lewis had written about the West Side of New York City. The student was talking about some buildings Mumford had criticized early in his career that are now "in" because of their ornamentation. She asked whether Lewis had revised his opinions, implying that he had been wrong in his assessment of these buildings. He had not heard her, but Sophia had. She told the woman, "Definitively Not!" I said that part of the half-lost and confused nature of so-called postmodern architecture was that in coming out of the "no-food diet" of radical asceticism, any little tasteless ornament can now be sanctioned.

A little later in the conversation, Mumford shook my hand and said he hoped we would meet again, and that we will meet one more time.

Mumford turned at various points to Sophia and said, "Is that all right dear?" This was another repetitive behavior, as though asking whether what he had said was appropriate and whether the discussion was over. He seemed very out of touch, yet seemed to understand more than he could say, and in places to want to say more than could come out clearly.

Sophia told me a doctor had wanted to do a brain scan recently. She didn't want to put Lewis through it, and the doctor said, "But you're living in the modern world." She said, "I told him about Lewis's lifelong concern with technology and modern conditions, how he had criticized the modern world for not limiting technology." I told her, "Yes, you may be *in* but you are not *of* the modern world."

I went on about another level of Lewis's work, how he had cut through to the premises of modernity and proposed new ones in their place. And this is why he seems practically alone in our time, another "last American." Sophia offered examples of her own. At another point she said one of the things she felt was distinctive about Lewis is his wisdom. She said that friends and acquaintances from early on would remark that he was so affable personally, not all seriousness as they had expected from his books.

Before leaving I went into the kitchen to get directions to Rhinebeck from Dick Coons, where I was to join friends camping. Then I met Sophia on the front doorstep and she expressed sorrow that it should come to this for him, whose mind and memory were so sharp. We spoke of how his work had not yet been understood at its deepest levels, and I said again that although I know he is world renowned, it seemed to me that the time for his vision has not yet arrived, and that his work will eventually grow in significance. I thanked Sophia again for her warmth and for making my visit to both of them possible.

P.S. I spoke to Don Miller, who is writing the biography of Lewis, a few weeks later and he told me that Mumford's present state of bad health and loss of contact is a more rapid deterioration within the last six months. He said that Lewis had recommended my discussion of his work in my "Reality, Community, and the Critique of Modernism."

Second Meeting with Lewis and Sophia Mumford, Amenia, September 1, 1986

I rented a car while attending the American Sociological Association meeting in New York, and drove up on a beautifully clear day to visit Lewis and Sophia for the second time. My expectations for the meeting were not high, since the previous visit showed me that Lewis's powers of concentration were severely limited. But to my complete surprise he was lucid for the entire meeting, which lasted one and one half hours, with a break in the middle when Sophia and I went out to the backyard.

Sophia met me at the front door and led me into the living room, where Lewis seemed at once to recognize me. He said, "I'm so pleased that you could make it." I jovially asked if the weather was always sunny, warm, and clear in Amenia, as it was when I visited in June and as it was on this day. Mumford said no, they had bad weather as well, and it just happened to be good on this day. I could see in him a much higher level of energy, attention, and consciousness.

I was not sure how long his attention would hold, so I wanted to get our discussion going right away. I had been thinking about some questions on the ride up to Amenia, and said, "I have a couple of questions I have brought with me this time. How did you come to medieval culture, to the medieval mind, early in your work. He said something to the effect that "I stumbled into it. It was something I had to deal with at a certain point and I found valuable ideas there." I said, "I ask because it must have involved going behind the veils, overcoming the prevalent stereotypes of the medieval culture as the dark ages, as undeveloped." He said yes, and that on the contrary, there was richness in medieval culture. I continued that Don Miller had told me that

Lewis's most recent work was on evolution, and on trying to view purpose in nature. This seemed to me to resonate with the tendency to view nature as general in medieval philosophy, in someone like Duns Scotus, as I have read him through Charles Peirce. And that I wondered whether this direction in Mumford's thought might have early on been influenced by the medieval mind. He seemed not to have thought of this, but to have found it possible.

Sophia Mumford said around this point that no one had been able to bring Lewis into discussion in this way, and that she was amazed. She later told me, as we were talking in her backyard, that when I asked my questions, she was apprehensive, because she did not think Lewis would be able to answer them, and was delighted that he could be drawn into such a serious discussion.

I felt very clear throughout our conversation, all the right words seemed continuously to come to my lips, and as I spoke of the need to "take care of" the world, the cultivation of an attitude of responsibility, early in the conversation, Sophia said that I had touched what is most dear to Lewis's heart, and told him that here was the fulfillment of his work. She said that he feels very strongly that an attitude of responsibility is sorely needed, and also worries that this way of thinking, which his work is all about, is not being carried out, and also, that his ideas are not having an active effect.

I spoke of my experience at a Pueblo Indian Corn Dance in New Mexico in 1982, and of how Alfonso Ortiz, himself a Pueblo and anthropologist, had explained that many whites think that the dance is supposed to make rain, as though it were a causal connection. Instead, he said that the sun does its part, the rain does its part, and the people must do theirs: the people's part is to dance and sing of the seasons, and that is how we uphold our responsibility in the order of nature.

I thanked Sophia for saying that here was the fulfillment of his work, but also that she was giving me too much credit. I said that the real fulfillment of Mumford's work is the shaping of a new way of thinking, of a new mind in the process of being formed, ecologically aware of civilizational and organic limits and possibilities, and that his legacy, the body of his work, will really find its fulfillment in the many people it touches and influences in this new way of thinking.

I said that this brought me to the other main question I wanted to ask, and turned to Lewis. I said to him that it seemed to me that a new mind is in the making, and indeed, his work not only suggested this but also showed what it might look like in possible outline. I asked whether he thought it possible that we might undergo the transformation to this life-enhancing mind from our present life-destroying culture without also suffering world catastrophe, or whether only large-scale catastrophic events would provide the jolt to present ways of thinking that could bring about new conditions. He began to answer by talking about the transformed mind. I then said that perhaps I should rephrase my question (it seemed to me and to Sophia Mumford too, as she told me later in the garden, that he had avoided the central part of my question, the catastrophe).

I asked Lewis whether we have insulted nature too much for a transformation to occur without deadly consequences needing to be paid, or also whether we have insulted nature too severely for human culture to survive, let alone to transform itself. He said he agreed with me, but that the possibilities were nevertheless out there for human transformation.

He said that we must live with hope, that we can only know the new mind vaguely and partially, and that he and I are of it. He said further that he and I would continue in it, "only, it is changed." Sophia took him to be wandering at this point, but I asked him, "Do you mean in the continuum of ideas?" He, in effect, said yes, by continuing to talk, as though from personal experience, of what I took to be a description of the afterlife. I don't believe that I was reading into his words; he seemed to me to be a man with one foot in the grave at that moment, fastened upon futurity and released from this world, literally *seeing hope* and the real world of possibility it produces. Lewis Mumford is, after all, a man who has lived in such a world throughout the sad twentieth century, concretely and prophetically. His words may have been too frequently ignored, but his perceptions of contemporary life were also profound perceptions of likely future conditions—likely yet potentially changeable.

I felt strongly that Mumford's words were a declaration of a man in the process of "giving up the body," yet in the name of hope: the hope of his vision. Hope, as he said in our conversation, is not something we can give up. I agreed and said that hope is that open-ended aspect of our existence, a kind of a synapse between what we are and what can be. I said that from one perspective the quest of modernity was to fill in that synapse with certainty. Indeed, hope, in the modern ideology, was to be transformed from its religious leaps of faith into science, which in its purest form would be a technique beyond hope ("beyond hope" meant as better than hope by its true believers, but shown to be hopeless in its consequences to those not capable of believing in the religion of techno-science). I'll take the "synaptic gospel"—as Max Lerner once put it in late-night bar conversation with me and Victor and Edith Turner—the synaptic gospel of hope, of the fluid inferential medium of the human life-spark, any day over the Moloch of modernity, who has so devoured the divine possibilities inherent in the human animal.

We went on to talk of the hard work it is to develop oneself, and of how long ideas sometimes need to accumulate. We connected throughout the conversation, and a few times Lewis held out his arms and said, "We embrace you." After a certain—or should I say hopeful—point in our conversation, Sophia suggested that we should give Lewis a rest, while she and I walked out to sit in the backyard. I noticed that Mumford was sitting on the edge of his chair, signaling to me how much more involved in our conversation he was this time.

Sophia Mumford and I went out to the backyard and sat down on some chairs. She told me how happy she was to see Lewis drawn into serious conversation, how she feared he would not be able to answer my questions. She said she had not seen him respond in this way for months at least. She added that she could not understand how he could not recognize his granddaughter, who visited a week or two earlier, and yet converse on such a serious level. Mumford's granddaughter had visited in the morning, and in the afternoon he asked Sophia, "Who was that lovely girl here today?"

Sophia also told me that she and Lewis had been fighting in recent weeks. She said he had taken off his wedding ring and was refusing to wear it, claiming that she had not been a real wife to him, or that she was not his real wife. Their housekeeper had tried to get Lewis to wear the ring but I seem to remember that Lewis claimed to have his "real" ring on, as opposed to the one he refused to wear. The "real" one was imaginary. Or perhaps it was that Lewis agreed to put the actual ring back on, but claimed it was not the real one.

Sophia asked me what I made of this. I said that I always believed Hawthorne's *Scarlet Letter* to be about Art, that art was the artist's mistress and that perhaps here, Lewis was expressing something about his dissatisfaction over his not being able to work, or something related. I wondered whether Mumford's childish fighting with Sophia was a sign that some of his vitality was returning (note: I did not know at that time about his love affairs, or perhaps I might have tempered my remarks about *The Scarlet Letter*! I also did not think that the argumentativeness could be an aspect of his dementia. Then again, perhaps my remarks were more on target than I could have possibly known).

While outside, Sophia mentioned that some of her friends ask her, "What will it be like in ten or fifteen years?" She said that question doesn't interest her. Instead, she would like to know what it will be like in a hundred or so years, because ten or fifteen years will only be more of the same as now, whereas a hundred years from now may have conditions vastly changed from those that dominate the present.

Sophia and I returned to the living room, and she asked if I would like a glass of wine. The three of us had glasses of New York State wine and continued talking, but at a much less intense level than before.

Saturday, June 27, 1987

I just finished meeting again with Lewis and Sophia Mumford, and there was a fellow there—I think his name was Jack Ricks—who was visiting. When I arrived, Jack opened the front door and then Sophia came to the door and greeted me. I went from the front into the living room where Lewis was sitting and he greeted me right away. She reminded him that I had been there last year. He said, "Yes," and was glad that I could be back again. He seemed very alert on greeting me. In actuality he had just awakened from a nap shortly before that and as we began to talk he was still kind of sleepy and gradually became more awake in the next five or ten minutes. Sophia asked what kind of work I'm doing now, and I mentioned some of my projects, such as trying to write about Chicago and modern culture. I explained some of the chapters that will be in my book, but especially the work on comparing Chicago and Vienna at the turn of the century: the social theories of architecture that were emerging out of Vienna through Camillo Sitte, Otto Wagner, and Adolph Loos, and comparing them with Daniel Burnham from Chicago and also Louis Sullivan and Frank Lloyd Wright and trying to look at alternating rhythms of modernity in the two cities by comparing the tensions of the different forms of modernity that emerged.

She wanted Lewis to hear some of what I was saying and asked him to listen, and he said it sounded very interesting. He kind of closed his eyes and I wasn't sure whether he was sleeping, but in fact he was listening because I went on for another minute or two describing what I was hoping to do in this work, and he said suddenly, "Well, you know, you've taken on a rather large task. It's a big project you hope to do." And I agreed that perhaps I had bitten off more than I could chew, but that's what I wanted to be doing this summer.

I mentioned to him that I was also dealing with his work for the conference on him next fall. I described how I wanted to deal with the theme of Lewis Mumford and the transformation of social theory by showing how, of twentieth-century social theorists, Lewis Mumford stands apart. I told him that Max Weber saw modern life as an inevitable growth of rationality. It could not be avoided. Whereas Mumford showed that all of the problems of modernity that Weber discusses—rationality or rationalization—were in fact avoidable because they were not a separate endeavor apart from human activity but were part and parcel of human choices.

I used the metaphor at one point that Weber saw clearly that the bureaucracy resulting from modernity was leading to many destructive directions, though he was loathe to criticize them, whereas Mumford showed how in effect we are hanging ourselves if we continue on this path. Where Weber sees us hanging ourselves from an objective scaffolding, Mumford sees us as hanging ourselves by ourselves and in that sense we cannot stop the scaffolding of modernity—the hanging scaffolding of modernity in Weber's view—but if we adopt Mumford's view we can stop this process. And in fact it's not a process of rationalization but de-rationalization. Rationality is not something that is suicidal in Mumford, only the perversion of it is. Weber unfortunately sees very clearly the direction of modern life but accepts that perversion of rationality as defining what rationality is.

I told Lewis and Sophia that I was interested in comparing his ideas with what the sociologists now call the "classical" tradition of sociology, that I had trouble with the word "classical" because to me "classical" means rightly proportioned; what sociologists mean is "old" and not very old at that, merely from the turn of the century. I told them that I preferred to use "canonical sociology," that these are the sociologists who have been canonized by the sociological profession and that Lewis Mumford can be seen in one respect as a noncanonical sociologist. He liked this. As far as the academy goes, I see Mumford in much the way he described Thorstein Veblen in his autobiography: "As an economist well-grounded in technics and anthropology, Veblen was as much a suspected heretic in the academic world as Patrick Geddes was; and those who were not able to cope with his immense scholarship covered their embarrassment by not paying sufficient attention to his ideas. . . . Not strangely the very traits that drew me to Veblen gave a special excuse to more pedestrian scholars to ignore him."[2]

We went back to the theme of the two worlds of German thought—the problem of the domination of social theory by German thought. I mentioned that much as I admire the varieties of ideas in German thought, the split between subjective and objective deriving from Kant that one finds in Weber, Durkheim, Simmel, and some other thinkers begins with the problem as if there were two opposing worlds, and the task of the sociologist is to put them together. I said that by contrast Lewis begins with one world, that he begins with a holistic approach, that we look first at a whole—whether it's a city or a person. The holistic approach begins in a more concrete way rather than a false abstraction of two worlds, yet can reach as far into subjective or objective directions, viewing them as a polarity instead of a dichotomy. But it was a tendency of German thought to dichotomize the world into two pieces and take that abstraction as primary.

I went on to mention how after reading his work intensely this spring I find dark statements in various places expressing a kind of pessimism and simultaneously statements of hope that express more of an optimism. I told him that when I try to sort these out, when I look at him in the context of social theory, it seems to me that he both is more optimistic and pessimistic than what I read in the rest of social theory. Weber again took a very dark view of the turn of modernity and saw increasing rationalization and bureaucratization as a cagelike world in which we would be living, and now we already are. But Weber still thought this was an inevitable development of the logic of rationality. Yet Mumford sees that it's not inevitable—that it is changeable—and yet ends up with a more pessimistic view. Why then must we continue to force ourselves to go in this direction? Is he even more pessimistic than Weber? Weber thinks it can't be helped, but Mumford poses to us the question: why then are we proceeding with these series of mistakes that lead us further in this path of restriction and constriction and destruction?

Mumford, in seeing that this is changeable has room to be more optimistic than other social theorists can be. It's not a blind optimism but it's something that has hope in it. Jack Ricks at this point said yes, it's hard to look at it as pessimism or optimism—it's something that defies the labels—and I had to agree with him that labels were really not the right way to put this into perspective. Somehow, Lewis ended up more encompassing than those labels. Sophia Mumford at that point said, "Well, maybe you could call it realism." And I had to agree with her that it is a realism. It's a realism that can stare negative consequences of current tendencies in the face and say we must avoid this direction or else we will bring catastrophe to our cities as he predicted in the late 1930s, followed shortly thereafter by the destruction of many of the European cities, and after that in the 1950s and 60s by destructive hollowing out of many American cities.

I said it was that theme of encompassing—being broader than the range of canonical social theorists—that also had an attraction and fascination for me in Mumford's work. I used Picasso as an example of someone who always encompasses the styles of the time and the styles that he helped to create and often generated. His Dada is more encompassing than the Dadaists. His art from 1930 or early 1930s was very geometrical and in some ways reminds me of late Paul Klee or Wassily Kandinsky. But where they have turned to a more rigid form from their earlier and freer work to more constricted geometrical work, Picasso always has life at the center of his work. It's always vibrant. It always jumps out at you with energy. And in the same way Mumford's work always carries an encompassing ability to see the big picture even in a particular piece or theme; it carries this larger context with it all the time. And perhaps in that sense it has that kind of life and energy that Picasso's work carries. So I tried to discuss this theme of encompassing that I see in Mumford's work.

I also mentioned again to him how his work seems to me so easily written. I knew from the last time I had met with him and spoke that it was not a very easy job to write, but that when you read his work, it just comes right off the page as though it were waved on there without any effort. He said, "No, no, no. It wasn't that way at all. It was a lot harder work than that," smiling. I said that I knew it was a very difficult task but that all the effort revealed itself in an effortless prose on Mumford's part.

Sophia Mumford told an anecdote at one point—perhaps it was when I had mentioned Vienna in the beginning of the conversation. She was in Vienna in 1930 and had met with the mayor of Vienna and they were talking about education in Vienna. The Montessori method of education was very popular in Vienna at that time. Sophia said that Montessori was old fashioned in the United States by then, that yes, it has come back again to become popular. And she was talking to the mayor of Vienna about this and he said, "Well in Berlin they have such and such kind of education more adapted to the individual perhaps, but here in Vienna we have a socialist government and we need a form of education that is social, that is not just addressed to the individual but is social because we don't have room for experiments here." We all laughed and I said that even as early as 1930 socialism had no room for experiments. And she said yes. She took it to be a very sorry state of affairs for socialism if it was so rigid it could not experiment even in education.

As I drive south now in Dutchess County, New York, taping these notes, the mountains are covered with either clouds or fog, or in many places wisps of fog that just come over the tops of the mountains and gradually evaporate.

At one point in discussing the encompassing nature of his work and this aspect of being both more pessimistic and more optimistic than other thinkers, I asked Lewis how this began. I don't think he fully heard the question, but Sophia answered—a terrific answer. She said that he was born that way, that she had observed from when they first met in 1919 that he had this kind of balance in him. He never took merely one side or the other. He always had a balance between a more objective and more subjective and a more scientific and a more literary approach to things. So she thought it was just what he is. She joked that he probably should not take credit for it because he was born that way. I said to her—also laughing—that at least he gives credit in his work to the concept of life—to the life concept that in effect is crediting his achievements to his own proclivities and impulses rather than to his conscious rationality of working them out. They met when she was the secretary for *The Dial* magazine and Lewis became an associate editor. Its board of editors included Dewey and Veblen. When Lewis returned from a half-year stint in London as editor of the *Sociological Review* a couple of years later they married. Her replacement was a young Kenneth Burke, later widely known as a literary critic.

I tried to take some note of the living room where we sat this time, because on my previous visits I was too engrossed in the conversation to really notice the surroundings. The living room was rather small. The walls were surrounded with bookshelves and crammed with books. The most interesting feature of the room to me was the ceiling, which had rough-hewn wood beams and unpainted wood. The whole ceiling was unpainted wood, giving it a rough and rustic quality. From where I was sitting facing Mumford in his chair I could also see the kitchen. I had been in there last time and noticed again the large fireplace. The house is a farmhouse from about 1837.

Early in the conversation Sophia was trying to fix the lamp next to her, to turn it on, and it was going on and off—perhaps the light bulb was loose—and she jokingly asked, "Who can explain how light bulbs work?" She would like to see someone write on light—the nature of light bulbs and how they work and don't work. We started joking a little bit about how light bulbs seem to work so that just when you need them they will go out. And we went into a discussion then of American culture and Sophia said she had to be careful sometimes in Amenia because people take certain things so seriously—the sending of cards on Mother's and Father's Day—and we got talking about the nature of greeting cards. She said that they have a German friend whose husband had recently died and who had received Hallmark sympathy cards. She said she just could not understand; she knew that the people who sent them did not know that form messages like this struck one as empty and inauthentic. I added, "or why people would prefer form messages to handwritten, heartfelt ones." I mentioned at that point, speaking of inauthentic and empty forms, of how I had been brought here via New York City by a magazine that wanted me to observe the phenomenon of the Wall Street brokers all congregating at the South Street Seaport (this was the heyday of Gordon Gecko greed, before the big crash). And I briefly discussed how they thronged, swilling beer in their three-piece suits and drinking Foster's Australian Lager beer in a kind of "Yupward Bound" yuppie ritual. I could not comprehend how people who have to congregate in frenetic conditions on Wall Street during the day could walk a few blocks away and again congregate in frenetic conditions, drinking beer and getting rowdy and acting corporate wild. It would seem that they might prefer to have a little bit of peace and quiet after such intensive daytime work, or at least a less high-stimulus environment, but they seem to want to continue the same frenzy after work as during the day.

At a couple of points in the conversation Lewis offered comments; they were not always clear and he was frustrated at some points. He said he was trying to say something and then he said, "Well, but that's nothing, I'm not saying it," and was expressing frustration with his ability to communicate his ideas clearly. In a couple of other instances, although he was speaking vaguely, I thought I could comprehend what he was trying to get at, and I asked him if such and such was what he meant. He said yes, in fact that was what he was trying to say. At the end of our conversation, when I was going out the front door, Sophia Mumford that this was such a wonderful occasion, that he can go for days and nothing will happen but when you present him with stimulating conversation he perks up and can be part of it. I said I hoped I wasn't putting words in his mouth trying to understand what he was saying. She said, "No, no." She was listening closely and thought I was picking up on what he was trying to say. At one point, for example, he said the materials are there but the inner world is not there now—something to that effect—and it seemed to me he was trying to say that we need to make a new inner life, that so much of our time has been devoted to outer aspects of existence, but that we need to remake the inner life and that all the materials might be there but they just have not been put to use. And he said yes, this was what he was trying to say.

I mentioned that this year I had read for the first time *The Condition of Man*, and it opened up a dimension of his work dealing with this history of Western civilization that I felt was also remarkable for its grasp and breadth and handling of the facts. I said that I had also begun another history of Western civilization written by D. H. Lawrence. Sophia was surprised. She said, "Did you say T. H. Lawrence?" I said no, D. H. She said that she had not been aware that he had written such a nonfiction work. I told her of some of his other nonfiction works; I said that to me, his work and Lewis's *Condition of Man* were two nonstandard accounts of Western civilization that I found fascinating to put together.

Sophia asked about other nonfiction works of Lawrence, and I told her that the one I find most interesting is his work *Apocalypse*, which is a commentary on the book of revelation attributed to John of Patmos. In *Apocalypse* Lawrence develops the idea that Jesus represents the inwardly strong—the inwardly powerful—who gives himself to the weak; who gives himself to those who do not have this inward power. But for Lawrence this was only half the story of Christianity. The other half involved the inwardly weak wanting to possess, destroy, and devour the inwardly powerful, and that this is the meaning of the apocalypse in the Judeo-Christian tradition. Perhaps also this is why we need to remake the inner life today in

Mumford's sense, not just as asceticism or "spiritualism" but also as the passions recentered.

Lawrence began this work after writing on Dostoyevsky's chapters on "The Grand Inquisitor" in *The Brothers Karamazov*. He saw the dark side of Christianity as an unrecognized destructive side, the legacy of a falsely idealizing love, one that seeks final judgment on the surface of things but in fact is seeking that inward power in a destructive way. For Lawrence, our time—the modern era—is the time of the apocalypse, the time in which the underside of idealized love comes to the foreground and the spontaneous life slides further into eclipse.

I went on to describe how in trying to talk about some of Lawrence's ideas with historians and others, they tended to see Lawrence as inclined toward fascism, thinking, in effect, that one man's Apocalypse is another's Götterdämmerung. And I said that so far in trying to look into this it appears to me that Lawrence had ideas that might seem to resonate with fascism but ultimately are diametrically opposed to fascism. In fact, Lawrence explicitly rejected fascism. He criticized Mussolini and the "uncanny danger" that he saw rising in Germany in the early 1920s. And he criticized "mass democracy," machinelike, as antidemocratic in his posthumously published writing on democracy gathered in *Phoenix*. I said that Lawrence was expressing an extramodern mind, just as Charles Peirce had. When I described my book (*Meaning and Modernity*), I realized that apparently Sophia Mumford had not received the published copy, so I again described how I had tried to use ideas from Peirce, how I thought that he was of a genuinely nonmodern mind, and how I saw connections between some of his ideas and Lewis's.

D. H. Lawrence had discussed blood—the significance of blood—and how some people thought this resonated with the Nazi ideology of "blood and earth," by which they meant, "my blood and my earth is better than yours." But Lawrence meant something far more radical: the sun has made our eyes and our blood resonates with the moon or is the nerves of the moon. Lawrence's poetic metaphors were animistic ideas that also were scientifically true in my opinion. Our eyes are made to be sensitive to visible light, the sun lights the earth and its growing forms, and in effect has created our eyes. Our eyes are attuned to the visual spectrum of existence that has its source in the sun, so Lawrence's animistic poetic metaphor can also be scientifically true.

I said these ideas seem to me to grate against the modern, dominant ideals, and the fact that the Nazis had perverted biology—perverted the human body to meet their ideology—made it difficult to talk about these ideas in Lawrence that are diametrically opposed to Nazism and fascism but also diametrically opposed to modern liberal rationalism.

Mumford broke in at this point and said in a rather long and coherent statement—very coherent—"Yes, there is a lot out there waiting. A lot to be used. The materials are there already." He mentioned Auden, saying that in W. H. Auden's poetry are nonmodern ideas waiting to be used and appreciated. I listened and said yes, I found that I keep discovering materials of our time—written in our time but not of our time—and I have to overcome certain prejudices in myself against our time in order to appreciate these materials: the work of D. H. Lawrence for example. I said I thought that Mumford's work was also part of the "blind spot" of our time, and he nodded yes.

I said that people cannot deny you your work on the city, but, while striking my fist, "that your work simply breaks through the constraints and repressions of our time. Everyone has to accept the power of that work, but when you express ideas about possible limits to the size of cities, critics might want to say that's a little off the mark, or that's 'nostalgic.' Or in your life philosophy when you claim that there are organic dimensions to human existence that have to be taken account of. Critics say, well he's thinking about old-fashioned biological concepts that are outmoded. They would either repress or not talk about those ideas or claim that he is off the mark in that area."

What is actually happening is that Mumford is touching areas of thoughts deeper than those critics can allow or can see. They are possessed by the dominant rationalist ideas of our time to such an extent that they are incapable of seeing that he is working out of a much deeper way of thinking. His discussion of biology involves a different conception of biology that is much more inclusive of the likely social, experiential conditions in which the human mind formed. I told Lewis that those sides of his thought that do not fit into the constricted tendencies of our time seem to have lain fallow so far.

Lewis went on to talk about an example of two elements of an organism. They might look simple and not seem to do much and then you put them together and . . . his voice gradually trailed off. He expressed frustration at not being able to say what he had wanted to say. I asked him whether he had meant to say that there could be two simple aspects of an organism that appear to be useless or just utterly simple but that in fact in some kind of combination can produce an unexpected transformation of the organism to bring about radically changed conditions from something that is not obvious, something that is so obvious it looks like it could never produce such a complex transformation. And he said yes, that was what he meant.

He talked about how we need to put together these materials for "the inner," the inner world, the inner existence. And I added that yes, it seemed to me our time is one of total attention to the externals. If someone were to discuss inner dimensions of existence as Mumford has, the critics would either dismiss it outright or turn it into just the externals, and he shook his head yes. He said we must in effect make this inner life appear, and he said that you two—looking at me—and that the other fellow there, Ricks—were doing this, and all of us here together—the four of us—were not enough. We needed a more general change of culture, in effect a change of cultural climate and conditions. I said again that the way he brings the inner life to the foreground was something that really attracted me to his work; I said how different his work is from social theory today.

I related that during my time in Germany I would hear people talk about why science or technology might be wrong, why we need to have the subjective life recognized, and why this was in many ways more important than the objective life. I was sympathetic to this, but there was something wrong about it that I could never really articulate while I was in Germany. It was when I read Mumford's letters to Germans written just after World War II (a war in which his son was killed in the last months) that I felt he really put his finger on the problem of German romanticism and again the two worlds of German thought—one being the objective and external, the other being the internal and subjective. He argued that we must have whole human beings, that we begin with whole human beings in our analyses and not just an inward subjective dimension that is correct because it is what we happen to feel, as happens in the worst of German "inwardness."

I told Mumford how much I had been attracted to his work on the transformation from animal into human, and how I had been turning to archaeological and anthropological sources for prehistoric man and the transformation to village and urban life. I had found some confirmation for his work in recent studies showing that there were decreases in protein and other nutritional levels after agriculture was introduced. Agriculture was not an advance in nutrition but rather a decrease of healthy food life, so that there had to be other mitigating factors that would lead us into organized village life. I also mentioned a study I read recently suggesting beer might have been part of this transformation. Beer was a source of high protein but also the altered state and sociability might have been something that people were willing to settle for—literally—in exchange for a richer diet from hunting and gathering.

At another point in the conversation, toward the end, Lewis looked at us and said, "Yes, our work is not done."

Last Visit with Lewis, November 1989

My last visit with Lewis was at the end of November 1989, about two months before he died. I arranged to go with Paul Goldberger, then the *New York Times* architectural critic. I was living that year in New Haven, and I ran into him in New York City. When I mentioned that I had been visiting Lewis and Sophia, he told me how, although he was led into architectural criticism by Vincent Scully at Yale University, Lewis's work had been an increasingly powerful influence on his own development over the years, primarily because of its "sustaining power." He wanted to meet Lewis if possible, even though he understood that Lewis's health had been failing. So we met in the town of Amenia, and I showed him the way to the house.

It was Sunday, and happened to be the day the *Times* published a review of Donald Miller's biography of Lewis, *Lewis Mumford: A Life*. The review was written by Ada Louise Huxtable, who had been Goldberger's predecessor at the *Times* and who had hired him right out of college. It was a real barn burner of a discussion, lasting a couple of hours. Lewis shook our hands when we entered the living room, but could not engage in the conversation. Paul reiterated to Sophia what I had told her earlier; he simply wanted to meet Lewis because he had been such an influence on him.

Sophia was upset with Huxtable's portrayal of her as the long-suffering wife, a Griselda, who put up with Lewis's self-absorption and extramarital affairs. Sophia was also upset with Don Miller for enumerating the affairs. As she put it, it wasn't as though Lewis hadn't included a couple of them in his autobiography, but that he did so to convey significant events in his life, including the ups and downs of their marriage, and not simply to list transgressions. She thought Miller had sensationalized Lewis in the biography, had, in effect, attempted to cut him down to size at the expense of showing his real place as an American and twentieth-century intellectual. She told us that she and Lewis put a date on his documents in the archive at the University of Pennsylvania Library to keep them closed well-enough into the future so that everyone mentioned in them would likely be dead by then. But the date was something like 1985! So they had already outlived it.

Sophia said that Miller had assured her he would show her controversial materials, such as Lewis's accounts of the affairs in the archives, if he meant to use them, but he had not. I could understand her anger, but this was also a delicate question. Should Miller have kept his word, as she described it, or should he have avoided censorship of what he thought should be published? It seemed to me that if he gave his word to check with her first then he owed it to her to do so. But I also don't know his side of the story. Even if he had permission to use the materials, should he have included them as he did?

Miller pointed in his biography to some disturbing traits in Mumford, not unconnected to his genius. His self-absorption and devotion to writing was so great that once, when his daughter Alison came home excited with a discovery she had made in her art class at school, he remained nonresponsive, deep in thought, and left to go type something. Alison was crestfallen and felt he didn't care about her discovery, but found out a couple of days later that he was so excited with what she had said that he wanted to write it down before forgetting it. This seems to me to be an example of his narcissism, perhaps just as his way of bringing his affairs into his marriage—into Sophia's face—is. This is the dark side of the "great man," who treats life as fodder for writing or art. Lewis himself described the chill that Herman Melville's self-absorption had on his family, even down through his grandchildren. Miller indicated something of that at work in Mumford, despite the fact that he did spend daily time with his children. His work was sacred, and his family members had to respect that, maintaining a kind of "radio silence" when he went into his study after breakfast to write.

Sometimes, it seems to me, the "great man" is one who makes a Faust bargain, gaining public fame by giving up the personal energies and connections of everyday life. Lewis gained fame as a public intellectual by the end of the thirties, and various commentators have described him as "noble," which in many ways his writings are, embodying an uncommon nobility of spirit. But sometimes that nobility can come off as aloofness, priggishness, or even as idealizing compensation for one's early life traumas. Lewis had idealized Patrick Geddes early in his career, perhaps as the father he never had, even naming his son after him. But he had come to realize that he could not be Geddes's son, especially after Geddes told Lewis how he reminded him of his own son, killed in the Great War. Still, he may have yet carried an idealized father image within; perhaps it was the great man he grew into.

Sophia also took offense to the "pauper" view of Lewis's mother, saying that her circumstances were not that grim. She also thought more proportion was needed, which would place Lewis's work as central. Although his account of Lewis's life and work is thorough and rich with detail and understanding, Miller could not fully grasp, in my opinion, the philosophical aspects of Lewis's work, perhaps because Miller, as a historian, preferred the trees to the forest. Lewis was a historian as well as a philosopher, he preferred to be called a generalist, and the deepest reaches of his philosophy, like those of Peirce and Melville, not only reveal the false underpinnings of the modern and civilized mind but also show the alternatives for a new mind and civilization. Mumford's moral outrage, especially in his later works, also rubbed Miller the wrong way. I can agree that some of it may have been Mumford's aloof "Olympianism," but what might have embarrassed Miller was simply an impassioned mind at work, unconstrained by academic mores.

Huxtable did draw attention to the compelling nature of Lewis's writings, but the "Griselda" tag still got under Sophia's skin. Huxtable claimed that because he lived in the country, Lewis was out of touch with city life, as though one had to live in New York City to say anything about it. Yet Mumford traveled frequently to the city, especially for his column on architecture he wrote for more than thirty-five years for the *New Yorker* magazine. His distance may have given him needed perspective to see the city freshly and critically.

Lewis died on January 26, 1990.

Letter to Sophia on Lewis's death, January 30, 1990

Dear Sophia,

I was deeply saddened to hear of Lewis's death. I know that this is a time of great sorrow for you, and my wife and I convey to you our heartfelt sympathies. You and Lewis struggled against this world to retain human warmth, simplicity, and dignity, and the fact that he died peacefully at home was itself a fulfillment of that struggle.

A great man has died, and the world has yet to know how great he was. I do not doubt that his work will endure the darkness of our life-negating time, but I mourn the fact that a man who gave himself to creating a new vision, a way out of this inhuman madness, could be so ignored and so little understood.

Lewis was a volcanic revolutionary erupting through the crust of the modern age. His vision cuts too deeply and broadly to be grasped in its full implications by contemporary "post humans." But it will live, if humanity does, as a vital contribution to the reservoir of human wisdom.

Sophia, please know in your loss that our feelings are with you and your family.

In sadness and love,

Gene

A few months later, in May, I saw Sophia at the memorial for Lewis held at the Hotchkiss School in nearby Lakeville, Connecticut, and visited her a couple of weeks later with my wife, my son Jacob, and my newborn daughter Gemma. I returned to visit Sophia two years later, in June of 1992, winding my way down from Kingston, Ontario. I was in the midst of a divorce, and Sophia told me that her daughter Alison Mumford Morss had been diagnosed with a terminal form of cancer.

Last Visit with Sophia, April 7, 1995

When I arrived and we sat down in the living room, Sophia told me how she had returned a few days earlier to find my book *Bereft of Reason* there, and my message asking if it would be okay to visit her. She thanked me for the book and told me what she had been reading lately. She said, "I'm ninety-five now and cannot read continuously, only in short chunks." I told her that being able to be engaged with things at the age of ninety-five was fantastic.

She said she is otherwise healthy, keeps in touch with friends, and feels alive. She asked how things were going for me now. I told her I feel more alive than ever, but after my divorce a couple of years earlier, and as a single custodial father of two kids, I've had trouble keeping in touch with correspondents.

I asked Sophia about a Japanese print in the corner of the living room near the front entry, a winter scene that looked to me like a treaty being signed. She told me that it had been a gift from Frank Lloyd Wright, and how Wright and Lewis had fought bitterly over American intervention in the Second World War. Wright was a libertarian isolationist, where Lewis actively called for U.S. involvement from at least 1939. The aftermath of Pearl Harbor eventually brought Wright around, but he and Lewis were not in contact again until 1950, when Wright sent Lewis a catalogue from an exhibition of his work in Florence, in which he inscribed, "In spite of all, your old F. Ll. W." Lewis, whose son Geddes had died in the war, allowed his bitterness to thaw, and wrote Wright back. Wright then sent him the Hokusai print. They remained friends for a few more years until Wright's ego intervened again; he became angry at reviews of his work Lewis had written in the New Yorker.

I also asked about another work, a sculpture in the living room that reminded me of the curving forms of Hans/Jean Arp. Sophia said her daughter Alison had done it, how much her teacher had admired it, and how Alison had not continued in art. Alison also wrote a paper in college that her teacher thought showed great promise, but she again did not develop that talent. I began to wonder whether she had been damaged from living in the shadow of "the great man." My motto for my just-published book came to mind: One cannot live by ideals, only with ideals.

In the three years since I had last visited I had come to see much more clearly how damaging to one's personal life living by ideals could be. I had come to see ways in which Lewis's combination of talents, drive, and iron will had helped him achieve great works and made him a great man, but how the hidden costs might have been a shadow cast on those around him, a Faustian reckoning. A "great man" does not necessarily a "good enough" man make, to those closest to him.

We are composite beings, our selves are comprised of personal, public, and even cosmic dimensions, and it is possible to reap great works by sacrificing the energies and empathies of the everyday in search of the great, the enlightened, the infinite. Buddha, after all, was an enlightened being who also happened to be a deadbeat dad. There is also the Isolato approach, immune to the greater world. The great task of life, as I see it, is how to body forth the various dimensions of self, yet still be in some kind of balance, true to one's spontaneous self, vulnerable to life.

I also came to see some blind spots in Lewis's works, a kind of indifference to the everyday world seemingly at odds with one who wrote so masterfully on architecture and town planning. But then there is his massive outpouring of letters over the course of his life, ranging from the most intimate and everyday to the great issues of the day.

We discussed Lewis's ideas further; I told Sophia how interesting I found his time at Stanford to be, given the recent culture wars involving the same Stanford Humanities Institute he helped start fifty years earlier, and how I discussed it in *Bereft of Reason*. Sophia talked about Lewis's time at the University of Pennsylvania in the early 1960s. He had suggested teaching a religion course with original source materials. No one was interested in it, though he spent a year preparing it. It probably would have gotten a lot more interest a few years later, when the sixties really hit. We spoke some more, and then it was time to go. I made my final goodbyes. Sophia was a remarkable woman, still fully engaged at ninety-five, and still at home. I knew this would be our final visit. Sophia died two years later in April 1997.

13

TELEPARODIES

Reality TV seems to me to correlate not only with the rise of surveillance culture, but, more generally, also with the loss of reality, public life, and private life in Western and globalizing techno-culture, with its consumption-inducing military-industrial-academic-entertainment-sport-food complex. Reality TV: Or, Nights of the Living Dead. It is the world of BIG Zombie: gaze-deprived, gaze-obsessed, engaged in a spectatorial voyeur-combat that is the virtual bread and circus of the electro-coliseums of TV. Why live for real, when you can watch The Screen for hours per day as voyeur, and in the process, deplete yourself of your real life? *Pax electronica*.

In the tradition of Stanislaw Lem's *Imaginary Magnitude*, a book of introductions to books not written, and David Lavery and Angela Hague's edited collection *Teleparody: Predicting/Preventing the TV Discourse of Tomorrow* (London: Wallflower Press, 2002), in which my review of Art Dimsdale's book, *On Temptation Island: The View from the Hot Tub*, first appeared, I include here Art Dimsdale's brief review of the reality television show, *Face Factor* (which originally appeared in *Post-Critical Inquiry*, special issue on "De-Facing"), as an introduction to this illustrious postcritic's postcritical take on things. I am grateful for his generous permission to republish it here. My essay on Mr. Dimsdale's book follows it.

THE SNUFF FACTOR: KILLING THE
GOOSE WHO GOT THE GOLDEN EGG LAID

by Art Dimsdale

Man is a natural polygamist: he always has one woman leading him by the nose, and another hanging on to his coattails.
—H. L. MENCKEN

God gave us a penis and a brain, but only enough blood to run one at a time.
—ROBIN WILLIAMS

Of course it was only a matter of time for TV to turn from the peeled-skin corpses of CSI and other crime lab series to live reality show versions. But with the death last week of Boiff Krauthammer, the blimpy, aggressive contestant on "Face Factor," reality entertainment has had to face the sobering prospect of a congressional inquiry into its behind the scene realities. This could spell the final autopsy of reality entertainment.

"Face Factor," as you know, combined elements of the extreme makeover shows with "Fear Factor," one of the early reality-daredevil commercial successes. Utilizing the latest technical advances in plastic surgery, plus the aura of the John Travolta–Nicholas Cage film *Face-Off*, "Face Factor" pitted contestants against each other in a kind of Mr. Potato-Head assemblage.

Genetic samples taken from each contestant are harvested for six weeks in the rapid-growth labs of Bioscab, the biotech giant which sponsors the show, and which revolutionized the plastic surgery trade. The Bioscab peel, which used genetic therapy to modify faces, did for the human face what Viagra did for the human penis, erasing the shrivel virtually overnight.

With spare parts now grown contestants then meet with the selected member of the opposite sex, having the full availability of ears, nose, eyebrows, mouth, chins, and hair of the other contestants available, as well as a personal "facial designer" for advice on how to "dress" appropriately. Rumors have surfaced about other body parts in jars available for use as well, especially after the Krauthammer Incident, as the media is calling it.

Though contestants are doused with ample antibiotics and steroids for the duration of the show, something went drastically wrong in Boiff's case. Two weeks into the shooting, a nose started growing on Krauthammer where it should not have grown. Way where it should not have grown! Way down in a place where The Organ is supposed to be, and which is supposed to grow only at those inspired moments of passion.

Worse, Krauthammer's facial nose began to act peculiarly, apparently perking up at mealtimes, when catering arrived. Despite Krauthammer's best attempts to save the appearances, the obvious soon became obvious. By some genetic fluke, Krauthammer was undergoing a case of transposed heads, so to speak. What should have been his ticket to ride turned into his facial freak show. Oddly, however, the female contestant, Virginia Dover, showed an initial interest in the new beak, at least until the growth factor went awry, and she realized what the emergent object of her affection in reality was. A dickhead.

The Bioscab people, on realizing the catastrophic effect such a genetic boo-boo could have on their livelihood cancelled shooting immediately and scheduled Krauthammer for surgery. At first he was reluctant, feeling himself a kind of reborn Cyrano de Bergerac, nosing for Roxanne. It took but the mention of two words from the surgeon, however, to bring Krauthammer around. "Michael Jackson," the surgeon stated, and before he could launch into the history of the lost nose of Michael Jackson, Krauthammer was sobbing: "OK, OK, I'll do it."

Krauthammer died on the table, between his severed nose and penis, a sad testimony to the skin-flick industry that is reality TV. Whether the entertainment complex can survive the congressional hearings is the story that will dominate the entertainment "news" for the next year. But don't hold your breath waiting to see how it turns out. Instead, try to see if you can find any wrinkles on the committee members' faces.

NO MAN IS AN ISLAND: IT TAKES A VILLAGE IDIOT

(Review of Dimsdale, *On Temptation Island: The View from the Hot Tub* [New York: Danaides and Baedecker, 2015], 261 & iv; 22 ani-photos and comp card)

MTV doesn't really package the show as "you'll love these kids." It is kinda like, "look at these fools" and then it creates this vicious kind of superiority thing. See, some people at home just sit there excited that they aren't you, and pass serious judgment. I know, I was once a viewer and I felt this way. Plus it's true.
—PRINCESS MELISSA, FROM MTV'S *The Real World*,
NEW ORLEANS

When I was younger I could remember anything, whether it had happened or not.
—MARK TWAIN

Mad, decadent, puerile, revolting, titillating, vomitous, cheesy, scummy, raunchy, kitschy, cruel, outrageous, indifferent, and desperate things go on ALL the time in most of the US, certainly on its universal "Big Eye" of TV. But people seem to think that the decadence is always greener on the other side of the fantasy island, so to speak. It all seems more real when it, as it were, seems more real. It seems as though reality in America floats somewhere between the "seems" and the "seamy."

To judge by the continued popularity of "reality" shows, decadence is alive and well today. After their initial burst of success with "Survivor," new shows continued appearing for a few years, then seemed to be on the wane. But now, fifteen years after the first "Survivor," the shows have reflourished with new vigor, stretching boundaries that many thought were already stretched to the limit. What gives? Why so?

Enter Art Dimsdale, the postpolitical pundit whose punchy polemics have previously parodied the presidency. Yes, the author of *From Marilyn to Monica: Mammaries Are Made of This*, and more recently, *A Bird in the Hand: Homoerotic Subtexts of the Bush Presidencies*, has now turned his rapier wit on the reality show phenomenon.

On Temptation Island: The View from the Hot Tub, is no mere deconstruction of the phenomenon. For that, Dimsdale reminds us, is not only easy, but has already been done, "*ad nauseum* by the numerous wits—dim and yet otherwise penetrating—of the present age."

I admit to a certain weakness for this sort of sharp-edged writing, especially when its author can go fully satirical without being a lit-snob. Unlike the postaesthetes, slashing, parenthesizing, and always obfuscating, Dimsdale chose to kick back and get it wet, to get himself out of the frying pan of journalism into the fire of the shows themselves. Well, sort of.

Do you remember George Plimpton, the author who became a real-life Walter Mitty? They called him a "participatory-journalist." He was a kind of renaissance celebrity man. He got to play professional football, hockey, golf, hang with celebrities, act in movies and on TV shows. Remember that series ER? Plimpton acted in one episode. The man also had heavyweight literary credentials that few celebrities could match, having founded *The Parisian Review* and continuing on as editor for decades during his escapades.

Well Dimsdale seems to fancy himself a new Plimpton in this work, a "virtual-participatory-journalist." Plimpton had to get his butt off his desk chair and out on the playing field, into the arena of sport and celebrity life. But Dimsdale has taken the virtual route, plunking his bottom in a hotbed of American fantasy reality, the hot tub.

Not just any hot tub, not for our Art. Ay, there's the rub-a-dub-dub!

Dimsdale is nothing if not savvy. He understands, as few postcritics have, that though the festering sleep-of-death fantasies of America may dislocate themselves in globalized exotic commodification zones, they emanate from Main Street.

Sherwood Anderson understood the second part of this "To sleep, perchance to nightmare" equation: Main Street the ideal is composed of Main Street the grotesque. But the first part, the *Exotica Projection*, as Dimsdale terms it, was yet to fully blossom in the second half of the last century. Surely this must give us pause, if for no other reason, then pause for the cause.

Main Street may have morphed into Main Street Mall, the placeless faceless one-size-fits-all Happyland of consumption, but the underlying grotesque only grew larger, like an unattended Golem.

You see, America used to be able to project its utopian desires a little closer to home. The Jersey shore could embody New York's fantasies, until air travel scattered them further. Asbury Park and Atlantic City gave way to the all-year-round tropics, and became emaciated little scumbag towns. Gambling goosed Atlantic City back to attention, but it was no city at all, merely a Potemkin money strip, a seaside mall of money.

Who would want to watch "reality" in Atlantic City or Asbury Park? Who would want to go there to share summer food, fun, and surf, when one could go to far more exotic places, all-year-round places, places that one could bring back as moneyed "souvenirs"? MTV once tried it, using Seaside Heights, NJ, as a summer location, but they still saved the hard-body onstage TV erotica competitions for the tropics.

Who, in short, would want to set a "reality" show in prosaic New Joisey, when one could go to fantasy island? Answer: nobody in their right commodified mind would want to, nobody, except Art Dimsdale that is.

Whatever one says about Dimsdale's shrewdness, slickness even (remember that chapter of his last book, "Bush Whacked?" Or just take a look at Dimsdale.com!), he understands the fundamental ratio of decadence to exotica: when it's *there* it's better than *here*, and even when it's *here*, it's better to pretend that it is really *there*.

Would "reality" shows set in Anytown, USA be watched more than those set on Fantasy Survivor Temptation Island? No way they would. Dimsdale knows this, but chose to play with it as postcritic by immersing himself, literally, in "Midwest Civ," as he calls it. Virtual George Plimpton meets Hunter S. Thompson in the matrix of magic that brings fantasy island to Anytown USA.

Figure 24. Dimsdale and Tania, crayon, by Fritz Janschka, 2001.

Dimsdale put himself into a hot tub in Normal, Illinois, a great big hot tub owned by Tom and Harriet Foley, a hot tub that for a few weeks became the evening gathering place for eight latter-day residents of "Main Street."

But Dimsdale also knew that "reality" shows required the exotica, so he and his seven tub mates watched the shows set in fabulous locations while sequestered, like a hung jury, in their Normal hot tub. Three nights each week they soaked it all up as the world's first reality show viewing team.

Dimsdale intuitively understood what the TV producers have yet, even to-day, to figure out: that it takes more than exotica, that it takes an island, what he calls *Isolato Island*, after Herman Melville. In *Moby-Dick*, Melville depicted the United States as comprised of *isolato* islanders, not from "the common continent" of humanity. And Dimsdale slyly cites Thoreau's journal entry of April 24, 1859, where he says, "Fools stand on their island opportunities, and look toward another land. There is no other land, there is no other life but this." And so what Dimsdale did was to create a little Gilligan's island of Main Streeters. More, he also "supplemented" the shows he and the Normal citizens were watching with ones of his own devising, formed in that imaginary domain between public TV voyeurism and private hot tub fantasy.

With Margarita Montoya, the aerobics instructor and massage therapist on his left, and Debbie Engel, the saucy lawyer on his right, watching the double digital TVs set at opposite ends of the tub and commenting on the antics of the real TV participants, their feet and thighs touching in tactile underwater repartee all the while, who would not drift dreamily to fabulous vicarious realities?

The first chapter, "Temptation Island Survivor Loser," sets the historical context for the reality revival, with Dimsdale describing the unplanned, but not unwanted, birth of the "hyper-reality" show in 2011. That was the year Jerry Springer was assassinated live on the air by the animal rights activist during the famous "Lovers Loving Lovers' Pets" episode of his show. It was also the year of the "Bacchae Incident," as the media named it, after the women followers of Bacchus, ancient god of wine and ecstasy, also known as Dionysus. The Bacchae Incident was one of the most significant moments in TV history, ranking, perhaps, with the Kennedy assassination. And to this day the debate continues whether the incident was unplanned or scripted.

Dimsdale reminds us that budgets of the few remaining reality shows had been cut, and that Fox had tried to scrimp by filming two separate shows simultaneously on one island. *Survivor 15: D.I.*, which was to be the last installment and grand finale of the show, was supposed to feature a cast of competitors made up entirely of male marine drill instructors.

This *Survivor* was supposed to have changed the question from "Who's tough and who is not," to "Who's the toughest and nastiest of them all." It was a good premise, since everyone knows that viewers love to hate the contestants, even while identifying with them. It even featured a competition based on the film *The Hunted*, released back in 2003, where Tommy Lee Jones played a master tracker who had to find and capture an expert commando gone bad, played by Benicio Del Toro. The cameramen couldn't keep up, so all the competitors were fitted with "third eyes," those tiny disc-cameras attached to the middle of the forehead, freeing the entire crew to shoot on the other side of the island.

Oddly, this should have been the most adrenalin inducing of all the Survivor series, yet it did not make for good TV. These were former professional combat soldiers, most of whom had served in Afghanistan, Iraq, Iran, or Venezuela, and watching them hiding, camouflaged green, in bushes for hours on end got to be boring.

Meanwhile, on the other side of the island, an all-female cast of competitors was assembled for "American Gladiatrixes," another retro-revival of the old "American Gladiators," a show that many feel was the first reality show— or first decadence show, depending on your view of reality.

Well, the women had just finished the mud wrestling event, which was to give the winners a bubble bath and the losers a trip to "The Penile Colony," a wicked Kafka maze of giant 2-meter male organs, life-like to the touch, waving like undersea ferns, obtrusive, in-your-face, through which the losers had to wander until they reached the exit.

Now understand that filming on the island had been going on for three weeks, and not all of the women found these symbols of patriarchal repression to be a negative experience. Quite the contrary.

It was after this event that the women revolted and bolted. They had heard from some of the crew about the marines on the other side of the island. So the "sisters," all twelve of the remaining contestants, joined together, commandeered the power boat, and drove to the other side of the island, where they made their amphibious assault. The rest is history.

What no military power on earth could do (the Iraq and Iran defeats notwithstanding), these women did in less than an hour. In less than one hour they held these sweating, woman-starved fighting machines under their complete domination. And in this fusion of shows, *Booty Camp* was born.

With camera crews on the other side of the island, two days away by foot, and the marines with "third eye" cameras in place and still rolling, the nervous producers had to sit back in their offices, out of communication with the island. But in those two days a TV miracle happened. The contestants spontaneously invented their own reality show, motivated by pure play and carnal desire.

Booty Camp: who could have imagined an island of marines dominated by women gone full Amazon? These women were whipped into a frenzy the marines could not resist, and they soon found themselves tied up in Bacchic bondage rites. It was no longer clear what constituted a "winner" or "loser," for spontaneous ritual had replaced calculating competition.

The women made up the game Semper Fido, in which each marine, stripped to jock strap and tied on a leash held by a woman, had to race against the others on all fours while obeying the commands of the woman as a "good dog." And this was after they had to carry the women on their backs a half kilometer to the staging area. Drill Instructor Yaney, the meanest marine before the women arrived, was the women's favorite target:

"You wanna do it, Yaney?" the bikinied sirens all chimed together.

"Do it? I'm dead," D.I. Yaney says resignedly. "I'll do it."

"We can't hear you, Yaney," they cooed back in mock marine talk.

"I'm dead," D.I. Yaney shouts back. "I'll do it."

"You will address us properly," the women shouted in unison.

"Arf, arf, arf!" Yaney barked back, having temporarily forgotten that this was Semper Fido.

"How bad could it be?" Yaney whispered to the marine next to him, looking into the camera, "What choice do I have anyway?"

The "top dog" got to give his bone to the woman that evening. Religious fundamentalists, animal rights groups, and militarists decried this irreverent behavior. Feminists lauded it.

The men in turn made up a rite for the women: they called this game Eager Beaver. Each woman had to spend the day building a floating damn-bed for their evening tryst. But watch out: if your water breaks while you're *in flagrante delecto*, "you're in for a ride down the river without a paddle, Baby," as Dimsdale put it.

This was hyperreality, for two days a synesthesia of pleasures and pains beyond anyone's expectations. It was raunchy. It was pure animal release. It even seemed real to a zombied viewing world already deadened by overstimulation. It was something that could never be scripted.

Yet, as Dimsdale documents, that is exactly what the TV bureaucrats later tried to do, with expected results. Deliberately allowing contestants to make up their own rules only brought in the old competitive greeds, not the spontaneity. But reality TV, following the rules of the megasystem, only tries to simulate spontaneity. The real thing is too dangerous, whereas simulated spontaneity helps keep the adrenalin up, the attention on the advertising, and the viewer on the couch.

Or in the hot tub. Art Dimsdale opened his hot tub experience by recounting this history for the folks in his tub, asking them what they would have done. What a brilliant move! Right at the start, before the first show appeared on the dual TVs, he had taken a TV Rorschach of his Normal companions, accurately sensing their likely desires.

Most said they thought it was too much for TV, but fun to watch anyway. Margarita said she liked Semper Fido, that the men showed good discipline and were in great shape. Debbie said she had originally watched it with her ex-husband, and that when she suggested that they try some of the games in their bedroom, he just rolled over and went to sleep. From that night it took about five months for the divorce to get settled.

Both of the guys, Lonnie Leveetra, a restaurant owner, and Kevin Anders, an African American plumber, felt that what the women did was cruel, and that it got in the way of the more interesting military games the men had been competing in. Dimsdale inferred, correctly, that Lonnie and Kevin were a bit light in the loafers.

The Foleys, weakest link in this daisy chain, both chuckled together and replied, "Arf, arf, arf." Missing link might be a better term for them, they were pathetic.

The last contestant, Tania Gryjz, a tall, dark-haired, voluptuous nurse, said that she watched the original in a hot tub, and that she thought it was "sexy and just so much fun." She didn't see or remember that much, however, because her boyfriend Bobby and her best friend Bobbi and she moved on to their own triple feature in the tub. "I was just a total mass of jelly after that!" she bubbled in her thick Croatian accent.

Dimsdale now knew the object of his game would have to be Tania—as he puts it, "I then sounded myself out my own mental Rorschach, and my response to Tania's words was simply 'Boiiing!'" I thought Margarita was going to be my 'drink of choice,' but you would have to be a complete village idiot not to feel the pure sex in Tania's words, in her voice, in her eyes." If "Boiiing" isn't a call to reality, what is? Thus in the following chapters he takes the reader into that magic matrix between tube and tub, spinning out commentary and fantasies.

His chapter on the short-lived show *X-posure* is a tour-de-force of post-criticism. Reminding us at the outset that the largest organ of the human body—whether male, female, or transgendered—is skin, Dimsdale argues that the show's producers missed a great opportunity in focusing on the virtual nakedness of the contestants—hard body thongs for the women and bulging racing briefs for the men—instead of focusing on the skin itself.

He takes us on a phenomenological tour of skin, of the wonders of touching. Tracing a brief history of skin and competition, Dimsdale reminds us:

Yes, the Assyrians were one of the finest examples of the specific murderous cruelty achieved by civilizational societies. Goethe once commented that, "Nature has neither core nor skin: she's both at once outside and in." Well the Assyrians showed how this could be true for civilization too: Would you rather have your flayed skin hung on the city walls, or have yourself cemented into the interior of the city wall itself, as they did to their enemies. Ah, civic pride!

Or remember that fine example of reality in Kafka's story "In the Penal Colony," when Kafka describes the execution machine: "When the man lies down on the Bed and it begins to vibrate, the Harrow is lowered onto his body. It regulates itself automatically so that the needles barely touch his skin; once contact is made the steel ribbon stiffens immediately into a rigid band. And then the performance begins. . . ." Now Kafka was one sonofabitch who really knew how to make a reality show, only producers today, a hundred years later, still don't have the balls to do it!

This is pure Dimsdale. And could any post-Marxist top this critique of touch in America: "If religion is the opiate of the people, both relieving the suffering and masking it, then pets are the opiate of touch in *tech-nolo mi tangere* America."

But Dimsdale is a postcritic, more playful than critical. He invents new sports that the producers of *X-posure* could have used to highlight the *touching* of skin rather than merely the *viewing* of it. Take his idea of "Scuba-Dooba," for example, which involves couples hooking up down under, having to share only one breathing tank, filmed close-up with slow-motion cameras. This follows a round of "Flipper" ("see him do tricks when excited"), where women judge the men, and "Flotation Devices," where men judge the women. The teams that succeed in "Scuba-Dooba" go on to the next degree of difficulty in a round of "Snorkel-Dorkel."

One of Dimsdale's more interesting points, here and throughout the book, is that the image of hard bodies that dominates these shows needs to be democratized with more diversity. America, after all, has been fattening up for the past few decades, yet all of that obesity tends to be filtered out. As he put it, "Consumption culture must mask production, hiding it just as the Morlocks' underground factories were hidden from the Eloi in H. G. Wells's *The Time Machine*. Similarly, commodity capitalism sells the fat food but must keep its consequences, the fat bodies themselves, invisible, off-screen, or reinvent those bodies as uncaused objects of diet ads."

The responses of the tubmates are particularly interesting here, especially Debbie, who tearfully confessed: "These people they get on these shows are like the damn athletes in my high school. They always made you feel bad for not being perfect. Who's the first to get thrown off the islands? It's usually the big ones."

Still, Debbie was not wildly enthusiastic about Dimsdale's proposal for *Bellybusters*, an updated version of *Big Diet*. Dimsdale suggested a new method for winning, combining how much weight people could gain with how much they could lose. The winner would be rewarded with his or her weight in food, and with the gain/loss ratio in gold. In any case, the winner could conceivably be the same weight at the end of the show as at the beginning. Dimsdale slyly suggested that this would truly be a reality diet show.

One of Dimsdale's most imaginative suggestions was also one of his most manipulative. Remember, he had set a goal of seducing Tania. But he also claims to have had the idea well before meeting her. *Libertas Peninsula* would be a hyperreality show set in Dubrovnik, Croatia, a Slavic-Italian jewel of a walled medieval city, jutting out on cliffs over the clear Adriatic, a beautiful Mediterranean place. Those huge medieval walls, over eight hundred years old, were sturdy enough to ward off the Serb offensive in 1992, when the city came under artillery and amphibious assault. In fact, the city boasted, with *Libertas* as its motto, that it had never been conquered.

Dimsdale pointed out that sex is relatively easy to set up in exotica, but that violence is more difficult on reality competition shows, even though it is regular fare on talk shows ("Witness the Springer show, right down to its final episode!"). So given the fighting that broke out between Croatia and Bosnia in the 1990s, Dimsdale envisioned a show to be called *Siege Mentality* set in the walled-in, warring city: it has the tropical exotica element, with added features of an old city, and the potential chance elements of Serb snipers and artillery as adding extra degrees of difficulty and death.

But, as Dimsdale told the tub, it would also have to be called off before finishing, because,

"People would discover that some of the competitors were being shot not by Serb snipers, but by the residents of Dubrovnik themselves, who were shooting them out of malice ..."

"And out of a sporting sense!" Tania chimed in, "Tourist Season!"

"Tourist Season!" Why yes, that's it!" Dimsdale exclaimed.

At that moment, Dimsdale knew he had her. They had spent two of the eight weeks in the tub, and though the rule was to not have any contact outside the tub (a rule that Lonnie and Kevin broke on the very first night!), Dimsdale knew that his time to transgress had come, and so would he!

After making love like weasels in heat the third time that night, Dimsdale and Tania had the first of their pillow-talk sessions, which Dimsdale uses as interludes throughout the book. Discussing the others, Tania confessed that not only had she sensed immediately that Lonnie and Kevin were closeted gays, but that she had nicknamed them to herself "Tinky" and "Winky." Dimsdale realized that he had more than a sex machine in his hands, that Tania was:

. . . a full woman and muse, all wrapped in one luscious, bedroom-eyed bombshell. "Tele-tubb-ies," I stammered in awe, completely under her spell, realizing that she had given me my private nickname for our whole group, for all of fat-assed America and our whole freaking camera civilization!

Sure, I had done my homework, I knew the history of the teletubbies, the research is now well-established in the media studies canon, but I began to see how turn-of-the-century America had to project its obesity epidemic in "alien" form, importing these creatures from England, as it had earlier imported its own Jimi Hendrix, denying that they were its own hidden "soft-body, telly-belly" reality!

It would not be right to tell you how the remainder of the book goes further and further inside the reality show through the dreams of the Normal people in the tub, for there are some real surprises there. I found myself really caring for these people by the end—except perhaps the chucklehead Farleys—even with Dimsdale's peppering of cynical comments. And I think he found himself at home there as well, at least temporarily, even if he also came off as the main character you love to hate. But most fascinating for me was Dimsdale's proposal in the last chapter, *Isolato Island*, for a show almost reminiscent of Hesse's novel, *The Glass Bead Game*.

Isolato Island's main "hook" is an event called Doors of Perception, taken from William Blake's line in *The Marriage of Heaven and Hell*: "If the doors of perception were cleansed everything would appear to men as it truly is, infinite. For man has closed himself up, till he sees all things thro' narrow chinks of his cavern." Contestants must choose either Door Number 1, the pleasure door, or Door Number 2, the pain door. Both doors, unknown to the contestants, lead into the same room, the Room of Unhappiness. This curious game—I can't see it ever working as a literal proposal, though Dimsdale seems to mean it that way—raises the question of whether life in our globalized twenty-first century is a matter of mind-forg'd manacles or manacle-forg'd minds. Either way seems to be an isolation from happiness.

The only way out of the Room of Unhappiness is through an exit door marked No Exit (perhaps Dimsdale is satirizing Sartre here?), which mysteriously opens as they near it. Contestants enter a new event, a walk-thru exhibit reminiscent of a spook-house and called Inferno, where they must guess the sins of the exhibitionists. Dimsdale describes it thusly:

The last exhibit reveals an apparent theologian–mountain climber wearing a back-pack, relentlessly climbing a stairmaster exercise machine. After a couple of minutes of exertion, the climber stops, removes the backpack, hands it to the contestant, and a circular chink in the wall opens, revealing a slide into darkness thro' which the tired climber exits, as the door quickly shuts. When the contestant looks inside the back-pack, all that is there are heavy tomes, weighty books, those great ennobling books one should read but never has time to.

The contestant slowly realizes over the next minutes, hours, days even, that the only way he or she can get out is by treading the stairmaster, which opens the door into the room, so that the next contestant can relieve the stepper of his or her burden. But the peddler never knows when the next contestant will arrive.

In this last, ultimate reality game, Dante's Ugolino, the guy who ate his children and who occupied the lowest rung in Hell, gets some company: the backpacked, bookpacked critic on the eternal stairmaster, unable to read any of the books. Yes, the critic, lost in eternal damnation, in that zone of unreal-ity somewhere between the metaphor and the literal. There, but for the grace of God and the brilliance of Dimsdale, go I.

As I mentioned, Art Dimsdale is perhaps the preeminent postcritic of our time, as fully articulate and breezy as any of the other celebrities in the Inter-national Theory Cartel. Yet his book has this strange, almost existentialist, almost mystical, downbeat concluding chapter. What are we to make of it? Consider, as another example, this excerpt, which I quote at length:

In this same sense the sophists of today, the Grand Inquisitors of the advertising and television industries, have not replaced word with image, as so many critics suggest, but have replaced image and imagining with the scripted image. They are attempt-ing to "persuade" away the living spark of public life by providing virtual-adrenalized substitutes—"scripted life"—toward an ultimate end of one vast McDonaldized reflex-arc. Their crypto-religious apparatus taps the deep levels of human entrancement, transforming it into mere stimulus—response pleasure—pain reflex-arc, and all that is human melts away as the mere flesh-covering of the machine.

Give me what used to be called the vices of the flesh any day over the virtues of the machine, for the machine is death, pure and simple. When flesh becomes automatic, it becomes death, it becomes machine. Read the signs: the sophist—Grand Inquisitor—Advertising Executive and his/her/its couch potato other half is nothing if not a semio-tician, in utter suicidal alienation from semiosis, reading the road-kill signs of death!"

When wily Willy Blake claimed that the old prophecy, "that the world will be consumed in fire at the end of six thousand years is true, as I have heard from Hell," he wasn't being some schizo. No, he envisioned what finally incarnates now, in our time. We are become that machine that is death, and it should not take but another 10, maybe 15, years of building this globally, electronically, virally, economically, and spiritually interconnected house of cards before it collapses—utterly and totally collapses—whoosh—all gone, and we with it.

Understand that I am not simply looking down my nose at Mega-Reflex-Arc-America, for no man is an island, isolate from the all-surrounding societal significations. But I do not want to leave out the gestural aspect of the sign, and so I will thumb my nose at it, I will flip it off: Friends, contemporary Mega-Reflex-Arc-America is a world-consuming bloated pig in a Brooks Brothers suit, anaesthetizing its loss of humanity by push-buttoning its own automatic flush down the toilet. No way I will let it tread on me and my American vision! Give me *Libertas Dubrovnik* or give me death! I would rather live hard the entrancing carnival games of life, than to be zombified into "remote."

Now is it me, or is Dimsdale suggesting that there are some sort of universal human "essences"? How could someone who understands so well how reality is socially constructed say this? Isn't this jeremiad theorizing, especially in relation to TV, not only passé, but pre-post-critical?

Or is this Dimsdale's ultimate trump card, a subtle, ironic commentary that appears on the surface to link him empathically to the common continent of humanity, while in reality he remains an island of post-Cartesian ego unto himself? Isn't he, in short, gazing into his own reflection in that hall of mirrors out of which "reality" is endlessly constructed while convincing us that we are seeing the real man objectively describing the real thing?

However it may be, this is a book well worth reading and viewing. I found myself going back to the animated photo sections repeatedly. Call me old fashioned, but I love to hold a book. But I also love the opportunity to see the scenes and people move and talk in the ani-photo sections as well. For all that I know Dimsdale's tub may be just a verbal sleight-of-hand, the ani-photos as real as that portrait of Captain Lemuel Gulliver that stands as frontispiece to his renowned *Travels*.

One thing is certain, however. Art Dimsdale himself is the real deal, a man who knows that being there here is what it's really all about.

14

HIS ONE LEG

Blow, winds, and crack your cheeks! rage! blow!
You cataracts and hurricanoes, spout
Till you have drench'd our steeples, drown'd the cocks!
—*KING LEAR*, ACT III, SCENE 2

Perhaps it was the Haitian voodoo painting I purchased in the spring of 2001. Haitian voodoo surrealism by Ezene Domond, with a couple in an interior on the left, a nude woman in the center foreground, emerging from a watery cloudlike bath-couch, half floating as her right leg merges into the waters overflowing toward the couple, toward the other woman's flowing gown, her eye fixed on this other woman, emanating dark energies through a visible aura: casting the evil eye, the hoodoo-voodoo. Toward the back, sexual enigmas are transposed in the frolic of humans and a horse, themselves emanations of the watery surrounds.

The painting was cheap, unframed, slightly damaged. I took it to get framed and cleaned, and did not pick it up until a few months later, after some encounters with the wind god. It was then that I began to notice Huracán, as the Carib people called him, visible in the painting. Huracán, from which the term "hurricane" derives, literally means "his one leg," and was used traditionally throughout the Caribbean, often connected with destruction. I don't know, maybe the idea is someone pivoting in a circle on one leg. Huracán has been linked through the Mayan god Kukulan with Quetzalcoatl, the Mexican plumed serpent god of the winds, a creator god, the "giver of breath." The background of the painting is his aquamarine watery wind world, imaging itself. A white cloud figure, perhaps a personification of Huracán, seems to be cracking his cheeks, blowing the cloud waves morphing into the horse play of the sexual puzzle: a naked female with her hands "milking" a horse whose hindquarter we see, while a second figure, amorphous, nuzzles her. A white horse, next to the couple in the foreground but in the frame of the water figures, directly beneath the cloud figure and facing the same direction, looks over at them, smiling at their game.

The naked woman in the foreground casting the gaze has her right hand on a bell-rope, a rope that merges into the amorphous watery figure. Could her right leg, already out of the tub and blending to water, be the connection to Huracán, to "his one leg?" Domond also did a painting in 1976 titled *Voodoo Ritual*, with a woman similarly seated centrally on a couch. The intensity of the naked woman's gaze in the painting I have seems connected to cyclonic powers, channeling the watery wonder-world energies to some desire in this world. For whom does the bell toll? For the other woman as her competitor? As her lover? As herself?

Yes, I have had some encounters with Huracán in my life, in various avatars. When I was four years old, my family was declared missing on the radio from our oceanfront apartment in Deal, New Jersey, just north of Asbury Park, after a huge one, Hurricane Hazel, ripped into the Jersey Shore on October 15. Hazel utterly devastated Haiti with 150-mile-per-hour winds, killed over a thousand people, and made it all the way to Toronto, where eighty-one more people perished. Inland Toronto, in Canada! As Vladimir Nabokov put it in Pale Fire: "It was a year of tempests, Hurricane / Lolita swept from Florida to Maine." This was not your average hurricane. Fortunately we had moved to the next town inland two weeks earlier, Neptune, and so we were not washed away with the departed.

We moved to Neptune, and avoided Huracán. Isn't Neptune the Roman name for the Greek Poseidon, the Mediterranean avatar of Huracán? Well, actually not. The Greek god of weather was Poseidon's brother, Zeus, though Poseidon kicked up his own storms from time to time. And so, from an early age my life was involved with the watery-wind worlds of Huracán/Neptune/Poseidon/Zeus, or whatever that energy be called.

The house in Neptune I lived in as a young child was kamikazied a few decades later by a man who stole a plane from a nearby airport and targeted his ex-girlfriend who lived there. Another *air* assault perhaps, a personal-

Figure 25. Oil painting by Ezene Domond, no date. This figure also appears in the color gallery as plate 5.

ized blitzkrieg from the god out of the machine, impersonated by a man in a mind-storm. Like an airborne techno-sperm aspiring to merge with the egg of its urges, plummeting in glorious fiery ritual suicide. Summon Air and Fire to the Earth, and douse with Water the charred remains: four elements, but what of the quintessence? And of course, as fate would have it, his intended and her family were not at home. No one was at home to join him flaming, including himself. Talk about autopilot! An event like this happened in fiction, I only discovered later, in the novel *The World According to Garp*. But my story actually happened in life. Happened in my life. I remember leaning back on a swing in those Neptune days of my nascent consciousness, looking up at the single-engine piper cubs flying overhead, listening to the advancing and receding motor, wondering what it was like to be in the clouds. I was not aware then that there were atomic bombs stockpiled at the Earle Ammunition Depot just about three miles away from my home, and only about one mile or so from the Shore Drive-In where my family would view Japanese movie monsters released by radiation.

I visited that early childhood neighborhood decades later, the day after I returned from tracker Tom Brown Jr.'s survival school standard class, and was stunned to see that the woods behind it where I played as a young child remained intact, despite the massive development of the Jersey Shore. The woods had been turned into a state park. As I walked in woods with sphagnum moss, I realized I had been living on the edge of the Pine Barrens from the age of four to six, at the same time as Tom Brown, who lived not that far away in Toms River. He prayed for a teacher and at the age of seven found one, an Apache master tracker and shaman. His teacher Stalking Wolf was a master of the ages, a wanderer of North and South America, who taught him the subtle ways to be a child of the earth, ways of sophisticated awareness attuned to the marvels of nature.

As this amazing story was unfolding just some fifteen miles away from me—of all places in the Pine Barrens of New Jersey—I moved within a year with my family to Bayonne, where I would play in the muck of the bay with all the flotsam and jetsam: the little killy fish, the toxic chemical bags that floated in from the factories. There was no master around to reveal the heart of life for me then, like lucky Tom Brown had found. My path of life has been roundabout, sometimes wandering, sometimes lost, sometimes idiosyncratic, but I would never trade it for another's. I have learned to find masters in my own way, wherever I can find them and learn from them.

I encountered Huracán directly in Puerto Rico in the summer of 2001. I learned of Huracán the day before from A, walking with her through the rainforest east of San Juan, listening to the tree frogs call "coqui." We were to have spent a couple of days that late August 2001, on the island of Culebra, just off Puerto Rico's east coast, where a Tropical Depression, named Dean, originated on the very day we were to have arrived there. The god Huracán spoke to us directly, even as we threaded our way through the fate entanglements—not going to Culebra in the east, but going to the north coast and to the west.

We went to the beach, and I went for the big waves, body surfing until a rainstorm began. I had bought a disposable underwater camera and took photos while in the big surf, which grew increasingly bigger and darker as the clouds thickened and the breezes blew stronger. I was in heaven, back in the sea, body surfing well over an hour in what was noticeably turning into storm surf. The skies were darkening and the sea with them. It began raining hard. In the very last photo I took of a big wave about to crash on me I would notice after developing the film months later a full round face with open, ample lips blowing my way, uncannily similar to the figure I found in my Haitian painting on my return from this trip (see figure 26).

When the storm finally released its rains we ran up from beach to car, then to restaurant-bar, enjoying the fierce weather with some locals and loud salsa. About forty minutes later, sun now returned, a woman burst into the restaurant all upset; vandals had broken the window of her auto and of the car next to hers.

I noticed that there were only two cars parked in the lot. I did the math.

Figure 26. Tropical storm wave about to crash on me, with face of Huracán right of center?

Surfers (I tracked their footprints to their towels) had smashed the window of our rental car, looking for something of value. In my rush in the rain, I had stupidly left my shorts and a plastic bag on the back seat floor, in view. Bait, you might say. At least that's what I would call it, from my Jersey Shore youth, where what appears as possibly valued is meant to be taken as valuable—emphasis on taken, if you know what I mean. Normally I cover my things with auto debris—old blankets, trash, and the like. The merest nothing is usually enough to ward off the impulsive thief. The surfer kids got only a half-used disposable camera. At any rate, we realized we must get back to San Juan, where we had rented the car, and return and exchange it.

The sky began churning gray-black threatening clouds around us, raining off and on, ever increasing in intensity, full gray-blackness descending. As we drove I could see lightning over the ocean, and I asked A whether Puerto Rico got lightning. She told me, "not until hurricane season." But we were in it, a thunderstorm cauldron. And this was hurricane season.

As we neared the airport the clouds burst wide open. We returned the car and exchanged it for another, and then wound back fifteen minutes more through howling rain-soaked sheets of wind to A's mother's place, surviving this reality show of "tropical depression." The outer storm receded. And the inner storm between A and me ended the next day, but only when I returned the auto to the airport, unable to find my way back to A, who had, at least as far as I could see, removed herself completely and utterly from me. She may have had good reasons, for I had broken with her seven years earlier, broken with her as the first woman I loved after a long-term marriage went belly-up. I was fledgling, still unsure of myself, unwilling to lock in. It was right woman wrong time. And now she was armored against relationships, as she told me. I should have followed the never look back rule.

Huracán spoke to me again only a few days later, when I went to pick up my daughter at O'Hare airport in Chicago. While riding there, I heard a slight click on the front window, as though a pebble might have hit it. When my daughter got in the car, she noticed an eight-inch crack on the right side.

I had never cracked or had a broken car window before in my life, except for the broken window a few days earlier. I wondered whether this was another omen of an approaching storm, while also realizing that it could just be "magical thinking" on my part. But sure enough, Huracán found us on the way back home. As we drove toward the skyway bridge from the Windy City into Indiana, the soft rain dramatically increased to downpour and the wind-howl began in earnest. By the time we were at the top of the bridge all hell cut loose, we and other autos blown suddenly en masse one lane to the left, and I found myself in the same sheets of blowing wind-rain that I had driven through on the way back from the San Juan airport just a couple of days earlier. After arriving back home, I discovered that four tornados had been launched nearby by that very storm.

Then about two months later, my place of meditation in the woods near where I live was hit by an F-3 tornado. Ten tornados touched down around 3:55 p.m. on October 24, 2001, a most unusual time for midwestern tornados (but not for hurricanes). The largest, the F-3, hit dead-on center my "sit-spot," the place where I went to meditate in the external world and in my mind. It blew across the river, straight into the bluff, slamming down large trees in a path about fifty yards wide. It tore down hundreds of trees past my site, a vast pick-up-sticks park, and it continued its damage in neighborhoods beyond for another thirty miles. Nowadays the ground growth makes it difficult to take in the field of flattened trees. But the canopy above is gone. I still feel the power of Huracán when I go there.

This season of windstorm proved to be an intense time, including a vision one night while in meditation of a burned-out corpse, and then an energized jolt awakening me at dawn, feeling something not right, and sickening unease from the vision the night before. The last time I had stayed up late and was urged to wake up early like that was the night of my vision of the hunter-gatherer's world's fair.

This time I found myself trying to envision another ex-lover who was with a group traveling out West. The last time she traveled there it was with me two years earlier when we were together, to attend to her son and identify his girlfriend's body. He was in intensive care. Her eighteen-year-old son crashed his car in southern Utah and his girlfriend was killed instantly. We had to fly to Las Vegas on a nightmare ride filled with hard partying gamblers and lovers.

A few days before that crash I saw what I thought was a beaver on the road in Pennsylvania, while driving home from visiting my dying father. It haunted me: why would a beaver be on the side of the road? Weeks later I realized that it was more likely a groundhog, a critter that seems given to roadside foraging. Yet in those few days I could not get beaver out of my mind. But I now found myself on a surreal death journey, driving into the desert night from Las Vegas. Around midnight we passed through Saint George, Utah, one of the most heavily contaminated towns in the world, from American nuclear bomb blasts, which I had written about just a few months earlier (in the essay that is now chapter 2 of this book). And my destination: the hospital where her son lay in serious condition, located in a little town called Beaver, Utah.

The night before that auto accident I had a dream of a lawn of owls walking toward me, after reading about the owl as a symbol of death. My ex-lover had a collection of owl statues throughout her house, and so I came to think of it afterward as having pointed toward upcoming death connected to her house. I also allowed the possibility, as usual, that it was simply chance. We may be such stuff as dreams are made of, but it is gossamer stuff, not always easy to untangle in the light of waking consciousness, where we can simply ignore or repress it, or, from the other direction, overinterpret it. A dream may be a mere dream, but sometimes it may be an epiphany.

In any case, two years after that journey to Utah, in my season of windstorm, I happened to read late at night an appendix in one of Tom Brown's nature guidebooks that described owls. Then I went on to read about owls in the body of the book itself, thinking of owls as harbingers of death. Then I went into deep meditation—sacred silence—before going to sleep. I tried to envision my ex-lover, wondering why she would return to that place of death, driving from Las Vegas through Utah and surrounding states. I could not envision her, but only a body with the back hollowed out, revealing the blood-red innards. I thought I might be coming down with a cold or something, because sometimes, disturbing images have appeared as I was getting sick.

Next morning I was urged to wake up early in dawn's light, tight and anxious, and again wondered whether I was getting sick, as that has also been a symptom for me—little sleep but waking up early, unable to sleep. Then again, that inner wake-up call has also been a harbinger on other occasions. Something was urging me awake, and it was not a cold. This occurred Tuesday morning, September 11, 2001, a couple of hours before the explosive catastrophe began.

Of course, hindsight is 20-20 you might say. Perhaps it was all chance, but I wonder whether the death-owl was signaling me the night before, in the way omens do, to Tom Brown himself this time, to his house where death would occur that day. Tom Brown's brother-in-law was pilot of the second plane to crash into the World Trade Center. The wind god appeared again in horrific guise, spewing fire and death, not that of the solo madman who had crashed into my former house at 300 Elm Drive, Neptune, in the 1980s, but through madmen turned suicidal murderous autopilots, mass murderers striking the prime symbol of axis mundi, the economic pivot of the world, hurtling toward Hades.

Enter the Socratic Beat

The following summer, during July 2002, I found myself in Athens, Greece, temporarily between ferry boats, en route to Atlantis. I was headed for Santorini Island, the likely source of the myth of Atlantis, whose volcano had erupted circa 1600 BCE with the greatest explosive force in all of human history, destroying Minoan civilization.

The previous week I had performed on harmonica with a jazz trio and belly dancer at the Troubador Hard Jazz Caffee in Dubrovnik (http://www.nd.edu/~ehalton/Eurotour022.html). From Dubrovnik I had ferried to Bari, Italy, and from Bari to Patros, Greece, meeting on board an Italian philosopher who was on her way to her Greek philosopher husband in Athens. She offered to give me a ride to Athens, as a fellow philosopher, and I would be lying if I said that I did not desire to sin against Athenian philosophy, so to speak, with her. But that is another story of itself, however, one not to be told here. Here I say that when the boat docked in Patros, on the Adriatic opposite Italy, we met in the auto area and drove off in her car, crossing Greece to Athens.

We journeyed through a highway littered with two separate fatal accidents, and at the second, she turned off the road at the sight of a still-smoldering body ahead, hanging from a burned-out auto that had hit a transport truck head on.

We drove along the coastal road for an hour, stopped for gas, and discovered that the auto was overheated and needed immediate repairs. But it was Mediterranean lunchtime—two p.m.—and the mechanic would not be back until six. So we sipped ouzo at a nearby café, and she told me that I must visit Socrates' prison cell, where he had been held before being put to death. We eventually made it to Athens.

For the next two days I did time at Socrates' prison, spending hours there, beneath the Acropolis. The location of the prison was part of Socrates' punishment: that he would be forced to gaze upon the holy Acropolis, his public life quashed, his corporeal life to be drowned by hemlock. Socrates' execution was delayed because of the sacred holidays commemorating the journey of Theseus to Crete and his defeat of the Minotaur and King Minos. Each year

Figure 27. Me viewing you viewing the view from Socrates' Prison, with the Parthenon in the distance to the left.

a ship was sent to Delos as part of the ceremony, and no one could be executed until it returned to port. The ship was also delayed that year by contrary winds, which gave Socrates extra time for contemplation and visits from his friends and students, including Plato.

For all of the magnificent glory of the Acropolis, arched above Athens, I found myself drawn more to Socrates' lowly prison, cut into a cliff across from the base of the Acropolis. It was hardly noticeable, as though Athenians still felt guilty about putting their great wise sage to death.

As I looked at the Acropolis from his prison entrance, an idea overwhelmed me, one that I have not been able to confirm or reject to this day: the worst aspect of Socrates' punishment, though unmentioned in Plato, might be that he literally helped to build the Parthenon and some of the other great works on the Acropolis, works built during the height of his powers as a stonecutter!

Socrates, like Jesus, was a stonecutter, a *Tekton*. Both breathed evanescent words, a tiny portion of which their followers immortalized in writing, giving us slight glimpses of them. Yet they hammered immortal stones still intact today, if only we knew where. As I gazed from Socrates' prison, I knew where some are today: in the Parthenon itself, his focal point while awaiting his poison, encased in a stone-cut prison. I realized Socrates must have worked on it and other buildings in the course of his long life, during which the Parthenon was built.

Socrates, who drank all others under the table in Plato's *Symposium*, forced to drink death in a prison of stone, viewing his anonymous stone handiwork. Now there's a punishment about as sick as nailing a carpenter to some wood!

Plato has Socrates say near the end of the *Phaedrus* that the true way of writing is found ". . . only in principles of justice and goodness and nobility taught and communicated orally for the sake of instruction and graven in the soul, which is the true way of writing." Consider "graven in the soul": Perhaps it was the stonecutter in him speaking, engraving the words in his own heart and in the souls of others in the living act of speech. A hammerhead!

I scribbled these notes there on the spot:

Socrates the *tekton*, the stonecutter, imprisoned finally in stone, doomed to view the Acropolis while awaiting his end. There stood in his vision and in ours today the Parthenon, temple of Athena, in all its glory, and the other great works from Socrates' own lifetime and well before.

The sacred Acropolis, what went on in Socrates as he gazed upon it?

What did he think of the Parthenon, for which Pericles emptied the treasury to build?

Did Socrates, himself a stonecutter, help build the Parthenon? Are his stones still there, standing immortal? Or scattered amid the ruins?

The man who would not write inscribed by his wordless deeds in the enduring stones?

And his prison. After a lifetime of working stones, only to be locked in a living tomb carved from the rock.

Did Socrates, unknown to his devoted students, do stonework on his prison itself, carving, say, the indentations in the floor of the left entry?

When I returned home I searched for references to Socrates' life as a stonecutter, but found nothing. Finally, a year ago, I came across Diogenes Laertius's account of the life of Socrates, where he relates: "But Duris says that he was a slave, and employed in carving stones. And some say that the Graces in the Acropolis are his work; and they are clothed figures. And that it is in reference to this that Timon says, in his Silli:

From them proceeded the stone polisher,
The reasoning legislator, the enchanter
Of all the Greeks, making them subtle arguers,
A cunning pedant, a shrewd Attic quibbler."[1]

Socrates the wise wordy philosopher may also have been a master sculptor, hammering stones, hammering the very Graces themselves, if we only knew more. But I felt his presence on the sacred hill as I gazed toward the Parthenon from his prison portal.

I returned to my hotel late in the afternoon of the second day of meditation in front of Socrates' prison, after contemplating and finishing a "new" and previously unpublished translation of Plato's *Symposium* by Percy Bysshe Shelley that my colleague David O'Connor had edited. I climbed seven stories in Athenian midsummer heat—the hotel had flooded from a fierce storm that had struck a day or two before my arrival and elevators and electricity were not yet working. It didn't matter; I loved it, springing two steps at a time. It was nothing compared to the walk up to the Acropolis, and besides, I was overflowing with Mediterranean energies, a wanderer who had just performed a week of music in Dubrovnik with a jazz trio and belly dancer, who had promenaded the city walls of Bari, Italy, two nights around midnight, who had driven through Greek highway death conversing on life, love, and wisdom, a wanderer on his way to Atlantis.

I had wandered most of that day in philosophic contemplation at the prison tomb of Socrates, considering life and death; the glorious sacred Acropolis and the powers-that-be who built it with the sweat of Socrates; Socrates who spoke truth to their lies, who honored the gods of the city and gave learning and wisdom to the youth, for which the powers-that-be, in their pomp and pathetic cowardice and Athenian justice, killed him. The truth does that to people.

I reached my room, jumped into a cold shower, toweled dry, and lay down. I descended into a deep meditative state, slowed breathing and heartbeat, and allowed myself to enter the hypnogogic envisioning world in the dreamtime between musement and contemplation. After some time a music came to me, a music with a Macedonian beat. Here it is, try counting it out:

1-2-3, 1-2, 1-2, 1-2-3.
1-2-3, 1-2, 1-2, 1-2-3 . . . repeats

Then a song was given to me in my vision by Socrates, who in this world spoke from the source of rhythm, not from critical reason. In my vision Socrates told me that though he had danced and sung in life, drinking life to the dregs, he had reasoned too much and rhythmed too little.

And then these words came to me in the song: *Kalos kane kairos.*

It was like a Ouiji board forming words. Yet were they not from my own brain? But they came from this place of music, not from me. I do not speak Greek.

As the words shaped themselves into the beat of the song, repeating in deepening groove, I recognized the first as a term for beauty. That much I knew. But I did not know what the second two words meant. A week later, on the volcanic island of Santorini, a taxi driver told me that *kane* (kon-nay?) was a word for a breeze or wind, but I don't know for sure.

I wasn't sure whether the third word was even Greek or whether it might mean the Egyptian city of Cairo. I later found somewhat similar words, *ker* and *keros*, which mean heart and wax, and which Socrates uses to discuss the soul in Plato's *Theaetetus*, drawing from a parable of Homer. But I finally got around to looking up *kairos* more than a year later and was delightfully surprised. Although I had not known what the term meant, *kairos* connects to some of my ongoing writing projects, and literally means "right season," or opportune moment, the moment when one draws bow and releases arrow, the living moment. I realized that it was a term that could meld my reasoning and rhythming worlds. And I realized something real had happened between Socrates and me, however it be defined, and that I was graced.

I was not conscious of it at the time, and was amazed to find out, more than a year later, that Socrates had come around in his last days to making mousiké, "music," in the Greek sense that included poetry, music, and dance. What he told me in my vision was what he had grasped in his last days, something that his own dream visions had told him earlier, that he should make mousiké, but which he reasoned to be philosophy. He had reasoned too much and rhythmed too little, as he put it to me, or as he says in Plato's *Phaedo*:

In the course of my life I have often had intimations in dreams "that I should make music (mousiké)." The same dream came to me sometimes in one form, and sometimes in another, but always saying the same or nearly the same words: Make and cultivate music, said the dream. And hitherto I had imagined that this was only intended to exhort and encourage me in the study of philosophy, which has always been the pursuit of my life, and is the noblest and best of music. The dream was bidding me to do what I was already doing, in the same way that the competitor in a race is bidden by the spectators to run when he is already running. But I was not certain of this, as the dream might have meant music in the popular sense of the word, and being under sentence of death, and the festival giving me a respite, I thought that I should be safer if I satisfied the scruple, and, in obedience to the dream, composed a few verses before I departed. And first I made a hymn [humnos] in honor of the god of the festival, and then considering that a poet, if he is really to be a poet or maker, should not only put words together but make stories, and as I have no invention, I took some fables of Aesop, which I had ready at hand and knew, and turned them into verse.

294

I had read Plato's *Phaedo*, his account of the last days of Socrates, before my visit to Athens, so it is possible my subconscious was primed with more information than I was aware of. But I had never thought of those last days as Socrates' own breakthrough in his philosophy, from his muse who only spoke to him in the negative, as he put it, his muse of the emergent critical reason bodying into being in the world, to mousiké per se, affirmative musicking.

Socrates the city philosopher who claimed to learn from men and not nature, needed to rhythm words to Aesop's animal-filled tales. But this was also something that revelers at a house party (my translation of the Greek term *symposium*) would do, reciting from memory the unwritten stories. In this sense this was Socrates' last symposium, his joyous departure. Would that he could have recited some of these verses to Plato. And yet there were those Greek words, given to me in rhythm in my song of Socrates.

Kalos kane kairos: Breeze of Beauty blowing at the right moment, or Beauty breezes in the right moment. The other side of Huracán. The song haunts me every time I feel the right moment breeze, when the here and now and the wonder of eternity coalesce as palpable epiphany and all things are enlivened.

It haunts me now, and so, in the spirit of Socrates at the end of the *Phaedrus*, when he offers a prayer to Pan and other gods of the place he is in, to find wealth in wisdom and beauty "in the inward soul," let me offer a thanks to epiphanies, American and otherwise.

Let us celebrate Tashtego, the Native American of Nantucket! Let us celebrate Dagoo of African Madagascar, let us celebrate Queequeg of Polynesia, let us celebrate these harpooning aristocrats of the American vessel, and cabin boy Pip too, and Melville and Moby-Dick too, who remind us that in this precious game of life, we floating islanders perning the world-gyre like crazy gone prayer wheels in pursuit of the Great Whale of Life share both a common continent of humanity and aristocracy of the soul. Let us celebrate the aristocracy of our ancestors and our descendants, of our fellow creatures, noble and wild, of the whirling globe of life that envelopes us and from which we bodied forth. Let us submit to the aristocracy of the others, and to their presence in us, and to our own inward aristocracy. And let us revel in the rapturous epiphanies that pour forth sporadically, suggestively presenting to our awareness more than we can know. The unepiphanied life, to twist Socrates, is not worth living.

How do epiphanies happen? Is it serendipity? Mere chance? Preconscious knowledge surfaced? The Poetic Imagination? The breath of Zeus or

Huracán? The fantastic reality of *Kairos*? Somehow it seems a little of each to me, a kind of dreaming into being in the cosmic fantasia of life.

But that is another story. This story ends with a Hurricane Haiku:

> Cyclonic winds spin
> Our fates beholden to them
> and all air we breathe.

NOTES

CHAPTER ONE

1 2001 National Household Travel Survey. Washington, DC: U.S. Department of Transportation. Available at http://www.bts.gov/publications/highlights_of_the_2001_national_household_travel_survey/.

2 Brad Edmondson, "In the Driver's Seat," *American Demographics* (March 1998).

3 Quoted in "At Colleges, Women Are Leaving Men in the Dust," by Tamar Lewin, *New York Times*, July 9, 2006.

4 *Executive Excess 2006*, the 13th Annual CEO Compensation Survey from the Institute for Policy Studies and United for a Fair Economy. Cited in G. William Domhoff, "Power in America: Wealth, Income, and Power," available at http://sociology.ucsc.edu/whorulesamerica/power/wealth.html.

5 Christopher Lasch, *The Revolt of the Elites and The Betrayal of Democracy* (New York: W. W. Norton, 1995), 41.

6 See Roper Center survey of "The Good Life," published in *American Enterprise* (May–June 1993). Also discussed in Juliet B. Schor, *The Overspent American* (New York: Basic Books, 1998).

7 Michael Pollan, *The Omnivore's Dilemma: A Natural History of Four Meals* (New York: Penguin, 2006), 23.

8 Pollan, *Omnivore's Dilemma*, 41.

9 Eric Schlosser, *Fast Food Nation* (New York: HarperCollins, 2002), 3.

10 Lasch, *Revolt of the Elites*, 6.

11 Eugene Halton, "Eden Inverted: On the Wild Self and the Contraction of Consciousness," *The Trumpeter* 23, no. 3 (2007), at http://trumpeter.athabascau.ca/index.php/trumpet/article/view/995/1387, and Halton, "Peircean Animism and the End of Civilization," *Contemporary Pragmatism* 2, no. 1 (2005): 135–66.

12 Lewis Mumford, *The Pentagon of Power*, vol. 2, *The Myth of the Machine* (New York: Harcourt, Brace, Jovanovich, 1970), 272.

13 Mumford, *Pentagon of Power*, 284.

14 Ibid., 272.

15 Victoria Rideout, Elizabeth Hamel, and the Kaiser Family Foundation, "The Media Family: Electronic Media in the Lives of Infants, Toddlers, Preschoolers and Their Parents," Kaiser Family Foundation Report #7500, May 2006 (Menlo Park, CA: The Henry J. Kaiser Foundation), available at http://www.kff.org/entmedia/upload/7500.pdf.

16 Lynette Clemetson, "Babies and TVs Making More Sense to Parents," *New York Times*, May 24, 2006.

17 Walter Gantz, Nancy Schwartz, James R. Angelini, and Victoria Rideout, *Food for Thought: Television Food Advertising to Children in the United States*, Kaiser Family Foundation Report #7618, March 2007 (Menlo Park, CA: The Henry J. Kaiser Foundation), available at http://www.kff.org/entmedia/upload/7618.pdf.

18 Pollan, *Omnivore's Dilemma*, 104, 108.

19 Juliet B. Schor, *Born to Buy: The Commercialized Child and the New Consumer Culture* (New York: Scribner, 2004). Schor illuminates the ways consumption-oriented practices are not simply a result of "at risk" or disturbed children, but also productive of them. She also criticizes marketing research that utilizes rigid developmental models of childhood as mistaking cultural practices for natural endowments. I don't disagree with that specific criticism, but she seems to think that childhood is simply a social construction, citing histories of the past few hundred years and changing views of the child while ignoring developmental or anthropological literature on children. She thereby neglects, in my view, the ways that biosocial developmental needs, such as mother-infant bonding and separation, or puberty, provide psychological vulnerabilities that are exploited by marketers.

20 Schor, *Overspent American*, 70; Schor, *Born to Buy*, 148–49.

21 Vaclav Havel, "The End of the Modern Era," *New York Times*, March 1, 1992.

22 Muller cited in Linda Holler, *Erotic Morality: The Role of Touch in Moral Agency* (New Brunswick, NJ: Rutgers University Press, 2002). Elvin Stackman, president, American Association for the Advancement of Science, address to the association, cited in *Life*, January 9, 1950.

23 Glenn T. Seaborg and William R. Coorliss, *Man and the Atom: Building a New World through Nuclear Technology* (New York: Dutton, 1971), 188.

24 Christopher Mason, *Undressed: The Life and Times of Gianni Versace* (New York: Little, Brown, 1999). The book has not yet been released at the time of this writing.

25 Quoted in Andres Viglucci, "Last Piece of the Puzzle Is Gone with a Gunshot," *Miami Herald*, July 25, 1997.

26 James Gorman, "Flight Test on Butterflies Disclose Free Spirits," *New York Times*, December 12, 2002.

27 Stanislaw Lem, "The Upside-Down Evolution," in *One Human Minute*, trans. Catherine Leach (New York: Harcourt, Brace, Jovanovich, 1986), 60–62. "Weapon Systems of the

Twenty-First Century; or, the Upside-Down Evolution" was published originally in Polish in 1984.

CHAPTER TWO

1 See Lizabeth Cohen, *A Consumers' Republic: The Politics of Mass Consumption in Postwar America* (New York: Knopf, 2003).

2 Ralph Waldo Emerson, *Essays and Journals*, ed. Lewis Mumford (Atlanta: Communication and Studies, 1968), 32.

3 Richard L. Miller, *Under the Cloud: The Decades of Nuclear Testing* (New York: Free Press, 1986), 262–63, 266.

4 Keith Schneider, "Uranium Miners Inherit Dispute's Sad Legacy," *New York Times*, January 9, 1990.

5 Stephen I. Schwartz, ed., *Atomic Audit: The Costs and Consequences of U.S. Nuclear Weapons since 1940* (Washington, DC: Brookings Institution Press, 1998).

6 William H. Whyte, *Organization Man* (New York: Doubleday, 1956), 14.

7 Paul Boyer, *Fallout: A Historian Reflects on America's Half-Century Encounter with Nuclear Weapons* (Columbus: Ohio State University Press, 1998), 90.

8 Boyer, *Fallout*, 93. See also Daniel T. O'Neill, *The Firecracker Boys* (New York: St. Martin's Press, 1994).

9 John. G. Fuller, *The Day We Bombed Utah* (New York: Dutton, 1984).

10 Paul Boyer, *By the Bomb's Early Light: American Thought and Culture at the Dawn of the Atomic Age* (Westminster, MD: Alfred Knopf, 1987).

11 Schwartz, *Atomic Audit*.

12 Daniel Belgrad, *The Culture of Spontaneity: Improvisation and the Arts in Postwar America* (Chicago: University of Chicago Press, 1998).

13 Jack Kerouac, *On the Road* (New York: Signet, 1957), 253–54.

CHAPTER FOUR

1 Colin Turnbull, *The Forest People* (1961; repr., New York: Touchstone, 1987), 17.

2 Turnbull, *Forest People*, 14.

3 Phillips Verner Bradford and Harvey Blume, *Ota Benga: The Pygmy in the Zoo* (New York: St. Martin's Press, 1992). My discussion of Ota Benga draws from this work.

4 Bradford and Blume, *Ota Benga*, 242, 244.

5 Tom Brown Jr., *Case Files of the Tracker* (New York: Berkley Books, 2003).

6 Bradford and Blume, *Ota Benga*, 28.

7 Marianne Weber, *Max Weber: A Biography* (New Brunswick, NJ: Transaction Books, 1988), 290.

8 Henry Adams, *The Education of Henry Adams*, ed. Ernest Samuels (1907; repr., Boston: Houghton Mifflin, 1973), 466–67.

9 Adams, *Education of Henry Adams*, 496–97.

10 Ibid., 498.

11 Henry Adams, letter to Henry Osborn Taylor, Washington, DC, January 17, 1905, in *Henry Adams and His Friends: A collection of Unpublished Letters*, ed. Harold Dean Carter (Boston: Houghton Mifflin, 1947), 558–59.

12 Robert Hume, *Runaway Star: An Appreciation of Henry Adams* (Ithaca, NY: Cornell University Press, 1951).
13 Paul Shepard, *Coming Home to the Pleistocene*, ed. Florence R. Shepard (Washington DC: Island Press/Shearwater Books, 1998), 77.
14 Paul Shepard, *The Others: How Animals Made Us Human* (Washington, DC: Island Press/Shearwater Books, 1996), 317.
15 Bradford and Blume, *Ota Benga*, 206.
16 Ibid., 207.
17 Ibid.
18 Turnbull, *Forest People*, 38.

CHAPTER FIVE

1 Henry Adams, *The Education of Henry Adams*, ed. Ernest Samuels (1907; repr., Boston: Houghton Mifflin, 1973), 343.
2 Lewis Mumford, *The Golden Day* (New York: Boni and Liveright, 1926); Perry Duis, *Chicago: Creating New Traditions* (Chicago: Chicago Historical Society, 1976).
3 Farrell later remarked: "Most of these manuscripts related to death, disintegration, human indignity, poverty, drunkenness, ignorance, human cruelty. They attempted to describe dusty and deserted streets, street corners, miserable homes, pool rooms, brothels, dance halls, taxi dances, bohemian sections, express offices, gasoline filling stations, scenes laid in slum districts. The characters were boys, boys' gangs, drunkards, Negroes, expressmen, homosexuals, immigrants and immigrant landlords, filling-station attendants, straw bosses, hitch hikers, bums, bewildered parents. Most of the manuscripts were written with the ideal of objectivity in mind. I realized then that the writer should submit himself to objective discipline. These early manuscripts of mine were written, in the main, out of such an intention." James T. Farrell, introduction to *Studs Lonigan: A Trilogy* (New York: Modern Library, 1938), x. Compare the themes of Farrell's manuscripts to those of University of Chicago sociologists of the 1920s: Ruth Shonle, "Suicide: A Study of Personal Disorganization" (PhD diss., 1926); Walter Reckless, "The Natural History of Vice Areas in Chicago" (PhD diss., 1925); Paul Cressey, "The Closed Dance Hall in Chicago" (master's thesis, 1929); Louis Wirth, "The Ghetto: A Study in Isolation" (PhD diss., 1926), published as *The Ghetto* (Chicago: University of Chicago Press, 1928); Nels Anderson, *The Hobo: The Sociology of the Homeless Man* (Chicago: University of Chicago Press, 1923); and Frederic M. Thrasher, *The Gang: A Study of 1,313 Gangs in Chicago* (Chicago: University of Chicago Press, 1927). Thrasher contributed the introduction to the first book of the trilogy, *Young Lonigan: A Boyhood in Chicago Streets* (New York: Vanguard Press, 1932).
4 Winifred Raushenbush, *Robert E. Park: Biography of a Sociologist* (Durham, NC: Duke University Press, 1979), 15.
5 Robert E. Park, "Notes on the Origins of the Society for Social Research," intro. Lester R. Kurtz, *Journal of the History of the Behavioral Sciences* 18, no. 4 (October 1982): 337, 338 (originally published in *Bulletin of the Society for Social Research* 1 [August 1939]: 1–5). For further information on Park and the Chicago school of sociology, see Robert E. L. Faris, *Chicago Sociology, 1920-1932* (1967; repr., Chicago: University of Chicago Press, Midway Reprint, 1979); Fred H. Matthews, *Quest for an American Sociology: Robert E. Park and the Chicago School* (Montreal: McGill-Queen's University Press, 1977); Raushenbush, *Rob-*

ert E. Park; Martin Bulmer, *The Chicago School of Sociology: Institutionalization, Diversity, and the Rise of Sociological Research* (Chicago: University of Chicago, 1984); and Lester R. Kurtz, *Evaluating Chicago Sociology: A Guide to the Literature, with an Annotated Bibliography* (Chicago: University of Chicago Press, 1984).

6 Max Weber, as quoted in H. H. Gerth and C. Wright Mills, eds., *From Max Weber: Essays in Sociology* (New York: Oxford University Press, 1946), 15.

7 Rudyard Kipling, "How I Struck Chicago and How Chicago Struck Me," in *The American City: A Sourcebook of Urban Imagery*, ed. Anselm L. Strauss (Chicago: Aldine Publishing, 1968), 46.

8 Upton Sinclair, *The Jungle* (1906; repr., New York: Penguin Books, 1965), 51.

9 Michael Pollan, "The Vegetable-Industrial Complex," *New York Times*, October 15, 2006.

10 Eric Schlosser, *Fast Food Nation* (New York: HarperCollins, 2002), 197.

11 Sinclair, *The Jungle*, 213, 214.

12 William T. Stead, *If Christ Came to Chicago! A Plea for the Union of All Who Love in the Service of All Who Suffer* (Chicago: Laird and Lee, 1894), 107–8.

13 Theodore Dreiser, *The Titan* (1914; repr., New York: Signet Classic, 1965), 68.

14 Dreiser, *The Titan*, 68.

15 Carl S. Smith, *Chicago and the American Literary Imagination, 1880–1920* (Chicago: University of Chicago Press, 1984); Sherwood Anderson, *Windy McPherson's Son* (1916; repr., Chicago: University of Chicago Press, 1965); Charles Ives, *The Unanswered Question, Music for Chamber Orchestra, Performable also as Chamber Music* (New York: Southern Music Publishing, 1953); Saul Bellow, *Humboldt's Gift* (New York: Viking Press, 1975).

16 Dreiser, *The Titan*, 186.

17 The full statement is: "If men define situations as real they are real in their consequences. The total situation will always contain more and less subjective factors, and the behavior reaction can only be studied in connection with the whole context, i.e., the situation as it exists in verifiable, objective terms, and as it has seemed to exist in terms of the interested persons." William I. Thomas and Dorothy Swain Thomas, "Situations Defined as Real Are Real in Their Consequences" (1928), reprinted in Gregory P. Stone and Harvey A. Farberman, eds., *Social Psychology through Symbolic Interaction* (Waltham, MA: Ginn-Blaisdell, 1970), 154–55.

18 William Isaac Thomas, *W. I. Thomas on Social Organization and Social Personality*, ed. Morris Janowitz (1917; repr., Chicago: University of Chicago Press, 1966), 171, 181.

19 Robert E. Park, "The City: Suggestions for the Investigation of Human Behavior in the Urban Environment," in *The City*, ed. Robert E. Park, Ernest W. Burgess, and Roderick McKenzie (1925; repr., Chicago: University of Chicago Press, 1967), 45.

20 Ernest W. Burgess, "Can Neighborhood Work Have a Scientific Basis?" in Park, Burgess, and McKenzie, *The City*, 143.

21 Burgess, "Can Neighborhood Work," 154–55.

22 Mary Jo Deegan, *Jane Addams and the Men of the Chicago School, 1892–1918* (New Brunswick, NJ: Transaction Books, 1988), 75.

23 Stuart J. Hecht, "Social and Artistic Integration: The Emergence of Hull-House Theatre," *Theatre Journal* 34, no. 2 (May 1982): 172–82.

24 Frank Lloyd Wright, "The Art and Craft of the Machine," in *Eighty Years at Hull-House*, ed. Allen Davis and Mary Lynn McCree (1913; repr., Chicago: Quadrangle Books, 1969), 85–88.

25 Walter Lippmann, "Well Meaning but Unmeaning," in Davis and McCree, eds., *Eighty Years at Hull-House*, 111.

26 Louis Wirth, "Urbanism as a Way of Life," in *Louis Wirth on Cities and Social Life*, ed. Albert J. Reiss Jr. (1938; repr., Chicago: University of Chicago Press, 1964), 60–83.

27 Louis H. Sullivan, *The Autobiography of an Idea* (1924; repr., New York: Dover Publications, 1956), 321–22.

28 Bulmer, *Chicago School of Sociology*, 181–84.

CHAPTER SIX

1 Ronald Reagan, *The Official Ronald Wilson Reagan Quote Book* (St. Louis Park, MN: Chain Pinkham Books, 1980).

2 Excellent accounts of these themes can be found in Elizabeth Hess, "A Tale of Two Monuments," *Art in America* (April 1983): 120–27; "America Remembers," *National Geographic* 67, no. 5 (May 1985): 552–73; Robin Wagner-Pacifici and Barry Schwartz, "The Vietnam Veterans Memorial: Commemorating a Difficult Past," *American Journal of Sociology* 97 (1991): 376–420. I am grateful to Barry Schwartz for helpful discussions concerning his research with Robin Wagner-Pacifici on the Vietnam Veterans Memorial.

3 Interview with Maya Lin in *Art in America* (April 1983): 123.

4 See the discussion in Wagner-Pacifici and Schwartz, "Vietnam Veterans Memorial."

5 Alexis de Tocqueville, *Democracy in America* (1840; repr., New York: Doubleday Anchor Books, 1969), 517.

6 Émile Durkheim, *The Elementary Forms of the Religious Life*, trans. Joseph Ward Swain (1915; repr., New York: Free Press, 1965), 264.

7 See Jay Mechling, "The Collecting Self and American Youth Movements," in *Consuming Visions: Accumulation and Display of Goods in America, 1880-1920*, ed. Simon J. Bronner (New York: W.W. Norton, 1989), 255–85.

8 Jean Baudrillard, *America*, trans. Chris Turner (London: Verso, 1989).

9 See Russell Belk, "Moving Possessions: An Analysis Based on Personal Documents from the 1847–1869 Mormon Migration," *Journal of Consumer Research* 19 (December 1992): 339–61.

10 Tocqueville, *Democracy in America*, 513.

11 Henry Adams, *Letters of Henry Adams, 1892-1918*, ed. Worthington Chauncy Ford (Boston and New York: Houghton Mifflin, 1938), 438.

12 Lewis Mumford, "The American Way of Death," (1966), in *Interpretations and Forecasts: 1922-1972* (New York: Harcourt, Brace, Jovanovich, 1979), 369.

13 Robert N. Bellah, Richard Madsen, William M. Sullivan, Ann Swidler, and Steven M. Tipton, *Habits of the Heart* (New York: Harper and Row, 1985).

14 See Roberto DaMatta, *Carnivals, Rogues, and Heroes* (Notre Dame, IN: University of Notre Dame Press, 1991); Victor Turner, *The Ritual Process* (New York: Aldine Press, 1969).

15 John MacAloon, *This Great Symbol: Coubertin and the Founding of the Modern Olympic Games* (Chicago: University of Chicago Press, 1980).

16 Lewis Mumford, "Utopia, the City, and the Machine," in *Utopias and Utopian Thought*, ed. Frank E. Manuel (Boston: Beacon Press, 1967), 3–24.

17 In 1990 there were 36,515 malls/shopping centers, which increased to 47,104 in 2003. *Statistical Abstract of the United States: 2003*, United States Census Bureau, 2003. Available at http://www.census.gov/prod/www/statistical-abstract.html, 2004-5 edition, table 1040.

18 "Scope U.S. 2004." International Council of Shopping Centers. See http://www.icsc. org/srch/about/impactofshoppingcenters/NationalImpact.pdf; http://www.icsc.org/ srch/about/impactofshoppingcenters/RetailSales.pdf.

19 John Gehm, "The Culture of Control: Electronic Monitoring of Probationers" (PhD diss., University of Notre Dame, 1990).

CHAPTER SEVEN

1 Cited in Jonathan Allen, "How to Feel Better If You Have a Cold: Get Paid for It," *New York Times*, February 7, 2006.

2 Stanislaw Lem, *His Master's Voice*, trans. Michael Kandel (New York: Harcourt, Brace, Jovanovich, 1983), 26–27. Subsequent quotes are cited in the text.

3 Richard Feynman gives a contemporary physicist's account of what Peirce calls abduction: "In general we look for a new law by the following process. First we guess it. Then we compute the consequences of the guess to see what would be implied if this law that we guessed is right. Then we compare the result of the computation to nature, with experiment or experience, to see if it works. If it disagrees with experiment it is wrong. In that simple statement is the key to science. It does not make any difference how beautiful your guess is. It does not make any difference how smart you are, who made the guess, or what his name is—if it disagrees with experiment it is wrong. That is all there is to it. . . . This will give you a somewhat wrong impression of science. It suggests that we keep on guessing possibilities and comparing them with experiment, and this is to put experiment into a rather weak position. In fact experimenters have a certain individual character. They like to do experiments even if nobody has guessed yet, and they very often do their experiments in a region in which people know the theorist has not made any guesses. For instance, we may know a great many laws, but do not know whether they really work at high energy, because it is just a good guess that they work at high energy. Experimenters have tried experiments at higher energy, and in fact every once in a while experiment produces trouble; that is, it produces a discovery that one of the things we thought right is wrong. In this way experiment can produce unexpected results, and that starts us guessing again. One instance of an unexpected result is the mu meson and its neutrino, which was not guessed by anybody at all before it was discovered, and even today nobody yet has any method of guessing by which this would be a natural result." Richard Feynman, *The Character of Physical Law* (1967; repr., New York: Modern Library, 1994), 156–57.

4 Charles Sanders Peirce, *The Collected Papers of Charles Sanders Peirce*, vols. 1–6, ed. Charles Hartshorne and Paul Weiss (Cambridge, MA: Harvard University Press, 1935), 6: paragraph 469.

5 Charles Sanders Peirce, *Charles Sanders Peirce: Contributions to* The Nation, ed. Ken Ketner (1893; repr., Lubbock: Texas Tech Press, 1975), 175–78.

6 Peirce, *Collected Papers*, 6: 295, 6: 293–94.

7 From "The Laws of Nature," written in 1901. Charles Sanders Peirce, *The Essential Peirce: Selected Philosophical Writings*, vol. 2, 1893–1913 (Bloomington: Indiana University Press, 1998), 72.

8 Lynn Margulis and Dorion Sagan, *Microcosmos: Four Billion Years of Evolution from Our Microbial Ancestors* (New York: Summit Books, 1986).

9 David Lavery, *Late for the Sky: The Mentality of the Space Age* (Carbondale: Southern Illinois University Press, 1992).

10 Tom Brown Jr., *Grandfather* (New York: Berkley Books, 1996).

11 Gerald Holton, *The Advancement of Science, and Its Burdens* (New York: Cambridge University Press, 1986), 122.

12 Henry Adams, letter to Henry Osborn Taylor, Washington, DC, January 17, 1905, in *Henry Adams and His Friends: A Collection of Unpublished Letters*, ed. Harold Dean Carter (Boston: Houghton Mifflin, 1947), 558-559

13 Holton, *Advancement of Science, and Its Burdens*, 291–92.

14 Richard L. Miller, *Under the Cloud: The Decades of Nuclear Testing* (New York: Free Press, 1986), 375.

15 John Ruskin, "Of the Pathetic Fallacy," in *Modern Painters*, vol. 3, part 4, 1856. Available at http://www.ourcivilisation.com/smartboard/shop/ruskinj/.

16 Eugene Halton, "Peircean Animism and the End of Civilization," *Contemporary Pragmatism* 2, no. 1 (2005): 135–66.

17 D. H. Lawrence, *Phoenix: The Posthumous Papers of D.H. Lawrence*, ed. Edward P. McDonald (New York: Viking Press, 1936), 300–301.

18 Cited in Lewis Mumford, *The Pentagon of Power* (New York: Harcourt, Brace, Jovanovich, 1970), 380.

19 James Glantz and Dennis Overbye, "Cosmic Laws like Speed of Light Might Be Changing, a Study Finds," *New York Times*, August 15, 2001. Here is an excerpt: "An international team of astrophysicists has discovered that the basic laws of nature as understood today may be changing slightly as the universe ages, a surprising finding that could rewrite physics textbooks and challenge fundamental assumptions about the workings of the cosmos. . . . The observations revealed patterns of light absorption that the team could not explain without assuming a change in a basic constant of nature involving the strength of the attraction between electrically charged particles.

"If confirmed, the finding could mean that other constants regarded as immutable, like the speed of light, might also have changed over the history of the cosmos. . . . The work relied on observations of light from distant beacons called quasars, which shine with a brightness equivalent to billions of suns. The light is probably emitted by matter torn from young galaxies by the powerful gravity of a black hole."

20 From "The Laws of Nature," written in 1901. Peirce, *Essential Peirce*, 2: 68.

21 See Lewis Mumford, "The Monastery and the Clock," in *The Human Prospect* (Boston: Beacon Press, 1955), 3–9; E. P. Thompson, "Time, Work-Discipline, and Industrial Capitalism," *Past and Present: Journal of Historical Studies* 38 (1967): 56–97; Morris Berman, *The Re-Enchantment of the World* (Ithaca, NY: Cornell University Press, 1981).

22 Eugene Halton, "The Cosmic Fantasia of Life," in *Integrative Learning and Action: A Call to Wholeness*, ed. David K. Scott, Susan M. Awbrey, and Diane Dana (New York: Peter Lang, 2006).

23 Eugene Halton, "Eden Inverted: On the Wild Self and the Contraction of Consciousness," *The Trumpeter* 23, no. 3 (2007), online at http://trumpeter.athabascau.ca/index.php/trumpet/article/view/995/1387.

24 See David Abram, *The Spell of the Sensuous* (New York: Vintage Books, 1997).

25 Owen Barfield, "The Harp and the Camera," in *A Barfield Reader*, ed. and intro. G. B. Tennyson (Hanover NH: University Press of New England; Wesleyan University Press, 1999).

CHAPTER EIGHT

1 Aristotle, *Politics*, book 1, chap. 9, 32–44. *Introduction to Aristotle*, ed. Richard McKeon (Chicago: University of Chicago Press, 1973), 611–12.

CHAPTER NINE

1 Henry David Thoreau, *Walden* (1854; repr., New York: Modern Library, 1946), 90.

2 Thoreau, *Walden*, 379.

3 Sam Maloof, "Wharton Esherick, 1887–1970," *Craft Horizons* 30, no. 4 (1970): 11.

4 In Noelle Backer, "Wharton Esherick: Expressionist in Wood," *The Crafts Report*, August 1996. Available at http://www.craftsreport.com/august96/esherick.html.

5 Renwick Gallery, *Woodenworks: Furniture Objects by Five Contemporary Craftsmen* (St. Paul: Minnesota Museum of Art, 1972), 38.

6 Cited in Gertrude Benson, "Wharton Esherick," *Craft Horizons* (January–February 1959): 33–37.

7 Hoag Levins, "A Thoreau in Wood: The Making of Wharton Esherick," available at http://www.levins.com/esh5.html. See also K. Porter Aichele, "Wharton Esherick: An American Artist-Craftsman," in *The Wharton Esherick Museum: Studio and Collection* (Paoli, PA: The Wharton Esherick Museum, 1977).

8 Marietta Johnson Museum, http://www.mariettajohnson.org/page2.html.

9 Marietta Johnson Museum, "The Concept," http://www.mariettajohnson.org/page4.html.

10 Gertrude Benson, "Wharton Esherick," 37. Two of these friends, Rose and Nat Rubinson, commented on Esherick's organic simplicity when I interviewed them on September 23, 1987:

Rose Rubinson: Let's start from another tack. Let's start from where we were before. Something you said. If you had the capacity, as Wharton did, with almost no effort, because he lived it, not so much that he had to be taught or he taught himself: he lived it. If you had the capacity to feel the organic nature of a structure, say, start with a natural structure, natural material, it shouldn't be difficult to transfer that insight into man-made structure and see that in organic terms. So that Wharton could look at a room and could identify precisely where it needed, what it needed.

Nat Rubinson: Well take here. When we would want something we would never ask for a sketch or a model. We understood him and knew that he could come through with it. The day he walked in—you see those two lamps sitting up there? When he had those out on his porch, you know what I did? I jumped in my car and drove away. I saw these huge things out on the porch. Where the hell is he going to put those things? I came back in. I couldn't find them. There they were. Now this is the truth. Rose and I were scared.

Rose Rubinson: From where I'm sitting, I don't see the lamp on the left. I see a body and an arm.

Nat Rubinson: If I were to move it over, you'd see the other part of it. . . . I think to put it in the simplest terms it's exactly what we said. I think he lived it. He had to have it.

Eugene Halton: So in other words, as you pointed out, he needed to make things at home. And so one might look at the essence of his art as growing out of needs.

Nat Rubinson: But the needs transformed—pushed his creativity up.

11 Selections from the Diary of Eleanor Anderson, 1933-40, compiled by Hilbert H. Campbell. Available at http://oncampus.richmond.edu/academics/journalism/eleanor.html.

12 Jerome Loving, *The Last Titan* (Berkeley: University of California Press, 2005), 264. His quotation from Esherick comes from an interview conducted by earlier Dreiser biographer W. A. Swanberg, on June 25, 1962, and is among the Dreiser papers at the Van Pelt-Dietrich Library, University of Pennsylvania.

13 Gene Rochberg, *Drawings by Wharton Esherick* (New York: Van Nostrand Reinhold, 1978).

14 See Hoag Levins, at http://www.levins.com/esh3e.html.

15 In Michael A. Stone, *Contemporary American Woodworkers* (Salt Lake City: Gibbs M. Smith, 1986), 4.

16 Ford Maddox Ford, *Great Trade Route* (New York: Oxford University Press, 1937), 222-23.

17 The Museum of Contemporary Crafts in New York held a retrospective of Esherick's furniture and sculpture in 1958-59, and the exhibition's brochure states, concerning his building of his workshop home:

> Nothing escaped his attention, with the result that a rare, unified decorative scheme, distinctly American and highly individual, came into existence. Further, with the completion of the new studio, a new artist of stature had emerged.
>
> The famous stairway in the studio incorporates perfectly the duality of Esherick as artist and craftsman. It is daring in concept, functional and thoroughly sculptural. It provides the keystone for the understanding of Esherick, perhaps better than any other single work. Schemes for stairways have commanded the attention of Esherick since the first one, notably the outstanding example in the Bok house.

"The Furniture and Sculpture of Wharton Esherick," Museum of Contemporary Crafts of the American Craftsmen's Council, New York, December 12, 1958 through February 15, 1959.

18 Cited in *The Wharton Esherick Museum Quarterly* 3, no. 4 (1987): 2.

19 Thoreau, *Walden*, 43.

20 Richard Slotkin, *Regeneration through Violence: The Mythology of the American Frontier, 1600-1860* (Middletown, CT: Wesleyan University Press, 1974), 526.

21 Renwick Gallery, *Woodenworks*, 24.

22 Benson, "Wharton Esherick," 37.

23 Ibid.

24 Joseph Esherick, cited in *The Wharton Esherick Museum Quarterly* 5, no. 3 (1990): 3.

25 *The Wharton Esherick Museum Quarterly* 3, no. 4 (1987): 2.

26 Stone, *Contemporary American Woodworkers*, 11.

27 Maloof, "Wharton Esherick," 11.

28 "Wood," interview of Wharton Esherick by Sam Maloof and Donald McKinley, *Craft Horizons* (May-June 1966): 20.

CHAPTER TEN

1 Lewis Thomas, "The Attic of the Brain," in *Late Night Thoughts on Listening to Mahler's Ninth Symphony* (New York: Bantam, 1984).

2 "Clark produced a significant number of pictures of great scope and originality. In addition to many small panels, he painted a number of large outdoor canvasses of the activity along the canal construction site as well as some scenes of Panama City, with the brilliance and immediacy that characterize his style during this period. In 1915 he showed eighteen of the Panama paintings at the Panama-Pacific International Exposition in San Francisco. . . . Clark showed the eighteen pictures again at the Art Institute in Chicago in 1916; he then removed them from their stretchers, rolled them up, and never exhibited them again. . . . The Panama pictures have been dispersed and are now in museum and private collections." Jean Stern, "Alson Clark, An American at Home and Abroad," in *California Light: 1900-1930,* ed. Patricia Trenton and William H. Gerdts (Laguna Beach, CA: Laguna Art Museum, 1990).

3 Michael F. Jacobson and Laurie Ann Mazur, *Marketing Madness: A Survival Guide for a Consumer Society* (New York: Westview Press, 1995), 15-16.

4 Thomas Gregor, "Dark Dreams about the White Man," *Natural History* 92, no. 1 (1983).

5 Told to me by Herbert Reid of the University of Kentucky at the conference Social Theory 2000, University of Kentucky, May 11-14, 2000. Mumford's words as later published were, "The do it yourself movement prematurely got bogged down in commercialism, but it pointed in the right direction, provided we still have a self to do it with." *Technology and Culture* 5 (Winter 1964).

6 Quoted in Dan Shaw, "Domestic Bliss," *House and Garden,* May 1997, 32-34.

7 Mihaly Csikszentmihalyi and Eugene Rochberg-Halton, *The Meaning of Things: Domestic Symbols and the Self* (New York: Cambridge University Press, 1981). See also Eugene Rochberg-Halton, *Meaning and Modernity: Social Theory in the Pragmatic Attitude* (Chicago: University of Chicago Press, 1986).

8 Albert Borgmann, "The Moral Significance of the Material Culture," *Inquiry* 35 (1992): 291-300, 294.

9 Suzanne Gannon, "Hooked on Storage," *New York Times,* March 8, 2007.

10 David Halle, *Inside Culture: Art and Class in the American Home* (Chicago: University of Chicago Press, 1993). The study is based on a sample of 160 houses from four areas in and around New York City, composed of upper- and upper-middle-class Manhattan residents, upper-middle-class suburbanites, and working-class residents from the city (Greenpoint) and suburbs (Medford), as well as subsamples including exclusive vacation houses in the Hamptons and a middle-class black suburb (Spinney Hill).

11 See my chapter, "The Cultic Roots of Culture," in Eugene Halton, *Bereft of Reason* (Chicago: University of Chicago Press, 1995).

12 Russell Belk, Güliz Ger, and Søren Askegaard, "The Fire of Desire: A Multisited Inquiry into Consumer Passion," *Journal of Consumer Research* 30 (December 2003): 326-51.

13 I remember an editor forcing me to change a reference to that event in an afterword I wrote to the first German translation of Turner's work, where I dealt with Turner's life; this editor wanted me to say that the event happened at a conference instead of in a home, presumably so that it would be more scholarly. Perhaps my American informality violated a more formal split between private and public spheres in the German context. Perhaps I am unwittingly doing that again in this footnote.

14 Walter Benjamin, "Unpacking My Library," in *Illuminations,* ed. and intro. Hannah Arendt, trans. Harry Zohn (1968; repr., New York, Schocken Books, 1969), 62. On collecting more generally, see Russell Belk, *Collecting in a Consumer Society* (New York: Routledge, 1995).

CHAPTER TWELVE

1 Lewis Mumford, *The Pentagon of Power* (New York: Harcourt, Brace, Jovanovich, 1970), plate 20.

2 Lewis Mumford, *Sketches from Life* (Boston: Beacon Press, 1982), 220.

CHAPTER FOURTEEN

1 Diogenes Laertius, *The Lives and Opinions of Eminent Philosophers*, trans. C. D. Yonge. Available at http://classicpersuasion.org/pw/diogenes/dlsocrates.htm.

ACKNOWLEDGMENTS

If you would like to read more about my work visit my Web site at: http://
www.nd.edu/~ehalton/. Information related to this book can be found there,
as well as other writings and upcoming projects.

I am grateful to the Department of American Studies at the University of
Notre Dame for the opportunity to present an earlier draft of "The Art and
Craft of the Home" in the American Studies seminar, and to the Institute for
Scholarship in the Liberal Arts of the University of Notre Dame for a sub-
vention for photographs. David Lavery invited me to contribute a chapter
to the book of teleparodies he edited with Angela Hague, through which I
became acquainted with the work of Art Dimsdale. I thank David for opening
me to new ways of predicting and preventing TV discourse. I am also grateful
for suggestions and criticisms from a number of people, and to name just
some of them, Bruce Wilshire, Russell Belk, Ben Giamo, John Monczunski,
Mark Gottdeiner, Erica Owens, Antonio Menendez, Dmitri Shalin, Barbara
Shinkos, Stepan Mestrovic, David O'Connor, Marek Szopski, Joseph Rumbo,
Doug Rice, and Henri Vaugrand.

I wish to thank Mansfield Bascom and the Wharton Esherick Museum for
photographs of Esherick's work and home, and Robert Wojtowicz for the
photograph of Lewis and Sophia Mumford.

Abbreviated versions or portions of the following chapters were published in the following: chapter 1, as "Brain Suck," in *New Forms of Consumption*, ed. Mark Gottdiener (New York: Rowman and Littlefield, 2000), 93–109; chapter 2, as "The Truth about That Quiet Decade," *Notre Dame Magazine* (Spring 1999), 43–48; chapter 5, "Life, Literature, and Sociology in Turn-of-the-Century Chicago," in *Consuming Visions: Accumulation and Display of Goods in America, 1880-1920*, ed. Simon J. Bronner (New York: W. W. Norton, 1989), 311–38; chapter 6, "Communicating Democracy, or, Shine Perishing Republic," in *The Sociosemiotics of Things*, ed. Stephen Riggins (Amsterdam: Mouton de Gruyter, 1994), 309–33; chapter 7, "Lem's Master's Voice," in *American Freedoms, American (Dis)Orders*, Conference Proceedings, ed. Zbigniew Lewicki (Warsaw: Polish Association of American Studies, 2005), 149–65; chapter 8, "An American Epiphany in Nashville," *New Observations* 72 (1990): 14–19; chapter 13, as "No Man Is an Island: It Takes a Village Idiot," "Review of *On Temptation Island: The View from the Hot Tub*," in *Teleparody: Predicting/ Preventing the TV Discourse of Tomorrow*, ed. Angela Hague and David Lavery (London: Wallflower Press, 2002), 99–108.

INDEX